P9-CMB-089

THE POLEMICS OF REVOLT

From Gandhi to Guevara

C. R. HENSMAN

ALLEN LANE THE PENGUIN PRESS

St. Philip's College Library

320.91724
H526f

Copyright © C. R. Hensman and contributors, 1969

—

First published in 1969
Allen Lane The Penguin Press
Vigo Street, London W.1

—

SBN 7139 0102 0
Library of Congress Catalog Card Number 76-107148

—

Made and printed in Great Britain
by Hazell Watson & Viney Ltd
Aylesbury, Bucks
Set in Linotype Times

FOR

ROHINI, JIMMY AND SAVI

72230

Contents

7

CONTENTS

PART THREE

The Situation: Description and Analysis of Conditions

PART FOUR

Goals, Objectives and Values

8

CONTENTS

PART FIVE

*What Has To Be Done: Tasks, Tactics, Programmes
and Ensuing Difficulties*

9

St. Philip's College Library

CONTENTS

Preface

THE study of the Third World, and therefore of the contemporary humanity of which it forms the largest and not least important part, is only in its beginnings. The subject is of some importance for serious students of the human sciences, for those who want to take responsibility for policy decisions affecting the future of mankind, and for those who, more simply, want to love their neighbours as they do themselves. The substance of study is not, as it too often tends to be, the opinions of people outside Latin America, Asia and Africa about the aspirations, values and actions of the diverse peoples of these continents; nor is it what Europeans and North Americans prescribe, prohibit, find convenient or regard as their problems in the Third World, or find in it to fit their academic pigeonholes. The Third World has a life of its own. It has to be discovered. In so far as this argument is correct, there is something to be gained by giving serious attention to what its peoples have already expressed of this peculiar life in their most significant words and actions. I hope that in writing the book largely in the words of the leading protagonists and intellectuals of the Third World I have better conveyed the shapes and flavours of what has to be discovered and studied than if I had merely discussed the subject. What I have regarded as pure rhetoric I have ignored, and that principle may account for some of the notable omissions. It has not been the aim here to be comprehensive, or to make selections from documentary material which goes back more than fifty years.

However successfully an author may have persuaded himself that a book is waiting to be written, and that he is the man to write it, he has to get sufficiently free of normal duties and responsibilities to work on it. How it was possible for me to do the needed research and writing, have the drafts scrutinized and criticized, get the typing done and the index prepared, and save myself from more mistakes than those that are left, had better remain a family secret.

C. R. HENSMAN

Acknowledgements

The editor wishes to thank the following for permission to reprint excerpts from their publications:

Allen & Unwin for *Nehru: An Autobiography* by Jawaharlal Nehru; Allen Lane The Penguin Press for *The Labyrinth of Solitude* by Octavio Paz; Asia Publishing House for *Against the Cold War* by Chanakya Sen, and *Essays on Economic Transition* by Surendra J. Patel; Cambridge University Press for 'The Outlook for Contemporary Africa' by Dunduzu Chisiza from *The Journal of Modern African Studies*; Jonathan Cape for *The Race War* by Ronald Segal; Centre for Agricultural Publishing and Documentation, Wageningen, for *The Role of Agriculture in Economic Development* by Mahmood Hasan Khan; Chatto & Windus for *The Attack on World Poverty* by Andrew Shonfield; Cuban Embassy, London, for *Cuba Information Bulletin*; Foreign Languages Press, Peking for *The Selected Works of Mao Tse-tung, The Correct Handling of Contradictions Among The People* by Mao Tse-tung, *The Struggle for New China* by Soong Ching-ling, *Long Live The Victory of People's War* by Lin Piao, *A Great Decade* by Chou En-lai, *Afro-Asian Solidarity Against Imperialism*; *Collected Works of Lu Hsun*; *Marriage Law of the People's Republic of China*; Foreign Languages Publishing House, Hanoi, for *Selected Works* by Ho Chi Minh, *The August Revolution* by Truong Chinh, *The Resistance Will Win* by Truong Chinh; Harvard University Press for *The Diplomacy of Economic Development* by Eugene R. Black; The Haslemere Group for *The Haslemere Declaration*; William Heinemann for *No Easy Walk to Freedom* by Nelson Mandela, *Not Yet Uhuru* by Oginga Odinga; The Institute of Economic Affairs, London, for *Two Views on Aid to Developing Countries* by Barbara Ward and Peter Bauer; Alfred A. Knopf for *The State of Latin America* by German Arciniegas; MacGibbon & Kee for *The Wretched of the Earth* by Frantz Fanon; Monthly Review Press for *Latin America and the Alliance for Progress* by Alonso Aguilar, *Lands Alive* by René Dumont; 'Argument of Latin America' by Carlos Fuentes; Mouton for *Li Ta-chao and the Impact of Marxism on Modern Chinese Thinking* by Huang Sung-K'ang; *New Republic* for 'The Dominican Revolution' by Juan Bosch; Martinus Nijhoff for *Aung San of Burma*, edited by Maung Maung; Oxford University

13

ACKNOWLEDGEMENTS

Press for *Freedom and Unity:Uhuru na Umoja* by Julius Nyerere, *Poverty and Capital Development in India* by D. K. Rangnekar, *Obstacles to Change in Latin America* by Claudio Veliz; Polish Scientific Publishers for *Agriculture, Land Reforms and Economic Development* by Ignacy Sachs; Frederick A. Praeger for *The African Nations and World Solidarity* by Mamadou Dia; Dr Frank Price for *San Min Chu I*; Progressive Publications for *Struggle for National Democracy* by José Ma Sison; Routledge & Kegan Paul for *Africa in Search of Democracy* by Kofi A. Busia; University of California Press for *Diagnosis of the Brazilian Crisis* by Celso Furtado, *Social Change in Modern India* by M. N. Srinivas; C. A. Watts for *An Introduction to Contemporary History* by Geoffrey Barraclough, *China in the Year 2001* by Han Suyin; Weidenfeld & Nicolson for *The Economics of Underdeveloped Countries* by Jagdish Bhagwati, *The Third World* by Peter Worsley; Yale University Press for *Oriental Despotism* by Karl A. Wittfogel; *Yojana* for 'Self Reliance in Agriculture' by V. K. R. V. Rao; *Young India* for 'Freedom for the People' by Mohandas Gandhi.

Acknowledgement is made to the following for permission to reprint in the United States excerpts from their publications: Alfred A. Knopf Inc. for *The State of Latin America* by German Arciniegas; Basic Books Inc. for *No Easy Walk to Freedom* by Nelson Mandela; Hill & Wang for *Not Yet Uhuru* by Oginga Odinga; McGraw Hill Book Co. for *The Economics of Underdeveloped Countries* by Jagdish Bhagwati; the Navajivan Trust for 'Freedom for the People' from *Young India* by Mohandas Gandhi; Octavio Paz for *The Labyrinth of Solitude*; Oxford University Press Inc. for *Nehru: An Autobiography* by Jawaharlal Nehru; Random House Inc. for *The Attack on World Poverty* by Andrew Shonfield; University of Chicago Press for *The Third World* by Peter Worsley; and Viking Press for *The Race War* by Ronald Segal.

PART ONE

THE STUDY OF THE THIRD WORLD

1. IS THERE A THIRD WORLD?

*

THE CREATION OF A WORLDWIDE SOCIAL ORDER

FROM a point in space directly above the heart of the continent of Africa – over Kinshasa, perhaps – our earth may be viewed as a hemisphere from which are excluded most of the North Atlantic *bloc* of countries as well as the greater part of the Soviet East European *bloc*. Recife (and the region of which it is the centre) will be clearly in view. Santiago de Chile, Caracas and La Paz less so; Kingston and Santo Domingo will be just out of view; in the other direction Colombo and Calcutta will be clearly in focus, with Phnom Penh and Chengtu on the rim of the curving hemisphere. One would have to shift one's position eastwards in order to bring into view Djakarta and Hanoi.

Geographical units of such great size are not, of course, to be defined predominantly by physical characteristics. The hemisphere which we have described can come into existence as the result, rather than be the cause, of a way of looking at the world which appears to be shared by the compatriots of Julius Nyerere, Gamal Abd al Nasser, Lazaro Cardenas and Nguyen Huu Tho. Geography, as we know, is part of human creation – not just in the sense that it is according to the maps of those in power that the world is transformed, but in the sense, too, that political, social and economic affinities and solidarities often precede the creation of communications systems, and of areas of intensive settlement and cultivation. If there is a 'Third World' of persons and communities living, in rough terms, south of a line which may be drawn westwards from Shenyang, through Kabul, Aleppo and Algiers, to Guadalajara, what is it that holds these persons and communities together?* Have

*The 'line' cuts through China, Afghanistan etc. and cannot be taken literally. The 'boundary' extends in fact along the northern limits of Korea, China, Afghanistan, Iran, Iraq, Syria and onwards to the north-western corner of Mexico. The sense of solidarity among Asians, Africans and Latin Americans may be savoured in readings from Mandela, Guevara, Paz, Ben Barka and Truong Chinh.

17

they not been integrated, partially or totally, with the peoples of the hemisphere north of the line? What are we to make of the great cultural diversity within it, of the virtual absence of lines of communication and of commercial and cultural interaction within the hemisphere? The rather loose use of the term 'Third World' leaves questions like these unanswered.

Those who discern a compactness in this 'world' of peoples, all living in the south, will have to describe and explain its features. What are the historical, political and cultural factors at work south of the Shenyang–Guadalajara line which bring the ongoing life, the renewed traditions, the struggles and difficulties, the aspirations and the creative achievements of the peoples in Chile and Korea, Iran and South Africa, Cyprus and China, into a single focus in the mind's eye? Are these factors more significant and powerful than those at work outside, north of this line?

The last question reminds us of an important implication of the distinctions we have implied of 'north' and 'south': the maps of the whole world that we draw must, to be complete, bring also into focus from another 'hemispherical' viewpoint the 'world' as it appears in the traditions, conceptions and achievements of other peoples – those living in the belt of countries stretching from Japan in the 'west' to Kamchatka in the 'east' with their respective centres of authority and power in Washington and Moscow.

But the sociological cartography which excludes *the* 'world', as it seems to many people in Europe and North America, from a whole hemisphere must appear strange and fantastic to them. The Third World then becomes more than a loose and vague expression, or even a 'cant phrase'* which is convenient to use

*J. D. B. Miller, *The Politics of the Third World* (Oxford: O.U.P., 1965), p. x. For a European Marxist view see Pierre Jalee, 1963. It may be worth considering whether the French have less difficulty with *Tiers Monde* than the Anglo-Saxons have with 'Third World'. With regard to the 'northern hemisphere', Louis Halle, in *The Cold War as History* (London: Chatto & Windus, 1967), writes: 'What we have today is an expanded Europe that stretches all round the world, to the Bering Straits in Siberia, and to the Bering Straits in Alaska.' p. 5.

for Asia, Africa and Latin America. It is, of course, common knowledge that south of the belt of economically developed, highly industrialized and affluent communities there are 'areas' of population in which over two thousand million poor people exist; and that these areas are almost coextensive with the non-industrialized continents of Latin America, Africa and non-Soviet Asia. Within these continents there are some eighty separate 'countries'; and these, for purposes of academic study, instruction or benevolent action on the part of Europe and North America are sometimes grouped together in areas – 'South-east Asia', 'the Middle East', 'East Africa', 'Francophone Africa', 'the Caribbean', 'South America' and so on. They are also 'backward areas', 'underdeveloped countries', 'emergent nations', 'societies in transition' and, as some United Nations documents put it, 'peripheral countries'.* On their history, social characteristics, and economic and political problems and possibilities the authorities are still Africanists, Orientalists, Sinologists, anthropologists, economists specializing in backward economies, and others who have done research in the 'field'; and they generally do not recommend our taking the view that a Third World of contemporary peoples follows an orbit of its own. The supposed boundary line (which we have mentioned) stretching from the northern limits of Korea and China to Mexico's northern border is, it is obvious, crossed freely and continually by the north in the exercise of its authority and the normal pursuit of its interests. The exclusiveness of the area south of the Shenyang–Guadalajara line is by no means an accomplished fact. For example, part of China's province of Kwangtung is the British colony of Hong Kong, and its Taiwan province is a United States protectorate. Stretching from Taipei, Manila, Ulan Bator, Saigon and Bangkok to Caracas and Managua are cities which testify to the active presence in Asia, Africa and Latin America of manufacturing and extractive industries, plantations, cultural institutions, military bases and much else that is vital to Europe, North America and Japan. The mere existence of what appear to be

* See Prebisch, 1964. Terms like 'new nations', 'developing areas', 'new states' are also frequent.

19

separate and autonomous economic, political and social units on the periphery of the Euro–American world does not constitute an independent southern hemisphere.

In considerations such as these we have reason for doubts and hesitations over talking seriously about a world divided into three major parts, of which the Third World is one. What is sometimes referred to as 'the end of colonialism' is not sufficient for assuming that there is in contemporary history a force, the Third World, making its orbit according to peculiar laws and principles, and that this sub-world forms an essential part of the secular context in which our humanity has to be tested and accomplished. Can it be assumed that the people of the southern hemisphere are taking their own initiatives? Do they have common values and interests and objectives, and are these antagonistic to those of the northern hemisphere? Has there been a decisive break in continuity with the colonial and imperial period, or has there been a significant continuance and development of the colonial traditions? In other words, can it be assumed that the people of the south are living authentically in a contemporary style without taking London, or Washington, or Paris, or Geneva, or Moscow, or Tokyo as their point of reference? If these peoples are indeed taking new initiatives, if these initiatives are destructive of the colonial heritage and traditions, if the centres of international power in the north are not their point of reference – what has been said and done in Asia, Africa and Latin America* provides the best evidence for us to go on – we then have to draw up a new agenda for the study of the contemporary world as a whole.

The way one community or group of communities of people exists in the imagination, thoughts and values of another derives largely from the relationship in which the former stands to the latter in actual practice – that is, in the structures formed by the interaction among peoples who have different or complementary economic and political roles and functions. Anyone interested in learning more than is commonly known

*The selection of material included in the readings is from over twenty 'countries'. In many of them the centres in the north from which extra-territorial power is exercised in the south are very much under attack.

about the southern peoples will find that 'Oriental Studies', 'African Studies' and other area studies which go on in European and North American universities do not portray the 'south' as an area belonging to autonomous and still-to-be-understood people with legitimate interests and mature values, which essentially differ from or conflict with those of the European peoples of the north. If he wishes to talk about these peoples and their societies collectively as the Third World he will then have to be prepared to explain his reasons to quite a number of his compatriots who think it safe to assume that for the greater part of mankind the focus of effective political and moral authority is still where before 1939 it used to be – in the North Atlantic region. A distinguished scholar like the British historian Geoffrey Barraclough may, in his *An Introduction to Contemporary History*,* produce facts and arguments to invalidate this notion; but those who think like him are still striking exceptions to the continued and general practice of identifying the worldwide authority and role of the present North Atlantic *bloc* of states with those of the Europe which at one time (to use the words of another scholar, the sociologist Peter Worsley) 'had accomplished a transformation which created the world as a social system ... a world order founded on conquest and maintained by force'.† For this majority in the north there seemed to be no valid reason to doubt that it was only the Soviet Union (or its 'international communist conspiracy') which threatened the continuing unity and stability of the world order the foundations of which were laid by European civilization, overseas discovery, colonization and commerce. On this premise there are no reasons why any part of this larger humanity which is not deceived or terrorized by Soviet agencies or forces should be conceived of as lying outside the worldwide social and economic system, whose creation by the Europeans was one of the most remarkable achievements in world history. One repeats: a good deal of explanation is called for if Latin America, Asia and Africa are to be con-

* Barraclough (1964) especially Chapter VI, 'The Revolt Against the West'.

† Worsley (1964), p. 14.

sidered not even just as 'independent' entities, but as virtually a hemispheric entity separate from Europe and North America. Some people would say that formerly subject peoples are moving into the present along paths mapped out and with means supplied by the mature, modernized European and North American world; that whatever civilization and modern economic and political existence the peoples of the southern regions have achieved have been, and perhaps still are, the gifts of the pioneers and leaders of modernization – the European peoples in Europe and North America – and that they are growths in non-European soil of seeds planted and fertilized by Europeans.* They would assume that these continents are still areas of backwardness and turmoil and ignorance and totalitarianism, too much so for their peoples to live civilized and modern lives by the light and power of their own creation and that the imperial responsibility of developing these areas technologically, industrially and culturally, as Great Britain, France or the United States were developed, is not finished. The opinions summarized here are widely shared, and in the light of the conclusions of orthodox scholarship appear to be sound.

The great empires of the nineteenth and twentieth centuries started the process of integrating the peoples of separate civilizations and territories into the first pattern of world order partly because the aims, values and technology of the imperialist powers had much in common. Even Japan, which subsequently (though briefly) became the greatest imperial power in

* 'In those countries that are sometimes called "underdeveloped" and sometimes, more hopefully, "developing", determined efforts are being made to raise living standards by adopting productive techniques that were invented in the Western World. The leaders of these countries have set themselves to accelerate a process that was set in motion when the command of machine technology enabled its original possessors to extend their economic and political relationships all through the world, and to organize large-scale production in countries that did not themselves have the means to do this ...' Lucy Mair, *New Nations* (London: Weidenfeld & Nicolson, 1963), p. 11.

In this book the term Europeans is used, except where it is otherwise defined, to include North Americans and Australians.

Asia, had of her own accord become part of greater Europe by modernizing herself like a European nation – constructing a national-capitalist economic base, engaging in the process of exploration, discovery and conquest necessary for growth and earning the status of a 'power'. The tremendous energy, skill and power with which the imperial powers had first transformed themselves and then the neighbouring or overseas territories they acquired was the achievement of middle-class, capitalist and technologically innovating elements which shared certain characteristics.*

About the beginning of the sixteenth century the area in which the European peoples lived was not one of special importance; in area it was only one twentieth of the world, in population it was only about one sixth. In terms of advanced moral ideas, art and architecture, invention and discovery, manufactures, administrative and political skill, it was not distinguished. A number of changes – a new dynamism, curiosity and adventurousness, a capacity for assimilating foreign ideas and techniques, technological innovations in communications, navigation, transport and industry, the tremendous advance of the capitalist system over feudal or other land-based economies – made Europe a radically different force in the world. In a period when the great non-European civilizations were beginning to decline, Europe virtually exploded in all directions.†

To get an idea of the scale and intensity of the operation of the new forces we can remind ourselves of what was accomplished. Except for Turkey and the areas ruled or dominated by imperial Japan, every area of the world was effectively penetrated, dominated economically or otherwise influenced

---

* See 'Sociological Categories of Economic Action' in Weber (1947); 'The Motivation of Economic Activities' in Talcott Parsons *Essays in Sociological Theory*, revised edition, Glencoe, 1949; Karl Marx: *Selected Writings in Sociology and Social Philosophy* (ed. T. B. Bottomore and Maximilian Rubel), (London: Watts, 1956) Part 3, 'Sociology of Capitalism', Dobb (1947).

† Whether the non-European peoples ever had a history, and what kind of history it was, is not the main question here. Some indication of what is referred to here may be found in Needham (1954, 1956), Lach (1968, 1965), Zimmer (1955), Coedes (1966).

by Europe, at one time or another, in one way or another.* The rulers of Spain and Portugal extended their sovereignty over the extensive area of the indigenous American empires and beyond them to the fringes of Asia. Portugal, though she lost Brazil (a hundred times her size) and part of Ceylon, retained African territory twenty times her size. Britain, after the loss of her American colonies, acquired a second overseas empire of about twelve million square miles, not to speak of her great power in China. The empire governed by the rulers of France (a country of about 213,000 square miles), after the loss of her American territory was in extent twenty-five times the size of France. Belgium's empire multiplied her territory eighty times over. In addition there were the Dutch, German and Italian empires overseas. The extension of Europe which became the United States (less than 800,000 square miles) grew westwards and southwards and across the seas to an extent, in land territory, of over $3\frac{1}{2}$ million square miles. Its counterpart, Russia, originally 14,000 square miles, a million square miles by the mid-sixteenth century, went on expanding her empire in all directions until it was a compact continent of nearly nine million square miles, with dominant influence in still more territory. Thus, for the person who is concerned with practical politics, as well as for the student of sociology, politics and history, the world which was to be known was an extension or continuation of Europe.† It was with the technological-indust-

* Thailand, Nepal, Afghanistan and Iran were exceptional in that no part of them became wholly a colony of one of the imperial powers. They survived by compromises which reduced their independence considerably.

† Of the four million in the United States at Independence, 700,000 were of African descent. On the new world order see Toynbee (1954), p. 111; 'From the failure of the second Ottoman assault on Vienna in A.D. 1683 to the defeat of Germany in the General War of A.D. 1939–1945, the West as a whole had been so overwhelmingly superior in power to the rest of the World in the aggregate that the fluctuations in a balance of power between Great Powers that were all either Western or Westernized in their culture had been the most important military, political and economic phenomena in the World during that quarter of a millenium. Throughout that period the Western Powers virtually had nobody to reckon with outside their own circle, and, on the material plane, the destiny of all Mankind outside the circle was therefore determined, in

rial revolution of the late nineteenth century, which created in the capitalist industries a voracious appetite for minerals, strategic bases and land all over the world, that the process of integration was most marked.*

HEIRS OF THE OLD EUROPEAN LEADERS

Europe, together with its counterpart Japan, by taking over every part of the world, subjecting it to European authority, permeating its ruling *élites* with European ideas, and weaving it together into an economic whole, had by the beginning of this century created something nearer to a single 'world' than had ever been seen before. European institutions and forms of organization were planted within the vast foreign territories controlled by Spain, Britain, Holland, France, Russia, Belgium and the United States; through political pressure, missionary activity and economic incentives European values and loyalties were inculcated. These institutions, values and loyalties, modes of production, notions of property and so on, inevitably became part of the social scene in Asia, Africa and Latin America – that part of it which was expected to have most significance in the future. A new kind of aspiration was encouraged by the introduction of a scale of progress in civilization which placed the achievements of non-European races several stages behind those of the ruling powers. A new uplifting influence was thus exerted in the form of a consciousness of various stages of development which all societies would have to repeat in order to become modern and civilized. The diffusion of European and North American influence and standards of judgement also appeared in the new educational institutions. Arrangements were devised by which it would be compatible with 'independence' for Europeans and Americans to continue in the role of mentors and guardians. Greater Europe became

that age, by the course of the mutual relations between those Western Powers. . . .' See also V. G. Kiernan's *The Lords of Human Kind* (London, Weidenfeld and Nicolson, 1969).

*See Barraclough (1964) Chapter II, 'The Impact of Technical and Scientific Advance'; Woodruff (1966).

the continued source of the modern techniques, ideas and forms of organization which are translated or adapted for use by the process known as 'indigenization'.* The ways and practices of pre-colonial traditions became more and more remote from the modern world.

Westernization of the world, where the native populations survived to any considerable extent, was conspicuous because it was manifested in the main cities of the colonial period and also brought into being a new middle class to perform functions and provide goods and services in colonial society which the feudal or other pre-colonial elements were unable to supply. The gradual decline of the power and wealth of the Western European countries began, for a number of reasons, early in the twentieth century. This growing debility, together with the growth of mass backing for the independence movements in the colonies, weakened the control and influence of Western Europe from the time of the First World War. With the nationalist challenge to the predominance of Britain, France, Holland and the other European powers it seemed likely that the First World would disintegrate – that social and political institutions, commercial and other enterprises owned by Europeans, with the ideology and values which made these seem normal in the hey-day of European world dominance, were going to decay or be destroyed, because of continental Europe's inability to maintain its military and administrative presence in distant lands. In opposition to the colonial bases in the cities there grew up, in the confused conditions of civil war and international war, counter-bases in the rural heartlands. But it could be argued that the destruction of the old empires by the end of the Second World War did not imply the inevitable emergence of a post-European order in the former colonial areas.

*It is in the period after 'independence' that most careful thought is being given to how European and North American ideas, techniques and institutions can most effectively and most permanently be made part of the local scene in countries which wanted not to be 'culturally' Western. This process of assimilation is the opposite of that which uses mastery of Western techniques and ideas to contest European power and influence on its own ground.

Though Europe (partly because of its internecine conflicts) lost the hold it once had over the non-European areas which were not settlement areas, there emerged a hope that under the leadership of the United States, with its phenomenal military, economic and technological resources, a new 'west' could bring to a conclusion (or at least up-to-date) in the post-colonial age what European annexation and colonization had begun in Latin America, Asia and Africa. In this extension of itself classical Western Europe had made a great leap forward in economic and military power, in technological 'know-how', in the ability to dominate the earth and make it yield its as-yet-unutilized resources and powers.* The hierarchy and order implied in the notion of stages of development, of European tutelage and world responsibility, of the diffusion abroad of its superior ideas and institutions and capital, of cooperation with it rather than revolt and conflict, could be restored. Non-European nationalism, under United States world leadership, could be handled in such a way that harmony and unity could be preserved.† The bid for world leadership which Woodrow

*Horowitz (1966) refers to the United States as 'the best example extant of the First World – of the highly mobile, commodity oriented, and ideologically egalitarian social system . . . the most perfect representative of parliamentary democracy and capitalist economics.' (p. 7). What Theodore Geiger (*The Conflicted Relationship*, New York: McGraw Hill, 1964) has called 'the sense of America's mission to serve as both a moral and a social paradigm for the rest of mankind' (p. 37) has made a European comeback possible. This almost revolutionary sense of a mission to reorganize mankind is different from crude presidential affirmations like this by Mr Eisenhower on 5 April 1954: 'America is the greatest force that God has ever allowed to rest on his footstool,' or this, also made on radio–television, by Mr Johnson on 12 July 1965: 'We will not retreat from the obligations of freedom and security in Asia.'

† It was not only Asian and African patriotism which led people to reject the notion of the harmony of interests and the unity of the powerful and the weak, and to contest it; Latin Americans felt the same in regard to the Monroe Doctrine. See the Latin American views included in Dozer (1965). The importance of restoring harmony and unity is explained by a leading contemporary policy-maker, W. W. Rostow: 'Indirectly, the evolution of the underdeveloped areas is likely to determine the fate of Western Europe and Japan and, therefore the effectiveness of those industrialized regions in the free world alliance we are

27

Wilson made at the end of the First World War,* and the sub-sequent bids of Franklin Roosevelt and his successors were designed to preserve European leadership of the non-European peoples. They would need to be written off as failures before there can be serious talk of the emergence of *three* worlds instead of one.

Are 'the turmoil and confusion' being mistaken for the end or break-up of the single world order – the first world, led and dominated by a renovated capitalist and liberal west? Is this not to be what Henry Luce called 'the American century',† the beginning of a new European phase? Should the modern development of Asian, Latin American and African communities not be studied in the context of a renewed, single, 'free world'? The American sociologist Talcott Parsons brings out the pertinent assumptions of the social sciences when he writes:

It is possible that the twentieth century will be characterized by future historians as one of the centuries of turmoil and transition – in the modern history of the West most analogous to the seventeenth. It is also likely, however, that it will be judged as one of the great creative centuries in which the major stages of the process of building a new society and a new culture will have occurred.‡

On the other hand, the question may be put to Professor Parsons whether or not he is failing to discern, beneath the disturbance of the old order and the stirrings in the southern

---

committed to lead. If the underdeveloped areas fall under Communist domination, or if they move to fixed hostility to the West, the economic and military strength of Western Europe and Japan will be diminished, the British Commonwealth as it is now organized will disintegrate, and the Atlantic world will become, at best, an awkward alliance, incapable of exercising effective influence outside a limited orbit, with the balance of the world's power lost to it. In short, our military security and our way of life as well as the fate of Western Europe and Japan are at stake in the evolution of the underdeveloped areas. We evidently have a major national interest, then, in developing a free world coalition which embraces in reasonable harmony and unity the industrialized states of Western Europe and Japan on the one hand, the underdeveloped areas of Asia, the Middle East, and Africa, on the other.' Quoted in Magdoff (1968).

* See Barraclough (1964), pp. 113 ff.
† Cited in D. F. Fleming (1961), p. 885.
‡ Parsons (1964), pp. 155–6.

hemisphere, the pattern of a new, more fully human order which, by its emergence in Latin America, Asia and Africa, is displacing, overturning or submerging much of that with which our fathers, in more placid times, were familiar. Of course, Parsons describes this century for Americans as one of 'challenge and danger', in which they are not permitted 'placid enjoyment of prior accomplishment', but, presumably, called to its defence against those who challenge or endanger its position. In the essay from which we have quoted he provides a perspective in which he would

like to sketch some of the problems of American youth, as the heirs of the next phase of our future, with both its opportunities and its difficulties.

In the course of this century, the United States has emerged at the forefront of the line of general development, not only because of its wealth and political power but also – more importantly in the present context – because it displays the type of social organization that belongs to the future. Since during the same period and only a little behind our own stage of progress a somewhat different and competing vision has also emerged in the Communist societies, it is not surprising that there is high tension at both political and ideological levels.*

The salient characteristics of this society are given as industrialism, 'a high evaluation of productivity, the free enterprise system, with the private, profit-oriented business firm as a conspicuous unit of organization, and with private consumption prominent in the disposal of the products of industry', and so on, through a long list, which includes 'a very large relative, as well as absolute, growth in the organization and functions of government', and 'great mobility as to persons, place of residence, and social and economic status'.

Now, if the best model for the future of the rest of all mankind has already been achieved in the United States – if, in the words of Daniel Lerner in a much-praised sociological work, 'what the West is ... the modernizing Middle East seeks to become'† – there is in post-1945 Asia, Africa and Latin

*Parsons (1964), p. 156.

† Daniel Lerner, *The Passing of Traditional Society* (Glencoe, Illinois: Free Press).

America no Third World but rather undeveloped populations which are in the process of development, with aims, objectives, values and so on which are already visible in developed form. Messrs Marcos, Syngman Rhee, Ngo Dinh Diem and Suharto could be said to represent the developing or 'transitional' societies, with centres like Manila, Bangkok, Caracas, as the microcosms of the emergent nations. There would be need for anthropological and linguistic study of these essentially pre-modern societies; and research into how the given goals of 'development' may most efficiently be reached, in view of the obstacles which the traditional culture places in the way of development. There would also be need to study how factors which create doubts and uncertainties about the given ideal of development, or encourage a preference for alternatives, and which thus inhibit or subvert development, can be dealt with. Studies of this kind have proliferated in recent years. And, of course, they contradict the notion that there is a Third World to be studied, distinct from the products of Western tutelage and authority.

The assumption of leadership of the capitalist democracies by the United States certainly affected non-European nationalist and other forms of anti-imperialist revolt in ways which have to be investigated. But the conflicts engendered by industrialism had given rise to a new phenomenon. Within the European*

---

*It is from Moscow that Europe set out on its mission of subduing the 'hordes' from Central Asia who had for so long menaced European civilization. The terms Europe, Greater Europe, Euramerica are used often to mean what Louis Halle (see footnote, p. 18) has described as an 'expanded Europe'. For an important Chinese anti-imperialist view of this Europe see Sun Yat-sen (1942): 'During her period of imperialism, Russia adhered to a policy of aggression and strove to expand her territory, with the result that it now occupies half of Europe and half of Asia, bestriding two continents. At the time of the Russo-Japanese War, the world feared a Russian invasion of Chinese territory, all the more because this might be a step towards world aggression. The Russian people once did have an ambition to conquer the world, and other nations were considering ways to thwart them. ...' Sun believed that Lenin had changed this. But the Soviet leadership's affirmation of their European identity, including the crudest attitudes of racial superiority and contempt, has been unmistakeable.

world which occupied and ruled over the non-European world an important split occurred which was much more fundamental than the rivalries among imperial powers which led to the two world wars of the twentieth century. There was a Europe which had not been shaped by the Roman Catholic Church, the Protestant Reformation, Puritanism, feudalism, Latin or Anglo-Saxon culture or the liberal democratic revolution; this was the Orthodox, largely Slavic, Eastern Europe, particularly Russia, which by the end of the nineteenth century formed the largest state the world had ever known, a continuous tract of land taking what had been part of Poland as well as what had been part of north-east China. In this vast country the traditional as well as the modernizing *élites*, who shared the assumptions and values of capitalist Europe, were overthrown by workers and peasants, in a revolution which initially threatened to spread to the centres of financial and industrial power. From Eastern Europe, after the Bolshevik Revolution of 1917 and the political mastery later achieved by Stalin, came the challenge to the universality and even primacy of the First World. The area of the latter contracted, providing a vast base for a new social order. Stalin and his successors departed considerably, it may be even fundamentally, from the original Marxist aims of the Bolshevik Revolution, but the power of the Soviet Union safeguarded, and later extended into parts of Eastern and Central Europe, a rival system to the one safeguarded and extended by United States power. Each came to see itself as the heir of those who had dominated the world until the First World War, and the model for modernization in the rest of the world. Under Stalin the worldwide organization of 'Communist parties' responsible to the Soviet Union was designed to get the workers in various countries who were oppressed by the ruling *élites* to defend the 'workers' state' and to follow its lead. Russia was able to beat back two external threats to its existence – invasion by its erstwhile imperialist colleagues in 1919, and the German invasion of 1941; at the same time it was able to surpass the rest of the old Europe in technology and industry. The Soviet Union's rivalry with the United States to take over the 'old' European role of the leader of a single world order has been expressed in the race to be in the forefront of industry, scientific technology and military power.

This is not the place to make any comment on the validity of Kremlinology and academic anti-Communism in the West. What is to the point is the need which arose to study a whole area of mankind which was characterized by a social structure, ideology, goals and values which did not prevail in the world order in the days before the Bolshevik Revolution. There has, in other words, indisputably been a Second World to study. But, in spite of the tremendous impression Lenin made on Asia, and, on another plane, of Russian domination of Mongolia and, for a time, of North Korea, the Second World, it may reasonably be argued, arose from a division within greater Europe. After the first few years following the Bolshevik Revolution and the successful attempt to prevent the other powers from overthrowing the new regime, Russia increasingly engaged in nationalist power-politics in the traditional sense. As the world-dominance of the Western European powers came to an end, socialist, soviet Europe, with its remarkable economic, industrial and military power, and its ideas and non-capitalist social system, challenged the other, western, extension of classical Europe, the United States, for the leadership of a Europeanized world. Within the industrially developed countries, as well as in the industrial-urban centres in Latin America, Asia and Africa, Soviet Communism created a new international organization, whose aim was presumably to see that Moscow rather than New York would be the centre of a post-1945 world order – or rather, to be more accurate, that Soviet Russia rather than the United States was to be the prototype of modernization. The future, it was believed, had been created, in the pioneering experience of Russian Communism, and not in the only alternative, United States monopoly capitalism and imperialism. Within the areas ruled by Europe and North America, the leaders of the new order would be the Soviet-oriented Communist parties and Communist-controlled unions of industrial workers, dockers, transport workers and the other urban intellectuals, and in some cases similarly-organised plantation- and mine-workers. Those who rejected the leadership of such

Communist Parties as these, and refused to join in the strikes and other struggles waged by Soviet-led forces, were assigned firmly to the enemy camp. Indigenous proletarian and other popular organizations who fought independently on behalf of the peasant masses and revolutionary-minded workless urban dwellers, or engaged in national liberation struggles or argued that generally in colonial situations industrial and white-collar union members were a privileged *élite*, were also treated as enemies. There is, for European Marxists and their non-European followers, no Third World.*

Is there, then, a Third World, which is neither Western nor Soviet? Many of those who see as normal the rivalry of the 'super-powers' would say that the countries of Asia, Africa and Latin America form an area which is confronted with a choice of two leaders in greater Europe. They constitute, in the aftermath of the nineteenth-century empires, an area of political, moral and intellectual vacuum; they are the field of contest between forces loyal to the United States – to freedom of private enterprise and individualism – and those loyal to the Soviet Union – to Communism. Hence the description of some countries in the 'south' as 'uncommitted', or 'non-aligned', and phrases like 'the battle for men's minds'. It is not assumed in these cases that there are modern human communities which freely and on their own initiative appraise the conduct and claims of two foreign groupings of states or foreign ideologies, but rather that in the given condition Latin American, African and Asian peoples belong to the 'free world', and by subversion or propaganda or terror are being won over to allegiance to the 'second world'. Stability, that is, continuity with the

---

* In the view of Horowitz (1966) 'The developmental process includes those social and economic changes which tend to make the nations of the Third World more closely resemble the nations of the First or Second Worlds or some combination of the two.' p. 60. The super-power role of the U.S.S.R., which has led paradoxically to the big-power consensus, finds its most serious critic in China. See also Tabata (1967). Even the anti-Stalinist Marxists incline to regard it as an affront that workers, peasants and Marxist intellectuals take revolutionary initiatives in Asia, without seeking guidance, leadership and authority from the (largely mythical) high command of a Europe-based workers' 'international'.

Westernization process already begun in the old colonial period, will be ensured by local *élites* loyal or obedient to the West; the alternative is conceived as the coming into dominance by subversion of *élites* ultimately loyal or obedient to Moscow.*

The assumption that untutored peoples may choose to create or enter a modern world other than Euramerica, an efficient social system conceived and organized in a radically different way, appears to present several problems of understanding. These problems have to be examined, but their existence is no reason for our not inquiring whether a unitary or a dual conception of world order and leadership excludes a large part of historical reality. As the actions of Sun Yat-sen, Gandhi, Mao, Ho Chi Minh, Castro, Mandela, Nasser and Nyerere indicate, there have been in the areas of enforced Europeanization a number of intelligent people, with very large followings, who have not wanted a world 'led' by the neo-European heirs of the old imperial powers. In spite of the impressive military and economic strength, and the vitality, of the new super-powers, there is a need to account for the decisive outcome of such encounters as the battles of Hsuchow and Dien Bien Phu between peasant armies and the technological and diplomatic might of Europe.† It may be part of the agenda for scholars to retrace the paths of history to account for such things as the successful Vietnamese and Laotian defiance of North Atlantic power. For if the Nankings and Shanghais have been taken from the Yenans – that is, if the revolution mounted from the caves and jungles could overwhelm the urban outposts of the First World – one is obliged as a student, whatever one may

*There is a similar dualistic view of the world in Jalee (1963). On the role of 'anti-Communism' see Jaguaribe (1965) pp. 181 ff. and Arciniegas in Part Three below.

† For a fuller discussion of the immense worldwide implications of the decisive victory in the Hsuchow Campaign of 1949 of the Chinese revolutionaries and their destruction of the U.S.–Soviet-sponsored post-war order see 'The Human Implications of the Revolution for the World' in Hensman (1968). The post-1945 political and military struggles between colonial and newly-liberated peoples and the new Europe cannot be described in terms of rivalries within a bi-polar Europe.

choose to do as a politician or a soldier, to inquire if the history which records only the creation of a modern, capitalist–democratic and middle-class-based order in Asia, Latin America and Africa is not fictitious.

2. THE SEARCH FOR HISTORICAL CONTEXTS

*

THE NEED FOR A 'NEW LEARNING'

WHETHER or not there is a 'third' world of peoples and societies is rightly the first question (if the substitution of a new set of slogans and academic clichés for the old ones is not the intention) when the study of the Third World is discussed. If it is true, as many believe, that it is ultimately from within Greater Europe that fundamental initiatives and decisions emanate, that long-term goals are defined, and that actions and policies are given shape, validity and legitimacy, then the notion of an independent southern tricontinental existence implied in the term Third World is a romantic one at best. It can be studied only as an idea, as a dream, as a myth, or as political speculation, and not as an historical, sociological and moral reality. The European expansion after the Renaissance integrated at least part of almost every community of people into a single world order, as we have noticed. Any major history-making, in the integrated world economy in which we live, which does not extend or consolidate the power and interests of either the First World or the Second World must therefore be considered more or less as a fresh departure in *world* history. For it unavoidably pulls and pushes mankind in directions not authorized or conceived in Europe. Therefore any suggestion that the world's future is being made in the impoverished and militarily vulnerable rural hinterland of countries which in spite of nominal independence have to be appendages of one or the other of the great super-power *blocs* into which Greater Europe has divided must seem fantastic. The 'immature', the 'underdeveloped', the 'dependent', cannot, by definition, be taken seriously or treated as equals by the adults. Communities in Latin America, Africa and Asia cannot, it seems reasonable to argue, contest the responsibility and power of the United States and the Soviet Union to build, guard and guide the world.

Is this writing off of the Third World realistic, however? Is there an element of wishful thinking about it? There is a considerable body of evidence to support the argument that Europeans and North Americans cannot make sense of the world in which they live without succeeding in a serious and systematic attempt to understand what has actually been going on south of the Shenyang–Guadalajara line, both in the form of social action and in the minds and imaginations of the peoples there. The ongoing life of historic communities in the southern hemisphere documented in the words of their spokesmen and leaders takes us into the heart of a 'world' of men, women and children, assumptions and values, hopes and fears, which does not originate in Europe, North America or Japan. Books like Peter Worsley's *The Third World* and Barraclough's *An Introduction to Contemporary History* may, in commending that hemisphere for study, and its aims and values for our respectful consideration, have sought in a rather disturbing and radical way to extend the whole range of the curriculum of those who try to be intelligently aware of the contemporary world, its problems and its possibilities. But people, especially those in the West, still find it difficult to believe that for decades intelligent people from China to Mexico, from India to Argentina, were building and living in the kind of world of which the readings included in this book give us a glimpse.*

To study the 'Third World' is then not to investigate the 'non-aligned States', or 'emergent peoples', or 'neutralism' or 'the developing countries'. (What this book indicates about the thoughts and actions of the southern peoples since Gandhi's and Sun Yat-sen's days hardly suggests that they are 'non-aligned' or neutral or emergent.) It is to seek a new learning for the reason that it does not make sense to try to understand the contemporary world exclusively or even primarily in Western, or in Western–Soviet terms. This may seem like a

---

*There was also much going on in the nineteenth century which is not represented in the readings.

pretentious argument for recommending what is after all a modest selection of readings and notes on Latin America, Africa and Asia in this century. It is, nevertheless, true that a corporate study of the Third World, and its relation to the Western and Soviet worlds, has hardly begun. Any contribution, however small, is useful if it gives assistance to the 'new learning' which is needed.

It has always been true that renewed study and understanding of human affairs would never have been accomplished if questions about the worth and relevance of a 'new learning' had not been argued beyond the resistance of popular prejudices and of academic orthodoxy. We may be missing exploration that is exciting, and intellectually illuminating, if we continued to look only at one, that is the European,* face of mankind, and assume that what lies at the centre of the other hemisphere is the 'heart of darkness'. We may be warned of the dangers of gratuitous and unwitting denigration by a remark of the philosopher Collingwood:

Certain historians, sometimes whole generations of historians, find in certain periods of history nothing intelligible, and call them 'dark ages', but such phrases tell us nothing about these ages themselves, though they tell us a great deal about the persons who use them, namely that they are unable to rethink the thoughts which were fundamental to their life.†

If the pundits find Central Africa or South-East Asia or the Caribbean in 'turmoil', is it possibly because their own minds are in turmoil as they encounter contemporaries whose lives are enriched and ordered differently from their own?

One may have cause to wonder if the assumptions of the Europe-centred view have pervaded historical studies of Asian, African and indigenous American peoples simply because of mistakes in the past, or lack of information. The obstacles in the way of historical curiosity and imagination have to be identified. It may be that the unbidden presence of the Third World in contemporary history may contradict the claims and

*See footnote on page 22.   † Collingwood (1946).

raison d'être of a world-dominant Euramerica. Does historical scholarship, in so far as it is a reflection of the relations of power, economic function and interests of an imperialist character, not get in the way of a fresh appraisal of the history that non-European communities have been making in their struggle – the struggle, that is, to produce what they need for a satisfying and dignified and secure modern existence, to replace an alien power with their own, and to develop in their own 'authentic' idiom experience of the possibilities of modern man and of nature?

United States scholarship labours under the disadvantage that the historical time-scale for North Americans is less than two hundred years, during which few of the experiences of the majority of mankind were shared by Americans. The distortions of European scholarship which assume that progress began for the non-European peoples as a result of colonialism are exaggerated in the shortened perspective of United States scholarship. It is therefore possible for a leading political sociologist to speak of the United States as 'the first new nation'.* It is also possible for the U.S. Council on Foreign Relations to sponsor a study which conveys information such as this: '... between the Neolithic revolution – which introduced settled agriculture many thousands of years ago – and the encounter with the West, historians have identified no revolutions in the traditional societies of Asia and Africa', and, 'the inception of fundamental changes in the traditional society has come only from outside – from the encounter with the West'.†

The notion that history began for the subject peoples only with the creation of the First World is hardly worth taking time and space to argue against. The high civilizations of pre-European America, Asia and Africa were the work of peoples who produced, created and invented. The blankness of the minds of historians who contemplate the millenia between the emergence of neolithic man and of westernized man can be

* S. M. Lipset, *The First New Nation* (New York: Basic Books, 1964).
† Theodore Geiger, *The Conflicted Relationship* (New York: McGraw Hill, 1966) pp. 56, 53.

filled by the reading of the work of those who have taken the trouble to do the research.*

For the student of the Third World the questions of substance about the colonial period are (a) whether it (the colonial period) is, except in a few special cases, an interlude, or an aberration, rather than the beginning of modern history, and (b) whether it was conceivable at all for the colonial officials, foreign businessmen, and the natives who had been assimilated into the European system, to be creators of history.

Where the indigenous population was virtually exterminated to make way for settlement, as in North America and Australia, the questions are not relevant. But in other cases, especially where the environment which throughout the period of colonial subjection sustained and shaped the inner and outer life of the mass of the people was that which had more or less elaborately been created over centuries or millenia by the hard work, ingenuity, intelligence and technology of their pre-colonial ancestors, was the colonial impact more than superficial and peripheral? For different countries the facts will differ. But, generally speaking, when power was transferred to or taken by the 'natives' at the time of the withdrawal of imperial rule, had the conditions for the creation of a post-colonial history – a cultivated and supple intelligence, mastery of the material environment, a proud sense of communal life, and the will and courage to fight against odds, self-confidence, and a leadership loyal to the nation – been produced among those who had accepted colonial rule? So far little convincing evidence exists for the view that imitations of parliamentary forms, westernized bureaucracies, foreign enterprises, incorporation in the capitalist system of the imperial powers, and other parts of the colonial inheritance have been the impetus for history-making in Asia, Latin America and Africa, or that colonial rule initiated in the colonies indigenous industrialization and capitalism. It is evidently the mass of the people who by their hard work and ingenuity created the past and will create the

* e.g. works by Needham (1954, 1956), Basil Davidson (1961), Coedes (1966). The way in which 'factors of civilization' work is discussed succintly in pages 118–23 of Gourou (1966).

future in any concrete sense. And their powers were not renewed or increased under colonial rule.

We must account for the fact that various people in the
southern hemisphere believe that with the end of imperial rule
they are resuming rather than just beginning (or aspiring to
begin) an authentic and autonomous existence in the front rank
of civilized peoples. Is this conception justified by objective
historical realities? It implies that major forces of world history
in our time which have broken with the feudal and other pre-
democratic societies of the past have been taking inspiration
and concrete shape outside greater Europe. It implies that a
new civilization is being created out of a non-European civilization. If the consciousness of independent history-making
which the Chinese, the Indians, the Guatemalans, the Ghanai-
ans, the Vietnamese and other peoples have is a reflection of
objectively verifiable events, then following Mr Barraclough we
should call for a new ground plan on which contemporary
world history must be reconstructed in the trained memory and
observation of the scholar and historian.*

THE NON-EUROPEAN ORIGINS
OF CONTEMPORARY HISTORY

It is a fact that the losers do not make history. But for those
communities for whom defeat and subjection does not lead to
oblivion but is a lesson in the realities of power that is effectively learned, there is still the difficulty about continuity of
past and future. How far back, and on what, does one stand
to perceive the emergence of the Third World in correct perspective? The past, however long and magnificent it may have
been (and often it wasn't that), continues to have significance
only if those who are active and creative in their own generation find its living presence a valuable and necessary resource
for building the future. Historic communities, however great
their span of life and expanse of home territory, can cease to
have a present when they are defeated in a critical struggle

* Barraclough (1964).

against being submerged by the overflow of an alien history, and against the forcible subordination to invading alien forces of what had once been sufficient authority, power and skill for continuing life.*

What happened to the civilized societies nurtured continuously for many generations by the Chinese or Hindu and Moghul or Aztec or Vietnamese traditions can be understood in these terms. Once they were overrun, physically or sociologically, by forces which would not exist alongside them, they either ceased to exist contemporaneously with the dominant societies or could continue only an underground, subterranean existence. Inasmuch as the authority and enlightenment and political experience of rulers and people enriched over generations were forcibly replaced by another authority, they ceased to have present validity or cause for celebration. The pre-European past in Asia, Latin America and Africa thus more or less ceased to be the heritage of the communities descended biologically from those who had once created it. Further, in so far as the creations of the past had proved inadequate as a resource for ensuring a secure, autonomous and prosperous (or at least bearable) collective existence in the face of fresh challenges and difficult conditions, the life-giving stream of history had been shown to be running out; and the pre-modern past was for that reason that much less vivid in the memory or in the things which sustained or dignified or shaped life, or restored it when it was failing. To some extent, therefore, failure to withstand foreign aggressions and invasions, occupations and subjections, made continuity with the past less significant. Such failures as the Indian Independence War of 1857 and the Yi Ho Tuan ('Boxer') uprising in China, like the Peruvian Tupac Amaru's great anti-Spanish revolt of 1780, showed how insufficient traditional resources were for overthrowing oppres-

*The students in Peking who began the May Fourth Movement of 1919 declared 'Our country is in imminent peril – its fate hangs on a thread.' For full text see Vera Simone (ed.): *China in Revolution* (Greenwich: Fawcett Publications, 1968), p. 141. Sun Yat-sen had the same fear that China would cease to exist. Colonialism compels its subjects to construct the means by which they are progressively deprived of the power to live and to control their lives.

sive rulers in the modern age. The past, of course, was rarely glorious. It was oppressive for the majority, and 'glorious' only for those who benefited by the social and economic systems. The desire to restore it could not inspire mass struggles for national liberation.

Indigenous existence, as we remarked, sometimes went underground when Europeanization was imposed by their conquerors. A memory persisted, past 'glories' were recalled by displaced *élites*. But is it not true that only those who make history afresh continue their past and keep it freshly relevant to contemporary life? The historical memories kept alive as consolation at a time of racial insult and oppression were sometimes a romantic myth, nourishing fantasies which took on as time passed and the world moved on even more deficiences of the kind which had led to loss of independence.* To recover the power of indigenous creation and invention and discovery and organization in productive work, technology, science, education, government and so on it is not enough to have kept alive a dead memory. Present power and dignity must be won for those who are living. Revolutionary reconstruction and development is profoundly ethical in character. To give an example: we may say that if they had not achieved the courage, the moral sense and the political and military skill, to beat back French and American attacks, it would be pathological for the Vietnamese to celebrate the fact that their ancestors successfully repelled the Mongol invasions of the thirteenth century, and thus saved Vietnamese society from earlier barbarities. Only a leadership responsible to living persons can celebrate what their ancestors saved for them.

All this discussion suggests that the 'resumption of history-

* Many of the *élites* who dominate the peoples of the Third World are those to whom power was 'peacefully' transferred before a war of national liberation could begin. Their nationalism makes much of restoration of traditional rituals, flags, languages and cults, while leaving economic and political realities much as they had been in colonial times. It is a matter for investigation if even Gandhi manipulated the masses rather than served them.

making' is an ambiguous notion. The distinctions, as the profoundly realistic discussion of it in China has shown, must be made carefully. Some of the non-European civilizations, as in America, were almost totally destroyed by the waves of invasion and colonialism from Europe; some, as in China and India and Vietnam, survived in a way. One must carefully distinguish the cases where anti-colonial or independence movements in their subterranean existence did maintain continuity with the peculiar historical traditions; often, it is interesting to note, it is where the resistance to foreign rule has been nurtured by the mass of the people, rather than organized by the colonial 'native' *élite*, that history has been continuous. The colonial and post-colonial *élites* who became agents of indirect foreign economic and political dominion never, however much they copied the traditional pomp and pageantry and native rituals of pre-colonial times, had the power to make post-colonial history. (Japan was unique in the non-European world, partly because she really had an independent capitalist–industrial *élite* free to take the course that modernizing countries like Germany were taking.) Their survival as a class required the destruction of the creative aspirations and powers of their people.

It is necessary to distinguish between the defeats suffered in pre-colonial times by declining 'feudal' authorities and the temporary or tactical retreats made by revolutionaries who sought in the name of an already subject people to bring to an end the dominance of alien authorities and peoples. What happened in the Spanish empire is significant. As we noticed earlier, this was one of the earliest of the great European overseas empires: in America it extended from where California is today to Cape Horn, virtually destroying the indigenous civilizations; it also included the Philippine Islands, off the coast of China. But the days when the Spaniards subdued the Moorish kingdoms, dominated western Europe and founded a distant empire long preceded the industrial revolution. Spain subsequently failed to keep pace with the rest of Europe in political organization, technological change and economic growth. At the end of the nineteenth century two colonial revolts against

44

the remnants of her imperial rule signified what we have good reason to identify as the beginning of a new 'history' outside greater Europe.

One of these anti-imperialist challenges was the attempt of Spain's Cuban subjects to throw off Spanish rule, which had become intolerably oppressive. The other, for the same reason, was the Filipino independence struggle. Both were fiercely fought, armed popular struggles against a decaying segment of a world-dominant Europe. The leaders – José Martí, José Rizal, Antonio Aguinaldo and others – were not the 'losers', though it is a fact that their names and their deeds appear not to have warranted mention in the history books. One must, nevertheless, regard the Cuban and Filipino revolutionaries of the 1890s as among the first of the peoples who, long before the weakening of Western European and Japanese imperial power in the war of 1937–45, fought their way towards the creation of a new society in Latin America, Asia and Africa – a society not built on European foundations, according to specifications laid down by the world powers of the imperial era. For the kind of existence for which the subject races were being prepared 'after independence' was not what 'the natives' favoured. It was not an accident that Sun Yat-sen, also a revolutionary, and the son of a Chinese peasant, was approached while in exile in Japan by a member of the Filipino revolutionary government, and that through Sun's efforts on their behalf the Filipinos were provided with arms from Japan. Imperial Spain was challenged by newly rising forces which in the years that followed were also at work against more formidable imperial powers in Egypt, Mexico, India and China.

To get the picture clearly in focus one must start farther back. Spain's rule had not been challenged and ended in Cuba in the first quarter of the nineteenth century as it had been elsewhere in Spanish America. The early nineteenth-century revolutionary movements against Spanish rule had left Spain with only Cuba and Puerto Rico of her possessions in America. A consciousness of their revolutionary potentialities developed in the Cuban people during the Ten Years' War with Spain which followed their declaration of Yara in 1868. It is significant that in this terrible war it was the son of a slave, Antonio Maceo, and not another Bolivar, who emerged as the outstanding revolutionary soldier. The war, which was expensive for both sides, was inconclusive. We must place it in a period when European imperial expansion was still going on, and when the economic and political conditions for national liberation of subject peoples were not ripe. At that time the failure of Arabia's attempt to rescue Egypt from European financiers and empire-builders was still to come, as well as the final conquest of Vietnam and Burma, the partition of Africa and the worst phase of the invasion of China. The non-European peoples were vulnerable and disorganized in relation to a Europe benefiting by the remarkable scientific and technological advances of the late nineteenth century. To say this is not to imply that conditions for national freedom can be prescribed. Is is hindsight, perhaps, which enables us to explain how peoples who had been vanquished and whose technological development was arrested became capable of achievements which were certainly not on the agenda of the ruling powers. Neither liberal nor Marxist historians have accounted for the emergence in the submerged colonial and semi-colonial world of forces whose generation was responsible for the wars of national liberation which, in turn, gave rise to the Third World.

In his speech at his historic trial, *History Will Absolve Me*, Fidel Castro in 1953 expressed the hope of the Cuban revolutionaries 'that once again we will live the days of Yara or Baire'. The Cuban Revolution reminds us that at Baire, in 1895, the Cubans, under José Martí and Antonio Maceo, declared their independence and resumed their war of liberation against Spanish attempts to suppress them; by then the world situation was significantly different from what it had been. That same year Sun Yat-sen had begun his revolutionary movement to overthrow the Imperial dynasty in Peking which he and his colleagues saw as the main obstacle to the freeing of China from foreign domination. In the Philippines a major revolt against Spain had been suppressed in 1872; but fresh movements against Spanish rule led by José Rizal, Emilio Aguinaldo, Andreas Bonifacio and a number of other Filipino nationalists,

46

found themselves forced into a bitter war of mass resistance against the same forces which were fighting Cuban independence. Rizal was executed by the Spanish in 1896, but having organized themselves into a more radically anti-imperialist organization known as the Katipunan (Sons of the People) the revolutionaries, who in 1897 formed an independent republic with Aguinaldo as President, fought on. Despite military setbacks they persisted.

Their will and determination precipitated a new phase of imperialism – that of the late-comers among the capitalist nations which at the end of the nineteenth century aspired to be world powers. The Filipinos (and the Cubans) found themselves, in the midst of their struggle with the forces from Madrid, confronting the United States. The infant Filipino republic, confronted with a threat to its independence, found itself fighting in the first of the modern wars of national liberation. It was only after large numbers of men, women and children had been slaughtered by the technologically superior United States forces that it lost its independence. The Filipino war looks forward to events many years later when the infant Vietnamese republic, which had got rid of French and Japanese rule, found itself in confrontation with a fresh French invasion, and then with the United States. China's experience was similar, after the defeat of Japan in 1945.*

This experience of the Philippines and of Martí's Cuba defines questions of general interest when the proper historical framework for the study of the Third World is discussed. In what circumstances and under whose auspices did the Third World originate? Is its emergence an irreversible process? The period from the beginning of the twentieth century to the end of the war which involved France, Britain, Belgium and Holland on one side and Germany, Italy and Japan on the other saw the fatal weakening of the grip of industrialized im-

*Pomeroy (1967) gives details of this first 'war of national liberation' in Asia. The brutality and racialism of the American conquest of the new republic are well-described. For views of the world situation as it developed after the Russian Revolution see, in addition to the readings, Tabata (1967).

47

perial powers who had followed in Spain's path. Could the indigenous anti-imperialist, anti-Fascist forces construct a post-war order? Did they have the power to prevent what happened in Cuba, the Philippines and China?

The struggles of the Cuban and Filipino masses were not only pioneering efforts in the national liberation of the colonized peoples; their anti-Spanish struggle had continuity with the revolutionary wars which threw Spanish (and Portuguese) rule out of the American mainland. The 'imperialism' of Europe which the peoples of America, Asia and Africa came under and then struggled to overthrow had changed its character in different periods and according to the 'power' which was its beneficiary, but not even Britain had sought to dominate the whole world. The partition of Africa and the joint domination of China had been an expression of a consensus among the powers. But the neo-European powers (which because of their ingrained contempt for the subject races, and the new economic, strategic and political needs of 'super-power' ambitions saw the areas from which the tired or defeated old-imperial forces retreated as a 'vacuum') could with an unmatchable vigour and single-mindedness aspire to be exclusive and universal inheritors of the old-European empires. As Albert J. Beveridge, one of the most forthright of the 'imperialists' put it when Americans moved in to forestall Cuban and Filipino take-overs in the Spanish colonies:

We will establish trading posts throughout the world as distributing points for American products. We will cover the ocean with our merchant marine. Great colonies governing themselves, flying our flag and trading with us, will grow about our posts of trade. Our institutions will follow our flag on the wings of commerce. And American law, American order, American civilization, and the American flag will plant themselves on shores hitherto bloody and benighted but by those agencies of God henceforth to be made beautiful and bright.

In the Caribbean and Latin America, in China and later in the rest of Asia, the United States was inclined less to collaborate with the old-imperial powers than join with local forces to expel them.* The franc and the pound were to make way not for local economic power, however, but for the dollar. What Senator Beveridge described in 1898 as 'a greater England with a nobler destiny' was on the scene.

The indigenous movements of regeneration in the areas suffering from the effects of foreign domination – beginning after 1900 with the Mexican Revolution of 1910 and the May Fourth Movement of 1919 in China – had therefore to contend with external forces which, unlike the British, French, Dutch and Germans, were increasing rather than diminishing in strength. The United States expansionist forces were more formidable than the Japanese. Carried thousands of miles across the Caribbean Sea and the Pacific Ocean by the vision of the new order expressed in the theology of Manifest Destiny, the business, military and other interests dominant in the United States, regardless of the protests of Americans who valued their democratic and revolutionary traditions, became a presence to be reckoned with in the areas of the old-European dominance. Its actions made it an open question whether the twentieth century was in fact going to be for the Asian peoples what the Dutch historian Jan Romein has called 'the Asian Century', and for the Latin Americans the Latin American Century; or rather, for Latin Americans, Asians and Africans 'the American Century'. The very forces who had dealt so effectively with the 'Indians' of America were driven, as if by irresistible forces, into action in Mexico and the Philippines, and then to establish a new kind of suzerainty over Latin America and Eastern Asia. To conceive the Third World as emerging peacefully out of the declining Old-European empires is a mistake. The last half-century has been characterized by another process, something unprecedented perhaps: in the most oppressed sectors of the European-dominated world the perennially submissive peasant masses have erupted in a series

*This view is not mere hindsight. Sun Yat-sen came to it by experience. José Marti, whose knowledge of the dominant forces in the United States was not equalled by any other anti-imperialist leader, had a remarkably prophetic knowledge of the new imperialism. See Roig de Leuchsenring (1967).

of spontaneous movements to create a social and economic order free from the ubiquitous expansionist capitalism which has made life intolerable for them; and a linking up of these movements has been taking place. Their threat to the colonial (or neo-colonial) towns and cities is a threat to the sector of the world economic order for which these are necessary. The desolate places of the Andes, the Thai north-east, Laos, Guatemala and other areas over whose economic transformation the struggle is being waged can hardly, in the new historical context, be called 'peripheral'. The new world-dominant powers may yet contain, in the aftermath of the destruction of the old order, the forces setting out to break out of the First and Second Worlds. We should be tentative when we attribute historical reality to independent Vietnam, China or Tanzania. It could be that 'Manifest Destiny' has made the far-flung United States an essential part, perhaps even the most important sector, of the southern hemisphere.*

To understand the forces shaping Asian and Latin American independence and liberation movements it is necessary to study the developments in Japan, Russia and the United States from the 1890s, or even earlier. What the movements had to contend with is explained in the policies of William Seward and Theodore Roosevelt, Josef Stalin and Baron Tanaka, as in those of Hideki Tojo and Harry Truman.

The task of what we have called history-making appears after the First World War no more as the struggle within a nation to overcome the remnants of a remote and declining imperial power. The course taken by the Mexican Revolution, the May

*For scholarly discussions of the ideology and practice of United States expansionism see Frederick Merk: *Manifest Destiny and Mission in American History* (New York: Vintage Books, 1963); Alstyne (1960); Dozer (1965); le Feber (1963); Weinberg (1935); Richard J. Barnet: *Intervention and Revolution: The United States in the Third World* (New York: New American Library, 1968); also excerpts in Williams (1956). The contributions in *Viet Report* (1968) and the Statement of fourteen leading 'Asia experts' (19 December 1967) are also relevant. The point at which the Third World clashes most fiercely with the super-power consensus is China. What has come to be called the 'Sino-Soviet Dispute' is centred on the issues discussed here.

Fourth Movement in China, the Indian independence movement, the Chinese Revolution, the Revolution in Egypt, the Vietnamese August Revolution, the Cuban Revolution and other similar mass movements makes the emergence of the Third World increasingly a universal phenomenon, involving the collaboration of many peoples in a common task. What began as the Mexican–Chinese-led Congress of Oppressed Nationalities in 1927, and elsewhere as the Bandung Conference of 1955, has grown into the tricontinental organizations of the 1960s. This process has interacted with an impressive apparatus for suppressing 'Communism'. Historical writing needs the breadth of focus which will take into account the whole range and profundity of the struggle which ensues when predominantly peasant peoples, in creating a modern history, find themselves called upon to mobilize resources of courage, skill in politics and economic reconstruction and moral authority to match the resources of the advanced technology, firepower and wealth of the super-powers. Nationalism, to be effective and to avoid being outflanked, has to be co-extensive with the imperial powers it challenges. It has to be conceived by the non-Europeanized proletariat in highly complex terms of an international order in which the local bases of First and Second world hegemony are destroyed. The 'world' for which people like Nehru, Mandela, Sison, Nyerere and Soong Ching-ling speak in this book is already a force in world history. But it is in the midst of a conflict the ultimate outcome of which is still a matter of faith rather than of accomplished fact.

3. SIGNIFICANT FACTS AND
VALID ASSUMPTIONS

*

THE discussion of world history in the last few pages is obviously controversial. It is offered as a hint of an authentic approach through the maze of blind alleys and false turnings confronting those who are truly curious about the Third World – that is, those who want points of entry which take them farthest and most comprehensively into the actual life and movement of the tricontinental 'South'. The correct answers about origins and starting points may have yet to be found. But it is important to recognize the fact that the conventional approaches of the North – in the United States, Britain, continental Western Europe and the Soviet Union – leave too many questions unasked about the true shape and proportions of the world society which has been coming into being, and about the social forces generated by the radical conflicts of values and interests between the two hemispheres.

Reference has continually been made in this essay to the tricontinental southern hemisphere, and to the line from Shenyang to Guadalajara as a boundary across which a distinctively new order, with new values and social and political forms, is in process of creation. In so far as this is a true observation, both contemporary mankind as a whole, and the various constituent members of the Third World itself, share some of the common characteristics of the 'revolutions' which are continually being discussed throughout this book.

Factual data, to convey the flavour of actual events, must be grasped by us in their authentic setting. The tricontinental south comprises well over a hundred contemporary nations and peoples, with a population, in 1966 terms, of around 2,400 millions – seventy per cent of the world's 3,400 millions. We would go far astray if we took the characteristics of any component unit we liked as typical. The variations within the southern hemisphere are vast: there are virtual continents like

Brazil, India and China, and tiny islands and city states; there are countries with very high literacy rates and free education, like Cuba and Ceylon, and those with almost universal illiteracy, like Haiti; there are traditional monarchies, and government by workers' and poor peasants' organizations. Countries like Bermuda or Botswana do not lead us to what is most significant. To select the truly significant countries, we must look for the peoples who have shown independent thinking, self-reliant activity and initiative. It is they who are doing and saying what needs to be reported and studied. It is these people who define what 'developing' means. Those outside the Third World need to be kept informed about the peoples whose political consciousness, mass initiative, creative intelligence, originality and hard work are deciding or will be crucial in deciding the shape of things to come. In just ten of the leading countries there are to be found the majority of the population: Cuba (7,800,000), Tanzania (11,833,000), Algeria (12,147,000), the United Arab Republic (30,147,000), Vietnam (36,000,000), Mexico (44,145,000), Brazil (83,175,000), Pakistan (117,000,000), India (498,680,000) and China (710,000,000). If we added to the 1,550 millions in these countries the peoples of Guiné, Laos, Bolivia, Guatemala, Chile, Peru, Argentina, Burma, Thailand, the Philippines and Indonesia, we have three-quarters of the Third World, and, incidentally, more than half the world's people. By the year 2000 the Third World will, it is estimated, make up nearly eighty per cent of the world's population. Already in the quarter of a century since 1945 much has happened. The productive resources of the Third World have yet to be surveyed and secured, the productive apparatus has to be built up so that this vast population can play its part; blockades and invasions, subversion and counter-revolutions, chemical warfare and destruction of crops and factories and dams, have all had to be coped with. But these are all peoples who have had experience of successfully creating indigenous organizations for wars of independence, national liberation struggles and revolutionary construction. A substantial part of them have shown that they can industrialize, and eradicate illiteracy, superstition, and deadly diseases, and

53

eliminate chronic hunger with a speed and efficiency which far surpasses what used to be thought possible. We could add a few more countries to our list, but not more than thirty peoples are now deciding what the south, and the world as a whole, will be like in the coming decades. What they are fighting for, and how determined they are to end the poverty and oppression they have known, have to be understood.

Study of the Third World pushes people into trying to recover forgotten but important facts which account for what happened and the force with which they happened. As they try to discover their contemporary relationship to the masses of the Third World, they also become sensitive to the need for fresh and reliable information. To be in touch with people who have a different collective experience and history, and who, evidently, have refused to follow Greater Europe in valuing highly the conduct, the goals of life, the personality traits, the moral standards on which they are enjoined to place the most value, is considerably difficult. Every word spoken outside the Western enclaves is spoken on a stage, as part of a drama, the subtleties of which may be as unfamiliar as, in a different context, Bharata Natyam or Noh theatre were. Its meaning and the force of its immediate impact must therefore be conveyed with care. For those of us who are Euramerican, every action or new event initiated by the peoples of Brazil, China or Mozambique takes place in a strange context, and is part of a sequence different from our own; what it adds up to or what weight it has we have to learn. There are no such things as 'bare facts'.

Among the difficulties of getting at the facts are some obvious ones. In some cases there is the physical remoteness of important countries, especially when for one reason or another communications are scanty; there is also the distance created by difference of language and culture and race. This distance has to be bridged, and simple 'translation' alone will not achieve this. Behind the obvious difficulties lie others. Most important of these is what we may call the unpalatable or shocking nature of truthful reporting of what goes on in the Third World, and also of what analyses of social structure and of conflicts of interests and values reveal. Openness to information may depend on our being prepared for more than casual or 'academic' knowledge. What we have access to in the information we get about the Third World is something living, active, and not subject to our power or censorship – a presence which may confront and challenge, gladden or hurt us. Curiosity can more easily than we suppose give way to the temptation to produce (or allege) facts more to our liking than those we hear.

There is no shortage of books, journals and broadcasts providing reports about the Third World to those in Europe and North America. If they conveyed more or less reliable and significant information about this or that aspect of it, we should know a great deal about what is going on in China, India, Latin America, the Arab lands, Vietnam and Africa. On China, which contains nearly one-third of the population of the Third World, a vast quantity of material is being published. In spite of the relative scarcity of North Americans and Europeans in China there is, for example, no dearth of 'reports' and 'explanations' about the origins, course and consequences of what the Chinese have called the Great Proletarian Cultural Revolution. Entire university departments, research institutes and government agencies, as well as specialist journals and publishers, are devoted to the study of Latin America, South Asia, tropical Africa, South-east Asia or China. Almost any week of the year more factual information about the 'south' is offered in books, journals and broadcasts in the 'north' than one can sift through in a month. It is important to ask what reliance can be placed on the information provided in this way. For the remarkable and heroic achievements of southerners are hardly ever reported. Who reports? What qualifications does he need? Are reporters or students from outside the Third World normally, after all, expressing in intellectual terms its confrontation by the alien values, hostile aims and interests, and superior material resources, of the First and Second Worlds?

We have now introduced the question of what academic detachment means in the study of the contemporary world. Some scholars may regard as inadmissible doubts about

55

whether all parts of the total human order are studied by them with equal impartiality. But it does seem very unlikely that the sympathetic understanding and ultimate moral approval with which in the human studies all but the most radical dissenters study the institutions and conduct of their own society, are there in equal measure in the study of a foreign society which, as we shall discuss below, has contrary interests. Certainly, if we are to take as a test of objectivity Western study of the Soviet world in the post-1945 period, we have good cause for not taking this scholarly virtue for granted in the study of the more antagonistic Third World.

'Truth' in the human studies is always an elusive quarry. When 'partisanship' in the scholar takes the form of an acceptance of the 'non-partisan' national consensus about another type of social order, the distinction between objective reporting and deliberate misrepresentation is easily blurred. One notices how in a predominantly white society which commends opposition to racial discrimination and prejudice the best scholarship is in favour of racial integration internally; but non-discriminating treatment of other races it finds difficult when conflicts between the dominant white minority and coloured majority peoples are being investigated or described internationally. A scholar committed to the view that in the long run only what we have labelled 'the First World' is entitled to prevail must find it extremely difficult to give much weight to or even to treat as significant historical fact what is being done to strengthen what we have labelled here as 'the Third World'. (He might be tempted to collaborate in flooding the libraries with the 'right' books, to submerge 'unscholarly' works.) A report or description from an 'imperialist' nation of phenomena, especially anti-imperialist revolts and revolutions, which challenge its status, will be remarkable if it is 'objective'. It is no exaggeration to say that the majority of books and reports on contemporary Vietnamese history, society and politics – that is, on a key aspect of the Third World – fall short of being factually dependable. The present situation in the study of politics, sociology and history calls for a good deal of thought about the problem of being objective in view of the loyalties, emotions and interests involved in the analysis of the Third World. But it will be useful to be aware that the free and orderly flow of factual information necessary as a basis for the study of the Third World can be maintained only if the contempt or hostility or fear in the reporter which can suppress, distort or invent facts is not allowed to intrude. It is not just objectivity which is necessary for academic integrity or for intelligent awareness. Courageous partisanship – on the side of civilized tolerance, truthfulness, justice – must inform objective study. The facts about living communities other than our own are known only in our interaction with them as people; and the truth about peoples who are our antagonists (or for whom we are antagonists) – which must include what we have done and are doing to them and their lands, and perhaps how much better they are at doing things than we are, and even perhaps how they are achieving moral and economic and military feats considered 'impossible' in our own society – is difficult, even impossible, to tell. When truthful reporting and scholarship requires the willing, even if only intellectual, suspension of belief in our own 'side', and perhaps disloyalty to 'our' cause, much more commitment is called for than is demanded in the study of exotic or primitive customs and societies. Study of the Third World undoubtedly leads Europeans and North Americans into the position of presenting information which puts their own communities in a bad light; for example, the most dispassionate account of what in the twentieth century French, British, Americans, Japanese and others in the 'north' have done to the people, land and society of Vietnam would be unbearable.*

* In regard to what is going on in Vietnam the 'credibility gap' prevented us from arriving at the fearful (as we discovered it to be) truth through the words of Western political leaders, scholars and journalists. The political and economic destruction and physical suffering hinted at in such works as Seymour Melman (ed.) *In the Name of America* (1968) and Edward S. Herman and Richard B. Du Boff, *America's Vietnam Policy. The Strategy of Deception* (Washington: Public Affairs Press, 1966) are more fully described in 'Unmasking Genocide' (*Liberation* Vol. XII Nos. 9 and 10, 1967–8). The credibility gap is just as great in the reporting on China.

The jargon and attitudes of Orientalists, Africanists, anthropologists and political sociologists preserves the illusion that the impoverishment and the insurgency are all going on in remote, perhaps quaint and exotic, underdeveloped nations. But analysis of the world society may indicate that it is in important ways a stratified society, and that the Third World communities which are being described stand to the European 'north' in a relation similar to that in which the 'inferior' classes stand to the ruling classes within a society. It will show that *nowhere* in the colonial or semi-colonial 'areas' did the expanding capitalist forces and their administrative bureaucracies initiate or cultivate the educational, technological and industrial processes which were responsible for the transformation and growing power and prosperity of European and Japanese society. Truthfulness about other races and peoples is in that case even more difficult than it would be if the conflicts were between 'nations' and peoples of equal status and independence.*

It is a platitude that to draw a picture of what has happened or is happening and what the scene was like, one has to convey the whole picture. The omission of significant details would turn what is sensible and rational into the

* To recommend the study of the Third World not only on the ground that we can learn more facts but also because we might profit from the example of others may sometimes cause offence. Admiration for what others have achieved can change us, can lead to imitation and discipleship of even 'lesser breeds'. Recognition of their power and capacity can induce us to give up trying to dominate them. Learning the truth about what one's own community has done to another can lead to 'repentance', because what one discovers may clearly be incompatible with justice as well as one's own humanity, self-respect and dignity. One can also study in order to destroy more effectively. As Charles Wolf in *United States Policy in the Third World* explains: 'A progressive reduction in the area of the world in which we could travel freely would significantly curtail our freedom, quite apart from the effect of such insulation on the quality of domestic society in the United States. ... A world of such piecemeal and sequential erosion would be one in which new generations of Americans would face increasing temptations to affiliate with the trend rather than oppose it. An inward-directed and withdrawn America might generate its own domestic opponents with an increasing disposition to overturn it from within.' (Quoted in *Viet Report*).

absurd and irrational. On the other hand, to clutter up a description without any distinction between insignificant and significant detail is to turn good sense into absurdity, too. The facts we require are a selection. The responsibilities that are entailed in the need for selection – which of course faces every serious reporter, social scientist, historian and creative writer even in his own society – cannot be exercised without some knowledge or premonition of what contemporary human life is about, for people of different statuses in world society, and what the significant issues of our time are. (And these responsibilities have also to be carried out in the selection of readings intended to convey the essential features of the Third World.) Third World studies make it very clear that reporters and scholars manifest their concern for accuracy and objectivity in the nature of the decisions which they make in what they choose to discover to their listeners or readers. Skill in the unearthing of trivial details and in the exegesis of irrelevant documents (sometimes reports of unimportant conferences) is no substitute for bold decisions on what the facts and issues are on which details of information are required at a time when large masses of men are presumably taking (or it may be failing in their attempt to take) world history in a new direction.

On these matters we must decide, too, whether or not to follow the example of the practice of scholars who for their own reasons concentrate, say, on facts of poverty, backwardness, crime, corruption, totalitarianism and similar other features which they allege or imply are characteristic of the important Third World countries; or who give great prominence to the presence or absence of features characteristic of the First or Second Worlds, or report in exaggerated detail the activity of their agencies (that is, the colonial or neo-colonial elements and the Communist Parties) within Latin America, Africa and Asia as *the* significant facts of the Third World. We are told that in this or that country parliamentary elections have virtuously been held or have viciously been denied, as though the spectacle of elections were the criterion of democracy. Or we may have regularly conveyed to us the views of a 'cross section' of the population, whose fundamentally European or American views, loyalties, conditions of living and interests may be representative of no more than five or ten per cent of a vast population. But it is precisely the nature of the historical realities that what happens in the offices, embassies and mansions of Bangkok, or Caracas, or Manila, or Rio de Janeiro is sociologically outside the Third World – that these are extensions or enclaves of the First World.*

But that takes us into questions of a different kind from those of how reliable information about post-European developments south of the Shenyang–Guadalajara line may be secured. Much that has been said in the last few pages has implied that (a) the structures and processes characteristic of the Third World can be understood only after systematic political and sociological analysis. Only then can the actual interconnections, the interrelationships, the flow and sequence of facts, events, actions, situations, be perceived and explained. What are these structures and processes? (b) For what reasons and in view of what alternative do the majority of the most sensitive Third World leaders (i.e. those represented in this book) estimate as less than most valuable what the majority consensus of Euramericans regard as the goals, objectives, institutions, attitudes and practices which are most precious, supremely worth fighting for; and (c) for what reasons, and with what finality of commitment, does the Third World find itself ranged in conflict against the aspirations, claims and authority of the First and Second Worlds in Asia, Africa, and Latin America?

*The character of the Western-oriented minorities who are conspicuous in the Third World is described later by Fanon. The extent to which the interests of foreign-trained officers and professional people, business men and financiers are identical with those of the top five per cent who own most of the wealth and get most of the local income has yet to be studied. Andrew Tully in *C.I.A. The Inside Story* writes: 'It is proper to seek to help Western-oriented groups to gain power in the strategic centres of the world'; but he also says: 'These Western-oriented leaders are not oriented to the needs of their people.'

4. SOCIAL STRUCTURE
AND PROBLEMS

*

FOR over seventy years the idea of revolutionary action has been a commonplace in what has come to be the Third World. The 'daring to rebel' which has destroyed the traditional uniformities and systems and sanctities, and frustrated the policies of colonialism old and new, has been more than just rhetoric or idealism. It is manifestly a historical phenomenon and the expression of social forces. Solidarities and collectivities foreign to indigenous and European traditions have come into being as part of the revolutionary process, to undertake action, now here, now there, in the southern tricontinent. They have created new social entities, based on distinctive conceptions of contemporary social reality, and engendered by characteristically new aspirations and aims. These new societies have found autonomy, coherence and authority according to visions and standards of their own. Revolutionary commitments, for what they are worth, have in their turn given rise to new problems: for example, how the continuity of the new societies over successive generations is to be maintained; and whether the rest of the world should adapt to them, or they should adapt to it.

When masses of people move beyond conventionally sanctioned, familiar and long-established systems and structures to realize new possibilities, we are in the presence of unprecedented situations. In this book we observe Nehru, Josue de Castro, Truong Chinh, Chou En-lai, Arciniegas, Furtado, Mao Tse-tung, Ben Barka and others surveying the social scene and the prospects from a variety of standpoints in the process of transformation. The calling into question of the whole social order, by drawing attention to all the elements and relationships and interactions and assumptions which make up society, reminds us of the immensity of social realities. But, immense

61

and unpredictably changing though the social and psychological processes in the Third World may appear to be, they are palpable and comprehensible.

A world centred on the European peoples has been ably analysed in terms of sociological theory developed by such major 'Western' sociologists as Max Weber, Emile Durkheim and Talcott Parsons, and also in the work of Soviet and other Marxist scholars. But new developments are needed to take into account the actual world of the twentieth century. The small-scale studies in 'political anthropology' of aspects of national and village economies, of societies supposedly 'in transition' to a Western model, and the like, provide interesting and useful information. But it would only multiply the confusions and fruitless ambiguities to be modelling our understanding of the Third World on the research done into 'closed' and 'undeveloped' societies. These societies may be 'developing' away from, not towards Western models. An inappropriate 'frame of reference' cannot, in an imperialistic manner, be imposed by sociologists of the 'north' who demand conformity to their respective 'Eastern' or 'Western' patterns. It has to be identified by close and detailed analyses which must indicate pragmatically what it is that is 'emerging' or 'developing' in the southern tricontinent, what the boundaries really are, what the hierarchy of roles is, what is the relative status of different functions and social groups, what the relationship between economics, politics, education, religion and the arts is, and so on. The formation and activity of the family, the village, the urban community, the school, the region, the factory and the 'kingdom' – how this formation and activity over periods of time are mutually related to form social wholes of wider or narrower span are subjects still to be studied in regard to non-Western peoples. We have yet to establish sociologically what such terms as 'China', 'India', 'Brazil' or 'Arab nation' mean, and what at various times the order is of which these are a part; and also what 'the unit' of society was in pre-modern times and in the phase of revolutionary modernization; how integration, order, stability and change were ensured at one time or another. When important 'actors' in any 'nation' are geographically outside 'the area', what should the unit of study be?

Sociologists use terms like 'differentiation' and 'specialization', but these can mean different things in the Third World. On these questions as well as on others such as what activity and elements constitute the 'economy', and what determines economic growth, Chinese society is today the most challenging intellectually. Revolutionary transformation beginning at the lowliest levels has been most far-reaching, and there has been a free and rich creation of new organizational forms and institutions. The 'separation of powers' in revolutionary China, the 'functions' of the People's Liberation Army or administration in factories in China are intelligible only if we devise sociological categories which will take account of strange realities. 'The family' also changes its meaning. Unfortunately, in academic sociology today there is too much of the provincialism which is ignorant of the fact that other peoples do things differently from the North Americans or Russians or British.*

THE VALUE OF DYNAMIC ANALYSIS

Fundamental to any scientific study of the economic and social structures of the Third World is an explanation of what some see as an area of 'turmoil' and 'anarchy'. Both this essay and the readings draw attention to the fact that the masses in such parts of the Third World as China, Mexico, India, Guatemala, Cuba, Peru and Portuguese Guinea were acting to change the forces responsible for the oppression and poverty they find unbearable. Readers will understandably be engaged on one side or another of the worldwide struggle. Since the systematic study of society and politics is a humanizing and civilizing action there is therefore much to be learnt by a sociological inquiry into the ordering of world society which produces on

* See Eric Wolf (1967), Dellinger (1964), Schurman (1966), Jaguaribe (1965), and Frank (1968). The richest field of study today is China, but its intellectual fascination is lost on the redundant kremlinologists and other cold warriors who have unfortunately associated this area of Third World study with Pekinology.

the one hand colonial and neo-colonial situations (with their highly affluent Western-oriented minorities) and on the other the insurgencies and rebellions. (The life histories of the 'makers' of the Third World are contrasted with those of 'Northern' leaders: imprisonment, exile, underground existence and persecution is 'normal' in their history.) What is involved, in terms of the modes of production, cultural activities, law, government and the relations among these, in the struggle to transform the order which creates what is seen as poverty and oppression into the desired order? If the one per cent who appropriate an inordinately large percentage of the wealth available and the means of producing wealth are not merely to be replaced by another privileged minority, if the existence of inequality is to be transformed into a more productive equality, what is the 'order' which makes an orderly process of this? What are the processes and systems which ensure the continuous exercise of revolutionary power by the masses? *

Non-sociologists sometimes confess that they find the language used by professional sociologists incomprehensible. It is true that even sociologists of major importance can and often do strain and contort their mother-tongue till it fails to say what needs to be conveyed; thought is cluttered up with a phraseology that is almost private to the sociologist. On the other hand, as we recognized a few pages earlier, systematic and methodical analysis of a society in its part or in its totality is impossible (for all but creative writers of rare genius) without a conceptual framework and a theory of how social systems work.

---

*There are indeed many distinguished people who have made pronouncements on world poverty and the very uneasy situation in the world today without bothering to try to understand what is happening in the world today. But enough published material is available to make it clear to anyone that a little napalm, some birth control and 'winning the hearts and minds' of the natives are not adequate to ensure that there is no problem or issue here to study. See Burchett (1965), Hinton (1967), Han Suyin (1966), Pike (1963), Lomax (1964), Fanon (1959), Juliao (1963), Dumont (1965), Fals Borda (1965), Sison (1967), Worsley (1964), Frank (1964) for specific situations. Also Georges LeFevre: *The Coming of the French Revolution*, Princeton, 1947.

By continually focusing attention on established systems and patterns and processes which have an autonomous existence, social theory tends to obscure the fact that the communal as well as individual human intelligence with its shaping and creative power is always at work and can, in history, create, destroy and re-create social systems. Social stability – the continuity of a social structure over a period of time – is viewed rather differently by those non-visible, submerged elements in society at whose expense it is maintained from the way in which it is presented by sociologists who regard what already exists as social order and what threatens it as disorder.

This fact is even more significant when we think of the global social system which came into being at the end of the nineteenth century. Sociology, Economics, Political Science and International Affairs of those who serviced the dominant stratum have tended increasingly to instil in us conceptions of 'systems' which in spite of their intellectual coherence have little to do with the actual world of the majority of people. And the more the 'First World' has ceased to be coterminous with the world society, the more partisan, propagandist and polemical the social sciences have of course become in arguing that it provides the models for 'modernization' and 'development'.

The effort to acquire a fresh understanding of the process going on in the Third World and its problems and prospects brings one up against these deficiencies in the intellectual apparatus with which one equips oneself in the First or Second Worlds. One comes to be aware that social and political and economic theories must have a place for the revolutionary and creative factor in the human intelligence which can carry entire societies further than or in a different direction from the point towards which they are moving; they must specify what relative importance unstructured or deviant 'man' has on the one hand, and social structure, economic organization, given political constitutions and processes, law and given moral principles have on the other. Society not only *is* but is all the time coming into being. Its future is not simply the extension onwards in time of what is now in process, but always is unpredictable.

Its different elements and components are all the time pulsating with life of differing intensities. The social sciences, in so far as they want to describe it in action, measure it, learn from it about what man is, and to be open to its possibilities, must be based on a much more dynamic conception of social systems than they now are, under the pressure of First World ideologies. This is especially true when we are dealing with the 'history without precedent' which is being made in the Third World; now, more than ever, it is true that we cannot approach living communities as though they were dead, and that we cannot unravel the mystery of what is new if we assume we know all that there is to be discovered.

The resistance to a change from static to dynamic conceptions of society is of course not simply an academic question. The distinguished Colombian sociologist, Orlando Fals Borda, makes this clear:

Structural-functionalism seems to be the idealization of the particular social conditions in which present over-developed capitalist societies operate. It furnishes a scientific rationale for the existing social order, for the American way of life. It seeks to justify and explain the stability sought in order to preserve a way of life that is imagined to be the best in the world. ... It seeks to give ideological and scientific foundations to the myths of the Great Society and orderly change. Structural-functionalism provides a good model for analysis of this type of society: the equilibrium model.

The conceptual frames of reference within which U.S. social scientists prefer to work are devised so as to demonstrate equilibrium or balance in society. Objectivity becomes anything that proves the equilibrium model is correct. Anything opposing it becomes a value judgement. It can readily be seen that this, in itself, is a bias. It overlooks the realities of life in a dialectical and Manichean world. It is inadequate in explaining the states of real conflict within society. After all, not all conflict is bad. Obviously, many of the revolutions of the world, including the American one, have been expressions of conflict. There are several works now, one of them by Professor Coser, a North American, which point to the positive sides of conflict. But Coser's work does not fit into the equilibrium model.

When all deviance is considered bad because it is incongruous with 'normal' tendencies, it may reveal a value judgement by a scientist who is reluctant to take a stand on controversial problems within his society. Such scientists do not want to commit themselves to something that will defy their society, their superiors, or general vested interests. They accommodate rather than risk their positions. They avoid the discussion by saying that to be objective is to be aloof and non-committed. This also is a bias, because it is a commitment to avoid change and conflict.

These biases have consequences in field work. Once in the field, of course, decisions must be made on how to tackle the technical problems. For example, should the study be cross-sectional or historical? The tendency has been to consider cross-sectional studies as paradigms of objectivity. But this is only the synchronic approach, which avoids an explanation of the diachronic, often cruder, realities of life. There has been a preference for making cultural inventories rather than studying what is behind cultural traits, or to concentrate on ancient archaeology or the ethnology of isolated, presumably contented marginal peoples who are free of the major schisms of civilization.*

If society, as we claimed earlier, is coming into being all the time, and is not a pre-existent state, then we make more sense of social realities. Poverty or world hunger is not a given condition; it is a social product of the world society of our time. 'Underdevelopment' is a term which may have the wrong implications; it is not something from which societies start, it is a state at which, like all other social phenomena not directly caused by totally unprecedented or very rare natural disasters, society arrives. The study of the phenomenon must trace the process. If this is true, Walt Rostow's theorizing in *The Stages of Economic Growth* is not only unrelated to actual historical examples of economic growth in the Third World, but is a theory of history based on the fictitious notion of a society moving from a static condition through non-revolutionary stages to 'take off'.†

* 'The Ideological Biasses of North Americans Studying Latin America', mimeographed, New York, 1966.

† The work of the orthodox schools of development theory is examined in Frank (1967). It would not be unfair to suggest that Rostow's capacities, intellectually and morally, for coping with the contemporary world are best indicated by the quotation in the footnote on page 27, and by his practical contribution to the well-being of the Vietnamese people.

OTHER PROBLEMS

One becomes conscious, in trying to understand the Third World, of so many problems of approach and attitude, that it would be tedious to write notes on them here. One need only point to some of these. One must decide whether to analyse developments and events in wide or narrow perspectives, and whether to show them in the long or the short run. The results may differ considerably if one changes the time-span from ten years to seventy years, as this book tends to do. Then, so much of what is written about the Third World consists of prescription, even of wishful thinking. In 'problem-centred' studies *whose* problems are being discussed? Those of the Western and Soviet Worlds are very different from those of decolonization. Is intelligent polemical writing valuable as analysis? Then, there is the importance to be given to conflicts: how relevant are terms like 'right' and 'left', solidarities and conflicts of 'class', the factor of race, neo-colonialism against 'national liberation'? In what ways has the status and function of 'peasants' in Third World countries differed from these in Europe? Is Modernization in post-colonial non-European societies different from what, according to various theories, it is in Europe and North America, or is it the same?

5. THE OTHERNESS OF
THE THIRD WORLD

*

DISTINCTIVE VALUES AND
CONFLICTS OF INTEREST

WHEN the mass of the people in any particular country come to feel that they are intolerably oppressed by the laws, institutions and values which the ruling minority have imposed on them, and when they organize themselves to rise up in revolt against the oppressive order, and overthrow it, what have they achieved? If, after overthrowing the beneficiaries of the oppressive system who have dominated them, they choose to end the system rather than make themselves the oppressors or 'dominators', what should they do? Supposing they believe that the old system was a tyranny, and want genuine democracy: what action do they take?

This kind of situation, like so many others which come under what has been called here the revolutionary 'making of history', leads us into questions about values and goals. A whole host of questions at the deepest level, of what communities are going to live for, challenge, even torment, the most sensitive spirits in the non-European world. Not for them the crude and vulgar rhetoric of a choice between 'the free world' and 'totalitarianism'. Given the revolutionary overthrow of a system which has been more or less sophisticated in its use of power actually to oppress and humiliate and impoverish, and the presence of the once-oppressed on the threshold of an era of freedom which has yet to be built, what does democracy mean? Should the experienced and well-organized group who are determined to recover the power to exploit and oppress, and those, as yet unorganized, who have just won, perhaps at great cost to themselves, the chance to create a new society, have equal political freedom? Is the denial of this freedom 'not playing the game' – a violation of democracy? Is the denial of the freedom of any group of men to appropriate the productive resources and work opportunities of the community a violation of what is most sacrosanct in a democracy?

Questions like these arise because the end of authoritarian and oppressive forms is a highly valued goal of many politically conscious people in the Third World. But we have in this rough sequence of questions not only a discussion of alternative values. We have one of the roots of conflict, one of the contradictions between the European world and the non-European world. There are others which are similar; and intelligent study of the Third World is perhaps impossible unless their importance is appreciated. Democracy which exalts the mass of *the people* as the creators of history, as the object of service, and beneficiaries of development, as the judges of good and bad government, *must* come into conflict with Western and Soviet conceptions of it; it is also irreconcilable with the freedom of Europeans and North Americans to operate politically and economically in the Third World.

Terms like 'non-aligned' and 'neutral' when attached to the Asian and African countries are misleading and nonsensical. No country can survive if it makes it a principle not to commit itself to special goals and values, and not to fight to defend its freedom and its people against attack, invasion and foreign occupation. In the struggle between the impoverished, subject peoples of the Third World and those who exploit them – the struggle for 'national liberation', that is – those who are neutral are either confused or opportunistic. The same judgement must apply to those who are non-aligned and neutral when the poor and the exploited are violently suppressed for demanding justice and equality. But what do these highly charged terms mean in the Third World revolutions?

CHARACTERISTICS OF THE THIRD WORLD

There is no point in listing the clashes of values and interests here.* An attempt to name the characteristics of the Third

* There is no uniformity of goals and values thoughout the Third World, but, as the readings indicate, the Third World is sharply distinguished by its interests and values from what it experiences of the First and Second Worlds.

World will provide some indications, as these notes on the study of the Third World conclude, of why it is a controversial subject.

The Third World is outside Europe and North America, and it is not an extension of the power, values and interests of greater Europe (Europe, North America, Japan and Australia), given local colouring in Asia, Africa and Latin America; it is an authentically independent and original creation of the peoples of the southern continents, conscious of their pre-colonial past and identity, but open to a 'future without precedent'. It is a future in which the primitive, peripheral or subordinate role its peoples played as producers and consumers is ended. During the period of the modern industrial and technological advance made by man, these societies were partly in decline, and were partly retarded by foreign conquest and colonial policies. The only modern sectors they had were developed as dependencies of economic, cultural and political centres elsewhere; and they have remained predominantly rural. They were at the end of the old colonial period unindustrialized, illiterate, and characterized internally by extreme inequalities of wealth, influence and power between the people and an *élite* minority. Their peoples are on the whole almost all racially 'non-white', and experience the effects of prejudice and discrimination by the world-dominant 'white' races of the north. Their lands are areas where it is normal for foreigners to claim the mission and responsibility of tutelage, and of deciding what is and what is not legitimate. But they have disavowed any dependent, inferior or satellite role. This disavowal leads in action to a conflict, as revolutionary actions against old and new forms of subjugation or subordination to Europe and North America are met with countering actions in defence of those who find stability and peace in the still-existing order of European dominance. It is regarded as normal in this order that the Third World is an area where foreigners may possess or monopolize vitally important economic assets and strategic positions. The Third World is an area of world society in which greater Europe can, by consensus, act as it wills, but which has no reciprocal rights. Within it are thousands of military bases, holdings of natural resources, agricultural and industrial enterprises, and cultural institutions ensuring free action by foreigners from greater Europe; there is no reciprocal opportunity or process. It contributes resources equivalent to a considerable proportion of its investment in development to advance the interests and welfare of groups outside. A large number of its national units are under foreign military occupation, without objection from organizations like the United Nations. To start with, these areas generally had foreign-oriented military and civilian *élites*, and in many parts of it *élites* loyal to Europe or North America are in conflict with nationalist revolutionaries. The area, in which two thirds of the world's population live, is, in contrast to the North Atlantic region or Eastern Europe, not monolithic, but an area of immense diversity, with a large number of centres of revolutionary initiative and action. It is marked by the emergence of a highly developed political consciousness, social dynamism, and determination outside the middle-class liberal groups to create a new social order; revolutionary thinking and activity is *normal* within it. There is a 'revolution of rising expectations' following what mass movements have achieved in *the* leading countries in the area. The present world economy is seen as one which breeds poverty. There is in the Third World much less individualism than has been cultivated in Europe and North America, and communal forms of organization still persist. Highly valued private and communal satisfactions have not been fully commercialized. Personal relationships are highly valued. Modernization is seen as a process by which all that is best in organization and technology can be used by all the people in their own way to realize the best of their values and satisfactions.

By the standards of greater Europe, all the peoples of the Third World fall into the category of those who are inferior in rights and abilities; what may be done in or to their countries may not be reciprocated. By the consciousness in the most dynamic areas of Latin America, Africa and Asia, the tricontinental southern hemisphere is a new world in the making. It has had a rich experience of what oppression, war, misrepresentation, foreign and economic exploitation can do to men, women and children, and a vision of what revolutionary solidarity, science and political wisdom can achieve to create a world free of oppression. But it has no blue-print for the new world, or the new man, in the making. Even people in the once-colonized continents may be surprised to discover how much the thinking of Chinese and Colombian, Indian and Tanzanian, Egyptian and Brazilian, Mexican and Vietnamese, have in common. It is an exciting, intellectually, and spiritually challenging world.

PART TWO

A NEW WORLD IN THE MAKING: NEITHER WESTERN NOR SOVIET

WHAT leaders of the struggle against European domination in Latin America, Asia and Africa had to say about conditions in their countries and continents; their discussion of their goals and aspirations; and their formulation and execution of policies and programmes of social and political action: once we have established as a fact that the Third World exists, these are crucial to its understanding, and are dealt with in the readings in later sections. But, first, are the social and economic awareness which they express indeed part of a *Third* World – and not, more or less marginally, still part of the structure of a world with only two parts, the international capitalist order ('the free world') and the Soviet *bloc*?

'Independence' is often taken as the starting point for a radically new existence for the nations the development of whose resources and people had been subordinated to the imperial powers of greater Europe and Japan. The transfer of governmental functions from the metropolitan imperial capitals – Lisbon, Madrid, London, the Hague, Paris, Moscow, Brussels, Washington, Rome, Berlin, Tokyo and so on – to national capitals in Latin America, Asia and Africa was seen to mark the end of 'colonialist', 'imperialist' forms of aggression, exploitation and subordination.

Accordingly, the distinguished Indian historian, K. M. Panikkar, ending his *Asia and Western Dominance*, chronicled what he believed was the close in Asia of 'the Vasco da Gama epoch'. He was presumably writing at a time when there would be no more of the invasions and domination of the non-European world by the merchants, soldiers, missionaries, manufacturers and administrators from the European nations. Other scholars as well as statesmen also treated the imperialism of the industrialized countries, with its characteristic ethos, institutions, social structure and ideologies, as a thing of the dead past. Developments after a given date were treated as though they belonged to a new social order. What had then to be presumed was that the former colonial and semi-colonial peoples had been initiated by their imperial rulers into a new experience – a contemporary or post-colonial development – outside the system of authority and values of which their colonial or semi-colonial existence had been a part. The 'end of Empire' or 'end of imperialism' could be evident only because it had decisively been succeeded by an ongoing, 'independent' national and international life for the once-subject peoples.

In seeking documentary material on the Third World which represents this view one is led therefore to look first in a particular direction. That is, in so far as it is the 'independence' allowed by the colonial powers which is the origin of the Third World one focuses one's attention on the words and acts of those to whom power and leadership were transferred. For it is presumably these words and acts which would establish and document what liberal nationalists like Dr Panikkar have taken for granted – the fact that the subject peoples have out of their constitutional independence circumscribed, contained, brought to a conclusion the extra-territorial dominion of British, French, Dutch, United States, Russian, Japanese, German and other European interests.

It turns out, however, that the task of the person who in this way wishes to document the end of empire and the emergence of the Third World is not as straightforward as all that. Our aim is to find material which is of more than literary interest. The educated nationalists who had inveighed against foreign rule and its humiliations for the native *élites* sometimes produced a vague and liberal rhetoric which did little to edify or inform. It was still the derivative, provincial expression of the imperial metropolitan culture. Its fantasies denied that there was any responsibility for an original, creative construction on new foundations. It was grand talk which provided no clue to any radical distinction between pre-independence and post-imperial society.

The material, much of it official, representing the 'orderly transition' conception of a new era of independence, is indeed useless as evidence of a transformation of the peoples and social structures of Latin America, Asia and Africa. It does not demonstrate the reversal of the processes and operations of imperialism – a reversal which must precede the establishment of the Third World. The 'transition' from foreign to native administrations, such 'nationalist' developments as the revival of pre-colonial ('native') religious and social customs and rituals, and the repression of the poorer masses, were all perfectly consistent with the pre-independence order. The imperial rulers had often functioned through loyal and 'responsible' intermediaries, usually traditional authorities. The transfer of administrative, legislative and police powers to native land-owners, colonels or businessmen occurred in some cases long before the date of formal 'granting of independence'. Even membership of the United Nations Organization is not a sign of a radically new and independent development. To take anything and everything said or written by nationalists as a demonstration of the existence of the Third World would be nonsensical. There is Asian, African and Latin American material clearly demonstrating the continued integration and subordination of elements within these continents into and to the Europeanized First and Second Worlds. It is interesting material, but it does not illustrate the emergence and existence of the Third World. But what does? Do the peoples of the tricontinental south have a post-colonial consciousness? And then there is the material we have rejected as irrelevant: of what social and historical phenomenon is it a reflection?

The Senegalese economist and statesman, Mamadou Dia, has some relevant clues to the answers. And so have several others who have been in the forefront of action and thought, whose work, too, is represented in the four sections of readings. Discussing the 'twentieth-century revolution' of the 'proletarian nations', M. Dia refers to 'neo-colonialism', and 'the effort of decolonization [which] must lead young nations [sic] to become principal creators of their own history by preparing themselves the technical and psychological conditions for that history'. His *African Nations and World Solidarity*, from which the first excerpt is taken, was written after 'independence' in French West Africa. He gave it as his considered view that the ascendancy of the West had never been 'so decisively effective as in this post-colonial period'.

It is, clearly, what has happened and what is happening in the tri-continental south (Latin America, Asia and Africa) that must provide evidence that the term 'Third World' is not a polite fiction – a face-saving label for non-white peoples who are sensitive about the exploitation and discrimination which is their lot in the world order. The fact that there are individual persons in the formerly subject areas who can conceive of a society with distinctively non-European standards and values, and who recommend independent policies and plans is not significant for our purpose; the Third World cannot be a set of ideas. Further, what was *expected* to happen in any colony as a result of the transfer of power on Independence Day is not evidence that a post-imperial order exists and functions and gives meaning to what happens among the formerly subject people. 'Independence' does not provide a dividing line. How, then, in the given social and historical conditions, did the Third World come to exist? If there is no continuity with the colonial order, how was the continuity actually broken? Historical events, we must suppose, cannot occur in the way they actually do except as products of human action. The phenomena we are observing are the result of action taken by human organizations and communities who have the determination, ability and the power to 'make history'; only then can they effect, or prevent, the carrying out of intended policies of change – only then can they decide whether what is decisive is conquest or liberation, oppression or revolution.

The governments whose power and interests had been decisive in the non-European world at the beginning of this century made (or endorsed) plans for the periods following both the First World War and the Second. But one finds no evidence in these arrangements that they envisaged or legitimized the creation of an international community and economy subject neither to the Atlantic powers nor to the Soviet Union, but, rather, bounding and contracting their former domains. One can, in other words, find no evidence that the creation of the Third World was on the agenda. The evidence is on the contrary.

Whether or not the moral, economic and political order represented and safeguarded by 'Versailles', 'Yalta', 'Suez', 'Saigon' and the invasion of the Dominican Republic is a good one is not at issue here. There is no doubt that, in spite of the great local variety within it, it served the interests of some social groups. And its preservation was backed by many. Our concern here, however, is how to get hold of what actually happened to justify taking seriously what is thought, said and done among the masses of Latin America, Asia and Africa. How does there happen to be a Third World? If the old order is not intact, it is not because its rejection and overthrow in the southern hemisphere has been achieved by literary fantasy or rhetorical anti-imperialism. (That kind of material is obviously of little value for students of the contemporary world.) The very essence of a decolonizing Third World, created by and 'belonging' to its people is an historical reality to which constitutional 'independence' is no door. It is the fact that the political consciousness, loyalties, interests and values of large masses of people within the subordinate, unilaterally exploited sectors of the former world economy and policy has been a contradiction of, led them into conflict with, what had kept the colonial order intact. The presence of the Third World is manifested in actions (some taking years and even decades) which change decisively the character of the history of the peoples of the formerly subject areas – bringing the era of European world domination to its conclusion, initiating on a totally different basis a new world order. The conflict has resulted in a decisive shift of power from alien to popular agencies. The new calculation of the rights and dignity and capacity of the non-European races and of the peasant masses, the new conception of social justice, have replaced the values and norms by which the Europeanized and bourgeois world order was stabilized, and respect for it maintained.

The readings grouped together in the first section therefore

81

focus attention on the conceptions, discoveries and actions which have been crucial for the emergence of the Third World. It is in the nature of things that we note the 'revolutions' of 'the age of liberation', not 'transitional societies' developing their orderly and sanctioned road to integration in an alien world order. Whether this world of peoples, making their own, and mankind's, history out of revolutionary conflict against what they see as humiliating and oppressive for all peoples has set out on an irreversible journey, one can only speculate.

1. MAMADOU DIA

*

The Twentieth-Century Revolution*

The Senegalese, Mamadou Dia, from whose book *The African Nations and World Solidarity* the following passage is taken, was born in 1910 in French-ruled West Africa. Outstanding both as an economist and as a nationalist leader in West Africa, he became Vice-President, then President, of Senegal in 1959. That same year he became Vice-President of the short-lived federation of Senegal and Soudan, Mali, which he had helped to create. In 1960 he became Chairman of the Senegalese Council of Ministers. But disagreements with conservative, traditional elements over his policies led to his being imprisoned by Leopold Senghor on the charge that he had been plotting to seize power. He remains in prison.

BÉCAUSE of its overseas nationalisms the twentieth-century revolution appears as a hitherto unknown sociological phenomenon. All the great revolutions of earlier centuries, from 1789 to the Fifth French Republic, and those that have freed the rest of Europe – the last being the Soviet Revolution – present common characteristics. They all have, necessarily, an ideology inspired by classic Western humanism, emphasizing notions of liberty and the universality of man's fate. But whether bourgeois or Marxist, these revolutions bear the imprint of a dated universalism different from an integral humanism that includes all mankind.

Some will surely protest, invoking the touching generosity of the leaders of the anti-slavery movement, to mention only the bourgeois revolution. As for the Marxists, they will never forgive so unexpected a *rapprochement*. One must nevertheless observe that despite the superficial universality that a certain amount of pre- and post-romantic philosophy confers upon it, the Revolution of 1789, for example, remains essentially a French revolution, whatever its repercussions abroad may

*From *The African Nations and World Solidarity*, translated by Mercer Cook (New York: Praeger, 1962).

have been. We must not forget that the project of the federalist Cloots for a 'universal republic' was rejected by the Convention after the intervention of the Dantonist Robert, who received wide support in the name of a realistic nationalism, selfishly French. Fichte's views on the closed nation exerted influence on the evolution not only of European nationalism, but equally of the countries of the socialist revolution, at least during Stalin's era.

All these revolutions generally present the spectacle of a dialectical, factual opposition between the notions of 'state' and 'nation' as defined by territory. This opposition stems from the tension between two internal forces in perpetual hostility. Whether it be a bourgeois or a socialist regime, the problem is for the state to justify its claim that it legitimately embodies the nation; otherwise, quarrels are multiplied and conflicts break out, ending sometimes in the triumph of the one, sometimes in the victory of the other. Neither Marxist nor bourgeois revolutions escape this classic duel, and the appearance of new concepts, such as the dictatorship of the proletariat, does not alter this fundamental principle. Bourgeois or socialist, the democracies created by these historic crises have no other national basis than the traditionally decisive elements: geographical area, cultural unity, and especially the zone of historical influence. Marxism–Leninism, despite all the resources of dialectics, has made no innovations in this respect. In the final analysis, it has built the Soviet state and the new socialist nation on no bases other than those of the classical theory, formulated in different language. It is interesting that though the slogans change, the borders of the national territory strangely coincide with those of the Tsarist Empire. Evidently, the revolution has not rejected all aspects of the old Greater Russia.

On the other hand, in the politically dominated countries of Africa or Asia, we are facing a new type of revolution. It is no longer a matter of applying Platonic or Hegelian ideology. If it is a question of freedom, this must be stripped of its metaphysical content, inherited from a current of romanticism. Changing the focus, freedom will be applied less to the indi-

vidual than to subjected collectivities. A nation-state establishes
its dominion over foreign territories, which, however retarded
their technical development may be, still contain nations or
homelands, even when captive. Whatever art may be deployed
to prolong their slumber, before long these nations become
conscious of their condition. We then begin to question the
relationship between one people and another, between the
dominating nation-state and the dominated nation or homeland. Because of historical circumstances that have made
colonial imperialism an affair between one continent and
another, between one civilization and another, the conflict in
human relations does not lack racial implications at the outset
and for a long time. But it is the consciousness of economic
inequality that gives birth to a proletarian national sentiment,
aligning the nations of Africa and Asia on the same battlefront
against the West. With the consciousness of underdevelopment,
a new idea appears, that of proletarian nations grouped 'on the
lifeline of imperialism' confronting rich nations with a geographical unity that widens the gap between them. Here,
evidently, is the most original feature of the twentieth-century
revolution. And this also underlines the importance of the
stakes on which the peace of the world depends.

2. LI TA-CHAO

*

The Dawn of 'The Age of Liberation' *

1919, the year of the peace conference in Versailles, was, whether
by coincidence or for deeper reasons, a turning point for the
peoples who had experienced subjection in one form or another to
those who ruled in Europe, North America and Japan, as well as
to the Turks. Very modest demands for consideration of and respect for the rights of subject peoples were addressed to the representatives of the leading powers assembled in Paris; and these
appeals (by Nguyen Ai Quoc [Ho Chi Minh] and the Egyptian
nationalist leader Said Zaghul, for instance) were based entirely
on the ideals and principles professed by the ruling powers, and not
on any radically new ones. In the event the Asian and African
nationalists were dissatisfied with the treatment they got. In Peking
the political movement started by the action of Chinese university
students and teachers on 4 May began a new phase of Chinese
history.

Among those affected was Li Ta-chao (1888–1927), a teacher at
the University of Peking, who was perhaps the first of the Chinese
leaders to realize the universal implications of the Bolshevik Revolution in Russia. As Dr Huang Sung-k'ang, from whose translations
of Li's work in *Li Ta-chao and the Impact of Marxism on Modern
Chinese Thinking* the following extracts are taken, writes: 'The
universalist outlook of Li Ta-chao always urged him on to seek a
solution for China which would at the same time encompass the
world beyond China. Time and again he cautioned the young
Chinese: "Since we are the youth of the twentieth century, we
must have a world vision. We must not be bound by corrupt family
ties. We must not be obstructed by narrow patriotism. Our new
life should begin with the development of personality, and then it
should go on to the promotion of happiness for the whole world.
The scope of our family has been widened to include the whole
world; the old restrictions are the traces left by evolution. We
should free ourselves from them. We should live the life of the

* From *Li Ta-chao and the Impact of Marxism on Modern Chinese
Thinking*, translated by Huang Sung-k'ang (The Hague: Mouton, 1965).

world as the life of our family. We should realize that the love-humanity movement is more important than the love-one's-own-country movement." '

Li was shot in April 1927 by the warlord who controlled the government in Peking.

(i) The European war has come to an end. We dreamt that humanity and peace had won and that from now on the world might cease to be a bandit world, and that perhaps there would be some human touch to it. Who knows but humanity and peace are nothing more than false signboards of the bandit-governments? We have but to look at the resolutions of the Paris Conference. Is there any shadow of humanity, justice, peace or honour in them? Is there anything that is not a sacrifice of freedom and the rights of the weaker nations for the benefit of the great bandit-powers?

(ii) The present age is the age of liberation, and the civilization of the modern age is the civilization of liberation. The people demand liberation from the state, the local governments demand liberation from the central authority, the colonies demand liberation from the colonizers, the weaker races demand liberation from the stronger races, the peasants demand liberation from the landlords, the workers demand liberation from the capitalists, the women demand liberation from the men and the young people demand liberation from the parents and elders. Every movement that arises in the political or social sphere is a movement of liberation.

3. CHANAKYA SEN

*

A New Post-War World*

The Second World War affected the peoples of Asia as deeply as it did those of Europe. The growing consciousness of the nature of imperialism and of the need to free Asia from it was responsible for the popular support given to leaders like Jawaharlal Nehru, Mao Tse-tung, Ho Chi Minh, Aung San and Soekarno. The war itself had begun in 1937 with the Japanese seizure of large parts of China, which were incorporated into its 'Greater Co-Prosperity Sphere'. The establishment of Japanese rule over peoples who had been under British, French, Dutch and American colonial regimes, and the anti-Fascist war, helped considerably to transform political and economic conditions in Asia. The organization of popular anti-Fascist guerrilla warfare in Indo-China, the Philippines and China, the resistance to British repression in India, all strengthened the anti-imperialist forces. The experience of the war, and the declarations of the Allied leaders, had led Asian nationalists to expect great changes in 1945 and the years following. Some of the expectations and anxieties are described by the Indian writer Chanakya Sen in his book *Against the Cold War*. He quotes Nehru, who, with a hundred thousand other Indian nationalists, had spent most of the war years in prison.

On 14 August 1945 came the complete collapse of the Axis Powers in the Second World War. Three days later, on 17 August 1945, a handful of Indonesians, meeting in hushed excitement at a modest corner of Djakarta, proclaimed the independence of Indonesia. Within six weeks, British troops landed in Indonesia to fight the post-war period's first colonial war. From that day till this, Asia or Africa has not been completely free from colonial war even for a single day.

But war is a strange alchemist. It contains in its hidden chambers unforeseen elements which tear down the dreams of the victorious and the vanquished. The Second World War

*From *Against the Cold War* (Bombay: Asia Publishing House).

which surpassed any other previous war by many times in its demand on the resources of the earth, released strange forces which strangely altered the face of continents. The world which had started the war almost completely perished with it. When the war ended, a new world took the place of the old. The balance of power changed totally. And in the new scheme of things, which continually baffled and surprised statesmen all over the world, an unforeseen development called for un-accustomed attention. This was the awakening of Asia and Africa. . . .

During the war the British Prime Minister had made it clear that the lofty ideals embodied in the Atlantic Charter were not meant for the enslaved continents of Asia and Africa. And after the war, the European imperial powers were determined to hold what they had and to regain what they had lost to Japan.

The Cold War started in Europe and over Europe. It was an undeclared global conflict which gathered momentum as the years passed until it became total in character. When it began, its authors took no notice of Asian–African sentiment; they did not pause to consider the pledges they owed to the millions of human beings struggling for better life.

When the war was drawing to its close with unmistakable signs of an Allied victory, a great Asian, locked in a British prison, asked agonizing questions tormenting the soul of Asia and Africa:

What will the leaders of the victorious nations say when they meet together after success in war has crowned their efforts? How is the future taking shape in their minds, and how far do they agree or differ between themselves? What other reaction will there be when the passion of war subsides and people try to return to the scarce-remembered ways of peace? What of the underground re-sistance movements of Europe and the new forces they have re-leased? What will the millions of war-hardened soldiers, returning home much older in minds and experience, say and do? How will they fit into the life which has gone on changing when they were away? What will happen to devastated and martyred Europe and what to Asia and Africa? What of the 'over-powering urge for freedom of Asia's hundreds of millions', as Mr Wendell Wilkie describes it? What of all these and more? And what, above all, of the strange trick that fate so often plays upsetting the well-laid schemes of our leaders?

From behind the prison walls that master mind could only guess what was happening in the chancellories of the warring nations. He knew that the end of the war would bring an unprecedented crisis in the British Empire, but he was also aware how deep-rooted was the imperial sentiment in the British ruling character.

He realized that in the post-war world, the centre of power would shift to Moscow and Washington. He also knew that 'whatever the future may hold, it is clear that the economy of the U.S.A. after the war will be powerfully expansionist and almost explosive in its consequences'. And he asked, 'Will this lead to some new kind of imperialism?'

The future policy of the Soviet Union was still shrouded in mystery. But from some revealing glimpses, he visualized that Russia in the post-war world would aim 'at having as many friendly and dependent or semi-dependent countries near its borders as possible'. He imagined that although the Soviet Union would work with other powers for the establishment of some world organization, it would rely 'more on building up its own strength on an unassailable basis'.

And other nations would try to do likewise as far as they could.

'That is not a hopeful prelude to world cooperation,' mused Jawaharlal Nehru while writing the last pages of *The Discovery of India*. 'Between the Soviet Union and other countries there is not the same struggle for export markets as between Britain and the U.S.A. But the differences are deeper, their respective view-points further apart, and mutual suspicions have not been allayed even by the joint effort in the war. If these differences grow, the U.S.A. and Britain will tend to seek each other's company and support as against the U.S.S.R. group of nations.'

Where do the hundreds of millions of Asia and Africa come in this picture? [he asked. And he hastened to add:] They have become increasingly conscious of themselves and their destiny, and,

90

at the same time, become world-conscious. Large numbers of them follow world events with interest. For them, inevitably the test of each move or happening is this: Does it help towards our liberation? Does it end the domination of one country over another? Will it enable us to live freely the life of our choice in cooperation with others? Does it bring equality and an equal opportunity for nations as well as groups within each nation? Does it hold forth the promise of an early liquidation of poverty and illiteracy and bring better living conditions? They are nationalistic, but this nationalism seeks no domination over, or interference with, others. They welcome all attemps at world cooperation and the establishment of an international order, but they wonder and suspected if this may not be another device for continuing the old domination. Large parts of Asia and Africa consist of awakened, discontented, seething humanity, no longer prepared to tolerate existing conditions. Conditions and problems differ greatly in the various countries of Asia, but throughout this vast area, in China and India, in South-east Asia, in Western Asia and the Arab world, run common threads of sentiment and invisible links which hold them together.

4. TRUONG CHINH

*

After Liberation from Colonial Rule –
What Kind of Society? *

Some of Nehru's questions about the post-war order were answered in very practical terms by the Vietnamese people as the Second World War drew to a close. The action by which they recovered their independence as a nation, their 'August Revolution' of 1945, turned out to be one of the decisive events of the post-war order. The Democratic Republic of Vietnam which the Vietnamese created and subsequently fought to defend indicated, almost before anything else, what kind of society the resurgent colonial peoples were creating.

It is clear that the Vietnamese revolution was rooted in a long memory of Vietnamese nationhood. Vietnamese civilization, which originated in the third century B.C., was one of the most ancient in the world when the French took possession of all of Vietnam in the nineteenth century. In writing in 1946 about the August Revolution, Truong Chinh, one of the Vietnamese leaders then, and more recently Chairman of the Democratic Republic of Vietnam's National Assembly, indicates what sort of national and world society the Vietnamese revolutionaries aimed to create. Its relation to the future the major powers of Europe and North America had prescribed or envisaged for the subject peoples after the Second World War is significant.

Truong Chinh (the pseudonym for Dang Xuan Khu) was born in 1909 in the town of Hanh Thien, in the province of Nam Dinh. Having started his political career by taking vigorous part in anti-colonial activity while still a student, and having been held by the French in a forced-labour camp for five years for his leadership of a peasant rebellion in 1930, Truong Chinh belonged to that generation of Asian leaders which had little to do with 'constitutional independence'. Like Ho Chi Minh, he had seen in Lenin's example a model for organized and disciplined leadership of the revolution by which Vietnam would become free. He was General

*From *The August Revolution* (Hanoi: People's Publishing House, 1946).

Secretary of the Indo-Chinese Communist Party at the time of the August Revolution, the analysis of which a year later (1946), in his book *The August Revolution* was closely related to the struggle then going on to prevent a French reconquest of Vietnam.

THE August Revolution was a revolution for national liberation. It aimed at liberating the Vietnamese people from the colonial yoke and making Vietnam an independent nation.

However, because it struggled against the Japanese and French fascists as well as their lackeys, the feudal reactionaries, and because it contributed a part, though small, in the great world anti-fascist struggle, it had the character of a democratic revolution, though it has not abolished all the vestiges of feudalism in Vietnam, nor realized agrarian reform so as to distribute the land held by the landlords to the peasants.

In the present historic conditions, a colonial revolution must have the following double character: first, it must be an *anti-imperialist revolution* aimed at overthrowing the imperialist domination, and second, it must be an *agrarian revolution* so as to confiscate the lands of the feudal landlords and distribute them to the peasants. The August Revolution has only aimed at overthrowing the imperialist rule and that of the feudal puppets, and setting up the democratic republican regime; but it has not abolished land-ownership by the feudal landlord class and all other vestiges of feudalism to create conditions for industrial and commercial development. Thanks to the August Revolution, a portion of the imperialists' and traitors' lands have been confiscated, land rents have been reduced by twenty-five per cent and some of the old compound-interested debts have been cancelled. However, in the agrarian field, generally speaking, the relations between landlords and peasants have not changed. Therefore we can say that, though the August Revolution has a democratic character, this character is not strongly marked enough.

Some people have said that, because the August Revolution has abolished the Imperial Government, with its machinery composed of mandarins and notables, it has a distinctly anti-feudal character. But by abolishing the Imperial Government,

93

we have abolished only one aspect of the feudal regime; because its basis, which is rooted now in the relations between landlords and peasants in the agrarian field, is still alive, the feudal regime is still in existence. We must see to it that we advance the anti-feudal struggle, and not be complacent about the achievements of the August Revolution.

It is clear that the August Revolution has established in Vietnam a democratic republic having the character of a new democracy. Popular representation has been widely established at all levels by universal suffrage; complete equality between the sexes, wide democratic freedoms, as well as personal liberty and equality between all nationalities big and small have been promulgated; the regime of popular assembly, ensuring the legislative and executive powers of the people, has been established and there exists a democratic regime completely different from bourgeois parliamentary democracy, which grants the people only limited rights in making proposals and in criticizing the government; the State economic sector is taking shape; the people's conditions of life are improved; attention is paid to the life of the worker and peasant masses; the eight-hour working day is officially recognized; the proletarian class now actually holds power, etc. All these facts make it amply clear that the Vietnamese regime is that of a democratic republic of a new style quite different from the old-style bourgeois democratic regime (for example, the French bourgeois parliamentary regime). However, the democratic regime in Vietnam guarantees the interests of all social strata, while the parliamentary republican regime in France is a disguised dictatorship of the bourgeoisie: under the cloak of democracy the bourgeois class exerts a dictatorial power which defends only the interests of a minority of exploiters, the capitalists. As for the Soviet democratic republican regime, it is a regime in which the proletarian class officially exercises the dictatorship, suppresses all vestiges of the exploiting class (landlords, bourgeois and kulaks) and guarantees the widest interests of all labouring people (workers, peasants, intellectuals) who liberated themselves and are cooperating to build a new life under the leadership of the proletarian class.

The republican democratic regime in Vietnam is in keeping with the stage of development of our country and with the present world democratic movement. Though it has been established in a backward agricultural country, it carries a new and progressive character, because it was born of the hard and fierce struggle against the French and Japanese fascists, out of the struggle for national liberation led by the proletarian class. A struggle led by the most revolutionary class against the most reactionary enemy must be crowned with the installation of a non-conservative regime, quite the reverse of the retrograde regime of the enemy.

The Historic Significance of the August Revolution

The August Revolution has highlighted the indomitable spirit of the Vietnamese people, a people who are struggling untiringly to shake off the foreign yoke. It is the completion of eighty years of uninterrupted struggle of the Vietnamese people against the French colonialists. It also constitutes the greatest historic event in our country since the victory gained by Quang Trung who drove the Manchu troops out of Vietnam in 1789. In fact, since then there has been no national movement which has, as fully as the August Revolution, given evidence of the indomitable heroism and of the strong unity of the Vietnamese people. Therein lies the great significance of the August Revolution; and President Ho Chi Minh, the first President of the Democratic Republic of Vietnam, the leader of the August Revolution, deserves the title of national hero.

Through the August Revolution, the Vietnamese people have clearly shown their anti-fascist spirit and their attachment to democracy and peace. The revolution constitutes the splendid completion of the great movement against the French and Japanese fascists in Vietnam during the Second World War, especially from March last year. Before the August Revolution, the Vietnamese people struggled in very hard conditions to harass and exhaust the rear lines of the Japanese forces. From the end of 1944, the Japanese sea-lines were attacked by the Allied forces; Indo-China had become a 'bridge' over the Japanese 'Great Oriental Asia Road', a bridge extremely important for the movement and supply of Japanese troops from the northern position to Indonesia. The blocking of this bridge to the Japanese forces was the task assumed by the Vietnamese people. Therefore, in March 1945, the Indo-Chinese Communist Party launched the great movement of struggle against the Japanese for national salvation, by organizing and actively leading the Vietnamese people to the attack on important Japanese strategic positions, thus causing a block in the traffic of the Japanese over the 'Great Oriental Asia' road.

From March to August last year, Japanese territory suffered more and more violent bombing raids. In Indo-China, the Vietnamese guerrillas were fighting the Japanese with increased strength. A free zone was established in the Highlands and Midlands of North Vietnam and constituted a permanent obstacle on the path of the Japanese from Southern China to Indo-China. In this zone, the guerrillas exhausted the Japanese forces, not allowing them a moment's respite. In this way the Vietnamese people had effectively contributed their part, beside the Allies, to speed the overthrow of the Japanese and indirectly, to hasten the Soviet army's victory. It is an indubitable fact that the Vietnamese people have made their share of sacrifices in the struggle against the fascist aggressors during the recent years.

The French reactionary colonialists purposely call the August Revolution 'pro-Japanese', 'Japanese-led' to belittle its significance. But there is plenty of evidence to smash their treacherous slanders. Today everybody has to admit that the reactionary attitude of the French colonialists with regard to the August Revolution is that of the robber who loots and at the same time cries 'Stop thief'. In point of fact, did not the French colonialists, assisted by the British imperialists, make use of the Japanese troops to counter-attack the Vietnamese Revolution?

Among the peoples oppressed by the Japanese, the Indonesian, Chinese and Vietnamese peoples have been the most successful in availing themselves of the Japanese capitulation last August to rise up and win democracy and freedom.*

By the fact of the August Revolution, the Vietnamese people have lodged this general claim to the UNO: *the Great Powers must recognize the right to self-determination of the Vietnamese people, in accordance with the Atlantic and San Francisco Charters.* As a natural consequence of the Japanese collapse, all peoples under the Japanese yoke must be liberated, and nobody must be allowed to replace the Japanese in oppressing and exploiting them. The Vietnamese people will resolutely oppose the return of the French oppressors as well as the regime of a 'mandated country', because they have already attained their majority.

The August Revolution and the war of self-defence waged for almost a year by the Vietnamese people against the French reactionaries have proclaimed these eager aspirations to the world. They show clearly that the colonial imperialist system is disintegrating and that the hour of liberation has struck for the oppressed peoples. The Vietnamese Revolution, like the Chinese and Indonesian Revolutions, strongly promotes the liberation movements of the Laotian and Cambodian peoples and other colonial countries in South-East Asia: this fact explains clearly why the British imperialists have done their best to help the French colonialists to repress the Vietnamese Revolution in South Vietnam and why the international reactionaries have made concessions to one another to allow the French to relieve the troops of Chiang Kai-shek in North Vietnam.

In fact, from 23 September last year and all through our struggle waged against the French, our forces have met the British, Indian, French and Japanese troops in many a battle.

* The peoples of Burma, Malaya and the Philippines also organized guerrilla forces to resist the Japanese invaders but when the Japanese surrendered, their forces were still insufficient to cope with the invasion of the U.S. and British imperialists, who were more powerful than their congeners, the French and the Dutch. Therefore, in spite of their relatively big efforts and sacrifices, their struggles have not brought as important results as those obtained by the peoples of Indonesia, China and Vietnam. (T.C.)

Our struggle of self-defence has unveiled the perfidious schemes of the international reactionaries. It has exposed before world opinion that from the start of their landing in Indo China, the British troops, only commissioned by the allies to disarm and repatriate the Japanese soldiers, instead of setting to this task of repatriation, used these soldiers to help the French colonialists to counter-attack the Vietnamese Revolution and repress the Vietnamese people's struggle of self-defence: thus we can say that *the Vietnamese people are not fighting for themselves only, but also to a certain degree, for the defence of world peace.*

At the end of the anti-fascist war, the task of all progressive world forces is to develop democracy and build peace. With the August Revolution and the present Resistance War, the Vietnamese people have shouldered a part of the responsibility to fulfil this mission side by side with the progressive and democratic forces struggling for a better world. Whether one likes it or not, the August Revolution is part of a great movement of mankind for the building of peace and democracy. The Vietnamese people fully understand their international role in this postwar period. They are determined to fulfil this task, whatever the obstacles may be!

This is precisely the reason why the August Revolution is warmly acclaimed by progressive opinion and why the Vietnamese people now enjoy tokens of solidarity and sympathy from all democratic countries throughout the world, especially from the oppressed peoples.

5. MAO TSE-TUNG

*

The Chinese People 'Stand Up' *

It had been the view of the Chinese revolutionary nationalist leader, Sun Yat-sen, that at the beginning of this century China was worse off than an ordinary colony – it was the colony not of one power but of all. More than twenty-five nations enjoyed special privileges in China. For the task of liberating the Chinese people from the oppression of the landlords, the officials, the warlords and foreign powers Sun had in 1924 set up a revolutionary government in Canton. Among the younger leaders was Mao Tse-tung, (b. 1893) who was to carry on Sun's revolutionary work. The *coup d'état* in 1927 by the head of the army, General Chiang Kai-shek, began the civil war in China. For the next twenty-two years the struggle of the predominantly peasant people of China to emancipate themselves was conducted by the revolutionaries as a fight on two fronts: (i) against any pre-empting by foreign powers or interests of what was regarded as the Chinese people's right to decide the affairs of their country, and (ii) against traditional and new forms of authoritarian rule and economic exploitation. In heading a revolutionary peasant society in Kiangsi province, in wresting control at the Tsunyi Conference of the Communist Party of China (conceived as the vanguard of the Chinese Revolution by Li Ta-chao, Mao and others) from the Moscow-line Communists and in creating in northwest China the first modern peasant-based regime in Asia (the Shensi–Kansu–Ningshia Border Region Government, with its capital in Yenan) Mao Tse-tung prepared the ground for the decisive phase of the revolution, in the post-war years. Chiang Kai-shek, who tried to eliminate the revolutionaries, had massive American aid, and his regime was backed by the Western powers and the Soviet Union as the sole, legitimate government of China. In making his proclamation of the new government of the People's Republic of China, Mao Tse-tung saw the popular overthrow of the Chiang Kai-shek dictatorship as the overthrow also of all the

*From *Selected Works*, vol. IV (Peking: Foreign Languages Press, 1961).

foreign decisions imposed on the Chinese people since their defeat in 1842 in the First Opium War.

WE have a common feeling that our work will be recorded in the history of mankind, and that it will clearly demonstrate that the Chinese, who comprise one quarter of humanity, have begun to stand up. The Chinese have always been a great, courageous and industrious people. It was only in modern times that they have fallen behind, and this was due solely to the oppression and exploitation of foreign imperialism and the domestic reactionary government.

For more than a century, our predecessors never paused in their indomitable struggles against the foreign and domestic oppressors. These struggles include the Revolution of 1911, led by Sun Yat-sen, the great pioneer of China's revolution. Our predecessors instructed us to carry their work to completion. We are doing this now. We have united ourselves and defeated both our foreign and domestic oppressors by means of the People's Liberation War and the people's great revolution, and we proclaim the establishment of the People's Republic of China.

Henceforth, our nation will enter the large family of peace-loving and freedom-loving nations of the world. It will work bravely and industriously to create its own civilization and happiness, and will, at the same time, promote world peace and freedom. Our nation will never again be an insulted nation. We have stood up. Our revolution has gained the sympathy and acclamation of the broad masses throughout the world. We have friends the world over.

Our revolutionary work is not yet concluded....

6. NELSON MANDELA

*

The Recovery of Freedom*

One of the organizations which took part in the Pan-African Congress of 1919, and also tried to make representations at the Versailles Peace Conference, was the body which became the African National Congress. In the years that followed, the situation for the coloured people of South Africa continued to grow worse, and action on behalf of the coloured people increasingly took on the character of mass political education and struggle. One of the most outstanding of the younger leaders to emerge was Nelson Mandela (b. 1918) and it is from a speech, 'No Easy Walk to Freedom', by him in 1953 that the next piece is taken.

Oliver Tambo, a colleague, had this to say of Mandela, who in 1964 was sent into life-long captivity on Robben Island by the South African government:

'As a man Nelson is passionate, emotional, sensitive, quickly stung to bitterness and retaliation by insult and patronage. He has a natural air of authority. He cannot help magnetizing a crowd: he is commanding with a tall, handsome bearing; trusts and is trusted by the youth, for their impatience reflects his own; appealing to the women. He is dedicated and fearless. He is the born mass leader.

'But early on he came to understand that State repression was too savage to permit mass meetings and demonstrations through which the people could ventilate their grievances and hope for redress. It was of limited usefulness to head great rallies. The Government did not listen and soon enough the tear gas and the muzzles of the guns were turned against the people. The justice of our cries went unrecognized. The popularity of leaders like Mandela was an invitation to counter-attack by the Government. Mandela was banned from speaking, from attending gatherings, from leaving Johannesburg, from belonging to any organization. Speeches, demonstrations, peaceful protests, political organizing, became illegal.

'Of all that group of young men, Mandela and his close friend and co-leader Walter Sisulu were perhaps the fastest to get to grips

*From *No Easy Walk to Freedom* (London: Heinemann, 1965).

with the harsh realities of the African struggle against the most powerful adversary in Africa: a highly industrialized, well-armed State manned by a fanatical group of white men determined to defend their privilege and their prejudice, and aided by the complicity of American, British, West German, and Japanese investment in the most profitable system of oppression on the continent. Nelson was a key figure in thinking, planning, and devising new tactics.

'We had to forge an alliance of strength based not on colour but on commitment to the total abolition of apartheid and oppression; we would seek allies, of whatever colour, as long as they were totally agreed on our liberation aims. The African people, by nature of their numbers, their militancy, and the grimness of their oppression, would be the spearhead of the struggle. He had to organize the people, in town and countryside, as an instrument for struggle.'

IN China, India, Indonesia, and Korea, American, British, Dutch, and French imperialism, based on the concept of the supremacy of Europeans over Asians, has been completely and perfectly exploded. In Malaya and Indo-China, British and French imperialisms are being shaken to the foundations by powerful and revolutionary national liberation movements. In Africa there are approximately 190,000,000 Africans as against 4,000,000 Europeans.

The entire continent is seething with discontent, and already there are powerful revolutionary eruptions in the Gold Coast, Nigeria, Tunisia, Kenya, the Rhodesias, and South Africa. The oppressed people and the oppressors are at loggerheads. The day of reckoning between the forces of freedom and those of reaction is not far off. I have not the slightest doubt that when that day comes truth and justice will prevail. The intensification of repression and the extensive use of its bans is designed to immobilize every active worker and to check the national liberation movement. But gone are the days when harsh and wicked laws provided the oppressors with years of peace and quiet. The racial policies of the Government have pricked the conscience of all men of goodwill and have roused their deepest indignation. The feelings of the oppressed people have never been more bitter. If the ruling circles seek to maintain their position by such inhuman methods then a clash between the forces of freedom and those of reaction is certain. The grave plight of the people compels them to resist to the death the stinking policies of the gangsters that rule our country. But in spite of all the difficulties outlined above, we have won important victories. . . .

The friends of the people are distinguished by the ready and disciplined manner in which they rally behind their organizations, and their readiness to sacrifice when the preservation of the organization has become a matter of life and death. Similarly, enemies and shady characters are detected by the extent to which they attempt to wreck the organization by creating fratricidal strife, disseminating confusion, and undermining and even opposing important plans of action to vitalize the organization.

The presence of such elements in Congress constitutes a serious threat to the struggle, for the capacity for political action of an organization which is ravaged by such disruptive and splitting elements is considerably undermined. Here in South Africa, as in many parts of the world, a revolution is maturing: it is the profound desire, the determination and the urge of the overwhelming majority of the country to destroy forever the shackles of oppression that condemn them to servitude and slavery.

To overthrow oppression has been sanctioned by humanity and is the highest aspiration of every free man. If elements in our organization seek to impede the realization of this lofty purpose then these people have placed themselves outside the organization and must be put out of action before they do more harm. To do otherwise would be crime and serious neglect of duty. We must rid ourselves of such elements and give our organization the striking power of a real militant mass organization. Kotane, Marks, Bopape, Tloome, and I have been banned from attending gatherings and we cannot join and counsel with you on the serious problems that are facing our country. We have been banned because we champion the freedom of the oppressed people of our country and because we consistently fought against the policy of racial discrimination in favour of a policy which accords fundamental human rights to all irrespective of race, colour, sex, or language. We

are exiled from our own people for we uncompromisingly resisted the efforts of imperialist America and her satellites to
drag the world into the rule of violence and brutal force, into
the rule of napalm, hydrogen, and cobalt bombs where millions
of people will be wiped out to satisfy the criminal and greedy
appetites of the imperialist powers. We have been gagged because we emphatically and openly condemned the criminal
attacks by the imperialists against the people of Malaya, Vietnam, Indonesia, Tunisia, and Tanganyika and called upon our
people to identify themselves unreservedly with the cause of
world peace, and to fight against the war policies of America
and her satellites.

We are being shadowed, hounded, and trailed because we
fearlessly voiced our horror and indignation at the slaughter
of the people of Korea and Kenya, because we expressed our
solidarity with the cause of the Kenya people.

You can see that 'there is no easy walk to freedom anywhere
and many of us will have to pass through the valley of the
shadow of death again and again before we reach the mountain tops of our desires'.* Dangers and difficulties have not
deterred us in the past; they will not frighten us now. But we
must be prepared for them like men who mean business and
who do not waste energy in vain talk and idle action. The
way of preparation for action lies in our rooting out all im-
purity and indiscipline from our organization and making it
the bright and shining instrument that will cleave its way to
Africa's freedom.

* Mandela quotes here from an article by Nehru 'From Lucknow to
Tripoli' reprinted in *The Unity of India.*

7. JAWAHARLAL NEHRU

*

The End of Camp-Following

The Congress of Oppressed Nationalities held in Brussels in 1927 had brought together people who were destined to play a leading role in the Third World – Soong Ching Ling (Madame Sun Yat-sen, widow of the Chinese revolutionary leader), Jawaharlal Nehru and Nguyen Ai Quoc. In 1947, on the initiative of Nehru, the Asian Relations Conference was held in New Delhi. At this meeting it was the delegates from Burma, Vietnam and Malaya who, in spite of some pressure by the Indians, made the voice of the radical nationalists heard.

Meeting in 1954 in connexion with the Geneva Conference on Indo-China, the Prime Ministers of the 'Colombo Powers' – India, Pakistan, Indonesia, Burma and Ceylon – set in motion the consultations and arrangements which led to the Asian–African Conference at Bandung in Indonesia. Twenty-eight nations (including Afghanistan, Cambodia, China, Egypt, Ethiopia, the Gold Coast, Iran, Iraq, Japan, Jordan, Laos, Lebanon, Liberia, Libya, Nepal, the Philippines, Saudi Arabia, Sudan, Syria, Thailand, Turkey, the two zones of Vietnam, and Yemen) took part, and there were representatives of the national liberation movements of the Algerian, Tunisian and Moroccan peoples.

In a speech at the Conference India's Prime Minister Jawaharlal Nehru expressed the widely-held view of the special position and status claimed or sought in the colonial or former colonial areas of Asia and Africa by outside powers, and of the contest of the 'super-powers' to secure the allegiance of Asia and Africa.

WE are great countries in the world who rather like having freedom, if I may say so, without dictation. Well, if there is anything that Asia wants to tell them it is this: No dictation there is going to be in the future; no 'yes-men' in Asia, I hope, or in Africa. We have had enough of that in the past. We value friendship of the great countries and, if I am to play my part, I should like to say that we sit with the great countries of the world as brothers, be it in Europe or America. It is not in any spirit of hatred or dislike or aggressiveness with each other in regard to Europe or America, certainly not. We send to them our greetings, all of us here, and we want to be friends with them, to cooperate with them. But we shall cooperate in the future as equals; there is no friendship when nations are not equal, when one has to obey the other and when one dominates the other. That is why we raise our voice against domination and colonialism, from which many of us have suffered so long, and that is why we have to be very careful to see that any other form of domination does not come our way. Therefore, we want to be friends with the West and friends with the East and friends with everybody because if there is something that may be called an approach to the minds and spirit of Asia, it is one of toleration and friendship and cooperation, not one of aggressiveness. . . .

Whether our influence is great or small, it must be exercised in the right direction, in an intelligent direction, in a direction which has integrity of purpose and ideals and objectives as shown in our Resolution. It represents the ideals of Asia, it represents the new dynamism of Asia, because if it does not represent that what are we then? Are we copies of Europeans or Americans or Russians? What are we? We are Asians or Africans. We are none else. If we are camp-followers of Russia or America or any other country of Europe, it is, if I may say so, not very creditable to our dignity, our new independence, our new freedom, our new spirit and our new self-reliance.

8. U NU

*

The Burmeseness of Burma *

U Nu (b. 1907) one of the convenors of the Bandung Conference, and at that time Prime Minister of Burma, visited the United States soon after it. Burma, a country with a long and distinguished history before Britain annexed it in 1886, had regained its independence early in 1948, refusing membership of the British Commonwealth. U Nu explained to his American audiences in his characteristically gentle manner how 'foreign invasion' and 'alien ways of life' were regarded by a formerly subject people.

BURMA has a long history. We had a great and flourishing civilization in Burma based on one of the great religions of the world, Buddhism, when William the Conqueror was crossing the English Channel. This civilization, passed on to us by our forebears, has now become our national heritage. It is our way of life. We prefer it to any other way of life on this earth. We do not say that it cannot be improved, or that it cannot be adapted to suit modern conditions, but we do not wish to change its basis. We are not prepared to exchange it for any other way of life. This is not a matter of conceit. We do not claim that our way of life is better than that of other people. We merely say that it is different, that it suits us better, and that we therefore cannot be induced to give it up in exchange for some other way of life, be that the Communist way, the Western European way, the American way, or any other way.

Now, I submit to you that if the citizens of any nation are deeply devoted to their culture, to their religion, to their way of life, to their country – as we in Burma are – then they will defend their way of life and their national frontiers with all the forces at their command. I can assure you that we are just as determined as any people to defend ourselves against foreign invasion or the imposition of any alien way of life by whatever

*From *An Asian Speaks* (Washington: Burmese Embassy, 1955).

method. And we have concluded that in the present phase of our history, and the present state of the world, the wisest and even the only course for Burma is to pursue an independent policy, unshackled by what George Washington called 'entangling foreign alliances'. ...

It is possible to disagree with this point of view. But whether one agrees or disagrees is immaterial, because in the present circumstances of Burma, her membership in any alliance with a great-power military *bloc* is incompatible with her continued existence as an independent state. This may seem to be putting it strongly, but it is a fact. Our recent history is such, our experience with great powers is such, that in the minds of the people of Burma an alliance with a big power immediately means domination by that power. It means the loss of independence. You may question the validity of that belief. But perhaps you will accept my statement that it is a political fact of life today that any government of Burma which aligned itself with a big-power *bloc* would at once lose the confidence and support of the people. In other words, the chances of subversion would be greatly increased. And if it is true that the real danger to countries like Burma lies in subversion rather than overt aggression, then it follows that membership in a big-power *bloc* would only tend to add to what is already said to be the greater of two dangers. ...

In this talk, I have been trying to explain how our love of independence – call it preoccupation if you will – leads us logically and inevitably to the foreign policy of independence from any alignment of major powers on the basis of a military treaty.

9. THE BANDUNG CONFERENCE

*

International Alignment with 'Liberation' Struggles *

In November 1954, six months after their defeat at Dienbienphu in Vietnam, the French were faced with a bitter 'liberation war' in their colony of Algeria. This bid to drive out French rule, led by the National Liberation Front, was supported by Egypt, as well as by the nationalists in Tunisia. The post-war objectives and interests of the colonial powers are here viewed in the light of those of the independent Asian and African countries which produced the report of the Bandung Conference.

Problems of Dependent Peoples

THE Asian–African Conference discussed the problems of dependent peoples and colonialism and the evils arising from the subjection of peoples to alien subjugation, domination and exploitation.

The Conference is agreed:

(a) in declaring that colonialism in all its manifestations is an evil which should speedily be brought to an end;

(b) in affirming that the subjection of peoples to alien subjugation, domination and exploitation constitutes a denial of fundamental human rights, is contrary to the Charter of the United Nations and is an impediment to the promotion of world peace and cooperation;

(c) in declaring its support of the cause of freedom and independence of all such peoples; and

(d) in calling upon the Powers concerned to grant freedom and independence to such peoples.

In view of the unsettling situation in North Africa and the persisting denial to the peoples of North Africa of their right to self-determination, the Asian–African Conference de-

*From *Report of the Asian-African Conference.*

109

clared its support of the rights of the people of Algeria, Morocco and Tunisia to self-determination and independence and urged the French government to bring about a peaceful settlement of the issue without delay.

10. GAMAL ABD AL NASSER

*

Military Alliances, Bases, and National Sovereignty *

Gamal Abd al Nasser (b. 1918) was, among all the Bandung participants, the most directly involved in helping the national liberation movements in North Africa. As the leader to whom Arabs seeking to end European and American supremacy in the Middle East tended to rally, he became a menace to Western interests in the area. On the other hand, his success in getting the British out of their military base at Suez, his undermining of the Western alliance based on the Baghdad Pact, his role at Bandung, his 'summit' meeting at Brioni early in 1956 with Nehru and Tito, and his firm diplomacy in negotiations for foreign financial assistance 'without strings' for the Aswan Dam added to his prestige in the Third World. It was out of this background of his record as a Third World leader that Nasser discussed current issues in his historic speech to a mass audience in Alexandria (on 26 July 1956). At the end of the long speech (excerpts from which follow) President Nasser announced that the Egyptian government had nationalized the Suez Canal Company. It was this act which led to the joint plan by Britain, France and Israel to invade Egypt and overthrow Nasser. Egypt successfully administered the Suez Canal and built the Aswan Dam.

THE ten principles of Bandung which were endorsed last year say that it is natural that all nations should have the right to choose freely their political and economic systems, and their mode of life in accordance with the purposes and principles of the U.N. Charter, and that the nations should, by being liberated from doubt and fear and through mutual faith and good intentions, exercise tolerance and live together in peace. The nations should live as good neighbours working for the consolidation of sincere cooperation on the following bases –

*From *B.B.C. Survey of World Broadcasts*, Part IV.

the bases of international relations laid down by the Bandung Conference.

(1) To respect basic human rights and the purposes and principles of the U.N.; (2) To respect the sovereignty of all nations and the integrity of their territory; (3) To acknowledge the equality of all races and of all nations, big or small. Then to abstain from any interference in the internal affairs of other countries. To respect the right of every nation to individual or collective self-defence. To abstain from using collective defence groupings serving the personal interests of any of the big Powers – the alliances which they contrive in the name of defence to serve their own purposes.

Every country should abstain from bringing pressure to bear on other countries. Then to avoid aggressive activities or threats or use of force against regional safety or the political independence of any country. To settle all international disputes by peaceful means. To develop joint interests and mutual cooperation. To respect justice and international commitments.

These are the principles of international relations approved by the Bandung conference so that the big nations might not use the small nations as puppets in their hands and as catspaws to implement their policy of domination and influence. . . .

Since the beginning of the revolution we have aimed at achieving political independence and the restoration of usurped prestige and dignity. Thank God we have been successful. On 18 June we succeeded in raising the Egyptian flag above Egypt's sky. We also succeeded in ensuring that an Egyptian command alone existed, thereby realizing a major part of objectives we aspired to and were demanding. But at the same time we did not forget to work for the sake of economic independence. This is a matter we have not neglected since 1952 – the year of the revolution – since we believe that political independence cannot exist without economic independence.

Since 1953 we have worked to increase production. Our aim thereby was to realize economic independence. We took this course and succeeded. We succeeded because we relied on ourselves, our work, sweat and efforts. We were able to raise the national income from 1952 to 1954 by about sixteen per cent. Following this, we were able to achieve from 1954 to 1956 an equivalent or larger increase. Therefore we work without thoughtlessness and are aware of the methods which victimized us, our fathers, and forefathers. Consequently when we were working for political independence, we were working at the same time for the sake of economic independence. When we felt economic independence, we turned towards the world at large and told ourselves: Let us forget the past. We also faced the imperialists and those who occupied us and departed, and who killed our fathers and forefathers.

On 19 June I said that I held out my hand to everyone and that Egypt held out her hand to everyone, and that she would make peace with those who would make peace with her and be the declared enemy of those who declared their enmity towards her. We move towards the realization of an independent policy which emanates from Egypt and not from London, Washington, Moscow or any other country. This policy emanates from our conscience and feelings. I said that we were prepared to cooperate with everyone, but that this cooperation could not be at the expense of our independence or dignity. These words I spoke on 19 June. These are the same words I have been wont to utter since the beginning of the revolution. Today I shall tell you everything that has happened since the revolution as regards negotiations and meetings; everything, so that you may become aware.

After the success of the revolution in 1952, Britain and the U.S.A. began to ask us to ally ourselves and come to an agreement with them. They asked us to conclude alliances and agreements with them. Our reply to them was that we could not conclude an alliance with them, and that we would conclude no alliance except with Arab states. I asked them – and this may be found in the minutes of the talks – if we should conclude an alliance with Britain whether Egypt could dictate to Britain. Furthermore, would the views expressed by Egypt count with Britain? If we sit at one table – Mr Eden representing Great Britain and I representing Egypt – how can a great Power ally itself with a small state like us? This would not be an alliance – merely subordination. I told them this was

113

subordination and we would not accept it. We can cooperate with you on equal terms; we can come to an understanding; we can be friends – but we will on no account agree to being an appendage or subordinate.

At the first meeting of the talks – I believe this was in April 1953 – General Robertson was present. He asked us to sign an alliance with Great Britain for a period of twenty-five years. We refused and the talks were suspended after two meetings. We rejected this alliance and said that we wanted to sign an evacuation agreement and that we would struggle for evacuation. We will not conclude an alliance, since our alliance will make us an appendage and subordinate. We say the same thing today as we said in 1952. I cannot see any difference. This was said in 1952 and in all the minutes and at all the meetings. In 1952 we began to speak about arming the Egyptian army. We told them: if you want us to be friends with you, supply us with the weapons we want. We are prepared to pay the price of these weapons. They replied: we will not supply you with weapons unless you sign a mutual security pact with us. Do you know the meaning of a mutual security pact? It means that an American mission will come and stay in Egypt, directing the affairs of the Egyptian army. Abd al-Hakim Amir will then have nothing to do with the Egyptian army. We told them that we had had experience – that as military men who had served in the army, we had considerable experience in this connexion. We had experience of the military mission. A military mission came to the Egyptian army in 1936, when we were young officers holding the ranks of second and first lieutenants and we were in contact with them. We found that their first objective was to weaken the Egyptian army. Their first objective was to spread the spirit of defeat and lack of confidence throughout the Egyptian army. We had an inferiority complex – a complex which cannot be cured by military missions – and we could not on any account accept a military mission. And thus we could not conclude a mutual security pact with them.

We want the Egyptian army to represent the principles of the revolution. We declared in our principles that we should establish a strong national army. We wanted the Egyptian army to be a strong national army, but we could never agree that the Egyptian army could be an army under the domination of foreign officers, be they American or non-American, or that it could operate under the direction of foreign officers. The army will only work for the interest of this people and the interest of the sons of this people. That was our conviction. That is why we refused to sign a mutual security pact. ...

Britain left Egypt believing – nay she was convinced – that she could have no place there. This was because the people of Egypt were awakened; because the people of Egypt had pledged themselves to achieve for Egypt freedom of life; because the people of Egypt pledged themselves that there should be no sovereignty in Egypt except that of the people of Egypt; and because the people pledged themselves to have no flag but the flag of Egypt flying in the sky. This was the true reason, and not the talks and the negotiations.

We were able to reach an agreement with Britain by which all British forces were withdrawn. It was a long battle, a bitter battle. But has this battle ended? This battle has not ended. Imperialism, brethren, has various forms. When imperialism started, it took the form of occupation by armed forces. Then it began to grow and develop. Today imperialism is represented by the agents of imperialism – imperialism without soldiers; force which can achieve its ends and purposes by means of its agents or traitors, who exist in every country. They deprive a country of its authority and influence, and then they take over office in the country. And thus the country becomes a mere appendage, placed at their disposal; and this without the use of armed forces, without an occupation, and without employing arms. Imperialism used to assume various kinds of forms; and we pledged ourselves to oppose imperialism of all kinds – unmasked imperialism; armed imperialism; imperialism coupled with occupation; and masked imperialism in the form of agents of imperialism, in the form of alliances and pacts in which countries are regarded as appendages. Imperialism began to plot around us and weave conspiracies so that it could gain control of the Arab states one by one. It placed its

115

hand on them, one state after another, aiming at besieging us from all sides – thus it could dictate its will to us. We resisted these plots, the Arab consciousness and Arab nationalism awakened, flamed and united in all Arab states everywhere, so imperialism was unable to achieve its purpose and its aims. . . .

Thus, brethren, we entered battles in Egypt and the Arabs entered battles outside Egypt. Battles rage throughout the Arab homeland. Imperialism wants France in Algeria, Tunisia and Morocco. NATO forces, which they set up and have been arming for five years or more, spending billions of dollars— all these forces moved from Europe to North Africa to fight the people which demand their right to freedom and to self-determination, people who demand their right to live. . . .

What does this mean, brethren? As I told you, Arab nationalism has been set on fire from the Atlantic Ocean to the Persian Gulf. Arab nationalism feels its existence, its structure and strength. It also believes in its right to life. These are the battles which we are entering. We can never say that the battle of Algeria is not our battle. Nor can we say that Jordan's December battle was not our battle. And we also cannot say that battles of alliances are not our battles. If we said that, we would be denying our Arabism and our nationalism and would be disloyal to ourselves and to Egyptianism. Our fates are linked. My fate in Egypt is linked with that of my brother in Jordan, in the Lebanon, Syria, and in every country, and also in the Sudan. Our fates are linked. We in this part of the world have our fates linked, one with another. Never can we say that these are not our battles. These are our battles, and the battles of every one of you and every member of Arabism.

What does imperialism want? Imperialism wants us to be lackeys so that when it gives an order we merely enforce it. What order? Any order. There are many countries which follow this method. You know them all, and I need not tell you about them. If I mentioned their names, I would be creating diplomatic or political crises. Every one of you knows these countries which take orders and obey them. In these countries the stooges and supporters of imperialism reign – you know. The stooges and supporters who have no faith in themselves or in their homeland and nationalism but rather put their faith in ambassadors, high commissioners, and so forth. They want us to languish in this state. This is impossible. Why was there a revolution? Why did the people fight? Why did the people struggle? Why did some of us die in 1919, in 1936 and throughout past years.* Would these people have been happy to die so that eventually we would revert to the old state and become lackeys taking orders from any country? They want us provided we hear their instructions. Of course, we hear their instructions in regard to Israel, for they say that Israel is a reality, that Israel's requests must be granted, that Israel's frontiers exist. But when you ask: what about the people of Palestine? they say: This is a subject which we shall talk about later – in other words a subject which must be postponed. These are Arabs like ourselves. Perhaps you do not have the same view of them as we do – the Palestinian Arabs who were dispersed. There are the rights of the Palestinian people. Give the beggar a little money. Not everyone will sell his country for money. Palestine is an ancient country, thousands of years old. Perhaps your country is only 100 years old; it is young and has no long history.

When Black,† the Director of the World Bank, arrived here he began to talk to me about the financing of the High Dam and to tell me: We are an international bank and we have no connexion whatsoever with the U.S.A. Black said he was independent, and expressed views he believed in. I told him that the managing board represented nations. How could it represent nations without being a political bank? His was naturally a political bank because he could not take any decision without approval by the managing board, which represented nations. This managing board is composed mainly of Western countries moving in the orbit of the U.S.A. I started to

---

*1919 was the year in which there was a countrywide revolt against British rule. It failed to achieve Egypt's independence, and the popular Said Zaghlul was banished, but anti-British activity continued. The Anglo-Egyptian Treaty of 1936 reduced considerably Britain's power and privileges in Egypt.

† Dr Eugene Black, President of the World Bank at that time.

117

look at Mr Black, who was sitting in a chair, and I saw him in my imagination as Ferdinand de Lesseps. I went back in my memory to what I used to read about the year 1854. In this year Ferdinand de Lesseps arrived in Egypt and went to Mohammed Sa'id Pasha, the Khedive, sat next to him and told him: We want to dig the Suez Canal. The Suez Canal will bring you untold benefit. The Suez Canal is a gigantic project which will give Egypt so much.

Whenever Black spoke, I could sense the obstacles behind his phrasing and simultaneously I went back in my mind to Ferdinand de Lesseps. I then told him: Look here, we don't like such things. We don't want a Cromer back in Egypt again ruling us. In the past there were loans and interest on loans, and the outcome was that our country was occupied. Therefore I ask you to take this into consideration in your conversation with me. We have a complex as a result of de Lesseps, Cromer and political occupation by way of economic occupation. This is the picture I had in my mind – the picture of de Lesseps when he arrived in Egypt. ...

The income of the Suez Canal in 1955 amounted to £35,000,000, the equivalent of 100,000,000 dollars. This is the income of the Egyptian company, the Suez Canal Company. In return for the 120,000 Egyptians who perished digging it and for the money we spent on building it, we get £1,000,000 or 3,000,000 dollars. On the other hand, the British and the Americans want to give us 70,000,000 dollars over five years. It is they of course who take those 100,000,000 dollars. Of course it is no shame that I should pay and try to get a loan and build my country to try to find help for my compatriots. What is a shame is that I should suck the blood of peoples and usurp their rights. We shall never let the past be repeated, but we shall eliminate the past. We shall eliminate the past by regaining our right to the Suez Canal. This money is ours and this Canal belongs to Egypt, because it is an Egyptian limited company.

The Suez Canal was dug by the efforts of the sons of Egypt – 120,000 Egyptians died in the process. The Suez Canal Company, sitting in Paris, is a usurping country. It usurped our concessions. When he came here de Lesseps acted in the same manner as do certain people who came to hold talks with me. Does history repeat itself? On the contrary! We shall build the High Dam and we shall gain our usurped rights. We shall build the High Dam as we desire. We are determined. The Canal Company annually takes £35,000,000. Why shouldn't we take it ourselves? The Suez Canal Company collected 100,000,000 dollars annually for the benefit of Egypt. We desire to make this statement come true and that we should collect this 100,000,000 dollars for the benefit of Egypt.

Thus today, when we build the High Dam, we are also building the dam of dignity, freedom and grandeur. We are eliminating the dams of humiliation and servility. We, the whole of Egypt in one front, a united national *bloc*, announce that the whole of Egypt will fight until the last drop of her blood. As I told you, all of her sons, in the manner of Salah Mustafa and Mustafa Hafiz,* each one of us, will fight to the last drop of our blood for the construction of our homeland and for the construction of Egypt. We shall not permit the warmongers, the imperialists and the slave-traders to have a grip upon us. We shall depend on our working hands, our blood and our own working men. We are rich. We were lax about our rights and now we are regaining them. I told you before that our battle goes on. We shall regain these rights step by step, and we shall achieve everything. We shall construct a strong and dignified Egypt. Accordingly, I have signed today and the Government has approved the following law. ...

Citizens, we shall never allow the imperialists or the oppressors to have a hold over us. We shall never allow history to repeat itself. We have marched forward to build Egypt strongly and surely. We march forward to political and economic independence, we march forward towards a strong national economy for the masses of the people. We march forward to work. If we look back, we do so only to demolish the relics of oppression, servility, exploitation and domination. We look back at the past only to put an end to its effects. Now, O

*Two soldiers who had presumably been killed during the Egyptian campaign to end the remnants of the British occupation of Egypt.

citizens, as the rights revert to their owners, now that our rights in the Suez Canal have reverted to us after 100 years, we are building the real foundations of sovereignty and the real edifice of grandeur and dignity. The Suez Canal was a state within a state; it was an Egyptian limited company which depended on foreign plots and on imperialism and the supporters of imperialism. The Suez Canal was built for Egypt and for Egypt's interests, but it was a source of exploitation and extortion. ...

Today, O citizens, the Suez Canal has been nationalized and this decree has in fact been published in the Official Gazette and has become law. Today, O citizens, with the annual income of the Suez Canal amounting to £35,000,000 – that is 100,000,000 dollars a year, and 500,000,000 dollars in five years – we shall not look for the 70,000,000 dollars of American aid. Today, citizens, with our sweat and tears and with the lives and skulls of our martyrs – the martyrs who died in 1956 – after 100 years in bondage – we shall be able to develop this country. We shall work and produce and shall increase production, despite all these plots and chatter. And whenever any talk comes from Washington I shall tell them: You can kill yourselves. We shall set up industries in Egypt and compete with them. They do not want us to be an industrialized country – they want their products to be sold here and to find a market in this country. I have never seen any American aid to help industrialization. The reason is that aid given for industrialization would constitute competition. American aid is always designed for consumption.

After the past four years, as we celebrate the fifth year of the revolution, we feel, as I told you earlier, that we are stronger and more resolute in our determination, power and faith. Today we greet the fifth year of the revolution, and in the same way as Farouk left on 26 July 1952, the old Suez Canal Company also leaves us on the same day. We now feel that we are realizing our glory and our grandeur. The people of Egypt alone shall be sovereign in Egypt. We shall march forward, united and in solidarity like one nation having faith in itself and in its homeland, and faith also in its strength. We shall march forward as one people who have vowed to work and to proceed on a holy march of industrialization and construction – nay, as one people who are solidly united in opposition to treachery and aggression, and to imperialism and the supporters and antics of imperialism. In this way, O citizens, we shall be able to achieve much. We shall be conscious of grandeur and dignity, and we shall also feel that we are truly building our homeland. That is what we want. We want to build in our own fashion and build what we like. We want to do what we like. We want no partner. As we retrieve our usurped rights, we gain strength. Our strength shall increase year after year. God willing, we shall be stronger next year, with higher production and more factories.

At this moment as I talk to you some of your Egyptian brethren are proceeding to administer the Canal Company and to run its affairs. They are taking over the Canal Company at this very moment – the Egyptian Canal Company, not the foreign Canal Company. They have started to take over the Canal Company and its property and to control shipping in the canal – the canal which is situated in Egyptian territory, which goes through Egyptian territory, which is part of Egypt and which is owned by Egypt. They are now carrying out this task so that we can make up for the past and build new edifices of grandeur and dignity. May the Almighty grant you success, and may the peace and blessing of God be upon you.

11. ERNESTO (CHE) GUEVARA

*

The 'Way of Dignity' for the
Inferior Peoples*

26 July, the day on which in 1952 the monarchy in Egypt was abolished and on which in 1956 President Nasser announced the nationalization of the Suez Canal Company was, by coincidence, the day in 1953 on which a group of young Cuban patriots began their attempt to overthrow the corrupt and, as they saw it, pro-imperialist, dictatorship of Fulgencio Batista. Their attempt, that day, under their leader Fidel Castro, to seize the Moncada Barracks failed. 1953 was the centenary of the birth of the great Cuban revolutionary nationalist, José Martí, and Castro in his trial speech 'History will Absolve Me' quoted his example and his words: 'The man who abides by unjust laws and permits anybody to trample the country in which he was born, the man who so mistreats his country, is not an honourable man. ... In the world there must be a certain degree of decorum just as there must be a certain amount of light. When there are many men without decorum, there are always others who bear in themselves the dignity of men. There are the men who rebel with great force against those who steal the people's freedom, that is to say, against those who steal human dignity itself.' The revolutionaries, joined by a young Argentinian who had been in Guatemala during 1954, made Latin American history when they succeeded in January 1959 in the revolutionary overthrow of the Batista regime, and then proceeded in defiance of the United States to establish a socialist regime. That man, Ernesto (Che) Guevara (1928–67), in the passage which follows, expressed in 1960 the sense of the Cuban revolutionaries that their action was part of a more universal phenomenon.

By a simple law of gravity, the small island of 114,000 square kilometers and 6,500,000 inhabitants is assuming the leadership of the anti-colonial struggle in America, for there are important conditions which permit it to take the glorious, heroic

*From *Studies on the Left*, vol. 1, no. 3.

and dangerous lead. The nations of colonial America which are economically less weak, those which are developing their national capitalism by fits and starts in a continual struggle, at times violent and without quarter, against the foreign monopolies, are gradually relinquishing their place to this small new power for liberty, since their governments do not find themselves with sufficient strength to carry the struggle to the finish. This is because the struggle is no simple matter, nor is it free of dangers nor exempt from difficulties. It is essential to have the backing of an entire people, and an enormous amount of idealism and the spirit of sacrifice, to carry it out to the end under the almost isolated conditions in which we are doing it in America. Small countries have previously tried to maintain this position; Guatemala, the Guatemala of the quetzal bird which dies when it is imprisoned in a cage, the Guatemala of the Indian Tecum Uman who fell before the direct aggression of the colonialists; and Bolivia, the Bolivia of Morillo, the prototype of martyrs for American independence, who yielded before the terrible difficulties of the struggle, in spite of having initiated it and having given three examples which are fundamental to the Cuban revolution: suppression of the army, the Agrarian Reform, and the nationalization of mines – a maximum source of wealth as well as of tragedy.

Cuba knows the previous examples, it knows the failures and the difficulties, but it also knows that it stands at the dawn of a new era in the world; the colonial pillars have been swept away before the impulse of the national and popular struggle, in Asia as in Africa. Now the tendencies to unification of the peoples are no longer given by their religions, by their customs, by their appetites, by their racial affinities or lack of them; they are given by the economic similarities of their social conditions and by the similarity of their desire for progress and recovery. Asia and Africa have shaken hands at Bandung, Asia and Africa are coming to shake hands with colonial and indigenous America by means of Cuba, here in Havana.

On the other hand, the great colonial powers have given ground before the struggle of the peoples. Belgium and Holland are but two caricatures of Empire; Germany and Italy have

123

lost their colonies. France debates in the midst of a war she has lost, and England, diplomatic and skilled, liquidates her political power while maintaining economic connexions.

North American capitalism has replaced some of the old colonial capitalisms in those countries which have initiated their independent life; but it knows that this is transitory and that there is no real rest to be found in the new territory of its financial speculations. The claws of the imperial eagle have been blunted. Colonialism has died in all those places of the world or is in process of natural death.

America is another matter. It was some time ago that the English lion removed his greedy paws from our America, and the nice young Yankee capitalists installed the 'democratic' version of the English clubs and imposed their sovereign domination in every one of the twenty republics. These nations are the colonial feudal-estate of North American monopoly, 'right in its own back yard'; at the present moment this is their *raison d'être* and the only possibility they have. If all the Latin American peoples were to raise the banner of dignity, as has Cuba, monopoly would tremble; it would have to accommodate itself to a new politico-economic situation and to substantial cuts in its profits. But monopoly does not like to cut its profits and the Cuban example – this 'bad example' of national and international dignity – is spreading among the American countries. Every time that an upstart people sets up a cry of liberation, Cuba is accused; somehow or other Cuba is guilty, guilty because it has shown a way, the way of armed popular struggle against the supposedly invincible armies, the way of struggle in difficult terrain in order to exhaust and destroy the enemy away from his bases; in short, the way of dignity.

12. JULIUS NYERERE

*

A World Without False Discrimination *

Castro's and Guevara's convictions about the kind of world which the peoples of Latin America, Africa and Asia must create in order to experience 'the dignity of man' was shared by Julius Nyerere (b. 1921). Nyerere and his colleagues in the Tanganyikan African National Union (TANU) succeeded by the end of 1961 in their efforts to achieve the withdrawal of British rule from Tanganyika. Nyerere's clear-sightedness, sober determination and integrity has made him one of the most highly respected political leaders among former subject peoples. This is an extract from his address to the United Nations General Assembly on 14 December 1961.

OUR pleasure at being accepted as a Member of the United Nations is a recognition that we have been given the right to join in the search for greater understanding and greater harmony between the peoples of the world. In trying to meet this responsibility the policies of my government will be based on an underlying faith in humanity and on four principles of action which follow from it. With your indulgence, Mr President, I would like to state those principles.

The basis of our actions, internal and external, will be an attempt, an honest attempt, to honour the dignity of man. We believe that all mankind is one, that the physiological differences between us are unimportant in comparison with our common humanity. We believe that black skin or white, straight or curly hair, differences in the shape of our bodies, do not alter or even affect the fact that each one of us is part of the human species and has a part to play in the development of mankind. We believe that the differences in our religions or our political ideologies may cause difficulties for our small minds, but do not, to our way of thinking, affect the rights of every individual to be treated as a man, with dignity and honour.

* From *Freedom and Unity – Uhuru na Umoja* (Oxford: O.U.P., 1967).

125

It may be, because of the history of Africa, that we are particularly conscious of the need to reaffirm this basic faith in relation to the racial divisions of mankind. Yet we believe this is of fundamental importance. We believe – we know as a fact – that a man may change his religion, that a man may change his ideological belief, but he can never change the shape of his face, nor the race into which he was born. That is why we believe that it is evil for any people to ill-treat others on the grounds of race. What we are in fact saying is that we shall try to use the Universal Declaration of Human Rights as a basis for both our external and our internal policies.

That declaration confirms the right of every individual to many things, which we cannot yet provide for the citizens of our own country. In that respect this document, the Universal Declaration of Human Rights, that of human brotherhood, regardless of race, colour or creed, is the basic principle which we ourselves, in Tanganyika, and we believe other peoples in Africa and other parts of the world, have been struggling to implement.

We accept without question as a basis, a basic article of faith, that every individual has an equal right to inherit the earth, to partake of its joys and its sorrows and to contribute to the building of the sort of society which he desires for himself and also for his children. In saying this, we have committed our country to a grand endeavour. We are conscious that the implementation of the spirit underlying lofty ideas is not always achieved without some difficulty, that we shall sometimes fail in our efforts. But any apparent deviation from the articles of this Declaration will be an honest attempt on our part to balance conflicting interests while preserving the major principle itself. It will be in the light of this principle that we shall try at times to determine our stand on every international issue which we shall be called upon to consider in this Assembly or elsewhere.

We shall always try to understand the practical difficulties which face governments and nations in the implementation of this principle, but we shall never compromise with those who deny this basic principle of human brotherhood. We accept that the United Nations cannot interfere in the internal affairs of any state, and we believe that, under present circumstances, that is as it should be. But we also believe that it has an over-riding interest in the preservation of peace throughout the world, and further, that there is no internal conflict now which does not have external repercussions.

My Government has unfriendly feelings towards no people, but it entertains bitter hostility towards governments whose policies are based on racial discrimination. On this issue we cannot compromise. We have inherited some racial difficulties in our own country and we believe that our own efforts to exorcize the evil spirit of racial prejudice from every one of our citizens would be jeopardized by the slightest compromise on our part on this matter of racial discrimination in other parts of the world; and we believe that our struggle for our own individual and national dignity would be invalidated by the spread of such poisonous spirit among our own people of Tanganyika.

We believe, in fact, that the individual man and woman is the purpose of society. All great philosophies in the world do agree on this simple statement. The way they differ is how to carry out this principle in actual practice. And we believe that every country, because of the differences in history, the differences of other circumstances, is trying in a different way to organize itself in a manner that suits itself in carrying out this principle. We do not believe that on this matter an ideal solution has been found anywhere in the world. We are convinced that mankind is still groping forward in trying to find a solution, and it is our ambition simply to join mankind in groping forward together in finding a solution.

13. THE CAIRO CONFERENCE

*

Peace and International Cooperation *

The regimes which came into being as a consequence of revolutions and transfers of power in the colonial and semi-colonial countries differed in ideology and in the character of their policies. But meetings of heads of state continued to be held after the Bandung Conference (1955) to discuss problems of common interest. These meetings sometimes included the Asian, African and Latin American states, but also European countries such as Yugoslavia and Finland. Though the rulers of some of these countries were cautious and conservative they were aware of what public opinion in the Third World considered to be major issues. Under the nondescript banner of 'non-alignment', conferences were held in Belgrade in 1961 and in Cairo in October, 1964. The second conference came after the Geneva United Nations Conference on Trade and Development, for which a loose *bloc* of seventy-seven developing countries had been formed. The Declaration issued by the Cairo Conference of Non-aligned Heads of State or Government, part of which follows, indicates how 'non-aligned' or 'committed' in regard to revolutionary wars of liberation, the dangers of neo-colonialism, Vietnam and other controversial issues the moderates in the Third World claimed to be at the end of the second decade of the post-war period.

Introduction

THE Second Conference of Heads of State or Government of the following non-aligned countries: Afghanistan, Algeria, Angola, Burma, Burundi, Cambodia, Cameroun, Central African Republic, Ceylon, Chad, the Congo (Brazzaville), Cuba, Cyprus, Dahomey, Ethiopia, Ghana, Guinea, India, Indonesia, Iraq, Islamic Republic of Mauritania, Jordan, Kenya, Kuwait, Laos, Lebanon, Liberia, Libya, Malawi, Mali, Morocco, Nepal, Nigeria, Saudi Arabia, Senegal, Sierra Leone, Somali, Sudan, Syria, Togo, Tunisia, Uganda, United Arab

*From *The Cairo Conference* Papers.

Republic, United Republic of Tanganyika and Zanzibar, Yemen, Yugoslavia, and Zambia, was held in Cairo from 5 October to 10 October 1964. The following countries: Argentina, Bolivia, Brazil, Chile, Finland, Jamaica, Mexico, Trinidad and Tobago, Uruguay and Venezuela were represented by observers. The Secretary-General of the Organization of African Unity and the Secretary-General of the League of Arab States were present as observers. The Conference undertook an analysis of the international situation with a view to making an effective contribution to the solution of major problems which are of concern to mankind in view of their effects on peace and security in the world . . .

The Conference also notes with satisfaction the growing interest and confidence displayed by peoples still under foreign domination and by those whose rights and sovereignty are being violated by imperialism and neo-colonialism and the highly positive role which the non-aligned countries are being called upon to play in the settlement of international problems or disputes. . . .

The Conference notes with satisfaction that the movements of national liberation are engaged in different regions of the world in a heroic struggle against neo-colonialism and the practices of apartheid and racial discrimination. This struggle forms part of the common striving towards freedom, justice and peace.

The Conference reaffirms that interference by economically developed foreign states in the internal affairs of newly independent or developing countries and the existence of territories which are still dependent, constitute a standing threat to peace and security.

The Heads of State or Government of non-aligned countries, while appreciative of the efforts which resulted in the holding of the United Nations Conference on Trade and Development and mindful of the results of that Conference, nevertheless note that much ground still remains to be covered to eliminate the inequalities in relationships between industrialized and developing countries.

The Heads of State or Government of non-aligned countries,

129

while declaring their determination to contribute towards the establishment of a just and lasting peace in the world, affirm that the preservation of peace and promotion of the well-being of the peoples is a collective responsibility deriving from the natural aspirations of mankind to live in a better world.

The Heads of State or Government have arrived in their deliberations at a common understanding of various problems with which the world is now faced and a common approach to them. Reaffirming the basic principles of the Declaration of Belgrade, they express their agreement upon the following points:

Part One: Concerted Action for the Liberation of Countries Still Dependent: Elimination of Colonialism, Neo-colonialism and Imperialism

The Heads of State or Government of non-aligned countries declare that lasting world peace cannot be realized so long as unjust conditions prevail and peoples under foreign domination continue to be deprived of their fundamental right to freedom, independence and self-determination.

Imperialism, colonialism and neo-colonialism constitute the basic source of international tension and conflict, because they endanger world peace and security.

The participants in the Conference deplore that the Declaration of the United Nations on the Granting of Independence to Colonial Countries and Peoples has not been implemented everywhere, and call for unconditional, complete and final abolition of colonialism now.

At present a particular cause of concern is the military or other assistance extended to certain countries to enable them to perpetuate by force colonialist and neo-colonialist situations which are contrary to the spirit of the Charter of the United Nations.

The exploitation by the colonialist forces of the difficulties and problems of the recently liberated or developing countries, the interference in the internal affairs of these states, and the colonialist attempts to maintain unequal relationships, particularly in the economic field, constitute serious dangers to

130

these young countries. Colonialism and neo-colonialism have many forms and manifestations.

Imperialism uses many devices to impose its will on independent nations. Racial discrimination, economic pressure, interference, subversion, intervention and the threat of force are neo-colonialist devices against which the newly independent nations have to defend themselves. The Conference condemns all colonialist, neo-colonialist and imperialist policies applied in various parts of the world. . . .

The newly independent countries have, like all other countries, the right of sovereign disposal in regard to their natural resources and the right to utilize resources as they deem appropriate in the interest of their peoples, without outside interference.

The process of liberation is irresistible and irreversible. Colonized peoples may legitimately resort to arms to secure the full exercise of their right to self-determination and independence if the colonial Powers persist in opposing their natural aspirations.

The participants in the Conference undertake to work unremittingly to eradicate all vestiges of colonialism and to combine all their efforts to render all necessary aid and support, whether moral, political or material, to peoples struggling against colonialism and neo-colonialism. The participating countries recognize the nationalist movements of people which are struggling to free themselves from colonial domination, as being the authentic representatives of the colonial peoples and urgently call upon the colonial Powers to negotiate with their leaders. Portugal continues to hold in bondage by repression, persecution and force in Angola, Mozambique, so-called Portuguese Guinea and the other Portuguese colonies in Africa and Asia, millions of people who have been suffering far too long under the foreign yoke. The Conference declares its determination to ensure that the peoples of these territories accede immediately to independence without any conditions or reservations.

The Conference condemns the Government of Portugal for its obstinate refusal to recognize the inalienable right of the

131

peoples of those territories to self-determination and independence in accordance with the Charter of the United Nations and the Declaration on the Granting of Independence to Colonial Countries and Peoples.

The Conference:

1. Urges the participating countries to afford all necessary material support – financial and military – to freedom fighters in the territories under Portuguese colonial rule;

2. Takes the view that support should be given to the Revolutionary Government of Angola in exile and to the nationalist movements struggling for the independence of the Portuguese colonies and assistance to the special bureau set up by the O.A.U. in regard to the application of sanctions against Portugal;

3. Calls upon all participating states to break off diplomatic and consular relations with the Government of Portugal and to take effective measures to suspend all trade and economic relations with Portugal;

4. Calls upon the participating countries to take all measures to compel Portugal to carry out the decisions of the General Assembly of the United Nations.

The Countries participating in the Conference condemn the policy of the racist minority regime in Southern Rhodesià which continues to defy the Charter and resolutions of the United Nations in that it denies the fundamental freedoms to the people by acts of repression and terror.

The participating countries urge all states not to recognize the independence of Southern Rhodesia if proclaimed under the rule of the racist minority, and instead to give favourable consideration to according recognition to the African nationalist government in exile, should such a government be set up. To this effect the Conference states its opposition to the sham consultation through tribal chiefs envisaged by the present minority Government of Southern Rhodesia....

The Conference appeals to all participating countries to lend support and assistance to the Liberation Committee of the Organization of African Unity.

132

The Conference condemns the imperialistic policy pursued in the Middle East, and in conformity with the Charter of the United Nations decides to:

1. Endorse the full restoration of all the rights of the Arab people of Palestine to their homeland and their inalienable right to self-determination;

2. Declare their full support to the Arab people of Palestine in their struggle for liberation from colonialism and racism ...

The Conference condemns the manifestations of colonialism and neo-colonialism in Latin America and declares in favour of the implementation in that region of the right of the peoples to self-determination and independence.

Basing itself on this principle, the Conference deplores the delay in granting full independence to British Guiana and requests the United Kingdom to grant independence speedily to that country. It notes with regret that Martinique, Guadeloupe, and other Caribbean islands are still not self-governing. It draws the attention of the *ad hoc* Decolonization Commission of the United Nations to the case of Puerto Rico, and calls upon that Commission to consider the situation of these territories in the light of Resolution 1514 (XV) of the United Nations. ...

Part Five: Respect for the Sovereignty of States and Their Territorial Integrity: Problems of Divided Nations

1. The Conference of Heads of State or Government proclaims its full adherence to the fundamental principle of international relations in accordance with which the sovereignty and territorial integrity of all states, great and small, are inviolable and must be respected.

2. The countries participating in the Conference, having for the most part achieved their national independence after years of struggle, reaffirm their determination to oppose by every means in their power any attempt to compromise their sovereignty or violate their territorial integrity. They pledge themselves to respect frontiers as they existed when states gained independence; nevertheless, parts of territories taken

133

away by occupying Powers and converted into autonomous bases for their own benefit at the time of independence must be given back to the countries concerned.

3. The Conference solemnly reaffirms the rights of all peoples to adopt the form of government they consider best suited to their development.

4. The Conference considers that one of the causes of international tension lies in the problem of divided nations. It expresses its entire sympathy with the peoples of such countries and upholds their desire to achieve unity. It exhorts the countries concerned to seek a just and lasting solution in order to achieve the unification of their territories by peaceful methods without outside interference or pressure. It considers that resorts to threat or force can lead to no satisfactory settlement and cannot do otherwise than jeopardize international security....

The Conference, considering that foreign pressure and intervention to impose changes in the political, economic and social system chosen by a country are contrary to the principles of international law and peaceful co-existence, requests the Government of the United States of America to lift the commercial and economic blockade applied against Cuba.

The Conference takes note of the readiness of the Cuban Government to settle its differences with the United States on a normal footing and invites these two governments to enter into negotiations to this end and in conformity with the principles of peaceful co-existence and international cooperation.

14. RONALD SEGAL

*

The Worldwide Conflict of Rich Whites
and Poor Non-Whites *

At the time when the cultural and political movements instituted by
the non-European revolutions and revolts – in Mexico, China, Vietnam, India, Egypt, Ghana, Cuba and elsewhere – were merging in
a broad 'tri-continental' solidarity, at least among the political
militants – the former editor of the (now defunct) journal *Africa
South*, Ronald Segal (b. 1932) wrote *The Race War*. Like Oliver
Tambo (see page 101), in whose escape from South Africa he
helped, and several others active in Southern African politics, an
exile, Segal has done a considerable amount of writing and publishing based on an intimate knowledge of African politics and also
travel in India and other parts of the Third World. Towards the
end of *The Race War* (one of the most substantial studies of the
Third World by one of its members) Segal writes with feeling of
the conflict between revolutionaries and counter-revolutionaries in
the contemporary world: '*Show me a society that is overwhelmingly agricultural and poor, with the vast bulk of its peasantry
landless or in virtual servitude to rent; a society in which a tiny
élite owns enormous tracts of land, controls commerce and such
industry as exists, and commands political power; a society in
which mass illiteracy, undernourishment and hunger, disease and
early death exist alongside luxury and corruption; a society of
coloured people ruled in the past by whites and still dominated by
the economic or strategic interests of a white state; and I will show
you revolution.* One may suitably say no less of almost every revolution that has taken place in recent years or is taking place now.
One may reasonably predict no less from the condition in which
dozens of countries and hundreds of millions of people are today
placed. *Show me revolution, and in almost every instance I will
show you a Western attempt to crush or control it.*' The extracts
which follow are from the first chapter.

THE poor themselves inevitably see the collaboration of the

*From *The Race War* (London: Jonathan Cape, 1966).

rich as a 'ganging up' against them, an alliance to preserve and indeed increase the privileges of the past. Their mounting despair at ever being able to alter their condition by present endeavour must drive them, sooner or later, to the classic recourse of the desperate throughout history, revolution, and the division of rich and poor along broad colour lines must add immeasurably to the passion of the conflict. The cultural cohesion of a Europe stretching from the United States to the Soviet Union may be the pride and the promise of the rich and the white; it is the reminder and the menace of the poor and the coloured. Ghana and Mali, Aztec and Inca, Aśoka and Akbar, are not the less rousing for their presence behind the centuries than Athens or Rome, Renaissance and Reformation, Elizabeth and Peter the Great. As the Chinese Revolution has shown, an awareness of what was achieved and lost in the past is worth an abundance of artillery. Such poles, of course, fly separate flags, but together they may well produce a display of coloured self-assurance and solidarity against white domination.

Certainly a recognition must grow that in their separate poverty, the coloured peoples possess only a common vulnerability. When China therefore calls for an alliance of the poor, she may expect her call to be heard, if not by indigenous rulers who have risen above the condition of the mass, and who can sublimate their humiliation at national or racial weakness in personal power and wealth, then by the masses themselves, who have no such substitutes. This is not to say that the coloured poor of the world will rally round China's personal standard, uncritical recruits to a new power domination. There is a difference, and a vital one, between China and the 'Chinese line', though Western comment does not seem to recognize it. The Indian Communists of the 'Chinese line' have scored their popular successes against colleagues still loyal to the leadership of the Soviet Union, not because they have appeared to offer Indians the promise of Chinese suzerainty, but because the 'Chinese line' of militancy and revolution has corresponded more to Indian reality than has the 'Soviet line' of compromise and collaboration with the Congress government. The war in

South Vietnam is not about an expansion of Chinese power, though the Americans talk and behave as though it was; it is a national rising under communist leadership against the concentration of land and power in the grasp of a few, and against the foreign – first French and then American – presence that has dominated and divided the country for so long.

What the 'Chinese line' promises and promotes, therefore, is not an imperial China, with colonies all over Africa and Latin America as well as Asia, but a coloured world rising in revolutionary alliance to establish the millennium of the poor. The Chinese leaders have publicly proclaimed the strategy of the struggle. Their own revolution was conducted by the peasantry, recruited and trained in the countryside for the encirclement and eventual capture of the cities. In the world of the present, Western Europe and North America (even perhaps, if the 'Khrushchevite revisionists' continue to hold sway there, Eastern Europe and the Soviet Union as well) are the cities, rich in industry and weapons but cut off from the only real ultimate source of power, the people. Asia, Africa and Latin America are the world's countryside, their peasants desperate and ready for recruitment. Why should the Chinese revolution not be repeated then on a world scale, with the slow encirclement of the cities and their eventual capture? ...

In the very catholic nature of its composition, the revolutionary struggle in South Africa, encompassing African, Asian and Coloured (with a calamitously few whites), nationalists, liberals, socialists and communists, may well mirror, too, the broad base of racial upheaval in the rest of the world. And that is why the Western – and especially, of course, American – obsession with communism is so dangerously irrelevant. It provokes hostility to revolution in itself, as an extension of communist power. But Western attempts to contain revolution must promote it, as a natural response to foreign domination, just as the blind seeing of communism in every revolution must spread communist influence by provoking calls for the aid and protection of communist governments.

In the end this refusal to countenance revolution simply advances the prospects of racial struggle, for it perpetuates the

137

economic inequalities, the national poverty and the resentment at white domination in the present and the past that produce the coloured consensus of rebellion. And should the West and the Soviet Union really reach an agreement to police the world together, in an alliance of white communism and white capitalism to control unrest, it will increase, not diminish, the possibilities of race war.

The need for international peace is, of course, far more apparent to those who have much to keep than to those who have little to lose. Peasants in vast areas of the earth feel themselves somewhat closer to death from hunger or disease than from nuclear conflagration. And, doubtless unreasonably, some of their leaders see in the very proclaimed anxiety of the dominant peoples for peace an argument against it. If peace serves the interests of the rich and the strong, how then can it benefit at the same time the poor and the weak? Peace is a good thing, yes, but not at the price of preserving the world as it is. (And, after all, the rich are also devoted to peace only at a price – their own price. Or why is peace in any danger from the poor?)

What the world, therefore, has to face is a despair so deep among the poor, a resentment against established conditions so passionate, that normal fears are ceasing to exercise their expected restraint. That is why the war in South Vietnam goes on – however many new intimidating weapons the United States employs, and however high the casualty figures among the peasantry mount. And the violence must, surely, spread – till the rich and the poor, the dominant and the dominated, are alike, in the final accommodation of an equal humanity or an equal annihilation.

The waste of it all is stupefying. For poverty and ignorance and disease – as the leaders of the rich world themselves proclaim, when thinking of their own societies – are infinitely wasteful of the world's greatest asset, people, and their unused, indeed undiscovered potential. Does it not seem probable that a world without rich and poor striving against each other to preserve or escape their unequal circumstances – a world, instead, of people striving together still further to dominate

138

their environment – would be more efficient and creative, and far more free? For it is nonsense to talk of freedom for those who are captive to their circumstances, whether they are poor and so imprisoned by want, or rich and so imprisoned by fear. Would not the energies and resources of separate nations, now separately invested in degrading rivalries and a squandering on stockpiles of destruction, be better invested in a coordinated international endeavour? What does democracy mean if it exists only within the nation state and requires for its survival the perpetuation of privilege? How rancid humanity has become that such sentiments sound somehow absurdly unrealistic, the daydreams of a political Pollyanna. Yet they must be real, or the only reality left is the havoc of race.

It is the overwhelming reality now. And there is escape neither in the deceit of cumulative intimidation nor in the distracting probes of doctrine or space. Indeed, such distractions are the ultimate deceit, a distortion of the whole human purpose, since they attempt to conceal the terrors of life as it is. For it is only when the human condition is stripped down to its bones, when the basic needlessness of so much suffering and the inevitable extent of the violence that such suffering must excite are properly measured, that perhaps men will at last rebel against their past and themselves, and provide somehow an excuse, a resolve, and a method for their decent survival.

15. WESTERN VIEWS

*

How do Europeans, North Americans, Japanese and Australians, whether Western or Eastern in ideology, view the developments in Asia, Africa and Latin America? Do they see in the south a 'new world in the making', created and sustained by neither the Western nor the Soviet *bloc*? In what follows we give excerpts from two sympathetic accounts: (i) *An Introduction to Contemporary History* by the British historian Geoffrey Barraclough and (ii) Peter Worsley's *The Third World*. Professor Barraclough, formerly Professor of International History in the University of London, is a Fellow of St John's College, Cambridge. Peter Worsley, an Australian, is Professor of Sociology in the University of Manchester.

(I) A NEW GROUND PLAN
FOR WORLD HISTORY*

IF the retarding influence of conservative forces fighting to preserve as much as possible of the old European-centred world was one factor affecting the process of transition, another factor was the disruption of the heart of Europe through the rivalries and conflicts of the European powers between 1914 and 1945. No aspect of recent history has been more fully discussed. For most European historians the disputes and rivalries that gathered momentum after 1905 marked the beginning of the great civil war in which Europe, caught in the toils of its own past, encompassed its own destruction, and it was the failure of Europe to solve its own problems – in particular, the long-standing problems of nationalism – that ushered in a new age.

No one would deny that this view of contemporary history, with its emphasis on Europe and on the continuity of develop-

*From Geoffrey Barraclough, *An Introduction to Contemporary History* (London: Watts, 1964).

140

ments within Europe, illuminates certain aspects of the history of the period. The real question is whether it is adequate as a key to the process of transition as a whole. The years between 1890 and 1960 confront us with two interlocking processes, the end of one epoch and the beginning of another, and the conflicts of the European powers undoubtedly played a large part in the former. What we have to ask is whether historians who have made Europe the pivot of their story have not concentrated too exclusively on the old world that was dying and paid too little attention to the new world coming to life. It is no doubt true that, but for the wars which brought the old world crashing down, the birth of the new world would have been more protracted and difficult. Their course and outcome also throw light on the post-war situation in Europe. But as soon as we extend our view from Europe to Asia and Africa, the position is different. There, as we shall see, the conflicts and rivalries of the European powers were a contributory factor; but they do not help us to understand the character of the new world which emerged after 1945, any more than they explain the origins and growth of the forces that shaped it during the preceding fifty years. An interpretation which concentrates on the European predicament, in short, is too narrow for a process which was world-wide; it may not be wrong within its own limits, but it is misleading in balance and perspective.

Nor shall we understand the course of events in Europe itself, if we dissociate it from the world-wide process of change which began around 1890. The European conflicts of the first half of the twentieth century were more than a continuation of earlier European conflicts. From the end of the nineteenth century Europe was involved simultaneously in the problems inherited from its own past and in a process of adaptation to a new world situation, and both aspects of its history must be taken into account. . . .

Fascism and National Socialism, which claimed to be the only effective instruments for shoring up the old world – and which won mass support on that score – turned out, by the peculiar irony of history, to be instruments of its collapse. They played a part in the process of transition as factors forcing forward the march of events; but their positive contribution to the new world arising amidst the ruin of the old was small. Only the most superficial analogy, for example, would seek to derive the 'guided democracy' of Indonesia from the Fascist corporate state or to explain the political structure of Argentina after 1945 as a consequence of Péron's visit to Italy between 1939 and 1941 rather than in the context of the social changes in Latin America inaugurated by the Mexican revolution of 1910. If we wish to understand why, among the many possibilities opened up by the collapse of Germany and Japan in 1945, certain ones materialized and others did not, we must turn to developments which historians have too easily banished to the outer margins of history and which are only now slowly finding their way back to the centre. Today it is evident that much we have been taught to regard as central is really peripheral and much that is usually brushed aside as peripheral had in it the seeds of the future. Looked at from the vantage-point of Dien Bien Phu, for example, Amritsar* stands out with new and unaccustomed prominence among the events of 1919.

It is no doubt true that, down to 1945, the end of the old world was the most conspicuous aspect of recent history; it engrossed the attention of contemporaries and blinded them to the importance of other aspects. But it is the business of the historian, looking back over events from a distance, to correct their perspectives, and to draw attention to developments whose long-term bearing they could not be expected to see. Up to the present, on the whole, they have made little use of their opportunity. No doubt, this is due in part to the fact that many historians are still emotionally involved in the death-agonies of the old world, which they feel more deeply than

---

*On 13 April 1919 a large assembly of unarmed Indians in a public park, Jallianwallah Bagh, in Amritsar, found their only exit blocked by troops, who were ordered by General Dyer to open fire. 379 people had been killed by the time the ammunition was exhausted. 'The Massacre of Amritsar' and other British measures to humiliate and terrorize Indians had a decisive effect on the anti-imperialist movement in India.

the birth-pangs of the new; it is due, also, to the fact that, until very recently, we were unable to stand outside the period of transition and look back over it as a whole. Today that is no longer the case. If, as I have tried to indicate, the long transition from one age to another is now over, if we can say that between 1955 and 1960 the world moved into a new historical period, with different dimensions and problems of its own, it should no longer be impossible to restore the balance between the old world which has passed and the new world which has emerged.

To do so is also a matter of urgent practical necessity. The rising generation will inevitably look back over the twentieth century with different priorities from ours. Born into a world in which – as all present indications suggest – the major questions will not be European questions but the relationships between Europe, including Russia, and America and the peoples of Asia and Africa, they will find little relevance in many of the topics which engrossed the attention of the last generation. The study of contemporary history requires new perspectives and a new scale of values. We shall find more clues, for example, in Nkrumah's autobiography than in Eden's memoirs, more points of contact in the world of Mao and Nehru than in that of Coolidge and Baldwin; and it is important to remember that, while Mussolini and Hitler were prancing and posturing at the centre of the European stage, changes were going on in the wider world which contributed more fundamentally than they did to the shape of things to come. The tendency of historians to dwell on those aspects of the history of the period which have their roots in the old world sometimes seems to hamper rather than to further our understanding of the forces of change. Here we shall try to strike a different balance. We shall not forget that the end of one epoch and the birth of another were events happening simultaneously within the same contracting world; but it is with the new epoch growing to maturity in the shadow of the old that we shall be primarily concerned.

(II) THE NEW INTERNATIONAL
CLASS STRUGGLE*

The African countries can help each other little. Capital is accumulated internally all too slowly. Recourse to external aid seems inevitable. Yet here, once more, the 'proletarian nations' find themselves in the same life-situation. They come with palms outstretched to ask for bread, and they are offered – capitalism or communism. They get aid largely as part of the world strategies of the two rival *blocs*. 'Aid' is neither disinterested Christian charity, nor proletarian internationalism; it is a political and military weapon in the world power-struggle.

At this point, the new states boil over. Between their society of hoes and goats, and the Euro-American world of space-rockets and blast-furnaces, there is a Grand Canyon full of bitterness and mutual mistrust. This is the great 'alienation' of the twentieth century, to them far more vicious and dehumanizing than any gulf between worker and bourgeois in capitalist society. On the one hand, the capitalist *and socialist* 'millionaires', to use Nyerere's words; on the other, 'the damned of the earth', as Fanon calls them.

Sékou Touré † has expressed this view most explicitly of all: 'The major division in the the world today,' he remarks, 'is not between East and West, but between the under-developed and the developed countries of the world.' Senghor goes further, and asserts that although the European or American worker is oppressed and alienated under capitalism, he, like the capitalist and everyone else in the 'over-developed' world, benefits from the exploitation of Afro-Asia, and Latin America. His formulation is important: 'In brief, the proletarians of Europe have benefited from the colonial regime; *therefore they have never really – I mean effectively – opposed it.*' This view has also been expressed by some left-wing European writers on the Third World, notably by Sartre and by the geographer

---

*From Peter Worsley, *The Third World* (London: Weidenfeld & Nicolson, 1964).

† Sékou Touré (b. 1922) President of the Republic of Guinea since its creation in 1958.

Buchanan, who cites with approval Moussa's statement that the 'efforts of Western workers to raise their standards of living have contributed more to the deterioration of the position of the under-developed countries than has the profit motive of industrial or commercial leaders'.

Such views have, of course, long been current on the Right, when they have been used as an argument from self-interest to 'justify' the retention of imperial holdings. They now occur on the Left. More extreme forms of these theories circulate in the Third World itself; in essence, traditional socialist internationalism has been replaced by a new kind of revolutionary theory in which the major conflict is seen as one between the hungry 'proletarian nations' and affluent Euro-America, capitalist or communist. A mystique of 'the colonial disinherited' replaces the solidarity of *all* the exploited in class-society. There is too, a kind of Sorelian celebration of 'cleansing' violence which will rejuvenate the earth and transform former slaves and former masters alike into human beings. Though the socialist terminology remains, in the course of this argument, international class solidarity has been subtly transformed into inter-*national* antagonism.

The temptations of such a view are obvious enough, especially in countries like Fanon's adopted Algeria, where the betrayal of the French Left has been so patent.

When the new states speak of themselves as 'proletarian nations', they see themselves in the image of Marx's working class, as an emergent social grouping which, under the politico-economic domination of the wealthy propertied states have been exploited and robbed of human status. Under this oppression, they have developed a consciousness of their common fate; they have thrown up, initially, 'defensive' organizations (the equivalent of Lenin's 'trade-union consciousness'). Ultimately, they have made the transition to revolutionary and collective *political* consciousness and action, through which they will bring about not only their own liberation, but also the world-historic destruction of the power-apparatus oppressing all humanity. The imperialists themselves will be freed from the curse of dehumanizing superiority which distorts their lives as much as inferiority distorts the lives of the oppressed. The particular struggle of the proletarian nations thus has a universal significance. Their revolution will be a *socialist* one which will permanently alter the 'human condition'.

Since the 'proletarian nations' have appropriated for themselves the role of Marx's proletariat, as grave-digger of capitalism, there is little historical role left for the proletariat of the advanced countries. In the new theoretical model, they are either passive or active accomplices of imperialism, so long corrupted that they have become historically insignificant as a revolutionary force.

If the proletariat of the advanced countries has been displaced by the revolutionary peasantry of the backward countries, so has the country which produced the first major revolution of our time. To thinkers like Ly,* capitalist imperialism is the primordial enemy, but Soviet imperialism is no less imperialism.

* Abdoulaye Ly, one of the outstanding younger politicians in Senegal.

PART THREE

THE SITUATION: DESCRIPTION AND ANALYSIS OF CONDITIONS

IT is clear that in important respects the peoples of the Third World do not share the outlook, aspirations and experiences of the forces which are dominant in North America, Europe and Japan. What they would regard as significant in their own situation – the place they occupy in the plans and activities of the others, the way they have been treated, the difficulties they face, and so on – would differ.

In what we have described as the tri-continental south there live seventy per cent of the world's population. The percentage of the world's area in which they live is smaller, and that from which they derive their sustenance is considerably smaller. But the countries in which they live are stretched out over a wide area. If we look at the nations which have developed the modern capitalist system we notice that there are a variety of social and political structures; for example, England, France, the United States, Japan and Germany are capitalist democracies or are 'liberal' in different forms. In a similar sense, the nations which were (or are) related peripherally to metropolitan economies in France, Spain, Britain or the United States, and are heirs of more or less highly developed non-European civilizations, inevitably emerge into the Third World in a variety of forms. The indigenous revolutionary leadership, the specific local conditions (including the local impact of the world economic system), have given different shape to what is conceived as a struggle for liberation or for modernization.

The diversity of backgrounds and situations, together with the varying intensity of political consciousness, and the multiplicity of the phases of the different Third World revolutions, tend to make the Third World almost inconceivably complex. Yet there are important features of social and economic structure which these countries share. With the exception of an

149

insignificantly small number of affluent people (some multi-millionaires, nearly all landlords or businessmen or agents and partners of foreign enterprises) most people are predominantly rural in outlook, and their material standard of living is very low. Outside the foreign-oriented enclaves, social and economic realities have a different aspect from those described in the industrialized countries. Events are viewed as desperate or promising, as failures or successes, as progressive or reactionary, as constructive or destructive presumably according to the new non-European histories in which the speakers or writers hope to participate as creators – organizers, builders, inventors. The view is, of course, no more universal than the Western view.

Given the decision of the militant peoples of the Third World to repossess the means, resources and making of their common destiny, what kind of situation is it that they come up against at one or another of the critical moments in their new history? What is there which the feudal or semi-colonial past has handed down to them – in the form of institutions, psychologically, as moral norms, and ideologically – which they have in the process of reconstruction to contend with? What is there in it that they can make use of? In surveying the scene with questions such as these in mind thinkers and leaders in the Third World appear at times to wonder if the social and political soil, as it were, in which in the previous era their lives were rooted, is any good at all. Have the plants which grew out of it not fructified and flourished as retarded and distorted economies, political disorganization, ignorant minds and stunted, sickly bodies, vulnerability to external attack or subversion, disunity, and so on?

The more searching the inquiry into the conditions, the more distinctly 'different' the descriptions and analyses are from the scholarly or polemical accounts of 'northern' writers. Practical men, revolutionary leaders, men and women with a passion to achieve 'liberation' for their people, probe the situation, waiting to know how the pace and direction of change and hierarchies of authority and status in the given world order accords with what they seek to create; how malleable the inheritance and what its potentialities are; what the bonds are which need to be broken to set the people free, and, indeed, what is needed to break them or to make those in bondage break them; whether the immediate situation for action is bounded by national boundaries or transcends them; whether the differences in conditions for different classes or groups are significant enough to require differences of approach and diagnosis.

What some of these writers (and those for whom they speak) are by this evidence sensitive to, the things which move them to passionate revolt or action are perhaps not easy to understand or appreciate. The selections have been made so that one or two particular regions can be kept under scrutiny for as long as possible. As the analyses of the peculiarities of politics, social structure and the economy indicate, Latin America could provide useful keys to the situation in other parts of the Third World. What is said here about the 'dynamics' of Brazilian, Colombian or Peruvian economics or politics suggests lines of research for those who are familiar with Southeast Asia, or South Asia or parts of tropical Africa. A methodical survey of the situation would no doubt have to range over such matters as education, the family, industry, food production and distribution, non-food agriculture, defence, health, the countryside and the cities, class divisions, the role and status of women, systems of authority, administration, political consciousness, law and much else. The readings that follow in fact take note of these elements of the historical situation in their relationship to one another.

1. JAWAHARLAL NEHRU

*

The Record of British Rule in India*

There were many distinguished Indians who worked for the over-throw of British rule in India. The one who was most interested in world history and world politics, and probably made the greatest impact on world politics, was Jawaharlal Nehru (see page 105). The fact that India was the most important of all the European colonies had something to do with the international importance of Nehru. He was at the height of his powers as a political leader, thinker and writer in the 1930s, and during one of his many periods spent in a British jail he wrote *An Autobiography*. In it he looked at what was happening with the eyes of someone who was certain that India would regain her independence. His assessment of the heritage of British dominion in India is given here. It is milder than that of his mentor, Mahatma Gandhi, who, for example, at his trial for sedition in 1922 indicted Britain of 'a crime against humanity which is perhaps unequalled in history' for what it had done to the Indian people.

WHAT has been the record of British rule in India? I doubt if it is possible for any Indian or Englishman to take an objective or dispassionate view of this long record. And even if this were possible, it would be still more difficult to weigh and measure the psychological and other immaterial factors. We are told that British rule 'has given to India that which throughout the centuries she never possessed, a government whose authority is unquestioned in any part of the subcontinent';† it has established the rule of law and a just and efficient administration; it has brought to India Western conceptions of Parliamentary government and personal liberties; and 'by transforming British India into a single unitary state it has engendered among Indians a sense of political unity' and thus

*From *An Autobiography* (London: Allen & Unwin, 1936).
† The quotations are from the Report of the Joint Parliamentary Committee on Indian Constitutional Reform (1934).

fostered the first beginnings of nationalism. That is the British case, and there is much truth in it, though the rule of law and personal liberties have not been in evidence for many years.

The Indian survey of this period lays stress on many other factors, and points out the injury, material and spiritual, that foreign rule has brought us. The viewpoint is so different that sometimes the very thing that is commended by the British is condemned by the Indians. As Dr Ananda Coomaraswamy writes: 'One of the most remarkable features of British rule in India is that the greatest injuries inflicted upon the Indian people have the outward appearance of blessings.'

As a matter of fact the changes that have taken place in India during the last century or more have been world changes common to most countries in the East and West. The growth of industrialism in Western Europe, and later on in the rest of the world, brought nationalism and strong unitary states in its train everywhere. The British can take credit for having first opened India's window to the West and brought her one aspect of Western industrialism and science. But having done so they throttled the further industrial growth of the country till circumstances forced their hands. India was already the meeting place of two cultures, the western Asiatic culture of Islam and the eastern, her own product, which spread to the Far East. And now a third and more powerful impulse came from farther west, and India became a focal point and a battle-ground for various old and new ideas. There can be no doubt that this third impulse would have triumphed and thus solved some of India's old problems, but the British, who had them-selves helped in bringing it, tried to stop its further progress. They prevented our industrial growth, and thus delayed our political growth, and preserved all the out-of-date feudal and other relics they could find in the country. They even froze up our changing and to some extent progressing laws and customs at the stage they found them, and made it difficult for us to get out of their shackles. It was not with their goodwill or assis-tance that the *bourgeoisie* grew in India. But after introducing the railway and other products of industrialism they could not stop the wheel of change; they could only check and slow it down, and this they did to their own manifest advantage.

'On this solid foundation the majestic structure of the Government of India rests, and it can be claimed with certainty that in the period which has elapsed since 1858 when the Crown assumed supremacy over all the territories of the East India Company, the educational and material progress of India has been greater than it has ever been within her power to achieve during any other period of her long and chequered history.' This statement is not so self-evident as it appears to be, and it has often been stated that literacy actually went down with the coming of British rule. But even if the statement was wholly true, it amounts to a comparison of the modern industrial age with past ages. In almost every country in the world the educational and material progress has been tremendous during the past century because of science and industrialism, and it may be said with assurance of any such country that progress of this kind 'has been greater than was ever within her power to achieve during any other period of her long and chequered history' – though perhaps that country's history may not be a long one in comparison with Indian history. Are we needlessly cantankerous and perverse if we suggest that some such technical progress would have come to us anyhow in this industrial age, and even without British rule? And, indeed, if we compare our lot with many other countries, may we not hazard the guess that such progress might have been greater, for we have had to contend against a stifling of that progress by the British themselves? Railways, telegraphs, telephones, wireless and the like were hardly tests of the goodness or beneficence of British rule. They were welcome and necessary, and because the British happened to be the agents who brought them first, we should be grateful to them. But even these heralds of industrialism came to us primarily for the strengthening of British rule. They were the veins and arteries through which the nation's blood should have coursed, increasing its trade, carrying its produce, and bringing new life and wealth to its millions. It is true that in the long run some such result was likely, but they were designed

154

and worked for another purpose – to strengthen the imperial hold and to capture markets for British goods – which they succeeded in achieving. I am all in favour of industrialization and the latest methods of transport, but sometimes, as I rushed across the Indian plains, the railway, the life-giver, has almost seemed to me like iron bands confining and imprisoning India.

The British conception of ruling India was the police conception of the State. Government's job was to protect the State and leave the rest to others. Their public finance dealt with military expenditure, police, civil administration, interest on debt. The economic needs of the citizens were not looked after, and were sacrificed to British interests. The cultural and other needs of the people, except for a tiny handful, were entirely neglected. The changing conceptions of public finance which brought free and universal education, improvement of public health, care of poor and feeble-minded, insurance of workers against illness, old age and unemployment, etc., in other countries, were almost entirely beyond the ken of the Government. It could not indulge in these spending activities for its tax system was most regressive, taking a much larger proportion of small incomes than of the larger ones, and its expenditure on its protective and administrative functions was terribly heavy and swallowed up most of the revenue.

The outstanding feature of British rule was their concentration on everything that went to strengthen their political and economic hold on the country. Everything else was incidental. If they built up a powerful central government and an efficient police force, that was an achievement for which they can take credit, but the Indian people can hardly congratulate themselves on it. Unity is a good thing, but unity in subjection is hardly a thing to be proud of. The very strength of a despotic government may become a greater burden for a people; and a police force, no doubt useful in many ways, can be, and has been often enough, turned against the very people it is supposed to protect. Bertrand Russell, comparing modern civilization with the old Greek, has recently written: 'The only serious superiority of Greek civilization as compared to ours

155

was the inefficiency of the police, which enabled a larger proportion of decent people to escape.'

Britain's supremacy in India brought us peace, and India was certainly in need of peace after the troubles and misfortunes that followed the break-up of the Moghul empire. Peace is a precious commodity, necessary for any progress, and it was welcome to us when it came. But even peace can be purchased at too great a price, and we can have the perfect peace of the grave, and the absolute safety of a cage or of prison. Or peace may be the sodden despair of men unable to better themselves. The peace which is imposed by an alien conqueror has hardly the restful and soothing qualities of the real article. . . .

It is a futile task to consider the 'ifs' and possibilities of history. I feel sure that it was a good thing for India to come in contact with the scientific and industrial West. Science was the great gift of the West, and India lacked this, and without it she was doomed to decay. The manner of our contacts was unfortunate, and yet, perhaps, only a succession of violent shocks could shake us out of our torpor. From this point of view the Protestant, individualistic, Anglo-Saxon English were suitable, for they were more different from us than most other Westerners, and could give us greater shocks.

They gave us political unity and that was a desirable thing, but whether we had this unity or not, Indian nationalism would have grown and demanded that unity. The Arab world is today split up into a large number of states – independent, protected, mandatory and the like – but throughout all of them runs the desire for Arab unity. There can be no doubt that Arab nationalism would largely achieve this unity if Western imperialist powers did not stand in the way. But, as in India, it is the purpose of these powers to encourage disruptive tendencies and create minority problems which weaken and partly counteract the nationalist urge and give an excuse to the imperialist power to stay on and pose as the impartial arbitrator.

The political unity of India was achieved incidentally as a side-product of the Empire's advance. In later years, when that unity allied itself to nationalism and challenged alien rule, we witnessed the deliberate promotion of disunity and sectarianism, formidable obstacles to our future progress.

What a long time it is since the British came here, a century and three-quarters since they became dominant! They had a free hand, as despotic governments have, and a magnificent opportunity to mould India to their desire. During these years the world has changed out of all recognition – England, Europe, America, Japan. The insignificant American colonies bordering the Atlantic in the eighteenth century constitute today the wealthiest, the most powerful and technically the most advanced nation; Japan, within a brief span, has undergone amazing changes; the vast territories of the U.S.S.R., where only yesterday the dead hand of the Tsar's government suppressed and stifled all growth, now pulsate with a new life and build a new world before our eyes. There have been big changes in India also, and the country is very different from what it was in the eighteenth century – railways, irrigation works, factories, schools and colleges, huge government offices, etc., etc.

And yet, in spite of these changes, what is India like today? A servile state, with its splendid strength caged up, hardly daring to breathe freely, governed by strangers from afar; her people poor beyond compare, short-lived and incapable of resisting disease and epidemic; illiteracy rampant; vast areas devoid of all sanitary or medical provision; unemployment on a prodigious scale, both among the middle classes and the masses. Freedom, democracy, socialism, communism are, we are told, the slogans of unpractical idealists, doctrinaires or knaves; the test must be one of the well-being of the people as a whole. That is indeed a vital test, and by that test India makes a terribly poor show today. We read of great schemes of unemployment relief and the alleviation of distress in other countries; what of our scores of millions unemployed and the distress that is widespread and permanent? We read also of housing schemes elsewhere; where are the homes of hundreds of millions of our people, who live in mud huts or have no shelter at all? May we not envy the lot of other countries where education, sanitation, medical relief, cultural facilities, and production advance rapidly ahead, while we remain where we were, or plod wearily along at the pace of a snail? Russia in a brief dozen years of wonderful effort has almost ended illiteracy in her vast territories, and has evolved a fine and up-to-date system of education, in touch with the life of the masses. Backward Turkey, under the Ataturk, Mustapha Kemal's leadership, has also made giant strides towards widespread literacy. Fascist Italy, on the very threshold of its career, attacked illiteracy with vigour. Gentile, the Education Minister, called for 'a frontal attack on illiteracy. That gangrenous plague, which is rotting our body politic, must be extirpated with a hot iron.' Hard words, unseemly for a drawing-room, but they show the conviction and energy behind the thought. We are politer here and use more rounded phrases. We move warily and exhaust our energies in commissions and committees.

Indians have been accused of talking too much and doing little. It is a just charge. But may we not express our wonder at the inexhaustible capacity of the British for committees and commissions, each of which, after long labour, produces a learned report – 'a great State document' – which is duly praised and pigeon-holed? And so we get the sensation of moving ahead, of progress, and yet have the advantage of remaining where we were. Honour is satisfied, and vested interests remain untouched and secure. Other countries discuss how to get on; we discuss checks and brakes and safeguards lest we go too fast. ...

It would be absurd to cast the blame for all India's ills on the British. That responsibility must be shouldered by us, and we may not shirk it; it is unseemly to blame others for the inevitable consequences of our own weaknesses. An authoritarian system of government, and especially one that is foreign, must encourage a psychology of subservience and try to limit the mental outlook and horizon of the people. It must crush much that is finest in youth – enterprise, spirit of adventure, originality, 'pep' – and encourage sneakishness, rigid conformity, and a desire to cringe and please the bosses. Such a system does not bring out the real service mentality, the devotion to public service or to ideals; it picks out the least public-spirited persons whose sole objective is to get on in life. We see what a class the British attract to themselves in India! Some of them are intellectually keen and capable of good work. They drift to government service or semi-government service because of lack of opportunity elsewhere, and gradually they tone down and become just parts of the big machine, their minds imprisoned by the dull routine of work. They develop the qualities of a bureaucracy – 'a competent knowledge of clerkship and the diplomatic art of keeping office'. At the highest they have a passive devotion to the public service. There is, or can be, no flaming enthusiasm. That is not possible under a foreign government.

But apart from these, the majority of petty officials are not an admirable lot, for they have only learnt to cringe to their superiors and bully their inferiors. The fault is not theirs. That is the training the system gives them. And if sycophancy and nepotism flourish, as they so often do, is it to be wondered at? They have no ideals in service: the haunting fear of unemployment and consequent starvation pursues them, and their chief concern is to hold on to their jobs and to get other jobs for their relatives and friends. Where the spy and that most odious of creatures, the informer, always hover in the background, it is not easy to develop the most desirable virtues in a people.

Recent developments have made it even more difficult for sensitive, public-spirited men to join government service. The Government does not want them, and they do not wish to associate with it too closely, unless compelled by economic circumstance.

2. HO CHI MINH

*

The Burden of Empire *

If there is anyone who has earned the title of 'grand old man' of the Third World it is Nguyen That Thanh (b. 1890) alias Nguyen Ai Quoc, alias Ho Chi Minh, of Vietnam. Beginning his career as a servant he is now President of an independent Vietnam. Born in the Nghe-An province of Annam (as it then was), Ho moved when quite young to Britain and then Europe. He thus got to see the workings of the European empires from the metropolitan centres in Europe. He was also in Europe at the very time when the Bolshevik Revolution split Europe into two, and the anti-colonial, anti-imperialist cause to which he had committed himself was taken up in Europe itself by Lenin and his colleagues. Ho was already a revolutionary and a 'proletarian' socialist at a time when in most colonial countries moderate, middle-class liberals were leading the movements for a greater share in constitutional government for native leaders. He was one of the first nationalists to conceive of the liberation of colonial peoples in international perspective. The article on Indo-China and the Pacific reproduced here was written in 1924.

AT first sight, it seems that the question of Indo-China and the Pacific is of no concern to European workers. But it must be remembered that:

1. During the revolution, the Allies, not having succeeded in their attack on Russia from the west, tried to attack it from the east. And the Pacific powers, the United States and Japan, landed their troops in Vladivostock, while France sent Indo-chinese regiments to Siberia to support the Whites.

2. At present, international capitalism draws all its vital forces from the colonial countries. It finds there raw materials for its factories, investments for its capital, markets for its pro-

*From *Selected Works of Ho Chi Minh* (Hanoi: Foreign Languages Publishing House, 1960).

160

ducts, cheap replenishments for its labour army, and above all, native soldiers for its counter-revolutionary army. One day, revolutionary Russia will have to cope with this capitalism. It is thus necessary for the Russian comrades to realize the full strength and all the immediate and long-term manoeuvres of their adversary.

3. Having become the centre of attraction for imperialist ambitions, the Pacific area and the neighbouring colonies are likely in the future to become the seat of a new world conflagration, whose proletariat will have to bear the burden.

These statements of fact prove that the Pacific problem will concern all proletarians in general.

Therefore, to reconstruct France ruined by an imperialist war, the French Minister of Colonies has worked out a plan for developing the colonies. The plan aims to exploit the resources of colonized countries for the benefit of the colonizing country. This plan states that Indo-China must help the other colonies in the Pacific to intensify their production so that, in their turn, they too can be useful to the mother country. If the plan were carried out, it would necessarily lead to the depopulation and impoverishment of Indo-China.

Lately, however, the Government Council of Indo-China, despite the resistance of Annamese opinion, unanimously voted for the carrying out of the plan. To understand the importance of this unanimity, it is useful to know that this council is composed of the Governor General of Indo-China, and about thirty high-ranking French civil servants, as well as five native mandarins, tools of the Governor. And all these gentlemen pretend to act for Indo-China and in the interests of the Annamese people. Imagine Eskimos or Zulus deciding the fate of a European people.

According to an official avowal, the colonies in the Pacific are afflicted with debility, and are living – if we can call it living – at a slower and slower rate. The truth is that populous islands are being entirely depopulated, in a short time, by alcohol and forced labour. Fifty years ago, the Marquesas had more than 20,000 souls, but now have only 1,500 weak and debilitated inhabitants. Tahiti had its population reduced by twenty-five per cent in ten years. From these declining populations, French imperialism has further taken more than 1,500 men to serve as cannon fodder during the war. This rapid extinction of a race seems unbelievable. However, it is a fact to be observed in many colonies. (In the regions of the Congo, populations of 40,000 inhabitants fell to 30,000 in the space of twenty years. Saint-Pierre et Miquelon islands had 6,500 inhabitants in 1902; in 1922 this colony had only 3,900, etc.)

Most islands in the French Pacific have been yielded to concessionary companies which rob the natives of their land and make them work as slaves. Here is an example showing how the native workers are treated. Two hundred mother-of-pearl divers were sent by force by the French Company of Oceania to plantations 800 miles from their native districts. (It is as if tailors were sent to work in mines.) They were penned up in a small schooner fitted up for ten passengers and lacking any life-saving equipment, and embarked without being allowed to see their wives and children. For two years, these unfortunate toilers were kept prisoner in the company's jail. Many were harshly treated. Others died.

Add to this inhuman exploitation the immorality of the rascals to whom French imperialism entrusts the administration of these islands, and you will see in all its beauty the regime of exploitation and oppression which is leading the colonized countries in the Pacific to death and extinction.

Imperialism has now reached a degree of almost scientific perfection. It uses white proletarians to conquer the proletarians of the colonies. Then it hurls the proletarians of one colony against those of another. Finally, it relies on the proletarians of the colonies to rule white proletarians. Senegalese had the sad distinction of having helped French militarism to massacre their brothers of the Congo, the Sudan, Dahomey, and Madagascar. Algerians fought in Indo-China. Annamese were garrisoned in Africa. And so on. During the great slaughter, more than one million colonial peasants and workers were brought to Europe to massacre white peasants and workers. Only recently, French soldiers in the Ruhr were surrounded by native soldiers, and native light infantry were sent against German strikers. Almost half of the French army is composed of natives, to the number of about 300,000.

Beyond this military usefulness, capitalism uses these colonies for the most skilful economic exploitation. It is often noticed that a decrease in wages in some regions in France and in some trades is always preceded by an increase in the proportion of colonial labour. The natives are employed as strikebreakers. Capitalism now uses one colony as a tool for exploiting another; this is the case of Indo-China and the Pacific area. Indo-China, despite the noisy untruths of the officials, is exhausted. During 1914–18, almost 100,000 Annamese (official number: 97,903 men) were dragged from their homes to be sent to Europe. Although deprived of so many hands for production, Indo-China was obliged to send, for the defence of its oppressors, more than 500,000 tons of edible grains. Hundreds of millions of francs were raked off in 'victory loans'. Each year, the Annamese sweat blood to yield up about 450,000 francs, a sum which is almost entirely used to fatten spongers. Moreover, Indo-China is responsible for big military expenses, elegantly called a 'filial contribution' by the Minister of Colonies.

It is from this oppressed, weakened, and emaciated country that millions of piastres and several thousand men (40,000 to begin with) are further going to be wrung to satisfy the insatiable appetites of the concessionaries and the personal ambitions of a gang of unscrupulous politicians.

It is not enough to demoralize the whole Annamese race with alcohol and opium. It is not enough to take 40,000 'volunteers' yearly for the glory of militarism. It is not enough to have turned a people of twenty million souls into one big sponge to be squeezed by money-grubbers. We are, on top of all this, to be endowed with slavery.

It is not only the fate of the proletariat in Indo-China and the Pacific area, but also that of the international proletariat, which is threatened by these actions. Japan commands the telegraphic stations on Yap Island. The United States is spending millions of dollars on improving the turret guns of its warships in the Pacific. England will turn Singapore into a naval base. France finds it necessary to build a Pacific Empire.

Since the Washington Conference,* colonial rivalries have become sharper and sharper, imperialist follies greater and greater, and political conflicts more and more unavoidable. Wars have been launched over India, Africa and Morocco. Other wars may break out over the Pacific area if the proletariat is not watchful.

*The conference held from 12 November 1921 to 6 February 1922, and attended by the United States, the United Kingdom, Japan, France, Italy, China, Belgium, Portugal, and the Netherlands.

3. KOFI BUSIA

*

The Colonial Inheritance in Africa *

How does the colonial record in Africa appear to one of the Westernized liberals among the African intellectuals and leaders? Kofi Busia (b. 1914), a Ghanaian sociologist, has been a don at Oxford and was earlier leader of the Parliamentary Opposition in Ghana until it became a one-party state and he was forced into exile. After Nkrumah was overthrown he returned to Ghanaian politics. He discusses his view of developments in the African continent in his *Africa in Search of Democracy*, from which the following is taken.

WE may ask what contribution colonialism has made to the development of democratic regimes in Africa. It is easier to see the contributions which could have been made but were not made, since these are shown in the weaknesses and needs of the states which have gained independence. In all of them, we find that neither agricultural nor industrial development was at a stage where the standards of living of the bulk of the population were much above subsistence levels. All the countries are classified as poor and underdeveloped. In all of them the raising of the standards of living is a major task which must have priority. That situation also discloses the inadequate development of human resources to which we have referred. There are not enough men with the necessary skills. Education has not been regarded as an essential investment for development. The newly independent states have been faced with severe shortage of manpower for the civil and defence services and their development projects. In some this has made independence more formal than real.

All this is apt to diminish the importance of the contribution that colonial powers have made. Works dealing with the early

*From *Africa in Search of Democracy* (London: Routledge & Kegan Paul, 1967).

165

history of colonial administration give a picture of what has been done. In the Gold Coast, for example, personnel was brought from Sierra Leone and the West Indies during the nineteenth century to fill posts in the clerical and administrative services, and in the police and military forces, because no literate persons were available in the country, and malaria took heavy toll of Europeans. Then schools were opened, and people were trained first for junior posts, and later for more senior ones. By the time of independence in 1957, there were Africans in all branches and at all levels of the civil service, headed by an African. An administrative framework had been provided. In all the colonies, there are accounts of the establishment of law and order, which was necessary for the development of trade and commerce. The cities of Africa and the big commercial centres are symbols of the development of commerce and industry. The contribution of colonialism was the provision of a stable political framework within which development could take place.

This contribution can be frankly acknowledged, as the supporters of negritude have done. But what contribution was made towards the development of democratic regimes? The colonial regimes were themselves authoritarian and paternalistic. They operated institutions which made it possible for a minority of whites to rule large African populations.

The administrative system in the rural areas, whether under the French or the British, did not allow local participation in decision-making. The British, under the system of indirect rule, worked through traditional institutions, but in the process changed their character. The chiefs were placed in a position where they were partly representatives of their people, and partly agents of the imperial power, and the checks and balances of the indigenous system could no longer operate democratically. They were undermined by the control of the administering power.

The French followed a policy which destroyed the existing tribal systems. They divided each colony into districts and cantons, often without regard to ethnic ties, and appointed so-called chiefs who were agents of the government. Where chiefs belonging to old 'royal' lineages were used, they acted more as agents of the colonial regime than in their hereditary roles. So in both British and French territories, the chiefs became identified as 'stooges' of the colonial government. In no territory in Africa did the colonial regimes establish local self-governing institutions. Local administration was under the control of appointed agents.

British policy followed a series of constitutional changes which led to the granting of 'internal self-government' as the last stage before independence. This was marked by elections to a Legislative Assembly, and parliamentary government by a Cabinet of ministers, usually with the ministerial posts of Justice, Finance, and Defence held by colonial administrators. The leader of the party that won the elections became the Leader of Government Business. The party in power was thus given experience and was helped in many ways. The new ministers had expert help from experienced civil servants and from their ministerial colleagues; they had the prestige and patronage of office for building up and strengthening their party. They could use official positions and appurtenances for party purposes.

The British teach that an opposition is an essential part of the parliamentary democratic system; yet their policy for helping the institution of the parliamentary system at this final stage never included any official help to the opposition. Three British administrators sat on the front bench with the government; and an array of experienced civil servants sat behind the government benches, always ready to send notes and answers to the members of the government to save them from being shown up by the opposition, while members of the opposition had to fend for themselves, without any help. Handicapped in many ways, held up to the country by the propaganda of their opponents as 'enemies of the people', and with the civil servants and administrators of the colonial regime weighted against them, it is no surprise that the opposition was often crushed. Yet explanations of opposition failures and weaknesses do not take account of the fact that the policy of the colonial government included help for the party that won elections, and no help for the party that formed 'Her Majesty's Loyal Opposition'. Neither at the centre nor at the local level can it be said that strong foundations for democratic rule were laid. The shoot was very tender, easy to smother under the authoritarian framework that is bequeathed at independence.

Under the French system, some of those who later led independence movements in the colonies, or headed the governments, such as President Houphouet-Boigny of the Ivory Coast, or President Senghor of Senegal, received experience in official posts in France. But the French colonies that have received independence since 1960 have done so at a time when, as French political scientists have themselves pointed out, France has been moving towards a type of monarchical republic, in the Fifth Republic under General de Gaulle, with a dominant executive and a weak, almost powerless parliament. This evolution has set an example not markedly different in effect from the one-party constitutions which have been adopted in the French-speaking states.

The more remarkable contribution to democratic rule is provided by ideas and techniques: ideas of justice, of impartial and independent courts; ideas of freedom of speech, discussion, worship and travel; ideas of the rule of law, and the idea of social justice which is only a sham without these essential freedoms and civil liberties. To the contribution of ideas must be added the techniques of voting, of administration, or running modern enterprises, and a modern state. For administration, language is necessary, and since African states are divided by many languages, the legacy of French or English which brings different tribes into conversation with one another within their common state, and brings Africans into conversation with the world outside, must be reckoned one of the contributions to democratic rule.

It cannot be said of colonial regimes that they were shining examples of democracy; nor can it be justly claimed that the newly independent States inherited from them democratic institutions suited to their condition. What the colonial powers have left is a foundation of democratic ideas and techniques which can help a country whose leaders wish to establish a democratic form of government; they have also left institutional frameworks of centralized administration with a tendency towards authoritarianism which can be, and in some states have indeed already been adapted to that end.

4. D. K. RANGNEKAR

*

The Statistics of Indian Poverty *

The crucial importance of India's problems and successes for the whole of the Third World has already been referred to. Some of the conditions in which Jawaharlal Nehru and his colleagues had to work in the years immediately following India's Independence were described by an Indian economist, D. K. Rangnekar, as he began his study *Poverty and Capital Development in India*. (The situation described below has, of course, changed. India's population was five hundred million by 1966, and there has been considerable increase in production. The number of literates has doubled; 76 per cent of children between six and eleven years go to school; hospital beds have trebled; life expectancy is 50.)

STATISTICAL comparisons of living standards are not easy and, in any case, do not lend themselves really well to explaining the material deficiencies in Indian life. But it gives some idea of the depth of poverty by Western standards to say that real income per head in India is probably no more than about one-eighth of that in the United Kingdom. The estimated national income per head was only Rs 265 (less than £20) in 1950–51. The National Sample Survey (N.S.S.) recently revealed that only 9½ per cent of households in rural areas spent above Rs 200 (£15) a month; more than half of all rural households had less than Rs 100 (£7½), one-fifth had only up to Rs. 50 (75s.). In the major cities of Bombay, Calcutta, Delhi and Madras the average consumer expenditure per household is only Rs. 55 (c. £4) a month. In India's wealthiest city, Bombay, only about eight per cent of the people spend over Rs 300 a month, nearly fifty per cent having only about Rs 100.

In actual life these figures reflect material standards lower

*From Poverty and Capital Development in India (Oxford: O.U.P., 1958).

than can be visualized in emergency conditions in the West. It is estimated that nearly thirty per cent of the population is normally undernourished and, even when the diet is quantitatively adequate, it is almost invariably ill-balanced. In a good crop year, such as 1953-4, the average Indian may get about 2,000 calories a day, about two-thirds as many as an average Briton, and about twelve per cent less than the estimated minimum necessary in Indian conditions; in a bad year, such as 1950-51, he may have to be content with only about 1,500 calories or even less, and traditionally there is at least one bad crop year in four. The normal diet, besides being quantitatively inadequate, is painfully short of essential protective foods. Cereals and potatoes supply most of the calorie intake; protective foods, including milk and eggs, provide little more than about ten per cent. Average consumption of meat, fish and eggs is less than one eighth of what it should be, of milk one half, of vegetable protein one fifth, of fruit one third.

Poverty, also means, for most of the population, inadequate clothing, impossibly bad housing, and a veritable lack of nearly all the amenities and services which in modern life in the West are taken for granted. Food absorbs more than half the average Indian's total expenditure. So there is little left for other purposes. He can, for example, scarcely afford 12–15 yards of cloth per annum. Only sixty million Indians can read and write. Even in urban areas less than half of the inhabitants are literate. In 1950–51 only forty-one per cent of the children of school-going age were at school – there were only 209,671 primary schools and 20,844 secondary schools for a population of over 356 million!

The inadequacy of medical facilities is grotesque: in the whole country there were in 1950–51 only 106,478 hospital beds; hardly one qualified physician was available for each 30,000 of village population. The average expectation of life at birth is probably no more than thirty-two years as compared with sixty-six in the United Kingdom. The death rate has fallen over the years, but it is still very high – unofficially estimated at thirty per thousand (officially recorded at twenty-two per thousand). Even on the basis of incomplete official records, it

171

appears that more than ten million Indians die every year: nearly one fourth of the babies die during their first year, and 100 out of every thousand girl-wives are doomed to die in child-birth. Official returns list a considerable number of deaths under 'fever' – for the simple reason that the precise cause is unknown owing to the sheer inadequacy of medical attention. In actual life today, tradition of a great, cultured civilization is perhaps the only major factor that separates Indians from the peoples of other so-called 'underdeveloped' countries.

Not only are the people too poor to afford education, medical aid, and reasonably decent living conditions, but the state also, for the same reason, cannot do much. The incomes of the great majority leave little surplus to tax. Less than one per cent (0.2) of the population have incomes above the income-tax minimum, and nearly two thirds of the tax comes from some 5,000 assessees, many of them big businesses. Taxes are high, but total taxation amounts to no more than eight per cent of the national income. In 1954–5 the total revenue of the Centre (i.e. Central Government) and states together was less than Rs 10,000 million (£750 million), not even half of Britain's defence expenditure.

India's basic problem, therefore, is the widespread poverty and sub-human standards of living of the masses. The essence of the problem is that, while over seventy-two per cent of the inhabitants live off the land, practising more or less static peasant agriculture, the population rises every year by over $4\frac{1}{2}$ million. Indian industry, just finding its roots, cannot absorb these millions. As things are, the feeding of the urban population is no easy matter. Moreover, the poverty-stricken villages provide only a poor and limited market for industry. Obviously, therefore, the first task is to tackle the agricultural problem: to step up agricultural production, to plant some dynamism in the rural economy and so to balance the surge of population. For so long has this problem remained unsolved that millions in India seem to have accepted undernourishment and misery as an inevitable part of life.

5. MAO TSE-TUNG

*

Conditions in China *

No other Asian leader in the crucial period between the world wars equalled Mao Tse-tung's ability to combine grasp of the concrete and minute details of history, geography and social formations with insights into the possibilities of revolutionary action. His closeness to the China of the peasants is matched by his analytic skill. Mao was in 1926 principal of the Peasant Movement Training Institute run by the Canton Revolutionary Government, but he seems, as the 'specialist' on the peasantry, to have been learning more from the Chinese peasants than he was teaching them. The works from which the three following excerpts are taken were written at different times. The first is from the report he made on his study of the spontaneous peasant revolutionary movement of 1927 in Hunan province (*Report on the Investigation of the Peasant Movement in Hunan*); it is a document of major importance, historically and sociologically. The second is from a letter written in 1930 (*A Single Spark Can Light a Prairie Fire*). The revolutionaries, facing Chiang Kai-shek's troops, were in considerable difficulties at this time. The third, written in 1936, after the famous 'Long March' had taken the revolutionaries to Yenan, is taken from an extended analysis of problems which arose and were solved in the course of the revolutionary civil war in China (*Problems of Strategy in China's Revolutionary War*). In one sense the China that is described belongs to the past; in another sense these excerpts from the Third World tell a present story.

(i) A man in China is usually subjected to the domination of three systems of authority: (1) the state system (political authority), ranging from the national, provincial and county government down to that of the township; (2) the clan system (clan authority), ranging from the central ancestral temple and its branch temples down to the head of the household; and (3) the supernatural system (religious authority), ranging from

*All three extracts from *Selected Works Vol. 1* (Peking: Foreign Languages Publishing House, 1965).

173

the King of Hell down to the town and village gods belonging to the nether world, and from the Emperor of Heaven down to all the various gods and spirits belonging to the celestial world. As for women, in addition to being dominated by these three systems of authority, they are also dominated by the men (the authority of the husband). These four authorities – political, clan, religious and masculine – are the embodiment of the whole feudal–patriarchal system and ideology, and are the four thick ropes binding the Chinese people, particularly the peasants. How the peasants have overthrown the political authority of the landlords in the countryside has been described above. The political authority of the landlords is the backbone of all the other systems of authority. With that overturned, the clan authority, the religious authority and the authority of the husband all begin to totter. Where the peasant association is powerful, the clan elders and administrators of temple funds no longer dare oppress those lower in the clan hierarchy or embezzle clan funds. The worst clan elders and administrators, being local tyrants, have been thrown out. No one any longer dares to practise the cruel corporal and capital punishments that used to be inflicted in the ancestral temples, such as flogging, drowning and burning alive. The old rule barring women and poor people from the banquets in the ancestral temples has also been broken. The women of Paikuo in Hengshan County gathered in force and swarmed into their ancestral temple, finally planted their backsides in the seats and joined in the eating and drinking, while the venerable clan bigwigs had willy-nilly to let them do as they pleased. At another place, where poor peasants had been excluded from temple banquets, a group of them flocked in and ate and drank their fill, while the local tyrants and evil gentry and other long-gowned gentlemen all took to their heels in fright. Everywhere religious authority totters as the peasant movement develops. In many places the peasant associations have taken over the temples of the gods as their offices. Everywhere they advocate the appropriation of temple property in order to start peasant schools and to defray the expenses of the associations, calling it 'public revenue from superstition'. In Liling County, prohibiting superstitious prac-

174

tices and smashing idols have become quite the vogue. In its northern districts the peasants have prohibited the incense-burning processions to propitiate the god of pestilence. There were many idols in the Taoist temples at Fupoling in Lukuo, but when extra room was needed for the district headquarters of the Kuomintang, they were all piled up in a corner, big and small together, and no peasant raised any objection. Since then, sacrifices to the gods, the performance of religious rites and the offering of sacred lamps have rarely been practised when a death occurs in a family. Because the initiative in this matter was taken by the chairman of the peasant association, Sun Hsiao-shan, he is hated by the local Taoist priests. In the Lufeng nunnery in the North Third District, the peasants and primary school teachers chopped up the wooden idols and actually used the wood to cook meat. More than thirty idols in the Tungfu Monastery in the Southern District were burned by the students and peasants together, and only two small images of Lord Pao * were snatched up by an old peasant who said, 'Don't commit a sin!' In places where the power of the peasants is predominant, only the older peasants and women still believe in the gods, the younger peasants no longer doing so. Since the latter control the associations, the overthrow of religious authority and the eradication of super-stition are going on everywhere. As to the authority of the husband, this has always been weaker among poor peasants because, out of economic necessity, their womenfolk have to do more manual labour than the women of the richer classes and therefore have more to say and greater power of decision in family matters. With the increasing bankruptcy of the rural economy in recent years, the basis for men's domination over women has already been weakened. With the rise of the peasant movement, the women in many places have now begun to organize women's associations; the opportunity has come for them to lift their heads, and the authority of the husband is

---

*Lord Pao (Pao Cheng) was prefect of Kaifeng, capital of the Northern Sung Dynasty (A.D. 960–1127). He was famous in popular legend as an upright official and a fearless, impartial judge with a knack of passing true verdicts in all the cases he tried.

getting shakier every day. In a word, the whole feudal–patriarchal system and ideology is tottering with the growth of the peasants' power. At the present time, however, the peasants are concentrating on destroying the landlords' political authority. Wherever it has been wholly destroyed, they are beginning to press their attack in the three other spheres of the clan, the gods and male domination. But such attacks have only just begun, and there can be no thorough overthrow of all three until the peasants have won complete victory in the economic struggle.

(ii) The question whether there will soon be a revolutionary high tide in China can be decided only by making a detailed examination to ascertain whether the contradictions leading to a revolutionary high tide are really developing. Since contradictions are developing in the world between the imperialist countries, between the imperialist countries and their colonies, and between the imperialists and the proletariat in their own countries, there is an intensified need for the imperialists to contend for the domination of China. While the imperialist contention over China becomes more intense, both the contradiction between imperialism and the whole Chinese nation and the contradictions among the imperialists themselves develop simultaneously on Chinese soil, thereby creating the tangled warfare which is expanding and intensifying daily and giving rise to the continuous development of the contradictions among the different cliques of China's reactionary rulers. In the wake of the contradictions among the reactionary ruling cliques – the tangled warfare among the warlords – comes heavier taxation, which steadily sharpens the contradiction between the broad masses of taxpayers and the reactionary rulers. In the wake of the contradiction between imperialism and China's national industry comes the failure of the Chinese industrialists to obtain concessions from the imperialists, which sharpens the contradiction between the Chinese bourgeoisie and the Chinese working class, with the Chinese capitalists trying to find a way out by frantically exploiting the workers and with the workers resisting. In the wake of imperialist commercial aggression, Chinese merchant–capitalist extortions, heavier government taxation, etc., comes the deepening of the contradiction between the landlord class and the peasantry, that is, exploitation through rent and usury is aggravated and the hatred of the peasants for the landlord grows. Because of the pressure of foreign goods, the exhaustion of the purchasing power of the worker and peasant masses, and the increase in government taxation, more and more dealers in Chinese-made goods and independent producers are being driven into bankruptcy. Because the reactionary government, though short of provisions and funds, endlessly expands its armies and thus constantly extends the warfare, the masses of soldiers are in a constant state of privation. Because of the growth in government taxation, the rise in rent and interest demanded by the landlords and the daily spread of the disasters of war, there are famine and banditry everywhere and the peasant masses and urban poor can hardly keep alive. Because the schools have no money, many students fear that their education may be interrupted; because production is backward, many graduates have no hope of employment. Once we understand all these contradictions, we shall see in what a desperate situation, in what a chaotic state, China finds herself. We shall also see that the high tide of revolution against the imperialists, the warlords and the landlords is inevitable, and will come very soon. All China is littered with dry faggots which will soon be aflame. The saying, 'A single spark can start a prairie fire', is an apt description of how the current situation will develop. We need only look at the strikes by the workers, the uprisings by the peasants, the mutinies of soldiers and the strikes of students which are developing in many places to see that it cannot be long before a 'spark' kindles 'a prairie fire'.

(iii) China's revolutionary war, which began in 1924, has passed through two stages, the first from 1924 to 1927, and the second from 1927 to 1936; the stage of national revolutionary war against Japan will now commence. In all three of its stages this revolutionary war has been, is and will be fought under the leadership of the Chinese proletariat and its party, the Chinese Communist Party. The chief enemies in China's revolutionary war are imperialism and the feudal forces. Although the Chinese bourgeoisie may take part in the revolutionary war at certain historical junctures, yet its selfishness and lack of political and economic independence render it both unwilling and unable to lead China's revolutionary war on to the road of complete victory. The masses of China's peasantry and urban petty bourgeoisie wish to take an active part in the revolutionary war and to carry it to complete victory. They are the main forces in the revolutionary war, but, being small-scale producers, they are limited in their political outlook (and some of the unemployed masses have anarchist views), so that they are unable to give correct leadership in the war. Therefore, in an era when the proletariat have already appeared on the political stage, the responsibility for leading China's revolutionary war falls on the shoulders of the Communist Party. Of all the social strata and political groupings in semi-colonial China, the proletariat and the Communist Party are the ones most free from narrow-mindedness and selfishness, are politically the most far-sighted, the best organized and the readiest to learn with an open mind from the experience of the vanguard class, the proletariat, and its political party throughout the world and to make use of this experience in their own cause. Hence only the proletariat and the Communist Party can lead the peasantry, the urban petty bourgeoisie and the bourgeoisie, the destructiveness of the unemployed masses, and also (provided the Communist Party does not err in its policy) the vacillation and lack of thoroughness of the bourgeoisie – and can lead the revolution and the war on to the road of victory.

The revolutionary war of 1924–7 was waged, basically speaking, in conditions in which the international proletariat and the Chinese proletariat and its party exerted political influence on the Chinese national bourgeoisie and its parties and entered into political cooperation with them. However, this revolution failed at the critical juncture, first of all because the big bourgeoisie turned traitor, and at the same time because

178

the opportunists within the revolutionary ranks voluntarily surrendered the leadership of the revolution.

The Agrarian Revolutionary War, lasting from 1927 to the present, has been waged under new conditions. The enemy in this war is not imperialism alone but also the alliance of the big bourgeoisie and the big landlords. And the national bourgeoisie has become a tail to the big bourgeoisie. This revolutionary war is led by the Communist Party alone, which has established absolute leadership over it. This absolute leadership is the most important condition enabling the revolutionary war to be carried through firmly to the end. Without it, it is inconceivable that the revolutionary war could have been carried on with such perseverance.

The Chinese Communist Party has led China's revolutionary war courageously and resolutely, and for fifteen long years has demonstrated to the whole nation that it is the people's friend, fighting at all times in the forefront of the revolutionary war in defence of the people's interests and for their freedom and liberation.

By its arduous struggles and by the martyrdom of hundreds of thousands of its heroic members and tens of thousands of its heroic cadres, the Communist Party of China has played a great educative role among hundreds of millions of people throughout the country. The Party's great historic achievements in its revolutionary struggles have provided the prerequisite for the survival and salvation of China at this critical juncture when she is being invaded by a national enemy; and this prerequisite is the existence of a political leadership enjoying the confidence of the vast majority of the people and chosen by them after long years of testing. Today, the people accept what the Communist Party says more readily than what any other political party says. Were it not for the arduous struggles of the Chinese Communist Party in the last fifteen years, it would be impossible to save China in the face of the new menace of subjugation.

6. SOONG CHING-LING

*

China in 1933 *

In 1914, Dr Sun Yat-sen (see page 275), the man who began the historical process we know as the Chinese Revolution, married as his second wife Soong Ching-ling (b. 1890). She was one of a wealthy family – three sisters and a brother, T. V. Soong – who were to play a variety of leading roles in China in the period following the establishment of the Revolutionary Government in Canton in 1924. Soong Ching-ling was a well-to-do Christian, educated in Western-style schools in China, and had been to college in the United States. But because of her admiration for what Sun was trying to achieve she went to work for him (1912) as his secretary while he was in exile in Japan. After Sun's death in 1925 she became the leading exponent of his revolutionary ideas and ideals, and her courage and outspokeness in the years following the *coup d'état* in 1927 of General Chiang Kai-shek (who married her sister) and her support for the liberals and revolutionaries who were his victims made her a political figure of major importance in China. Following the seizure of China's north-eastern provinces (Manchuria) in 1931, Japan had attacked Shanghai and started moving into North China. What follows was written in 1933. In September 1949 the author was elected Vice-Chairman of the People's Republic of China.

WHAT are the conditions in China? Economically, the workers are unemployed, or starving with miserable wages. They work long hours and have no protection. Peasants suffer, starve, and are robbed by high rents, usurious interest rates, and taxes. They have not sufficient land, and they groan under feudal exploitation by the landlords and gentry. They suffer by the wars of the generals and the marauding armies of the warlords. Politically, there is no right of free speech and free press, no right of assembly and organization. Radicals and revolutionaries are imprisoned, tortured and killed. Culturally,

*From *The Struggle for New China* (Peking : Foreign Languages Press, 1952).

there is no money for the education of the people, because ninety per cent of the revenue is squandered by the various local and provincial governments for the maintenance of their armies.

All of these conditions are aggravated by the war of Japanese imperialism against China. How is it possible that Japan can wage a war against China? There are two reasons: first, Japanese imperialism is assisted by imperialist England and France, which also aim at further dismemberment of China. The League of Nations has given Japan a free hand, making only such reservations as aim to guard the imperialist-robber interests of the other powers and to deceive their own and the Chinese people. The second reason lies in China itself. The Chinese people want resistance against Japanese and every other imperialism. The Chiang Kai-shek Government stifles this resistance by suppression of the boycott, sabotage of the Volunteers and abolition of the democratic rights of the people. The main forces of the country are employed to fight not the Japanese but the Chinese people, the workers and peasants of China. The leadership of the armies of China is in the hands of reactionary, treacherous generals.

Who 'defended' Jehol? The opium general, Tang Yu-lin, chairman of the Jehol Province. He opened the gates of China to the Japanese invaders. He left the Volunteers in the ditch without arms and supplies; he stabbed his own soldiers in the back. Who is responsible for this treason? The Chiang Kai-shek Government. Why? This government employs its main forces against the Chinese people; it puts treacherous generals in command and prevents their removal; it prevents the arming of the people and the organization of volunteer military detachments for the waging of a national revolutionary war against Japanese imperialism.

Today even members of the Chiang Kai-shek Government raise the cry: 'Death to Tang Yu-lin!' We agree, but we doubt that Nanking will shoot him. He should have been shot long ago. But did not T. V. Soong, Minister of Finance, declare a few weeks ago that the suggestion that Tang Yu-lin is on the Japanese side of the fence is an insult to the nation? So, only

181

when the Chinese people overcome the treason of their leaders will China live.

And now for the Chiang Kai-shek Government – the so-called 'central authority'. The time has come when its phrases about 'prolonged resistance' can no longer hide the facts of betrayal, cowardice and non-resistance. No preparations for real resistance were made by General Chiang Kai-shek and the Kuomintang leaders of Nanking. Only the utterly foolish hope was expressed that Japan might stop at the Great Wall, and that Japan's war of aggression would break down of itself owing to internal revolution and financial bankruptcy. But Japan will not stop. Jehol is the key for the invasion of Mongolia as well as of the north of China. Japan will not only take the territory north of the Yellow River, but will repeat its bombardment of Shanghai as well as other Yangtze ports, in order to win greater power in the Yangtze Valley and dictate terms to the Chinese people. In its future war against the Soviet Union, Japan will even attempt to use the Chinese masses as cannon-fodder, as it is already today using the Chinese soldiers of Manchuria against their brothers and sisters in Jehol and Hopei. When a nation can be driven to fight the robber wars of another imperialist power, it has reached the lowest depths of its humiliation.

7. GERMAN ARCINIEGAS

*

Fiction and Reality in Latin America *

In most of Latin America independence from rule by the original colonial powers, Spain and Portugal, had been achieved early in the nineteenth century. The condition of the Latin American countries, and the situation in which its people had to achieve the kind of existence to which they aspired in the twentieth century, were influenced by international and internal developments which took place after the period of Iberian dominance in America. A Colombian by nationality, and a leading liberal intellectual and statesman, German Arciniegas (b. 1900), has been his country's Minister of Education and an Ambassador. He wrote *The State of Latin America* in 1952. Dr Arciniegas was writing about conditions which at that time were giving rise to the revolutionary movements (such as those in Cuba and Guatemala) of the following year. It is not hindsight, but the remarkable Latin American political consciousness of the early 1950s, and the remarkably similar conditions in Eastern Asia, which still give value to these observations.

B y and large, the Latin American is a frustrated person. The demagogues have promised him democracy and a good standard of living. He has followed them blindly. But once the spell-binders have won power, their promises have gone up in smoke, leaving only the bitter bread of dictatorship. The old injustices continue, and administrative corruption thrives. Until well into this century the peasants lived in conditions no better than those of the Indian before Columbus crossed the Atlantic. Even today, tropical diseases, malnutrition, and lack of training prevent the common man from realizing his full economic and social potential.

Under a system of representative democracy these conditions would become a stimulus and a challenge for their alleviation. The problem would be thrashed out in the press, in the legislative chambers, in the streets and the homes. Everyone would

*From *The State of Latin America* (New York: Knopf, 1953).

express his opinion freely, and the course of social evolution would be expedited. That is what is happening today in Mexico. That is the way it used to be in Colombia. For the time being, that is the way it is in Brazil. But under the dictatorships the expression of opinion is stifled. Gradually the dammed-up criticism and indignation of the people collect around a hard, explosive core of resentment and distrust. The lion's share of the budget, which could be used to combat the social evils that exist in all Latin American countries, goes to the army, the dictators' praetorian guard, and the police, really an instrument of the government party. Under these circumstances, those countries which in the new terminology are known as 'underdeveloped' become highly developed breeding grounds of violence and revolution.

When the delegates to the 1948 Pan American Conference * arrived in Bogotá, the capital of Colombia, they paid slight, if any, attention to what appeared to be a routine maintenance of order by the army and police. But a long series of arbitrary government acts in the provinces had created between the people and the authorities a state of tension triggered for violence at any moment. At noon on 9 April the head of the opposition Liberal Party was killed in downtown Bogotá, and in three hours the heart of the city was reduced to ashes. Foreigners who witnessed the scene said that on the following day Bogotá looked like London after an air-raid. . . .

In many Latin American countries the masses have no arms and are practically naked. But this meant nothing as far as the latent possibilities of expression are concerned. The Mexicans who followed Pancho Villa against General Pershing in 1916 returned victoriously singing one of their ballads, or *corridos*, which went:

> *They've got airplanes by the dozens,*
> *But we've got what it really takes.*

The French, Russian and Chinese revolutions, and the independence of India and Indonesia, like that of the United

*The Ninth International Conference of American States, 30 March to 2 May 1948.

184

States and of Latin America, were achieved by the masses, by groups of ragged men who marched on empty stomachs and fought pitched battles, often with stones and sticks for weapons.

The problem of illiteracy raises some particularly interesting questions. Many of the civil wars in Latin America have been fought over a new constitution by masses who could not read. But this is not unprecedented. The North American colonies united around the figure of Washington and rallied the signers of the Constitution in Philadelphia, but it should not be forgotten that even 100 years later, in 1870, more than twenty per cent of the population of the United States was illiterate. The industrial revolution in England, though undoubtedly headed by educated leaders, took place in a country in which the great majority of men could communicate only by word of mouth.

But along with the illiteracy of Latin America goes an astonishing amount of writing and reading. It has been a surprise to many people to learn that *La Prensa* of Buenos Aires was, until Perón murdered it in 1951, one of the largest and best-informed newspapers in the world. Throughout Latin America many dailies have circulations in the hundreds of thousands. Magazines attain sales of 300,000 an issue. *El Mercurio* of Santiago, Chile, is older than *The New York Times*. In most of the capital cities the dailies give fuller international news coverage than their opposite numbers in the principal cities of Europe and the United States.

But in addition to serving as news media, the Latin American newspapers are media of opinion. In countries with problems as complex as those which confront all the Latin American republics, the voicing of opinion is perhaps the most vital function of the press. That is exactly what complicates the situation, because those who read and write are the very persons who are gagged by government censorship and control. . . .

The long experience of generation after generation deceived by the very men in whom they had placed the most hope has given the majority of the Latin Americans a sharper judgement and a keener awareness than might have been supposed. They know that they must wait, that as yet they have no im-

185

mediate means of defence. But a reserve of determination is building up which will surprise everyone when it can find expression. Bolívar knew how to make use of this reserve. One of the fundamental differences between the war of independence in North America and that in South America is that Washington had regular troops under his command whereas Bolívar's army was made up of the people, barehanded, with only their will, their determination to change things, as weapons. The outbreak that followed the assassination of Gaitan * in Bogotá at the time of the Pan American Conference is proof of the lengths to which the people will go once they burst through restraints.

There are two Americas, the visible and the invisible. The visible America, the America of presidents and embassies, expresses itself through official organs, through a controlled press. This America takes its seat at the conference table of the Pan American Union and has many votes in the United Nations. And there is the mute, repressed America, which is the vast reservoir of revolution. Both Americas are misleading in appearance.

Under its dictatorial regimes, visible America makes fervent protestations of its democratic faith, signs charters of liberties, manufacturing one line of goods for foreign and another for domestic consumption. This double personality has achieved a dexterity that is almost unbelievable. Even though everywhere and in all periods of history there has been something of this same split between what is said and what is done, the contrast has rarely been so brutal as that afforded today by the Latin American dictatorships. Laureano Gomez,† who had come to power on a wave of violence once said to a group of North American journalists: 'This is a people of savage Communists, they have killed one hundred police officers. Is there a civilized nation anywhere that would tolerate the killing of

---

*Jorge Eliecer Gaitan, the Liberal leader who was mysteriously assassinated on 9 April 1948, stood for radical change and had a mass following, and was expected to win the 1950 Presidential election.

† An ex-president who became a leading force in the Conservative Party.

186

one hundred police?' To understand this sophism we must analyse two words: 'Communism' and 'police'. For the purposes of their practical dealings with the United States the dictators describe as Communists all those who do not support them. According to General Odria,* the people of Peru are Communists; according to the military *junta* of Venezuela, the people of Venezuela; according to the dictator of Bogotá, the people of Colombia; according to General Trujillo, the people of the Dominican Republic. The 'police' likewise requires definition. A policeman in the United States or London is a human being who helps an old lady across the street, a guardian angel for the children coming out of school, the protecting arm of the law. A policeman under a Latin American despot is a shady character not too far removed from the criminal, a man of dubious past who is handed a uniform and revolver with orders to crush the opposition and maintain order by terror. The one hundred police officers over whom the North American journalists were asked to weep had been one hundred weapons turned on the peasants, members of a shock force that burned down homes, stole cattle, and attacked the wives and daughters of the peasants in scenes of barbarity that beggar description. When they got a chance the peasants fought back and killed. They were not Communists; the police officers were not police.

This arbitrary use of words has given rise to the' greatest confusion. The despots use the word 'democracy' to set up governments such as those described in the pages of this book. The common man asks himself if this can be democracy. The same thing holds true of the other words in the political lexicon: army, religion, freedom, Christianity, faith, republic, justice, judge, president, election, congress, priest, university, peace, public opinion. By turning words inside out, dictators destroy the natural medium of communication among people. When one of the presidents of visible America speaks, his every word must be analysed against the background of its accepted meaning and the application given to it by him inside his own country.

*Manuel Odria, military dictator of Peru 1948–56.

187

Although this theme may seem academic, its implications go very deep, because as a result of this deception moral principles are being undermined, good faith is being corrupted, and an atmosphere of cynicism and distrust is growing up. The story of the tower of Babel is not a fairy tale. At this very moment the greatest political campaign in the world is based on one word: peace. With special reference to Russia, her brand of peace is familiar to those Latin Americans who have suffered dictatorships. Paraguay enjoyed peace of this sort under Dr Francia,* this was the peace of Argentina under Rosas, of Venezuela under Juan Vicente Gomez.† This peace is the objective of their legitimate successors. We call it a living cemetery. There are peace and order because no one can talk or criticize or object or join his fellows in assembly. It is the kind of peace guarded by the family servant who acts as a spy on the household.

Latin America, like other parts of the world, has fought against the peace of the colony, the peace of slavery, the peace of servility. At times with maximum passion and heroism. In his war against these kinds of peace, man has grown in dignity, intelligence has had a mission to fulfil, people have learned that they are entitled to an existence better than that of the beasts of the field, and a little decency has been brought into the world.

Theoretically it would seem that Latin America is a fertile field for Communism. Yet it is amazing how few addicts this party has made. In fact, it may be said that in Latin America Communism is non-existent. France has many more Communists than all of Latin America, despite the fact that the people of Latin America, badly fed, badly dressed, badly housed and badly treated, are in much closer contact than any other with the capitalist world of their next-door neighbour. Why does Communism fail to take hold there? Because in Latin America the thirst for freedom is as great as the thirst for justice. Because there is a sense of national pride. The Mexican wants to be the master of his house, not the lackey

* Dictator of Paraguay from 1814 to 1840, when he died.
† Military dictator of Venezuela 1908–35.

of Moscow. What Schuyler said of the Negroes – that they cannot be Communists because they have emerged from slavery and are not buying a return ticket – holds true of the Latin Americans. They are through with being colonials. ...

Like visible America, invisible America lies. The humble folk know that they cannot say what they think, and the upper classes have learned this, too. ... This book has touched only lightly on instances of the brutality that is of constant occurrence. The full account of the violence, the tortures, the concentration camps has not been told outside the frontiers. But if in one of the most cultured countries of Europe Nazism could unleash the dark forces it did, why wonder that similar things have taken place in backward lands? In visible America, where a vast mass of the population lives with the cold breath of terror on its neck, the least word may bring reprisals. The part of prudence is to keep quiet, to wear a mask. Where machine-guns have the floor, a deep silence reigns. Life goes on under the cover of conventional phrases, lip-service, extorted votes. ...

8. M. H. KHAN

*

Land Tenure in Pakistan*

Pakistan, one of the two nations into which the Indian sub-continent was split in 1947, is one of the four countries in the Third World with a population of over 100 millions. With its two parts – East Pakistan and West Pakistan – separated by an unfriendly state, Pakistan has special problems in addition to those arising from its retarded economic development in the past. In what follows Mahmood Hasan Khan, a Pakistani agricultural economist, describes some of the general features of agrarian relations in Pakistan.

Adverse Land Tenurial Arrangements

THE importance of land tenure systems in a society cannot be over-emphasized: they determine the size and unit of ownership, thus directly or indirectly affecting the techniques of farming through a socio-economic lever of incentives or disincentives; they settle the share of the actual tiller of the soil in its total produce, hence they not only affect the volume of agricultural production, but also determine the distribution of the produce among the parties involved. . . .

Some of the major problems arising from the various tenure systems in Pakistan will be pointed out here. Two major types of farms can be distinguished: the landlord–tenant farms and the owner–operator farms. There is still a third category of farms in which some owner-operators rent part of their land to other share-croppers, but it is of negligible importance. Each of these types has its own peculiarities and problems, but from the point of view of this study there are four major problems which must be treated in some detail. The first three problems, namely, the concentration of land-ownership in a few hands, absentee landlordism and the exploitation of tenants, are to be

*From *The Role of Agriculture in Economic Development* (Wageningen: Centre for Agricultural Publishing and Documentation, 1966).

found in the landlord–tenant system prevailing in most parts of West Pakistan. The last problem relates to the size of cultivation units and their fragmentation; it refers both to the owner–operator types of farms and to the landlord–tenant system but especially to the former in East Pakistan. Each of these problems will be discussed in turn.

The landlord–tenant systems in East and West Pakistan have not been similar. In East Pakistan the percentage of owner–operator farms has been higher than in West Pakistan. Further, the extent of ownership concentration and landlord–tenant relations have also been less feudalistic in East Pakistan.

Concentration of Land-ownership

Whatever good one could say about the *zamindari* and *jagirdari* systems, for all feudalism is at best paternalistic, the fact remains that in Pakistan their social and economic effects have proved largely to be detrimental to progress in rural society. There is perhaps hardly any need to go into details to defend this contention, for even the most cursory survey of the extent of concentration of land-ownership (concomitantly the social prestige and political power) in a few hands and the relationship of landlords and their tenants in most parts of Pakistan will make it amply clear.

Though it is very difficult to give precise documentation of the extent of concentration, due again to the paucity of data, there are some broad figures which are quite suggestive.

According to one estimate, in West Pakistan about 3·3 million people (or about sixty per cent of the owners) had at one time only about 7·4 million acres of land (or about fifteen per cent of the total area) in holdings not exceeding five acres each as against about 60,000 people (or about 0·1 per cent of the owners) occupying as much as 7·5 million acres in estates of not less than 500 acres each. The situation was even worse in the former province of Sind: before the promulgation of the 1959 West Pakistan Land Reforms Act, it was estimated that about one per cent of the owners possessed as much as thirty per cent of the land in holdings of more than 500 acres each; and, against this, about sixty per cent of the owners possessed only about twelve per cent of the area in parcels of not more than fifteen acres each. In the former province of N.W.F.*, a similar condition could be seen: about 0·1 per cent of the owners had about twelve per cent of the area in estates of not less than 500 acres each.

Absentee Landlordism

The emergence of absentee landlordism, especially in West Pakistan, is the result of the concentration of land in the hands of a limited number of land-owners with large estates and varying degree of property rights. This absentee landlordism has been both physical and functional: in the physical sense it implies that the landlord lives away from the land and leaves the overall management of his estate in the hands of his functionaries; in the functional sense, it means that even if the landlord is present on the land he performs little or no productive function.

In addition to the concentration of land in a few hands, coupled with the high proportion of farm area cultivated by the tenants usually given to them in tiny parcels with varying degrees of security and charged to them at rates both legal and illegal – most of the *zamindar* and *jagirdar* supplied neither capital nor ready management nor any other significant assistance to promote the productivity of their land or of the labour engaged on it. Due to his socio-political influence, rather well-established historically, the landlord was interested primarily in the collection of his share in the produce through his functionaries. More often than not he enjoyed a luxurious life either in the towns or at his country house, and there he could afford to spare enough time and resources for his many hobbies, political adventures and local intrigues often being the most likely ones.

The peculiar social and economic consequences of such tenurial arrangements determine the attitudes of landlords and their tenants towards agricultural progress. . . .

*North-west Frontier.

The Exploitation of the Tenants

Turning to the landlord–tenant relationship, there are two types of tenants, namely, occupancy tenants and tenants-at-will.

The occupancy tenants are those who have a more or less permanent, heritable and transferable right to land so long as they continue to pay the fixed rent to their landlord. It was observed, in the former provinces of the Punjab and N.W.F., that they enjoyed most of the privileges that the owner–operators had.

The tenants-at-will had their tenancies fixed from year to year. Their share and rent were usually determined by custom or more often by the dictates of their landlord. These tenants could be ejected, as their name implies, by the landlord at his will, and often their dependence on the landlord was complete, not only for food but also for shelter. Most tenants in the former Sind province were in this category; in the former Punjab about fifty per cent of the area at one time was culti-vated by these tenants; the same was more or less true in the former province of N.W.F.

9. JACQUES CHONCHOL

*

Land Tenure and Development
in Latin America *

What work people do, what their responsibilities, status, powers and opportunities are in the places where they live and work, these are obviously important aspects of the situation within the countries which compose the Third World. The Chilean agronomist, Jacques Chonchol, is one of the leading authorities on rural conditions in Latin America, and here he describes in some detail the way in which the concentration of land-ownership in Latin America determines the living conditions of the masses, as well as the economy and politics of Latin America as a whole. This analysis has significance for other parts of the Third World, too. Jacques Chonchol has been adviser on programmes of agricultural reform to the United Nations Food and Agricultural Organization.

THE economies of Latin America have not evolved according to the theoretical sequence of development whereby industry, as it expands, should, as a result of the better wages offered, attract workers away from the land thus making it necessary to improve agricultural technology in order to maintain farm production at the required levels. In Latin America the flow of rural labour to the urban areas has been much greater than the number required for industrial expansion. Apart from the causes mentioned earlier in connexion with the economic limitations of the domestic market, there have been other factors contributing to the relative inability of industry to offer an adequate solution to the problem of the productive employment of an increasing labour force. These have included a rate of demographic growth, which is today more than twice as high as that of the European countries during the corresponding period of their industrial development; the fact that the present

*From Claudio Veliz (ed.), *Obstacles to Change in Latin America* (Oxford: O.U.P., 1965).

industrial technology created in the economically advanced countries, and introduced from them, shows a labour–capital ratio which is lower than that which prevails in the technologies of the initial stages of industrialization; the increasing flow of workers from the countryside to the cities owing to lack of prospects for social and economic advancement in the rural areas; and, finally, an evolution of agricultural mechanization and technology, which is frequently inappropriate to the stage of development reached by many Latin American countries. These four factors have likewise contributed to accentuate the lack of balance between the growth of the labour force and the opportunities for industrial employment.

Latin America, then, has begun its industrial revolution without having undergone an agricultural revolution. Its agriculture today is largely based either on traditional structures, methods, and systems, or else on modern systems which are not related to the present stage of development. Bearing in mind that viable prospects for future industrial expansion are to a large extent dependent on the incorporation of the rural sectors into the national communities, the improvement of the standard of living of these sectors and that of the large urban *Lumpenproletariat*, and the economic integration of the region, it is easy to see that industry alone, during the next few years, will not be capable of constituting the great energizing factor for development in the countries of Latin America. This can only be achieved by the combination of agrarian reform, industrialization and regional economic integration. It is on these three factors simultaneously – which basically imply the political conception of a new continental nationalism – that emphasis will have to be laid during the years to come.

The Structure of Land Tenure

The basic features of Latin American agriculture are the great concentration of land in the hands of a few people and the landlessness of great masses of the rural population.

The table below shows that in Latin America there are 105,000 agricultural and stock-breeding holdings of more than 1,000 hectares each, representing 1·4 per cent of all holdings

195

and covering 470 million hectares, or sixty-five per cent of the total included in the agricultural and stock-breeding land-rolls. This gives an average of 4,500 hectares for each of these holdings.

At the other extreme, there are 5,445,000 holdings, constituting 72·6 per cent of the total, with less than twenty hectares each and occupying twenty-seven million hectares, that is, 3·7 per cent of the total included in the rolls. This gives an average of less that five hectares for each of these holdings.

Distribution of Land in Latin America

Size-groups	Holdings			Areas		
	number (000s)	per cent of total	cumulative per cent	hectares (millions)	per cent of total	cumulative per cent
Below 20 hectares ..	5,445	72·6	72·6	27·0	3·7	3·7
20–100 hectares	1,350	18·0	90·6	60·6	8·4	12·1
100–1,000 hectares ..	600	8·0	98·6	166·0	22·9	35·0
Above 1,000 hectares ..	105	1·4	100·0	470·0	65·0	100·0
Totals	7,500	100·0	—	723·6	100·0	—

Source: Compiled on the basis of data quoted in 'Economic Growth and Social Policy in Latin America', *International Labour Review*, July–August 1961, p. 62.

In reality, there is an even greater concentration of land-ownership than would appear from the above figures, which relate to unit holdings. It is frequently the case that a number of these large holdings belong to one person or family, who manage them either directly or through indirect arrangements with administrators, tenants or partners.

These figures also show that of the one hundred and eleven million rural inhabitants in 1960 and the thirty-odd million making up the economically active agricultural population, only some 100,000 – and these are probably largely urban and not rural residents – own sixty-five per cent of the total agricultural land in the region. Disregarding the less than two million land-owners who may be considered to belong to the intermediate category since their holdings cover from twenty to 1,000 hectares, the balance – representing some twenty-eight million active men and, if we include their familes, a total rural population of some eighty million – is made up of small-holders with insufficient land to earn a minimum subsistence on their properties, and more especially of agricultural labourers who do not own any land at all.

The form taken by land concentration and the sizes of the large properties vary from country to country. These differences depend on the amount of land, the types of agriculture, and the historical evolution of the systems of tenancy, but in almost all countries the relative concentration of land in the hands of a few people is extraordinarily high. Among the most notable forms of land concentration in Latin America is, first, what has been termed the complex of estates and small-holdings which may be the subject of either direct or indirect forms of farming. Other characteristic forms of this concentration are the big cattle ranches, the big agricultural undertakings organized along capitalist lines, producing either for the external or the domestic market, and the large properties which are either not farmed at all or hardly so and are situated in remote areas.

The concentration of land in these different units is associated with other characteristics. These relate to extensiveness or semi-extensiveness of land use, single crop or diversification of production, the degree of capitalization, its integration with the market, and the mobility of the various factors of production. As it is not possible within the limitations of this work to analyse the specific peculiarities of each of these types of large agricultural enterprises, we shall merely examine in general terms the main effects of this great concentration of land and the characteristics which are found most commonly associated with it on the potential for agricultural progress and for the general development of the countries of the region.

197

Effects of Land Concentration

One of the most important negative consequences of the concentration of land-ownership in a few hands is the inefficient
use of the most abundant productive resources of agriculture
in Latin America: the land and the labour force. In the large
traditional estates which are the most typical, and also quite
often on the large modern plantations which rely mainly on
the cultivation of a single crop, we find an extraordinary degree
of under-employment of agricultural land and labour.

In the case of the traditional complexes of estates and
small-holdings and the large stock-breeding ranches, extensive
agriculture and cattle-breeding are practised on a large scale,
which results in the underemployment of labour and in a low
physical and economic return per unit of surface area. For
those who have available large land areas as well as an abundant supply of labour, extensive methods of farming are very
advantageous. With the use of only small amounts of labour
and capital – apart from the land – and very little risk, it is
possible to obtain a personal income which is more than satisfactory from the point of view of the owner's economic and
social requirements, and for his exercise of political influence.
Profits therefore result from the availability of a large quantity
of land in the hands of a single owner, accompanied by a
plentiful supply of labour which is usually not organized in
any way, and which possesses neither land nor any immediately
available alternative type of employment. These people are
therefore obliged to sell their services at the price imposed
by the few leading land-owners. Frequently the total value
of the wages paid on these large traditional-type estates represents less than ten per cent of their gross product. Moreover,
an important proportion of these wages is not paid in cash but
in concessions such as the temporary assignment of a marginal
plot of land for the worker's own crops or the right to graze a
few animals on the estate's pastures. This enables the land-
owner to carry on the productive process without the necessity of relying on any appreciable amount of working capital,
while exerting social and political power over the peasant

attached to his estate as a result of the concessions granted to him.

In such a situation there can be no incentive towards improving technology or increasing capital investment, the two basic conditions for a change-over from a traditional-type agriculture to modern methods. Nor is the land-owner, under these conditions, much influenced by possible economic stimuli from the market. Everything, indeed, tends to accentuate the desire and urge to accumulate land which, by virtue of the political influence of the owners, pays only a minimum in the way of taxation, and tends to maintain a high real value in the midst of the continuous devaluation process of many of the Latin American countries. In addition this system results in the land remaining as natural pasture or being subjected to a minimum of agricultural use: its value is greater as a source of personal income, social prestige and political power than as a factor of agricultural production.

Even among the large modern undertakings of the plantation type, it is not difficult to find many instances of large reserves of useful land being kept unproductive, as the owners are not interested in using them for crops or activities distinct from their main enterprises for the external market. On the other hand the single-crop system, which is typical of these modern properties, normally gives rise to acute seasonal underemployment among the labour force.

In the more remote areas the usually absentee owners of vast unused tracts are only interested in securing public works and improvements such as roads. The value which these add to their lands will enable them after a few years to reap a rich financial reward without any need for the slightest effort in operating them or incorporating them in the nation's productive processes.

The effects of land concentration on the potential for general social, political and economic development are, however, even more serious than those relating to the supply of agricultural products.

Land concentration gives rise to a very unequal distribution of agricultural income which is also – on average – well below the income obtainable in other sectors of the economy. This, in concrete terms, implies a state of sub-human living conditions for the majority of the population of the countryside. About one-third of the population of Latin America lives in abject poverty: this constitutes one of the main difficulties in the way of attempts to extend the domestic market, an essential condition for industrial growth.

Despite variations in average income *per capita*, there is considerable similarity in the uneven distribution of agricultural income. Peru, Chile and Costa Rica are three very dissimilar countries with widely different agricultures and economic systems, yet the three share more or less the same degree of inequality in the distribution of agricultural incomes. Although the categories used in the following tables are not precisely comparable, they do, none the less, provide a fairly clear idea of the relationship between social stratification and the distribution of agricultural income in these three countries.

In Peru, real income *per capita* is approximately $140. In Chile, according to the same United Nations source, annual *per capita* income is almost two-and-a-half times higher than in Peru – approximately $320 in 1960 – and only a little over thirty per cent of the population is directly engaged in agriculture as compared with well over sixty per cent in Peru. Nevertheless, the income distribution pattern in both countries is strikingly similar in its gross inequality. Costa Rica, one of the most progressive countries of Central America, provides the third case. There, in 1960, over sixty per cent of the population was classified as rural. And although the *per capita* income is one of the highest in the region – almost $250 per annum – the pattern of distribution again shows the same inequality evident in Chile and Peru.

The following picture, then, though schematic and somewhat simplified, is not far removed from actual reality. In Latin America there is a very small group of 'top people', consisting of the owners of large- and medium-sized properties with their traditional outlook, and of the capitalist operators in agriculture, who produce for export and occasionally for the domestic market. This small group, which represents only a tiny percen-

200

tage of the total agricultural population and which is in some cases largely made up of absentee landlords or persons who are primarily engaged in non-agricultural pursuits, concentrates in its hands the greater part of the landed resources and a substantial share in the income from the agricultural and stock-rearing sector. Moreover this is the group which benefits from all the social and political advantages of the existing system, which at best is typified by a social regime of benevolent paternalism, and at worst by a slave-like oppression of the lower groups.

Income Distribution in Peru

Social Groups	Percentage of active population	Percentage of income obtained
Large land-owners and capitalists	0·1	19·9
Technicians, top executives and small capitalists	0·4	6·3
Middle class (employees and skilled workers)..	20·0	46·7
Proletariat	22·8	14·2
Mountain-dwelling peasant class	56·7	12·9
	100·0	100·0

Source: Edgardo Seoane, *Surcos de paz* (Lima, 1963), p. 33.

Agricultural Income Distribution in Chile

Social Groups	Percentage of active population	Percentage of income obtained
Working classes	87·2	34·0
Middle classes	0·4	0·4
Upper classes	12·4	65·6
	100·0	100·0

Source: Marvin J. Sternberg, *Chilean Land Tenure and Land Reform,* University of California thesis, September 1962, p. 56.

201

Distribution of Net Income Derived from Agriculture in 1961 in the Central Tableland and the Province of Guanacaste in Costa Rica

	Percentage represented by each group	*Percentage of income obtained by each group*
Permanent labourers and small-holders ..	81·0	38·0
Family holdings	10·2	10·5
Large estates	7·9	29·8
Very large estates	0·9	21·7
	100·0	100·0

Source: Walter E. Chryst, *Land Tenure, Income Distribution, and Selected Aspects of Economic Development* (mimeo, 1962), p. 42. This document forms part of a study of the position of land tenure in Central America under the auspices of E.C.L.A., F.A.O. and I.L.O.

In certain countries, or in certain regions of some countries, between this tiny but dominant group and the lower groupings, there is a small rural middle class. It consists of independent family enterprises with adequate holdings of land, certain types of agricultural partnerships, or tenant farmers with a certain amount of capital, and some categories of employees responsible for supervision and accounts on the large estates. The numerical and social importance of this group is very small, except in certain special areas or places such as the northern part of the Argentine pampas region and the wine- and fruit-growing areas of that country, the horticultural areas and farms near cities such as Montevideo, São Paulo or Havana, and certain new settlement areas or irrigation lands, such as those found in Mexico.

Finally, there are those 'down below' who constitute the broad masses of the rural population, forming distinct groups with more or less specific characteristics. One of these groups is formed by the rural proletariat of the plantation areas (sugar-cane, cotton, bananas, rice); another by the horsemen of the great cattle ranches; a third by the under-endowed small-holders who are found as owners, tenants or squatters in practically all Latin American countries; and, finally, the great mass of wage-earners without land on the traditional properties, who are paid only by concessions or a combination of cash and concessions (the *huasipungueros* in Ecuador, the *inquilinos* in Chile, the *conuqueros* in Venezuela, the *colonos* in Brazil, the *peones* in the Argentine, or the Indians in Peru). This enormous mass, despite differences in income between the various groups of which it is comprised – which are determined by the demand for labour in each region, the degree of organization into trade unions in the small number of cases where this applies, and the greater or lesser social and political power of the small, land-owning, dominant group – constitute the 'pariahs' of the Latin American agricultural sector. This is the group with the fewest possibilities, expectations or opportunities of improvement. Their only real chance of breaking through the social and economic barriers which surround them is by moving to an urban area. For those who remain in agriculture, there is no other prospect under the existing order than to continue to lead the sub-human existence already led by the majority of them at the present time. The situation is aggravated in those places where the majority of the peasants consist of Indians still living for the most part according to traditional values quite different from those of the dominant community, with which they are not integrated. The reactions and way of life of these Indians are totally at variance with those necessary to people pursuing economic development as a rational aim. Attempts must be made to integrate them with the national community and to modernize their mentality. But if this is not accompanied by real prospects of improved conditions, the only result will be to create masses of uprooted and frustrated people, which is bound to have disastrous human and social consequences.

The existing situation, then, constitutes a basic obstacle to evolution or perpetuation of a democratic society. There is a profound contradiction between the existence of the present structure and the rural situation on the one hand, and the possible development of a democratic regime on the other. As has been rightly pointed out by Erich Fromm, the democratic character of a system can only be judged by the degree to which it allows of political liberty, personal liberty, an economic system operating in the interests of the great majority of the people, and a social system allowing the individual free and responsible participation in the life of the community. There is not the slightest doubt that the concentration of land in the hands of the few, together with its various economic and social consequences, represents the main obstacle to these four basic and complementary factors which are necessary to enable any true democratic society to exist in the Latin American countryside.

Finally it remains to say a few words regarding certain specifically economic effects of the concentration of land. There are two distinct sectors of agricultural production in Latin America: production for export and production for the domestic market. The former has always tended to enjoy priority in the eyes of governments and land-owners, and to attract the major share of investment funds; its growth has been restricted only by market conditions essentially outside the control of Latin American countries. Despite the increasing needs of a fast-growing population, production for the domestic market has expanded much more slowly than for export. This is mainly because the uneven distribution of income restricts demand, because the traditional agriculturists do not respond to the existing stimuli of the domestic market, and because there is little incentive to employ new and more efficient techniques. All these reasons are closely connected with the concentration of land in the hands of the few. The lack of dynamism in agriculture is an obstacle to the general development of the economy through its negative effects on the balance of payments and its inflationary pressures, and because it leads to a reduced state of physical well-being of the labour force.

10. JOSUE DE CASTRO

*

The Conditions Breeding Brazil's Underdevelopment*

One third of the population of Latin America is to be found in Brazil. Having been freed from Portuguese rule in 1831 Brazil had time to demonstrate in slow motion, as it were, the social and political features of ex-colonial countries in the periods following the end of direct rule by the imperial power. It was not till 1888 that slavery was abolished, and till 1889 that this vast territory became a republic. Such features as the relative status of the settlers and the Brazilian-born, the relation of racial groups, land-ownership, the power and influence of foreign-oriented *élites*, the relative strength of foreign nations interested in Brazil's resources, world economic conditions, and ideologies of modernization helped to shape the course of Brazilian history. One of the several internationally known social scientists and statesmen from Brazil's north-eastern provinces is Josue de Castro (b. 1908), the author of *The Geography of Hunger* and formerly President of the Food and Agricultural Organization, and Brazil's Ambassador to the U.N. at Geneva. What now follows is a sociological demonstration of how poverty and underdevelopment are produced in Brazil, taken from his essay, 'The Brazilian Dilemma: Bread or Steel?', another extract from which appears in Part Four.

SURPRISING as it may seem to many, Brazil is a place where people still go hungry. All surveys and studies made by experts in recent years point to this fact. In spite of the spectacular progress achieved in certain branches of activity, we continue to constitute one of the great areas of the world geography of hunger. In spite of our appreciable economic development, we continue to be a land of hunger, a country where two thirds of the people suffer the effects of dietary deficiencies.

The Brazilian hunger is a consequence, primarily, of our his-

*From Ignacy Sachs (ed.), *Agriculture, Land Reforms and Economic Development* (Warsaw: Polish Scientific Publishers, 1964).

205

torical past, which has found our human groups almost always in struggle against, almost never in harmony with, the natural environment. In certain cases the struggle may be blamed on the aggressiveness of the environment, which clearly opened the hostilities, but generally the fault lay in the incompetence of the colonizer, who was indifferent to anything that did not mean direct and immediate advantage to his mercantilist adventures. This opportunism developed in successive cycles of an economy that was destructive, or at least unbalancing, to the economic health of the nation: the brazilwood cycle, the sugar-cane cycle, the Indian-hunting cycle, the mining cycle, the 'nomad coffee culture' cycle, the rubber cycle, and finally, the cycle of a certain type of artificial industrialization, based on the fictions of protective tariffs and inflation. Always it is the same spirit of the adventurer slipping in, giving a push forward, and then immediately corrupting the processes of wealth creation. It is the 'Get rich' so keenly stigmatized by Sérgio Buarque de Holanda in his book *Raízes do Brasil*. It is the national impatience for profit clouding the consciousness of entrepreneurs and leading them invariably to kill all the possibilities of wealth that the land bears in its bosom.

In the final analysis, this situation of economic and social maladjustment has been a result of the incapacity of the Political State to serve as an equilibrating force between the private and public interest. Or worse, between national interests and those of foreign monopolies devoted to the exploitation of Brazil, colonial style. It is the foreign interests that have predominated, orientating our economy towards primary exploitation of the land and towards exportation of the raw materials thus obtained. In this way Brazil has developed her oceanic vocation, exporting all her potential wealth, the riches of her soil and her labour, for trifling prices. No resources have been left over to take care of the internal needs of the country: consumer goods for her people and equipment for her progress.

Under the orientation of European colonizers at first, of foreign capital later, an extensive agriculture of export products has developed, instead of an intensive subsistence agriculture capable of satisfying the hunger of our people.

206

The governments have almost always proved incapable of preventing this voracious interference of foreign monopolies in the development of our economy. Their political power has been totally inadequate to direct the adventure of colonization and the social organization of a nation along rational lines. The reason for this in the early days was the government's tenuousness and comparative weakness in face of the strength and independence of the land-owners, who acted as petty dictators in their own closed dominions, indifferent to any orders or regulations of the government that might threaten their private interests. Later the pendulum swung clear over the other way and there was an excessive centralization of power; practically all income and all rights were taken from the regional units and deposited in the arms – somewhat short when it came to distributing benefits – of the central government. In either case, the government has never had any adequate notion of the use of political force to carry out the administration of such an extensive territory.

In face of the weakness of the central political power, the colonialist interests manipulated affairs in such a way that economic progress was limited to increasing the profits of a small number of land-holders, associated in the colonial venture, without benefiting the bulk of the population at all. As the economist Gunnar Myrdal did well to bring out, the great powers, in the underdeveloped countries, have always used as instruments for their colonial exploitation 'the native oligarchies, themselves interested in maintaining the social and political *status quo*' and therefore hostile to genuine, emancipating development. On the other hand, one result of the centralization and show-window politics of the Republic was the almost complete neglect of the rural areas, of anything to parallel the surge of 'urbanization' that developed among us towards the end of the last century.

This development of the cities, coming on top of a situation in which there was no well-rooted rural civilization with a rational exploitation of the soil, aggravated alarmingly our existing food deficiencies. Not that the development of cities is bad in itself. It represents a necessary transition phase be-

207

tween a pure farming and a farming–industrial economy. The phenomenon occurred in the United States – indeed, it was a more violent social change there than among us – but still it did not upset the food supply of that country. On the contrary, it (was a factor of) stimulated farming and cattle-raising. It was the surge of industrialization and urban concentration in the East that led to the intensive grain and cattle farming of the Midwest, and made California, with its fruits and vegetables, the nation's leading agricultural state.

But among us, the imbalance aggravated evils that have always existed, ever since the day when the first European adventurers, financed in great part by Jewish capital, decided to create in these lands of America the industry of 'get rich quick' for the few, which was at the same time an 'industry of starvation' for the majority.

This is precisely the essential characteristic of colonialist economic development, quite different from authentic economic development of a nationalist type. Colonialism has promoted, here and there in the world, a certain sort of progress, but always at the exclusive service of the colonizers' profits. At most it is associated with a small group of the privileged, who have lost interest in the future of the nation and the political, social and cultural aspirations of the majority. The result is anomalous, sectoral development, limited to certain sectors that are more profitable and more attractive to speculative capital; but this development leaves other basic sectors, essential to real social progress, in complete abandonment.

As a result of this egoistic approach to economic progress there has developed in various dependent-economy countries what certain sociologists have called a 'dual social structure, with one well-developed layer separate from and super-imposed on another layer, which is characterized by absolute economic stagnation'. Faithful to colonialist traditions, this mental attitude persists in certain circles even today, as revealed in the tendency to conceive economic progress in terms of short-term profits, or as the simple injection of dollars for immediate exploitation of certain more abundant resources. The structural duality of Brazilian civilization – the two Brazils of Jacques Lambert – constitutes our living heritage, a survival of the political behaviour imposed upon us by European colonialists ever since the sixteenth century. Only now are we beginning to free ourselves from it.

Under the impulse of this anti-national policy and monopolized by half a dozen profiteers, export products were cultivated by soil-destroying, predatory methods. Railroads were built exclusively from production centres to ports of outlet for these products, and an exchange policy was set up to serve these economic manipulations. Behind this structure simulating progress – show-window progress really – remained the unproductive latifundium, the slavocrat system of great plantations, the backwardness, ignorance, pauperism, hunger.

Another aspect of our underdevelopment, with negative effects on the nutritional conditions of the people, has been the relative abandonment to which the poorer regions of the country have been relegated, and there hunger continues its ravages in full force. It is true enough that a country with limited resources, trying to develop itself principally with its own savings, cannot distribute these scarce resources except on a strict basis of priorities. Such a criterion is necessary to prevent dilution of investments to an impractical or unproductive level.

But this criterion cannot be one of concentrating all the resources in the more advanced areas, where germinating centres for expansion already exist, and of leaving by the wayside extensive areas potentially capable of participating in the economic process. And that is what has happened. The philosophy of Brazilian development in recent years has been conceived along the lines of *further development for the already developed*, rather than of integrating into the national economic system the present marginal areas, such as the North-east and the Amazon.

The case of the north-east is the most alarming, since a third of the Brazilian population is concentrated there; and these people live under extremely precarious economic conditions, as I have already had occasion to demonstrate. Nevertheless, the whole economic policy of Brazil has conspired against any genuine economic integration of this part of the country. Under this heading federal policy has been limited to certain measures of protection to the sugar economy, which alone can never emancipate the north-east, and to a paternalistic policy of 'help your starving brother' when the droughts reach the stage of calamity. And this aid, furthermore, has proved ineffective, even as simple relief, and has benefited local pork-barrel politicians rather than victims of the calamity as such.

What the north-east needs is something quite different, something that is not the treatment the mother country accords a colony. André Philip, speaking of the situation of underdeveloped countries *vis-à-vis* the great powers, says that such backward countries do not need help or financial assistance for development: that what they demand is economic respect for their economies. Respect is more important than aid. The same thing is the case within Brazil. It is necessary that the richer areas, those with greater economic and political power, should have more respect for the poorer regions and should seek to cooperate for their emancipation in the interest of the whole nation.

It should not be thought that these words are unconscious manifestations of a certain tendency towards lamentation and self-pity, something we have always condemned. No. We do not wish to divide Brazil with wailing walls. We wish to make it more and more unified, cementing its fragmented economy into one single system. But to do this we must throw down the walls of ancient prejudices, such as the idea that these poorer areas of the country are unredeemable, when in fact their progress has been held back by unfavourable historical conditions, by the absence of economic circumstances which could meet their potentialities. The north-east is not irremediably condemned to poverty and its people to hunger; there is no inexorable determinism about it. It is merely that in the play of economic variables, the colonial policy that has loosened in the south still remains in full force in the north-eastern region, which is a simple producer of basic products and raw materials.

I sometimes go so far as to think that what has been most

lacking in the north-east is a little more political force, a little more leadership, the courage to demand its basic human rights in dialectical terms, not as charity. If the north-east, or better, the whole North together, were to advocate an exchange policy of duties and of credit less harmful and unjust than the present one, which only benefits the economy of other parts of the country, its economy would expand much faster than it does as a result of limited budget credits, which are nothing but grains of sand in a sea of misery and quite incapable of cementing anything really solid. I shall give only two examples, but they seem to me to demonstrate very well the discriminatory treatment accorded the economy of the north-east.

The first is related to the problem of exportation of its basic products, such as cacao, sugar, carnauba wax, cotton, vegetable oils and certain ores, which generate a substantial volume of foreign exchange for our economy. But what happens to this exchange? Only a small part of it benefits the north-east; the greater part of it is drained off by the government and used to equip industry in the south. Or sometimes, what is worse, to pay for the importation of luxury products, show items – Cadillacs and perfumes – the kind of things with which underdeveloped countries think to disguise their misery, but which only make their underdevelopment more evident. Because underdevelopment is exactly that: it is economic imbalance, it is disparity between indices of production, income, and consumption between different social layers and different regions that make up the sociographic composition of a nation.

To promote authentic social-economic development would be rather to seek to close these gaps by a better distribution of wealth and a fairer basis of investment in the various regions and in the various sectors of the country's economic activity.

The economic development plans put into execution by the government of Juscelino Kubitschek*, although they had the patriotic objective of speeding up the economic development of the country, nevertheless did not provide adequate instruments for this balancing and levelling of the overall national eco-

* Kubitschek, who became President in 1956, was responsible for the construction of the new capital, Brasilia.

nomy, and therefore did not make their maximum contribution towards eliminating hunger from certain parts of the country.

The other example I wish to present, equally eloquent, is a comparison of the amounts of financing provided by an organ created precisely for the purpose of promoting the country's economic development: the National Bank for Economic Development. During the last five years this bank extended credit in the proportion of forty-nine per cent to the Eastern Region and forty-one per cent to the South, but it accorded the north-east only four per cent of its total financing.

It is this economy of dependence – total dependence of the north-east and the Amazon on the economic system of other parts of the country – which continues to maintain the dark blots of hunger in these areas.

After four centuries of human occupation we find a country that calls itself agricultural where only some two per cent of the land is productively worked; and of this insignificant area only a third is devoted to the production of food. As a natural result of this insufficient production, coefficients of consumption *per capita* can only figure, when they figure at all, at the bottom of the list in international consumption tables, principally as regards protective foods: meat, milk, cheese, butter, fruits and vegetables. Our annual meat consumption is only fifty-three kilos per capita, as compared to 136 in Argentina, 107 in New Zealand, sixty-two in the United States, sixty-four in England and sixty-seven in Denmark. Milk consumption is simply insignificant: thirty-seven litres a year, that is, about 100 grams, three or four ounces, a day. In other countries, meanwhile, milk consumption reaches such figures as 164 litres in Denmark, 108 in the United States, 101 in Australia and ninety-five in France. Figures for other sources of proteins – cheese and eggs – are equally insignificant: 600 grams of cheese, as compared to 5,500 in Denmark. We consume the same amount of butter as cheese – 600 grams – while the United States, England and Denmark consume, respectively, eighteen, ten and eight kilos. Consumption of the other protective foods occupies the same place in world statistical tables: our figures are among the lowest in the world.

If these data are interpreted in the light of the facts already set forth, the overall nutritional situation of our people may easily be inferred.

The picture here presented is not something out of the past, but a picture of existing conditions. This is our complex and confused social reality, the same that justifies the title Roger Bastide gave his book: *Brazil, Land of Contrasts*.

The contrasts are indeed shocking. For instance, between the splendour of city life in some of our great centres and the social sink-hole, the apathy of rural life a short distance away. Or the contrast of possessing a highly developed modern industry side by side with an agriculture in feudal style bound to the most conservative routine. Such is Brazil, and such is the explanation why, in spite of our surprising successes in the field of economic progress, in spite of our heavy industry, our automobile factories, our Brasilia and other goals set out and, amazingly, attained, we are still a land of hunger, we are still one of the great dark areas in the universal geography of starvation.

It is true that this blot of hunger has lightened a bit at certain points, has retracted its borders in others, but the general picture remains more or less the same. In recent years we have become more conscious of the reality of the problem. Government and people now discuss the question. The essential principles of nutritional hygiene are better known. But little has yet been achieved in the way of concrete results to improve the objective fact of our food situation. And in certain periods and under certain aspects, this situation even seems to grow worse, in contrast with the surge of industrial development the country is passing through. It is as though the men responsible for the destinies of Brazil had not yet taken the problem to heart, had not yet resolved to strike at its roots with courage and decision. Even those governments most devoted to our economic emancipation have not yet scored any successes in this sector so vital for the social well-being of our people. Let us see what has happened recently in terms of national economic development.

Economic development constitutes today an idea-force that

has taken dynamic hold of our people. They are anxious to take active part in this process of transforming our economy, and they are keeping a close watch on the results of this collective effort.

It was in 1930 that the reconstitution of our economy began to take shape and to develop the capacity for autonomous development. The rhythm of expansion has greatly increased since the last World War. A few figures will serve to demonstrate the momentum of our economic development, and how promising it is in certain sectors. For instance, real production in Brazil has practically doubled in the last fifteen years, the figure for industry being about 190 per cent. Agriculture, meanwhile, has grown only forty per cent. The country is becoming industrialized, and its productive capacity is increasing. It remains to be seen how efficiently this capacity is being used. Efficient use is the test of whether an economic development plan is adequate or not, because the rate of expansion of an economic system depends in large part on the criteria that guide investment.

What is happening in Brazil? What is the intensity of our economic growth, and what are the factors that are perhaps holding back its productive impulse?

The economic development of Brazil, if measured by the indices of average per head income, cannot be denied. But if we judge it by the actual distribution of income among the various social groups the picture is not so bright. And the fact is that social progress is not expressed by the volume of overall income alone, or by average income per head, which is a statistical abstraction, but rather by the distribution of such income in fact.

And this factor – distribution – instead of improving, instead of showing a tendency towards a beneficial dispersion, reveals an increasing concentration in certain areas and in the hands of certain groups. The government has lacked the courage to attack the basic structure responsible for this imbalance, and to promote, as part of the development process, a balancing and levelling of the overall economy of the country.

214

Even during the process of industrialization, our economy has followed the dictates of colonial-type thinking; it has shown no political interest in the fate of the majority, but has sought merely to develop further what was already developed and to enrich further those who had already become rich under the existing system. From the viewpoint of this lack of balance our economic development does not correspond to authentic social development, representing the genuine aspirations of the Brazilian masses.

Quite the contrary. In certain ways the policy of intensive industrialization concentrated in the southern part of the country, where there already existed an integrated economic system based on coffee exports and incipient industry, has still more accentuated and aggravated the already existing imbalance. There is the regional imbalance between the south on the one hand and the north and north-east on the other, and the sectorial imbalance between industry and agriculture. As a matter of fact, the imbalance between regions is nothing but a projection in geographical terms of the sectorial imbalance between industrial and agricultural economies.

It is this sectorial imbalance that I here wish to study, because in my opinion it constitutes the gravest distortion in the dynamic of our economic development, and the principle factor tending to strangle the industrialization of the country, which in turn is a fundamental goal of development. The whole process of directed development in an underdeveloped country automatically gives rise to a series of imbalances which constantly require corrective measures. The sociologist Costa Pinto very properly emphasizes the fact that 'in the social structures of the less developed countries the essential feature is not the lack of change, but rather the fact that different parts of the structure change at different rates, thus generating asymmetries and distortions, contradictions and pockets of resistance'.

That is why it is impossible to import pre-fabricated models of development for application *in loco*, as a valid transposition of the experience of other peoples. Each economic system in expansion must be oriented in its own original and to some degree unforeseeable manner, governed by the possibilities and potentialities of the various geoeconomic areas.

In the case of Brazil the most marked distortion has been the backwardness of agriculture as compared to the progress of the industrial sector. It is true that some contest this fact, pointing out that agriculture has grown faster than population in Brazil, in the proportion of three to two. But this is an extremely weak argument. It must not be forgotten that nutritional standards in Brazil have always been among the lowest in the world, with overall underconsumption of calories and specific under-consumption of various dietary elements, particularly the protective foods. Food production in Brazil has always fallen far short of taking care of effective needs, which in turn have been sharply limited by the low purchasing power of our people. It is clear that improvement of this purchasing power as a result of developing industrialization greatly increases the demand for food products, and requires an expansion of agricultural production on a far larger scale than anything accomplished up to the present. It is also well to remember that farming and stock-raising still supply sixty per cent of the raw materials for our industry, which for its own expansion requires a parallel expansion in the volume of these raw materials.

But it is not the volume of production that reveals the backwardness of agriculture most clearly; rather it is the indices of productivity, which are among the lowest in the world, both the productivity of the agricultural worker and the productivity of the land cultivated. It is the low production of the Brazilian farmer which makes it necessary to have millions of workers to cultivate only 20,000,000 hectares of land, whereas in the United States eight million workers cultivate 190,000,000 hectares, an area almost ten times as large. Productivity of the land for its traditional crops also shows a comparatively unfavourable situation. Average productivity per hectare for sugar-cane is thirty-eight tons in the north-east against seventy in Puerto Rico; for raw cotton it is 0·070 tons in the north-east, 0·124 in São Paulo, and 0·304 in the United States; for corn it is 0·676 tons in the north-east, 1·402 in Minas Gerais, and 2·271 in the United States. And so on. The weakness and backwardness of the agrarian economy in Brazil thus constitutes a factor that handcuffs the whole national economy, holding back, by various mechanisms, the momentum of industrialization itself.

Through scarcity of raw materials and high cost of production, agriculture tends beyond any doubt to strangle a large sector of the processing industries. A similar effect occurs as a result of the scarcity and high cost of subsistence products, which impose the establishment of wages for industrial workers that unnecessarily inflate the cost of industrial production – without even providing the worker with a type of rational diet that might improve his productivity indices. This food scarcity is more of a problem still when it comes to establishing great industrial complexes; in certain parts of the country food supply constitutes the biggest headache for planners and entrepreneurs. The rural citizen has been relegated to the position of a marginal economic element whose purchasing power is practically nil; and this prevents the formation of a domestic market capable of absorbing the increasing production of industry. Internal migrations, the flight from country to city, saturate the urban centres with great unproductive human masses, eco· nomically dead cells infiltrating the social structure, and this overloads the public treasury to pay for indispensable social services whose high cost necessarily absorbs a large share of the resources that ought to be applied to productive investment.

We suffer from a whole complex of restraining forces caused by the backwardness of the Brazilian rural economy and serving to limit our economic development.

11. M. N. SRINIVAS

*

Village and Family in the Process
of Secularization *

Intellectual, psychological or social elements which are present in society and act to dissolve or transmute or stimulate it are an aspect of conditions which needs to be described and analysed. One of these is what has been described as the 'secularization' process, and has been at work all over the world. How it has affected the Indian village and family is described by M. N. Srinivas, one of India's leading sociologists, in his book *Social Change in Modern India*, an extract from which follows.

THE changes that have occurred in the Indian village community have resulted in its more effective integration with the wider economic, political, educational, and religious systems. The vast improvement in rural communications that has taken place in the last few decades, especially since the Second World War, the introduction of universal adult franchise and self-government at various levels from the national to the village, the abolition of Untouchability, the increased popularity of education among rural folk, and the Community Development Programme – all these are changing the aspirations and attitudes of villagers. The desire for education and for a 'decent life' is widespread, and vast numbers of people are no longer content to live as their ancestors lived. Villages in India today are very far indeed from the harmonious and cooperative little republics that some imagine them to be; it would be more accurate to describe them as arenas of conflict between high castes and Untouchables, landlords and tenants, 'conservatives' and 'progressives', and finally, between rival factions. Everywhere social life is freer than before, as pollution ideas have lost some of their force. Secularization and politicization are

*From *Social Change in Modern India* (Berkeley: University of California Press, 1966).

on the increase, and villagers ask for wells, roads, schools, hospitals, and electricity.

It is easy, however, to exaggerate the increase in the secularization of village life. It is true that the unit of endogamy has widened somewhat, but this is more true of the higher castes than of others. The widening is, moreover, along traditional lines; a crude way of describing the situation would be that while barriers between sub-sub-subcastes or sub-subcastes are beginning to break down, marriages spanning wide structural or cultural gaps are rare. That is, peasants are not marrying shepherds or smiths or potters, but different peasant subcastes speaking the same language are coming together. (However, alliances involving structural and cultural leaps occur occasionally among the new *élite* in the big cities.) Interdining among castes is slightly more liberal than before, but only slightly. All the 'touchable' castes will unite against Harijans who want to exercise their constitutional right of entering temples and drawing water from village wells.

The processes which have affected caste and the village community have also affected the family system. This has happened at all levels and in every section of the society, but more particularly among the Westernized *élite,* that is, the upper castes living in the larger towns and cities. The traditional system of joint families assumed the existence of a sufficient quantity of arable land, and a lack of spatial mobility and diversity of occupations. The idea of selling land in the open market, which became popular during British rule, also contributed to the mobility of people. The development of communications, the growth of urbanization and industrialization, and the prestige of a regular cash income from employment in an office, factory, or the administration, dispersed kin groups from their natal villages and towns. Yet it would be a gross oversimplification to suggest that the Indian family system has changed or is changing from the joint to the nuclear type. The process is extremely complicated, and there are not enough studies of changes in family patterns in different regions and sections of the society. Enumeration of the size of households or even their kinship composition is not enough, as an urban household may

219

be perfectly nuclear in composition while kinship duties, obligations, and privileges overflow it in many important ways. Many an urban household is only the 'satellite' of a dominant kin group living in a village or town several hundred miles away. The Indian family system, like caste, is resilient, and has shown great adaptability to modern forces. It is still true, however, that significant changes have taken place in the family system of the Hindus, and these processes are most clearly discernible among the new *élite* groups. It is among them that there is great spatial mobility, and members who establish separate households in the large cities certainly live in a cultural and social environment significantly different from that obtaining in a traditional joint family in a small town or village. The urban household often lacks those elders who not only are tradition-bound but also have knowledge of the complex rituals to be performed at festivals and other occasions. Their mere presence exercises a moral influence in favour of tradition – as was vouched for by my Andhra Brahmin Communist informant, who said that he changed into pure clothes at meals 'because of his grandmother'. The education of women has produced a situation in which young girls do not have the time to learn rituals from their mothers or grandmothers, and the small households in big cities frequently lack the old women who have the know-how and the leisure. The educated wife has less of the traditional culture to pass on to her children, even should she want to. Still more significant is the fact that *élite* households have become articulators of the values of a highly competitive educational and employment system. Getting children admitted to good schools, supervising their curricular and extra-curricular activities, and worrying about their future careers absorbs the energies of parents.

These changes in family system occurring among the new *élite* groups are, however, somewhat offset by other forces. In large cities such as Bombay, Delhi, Calcutta, and Madras, voluntary associations tend to be formed on the basis of language, sect, and caste, and these make up in some ways for the loss of a traditional social and cultural environment. In a city such as Delhi, for instance, practically every linguistic group of India has voluntary cultural or other organizations which try to recreate for the speakers of each language their home environment. Concerts are held, plays are staged, *harikathas* are organized, regional festivals are celebrated, and regional politicians and other celebrities are welcomed. There is also a certain amount of residential clustering on the basis of language, and this is achieved even in housing projects built by the Government of India and which ostensibly do not recognize regional claims in allotting flats and houses! A homesick South Indian or Bengāli likes to rent an apartment in an area where other South Indians or Bengālis live, and soon there come into existence shops selling the spices, pickles, vegetables, household utensils, and cloth he was used to in his home area. The social network of an educated, white-collared South Indian or Bengāli who is living away from his linguistic area does include many people who speak a different language, but those who speak his language will perhaps preponderate in it. To obtain a seat in a school or college or a job for a relative or fellow-townsman, he may have to approach a Hindi- or Punjābi-speaker, but he does this usually through intermediaries who speak his own language.

Nevertheless, the traditional environment that is recreated in a big city differs significantly from the environment that has been left behind. It is a freer, more cosmopolitan and streamlined version, and it lacks the rich detail, complexities, rigidities, nuances, and obligatoriness of the traditional environment. Besides, it caters more to the parental generation of immigrants than to the offspring generation. The latter do not think of their parents' natal region as 'home', and many of them dislike visiting it even for brief periods. Their participation in the local culture and institutions is far greater than their parents'. Occasionally, marriages cutting across the linguistic and caste barriers occur between them and local folk.

12. CARLOS FUENTES

*

The Argument of Latin America:
Words for the North Americans*

In some respects the first of the Third World revolutions was the Mexican Revolution, which began in 1910, and continued for several years. In 1962 the Mexican novelist Carlos Fuentes prepared a text for a debate over United States television with Richard Goodwin, the U.S. Assistant Secretary of State for Latin American Affairs. The text, from which we extract the next reading, is polemical in tone. But it deals with the situation in which Latin America finds itself in regard to the international order.

SOUTH of your border, my North American friends, lies a continent in revolutionary ferment – a continent that possesses immense wealth and nevertheless lives in misery and a desolation you have never known and barely imagine. Two hundred million persons live in Latin America. One hundred and forty million of them work virtually as serfs. Seventy million are outside the monetary economy. One hundred million are illiterate. One hundred million suffer from endemic diseases. One hundred and forty million are poorly fed.

Today, these miserable masses have decided to put an end to this situation. Latin America, for centuries nothing more than an object of historical exploitation, has decided to change – into a subject of historical action. ...

You are much given to good wishes, to what you call 'wishful thinking'. You have always believed that what is valid for you is valid for all men in all nations and at all times. You forget the existence of specific historical factors. You fail to realize that in reality there are two worlds, one of rich countries and one of poor countries. You fail to recognize that, of necessity, the poor countries require solutions different from yours. You have had four centuries of uninterrupted develop-

*From *Monthly Review*, January 1963.

222

ment within the capitalistic structure. We have had four centuries of underdevelopment within a feudal structure.

A Feudal Castle with a Capitalistic Façade

You must understand this key word: *structure*. You had your own origin in the capitalistic revolution, liberal and Protestant. You were born without an anachronistic link. You founded a society that, from its first moment, was identified with the historical reason of the times. ... On the contrary, we were founded as an appendix of the falling feudal order of the Middle Ages; we inherited its obsolete structures, absorbed its vices, and converted them into institutions on the outer rim of the revolution in the modern world. ...

But you will ask yourselves: is a revolution necessary? Why not abolish these structures through evolution? The answer is simple: because the formulas of free-enterprise capitalism have already had their historical opportunity in Latin America and have proved unable to abolish feudalism.

During the nineteenth century, economic liberalism – *laissez faire* – was superimposed on the feudal structure in Latin America. Side by side with the landlord class of the colonial period, a new class of entrepreneurs sprang up to deal in the business of exploitation. Those capitalists turned us into single-product countries, exporters of raw materials to the occidental marketplace. The utopia of these entrepreneurs was the following: because of the international division of labour, it was appropriate for some regions to produce raw materials and for others to refine them; such an exchange would produce welfare for everyone. Now we know this is not true; we know that, in the long run, the price of manufactured goods will always be higher than that of raw materials. Now we know this is not true; we know that in a depression of the central economy, those who suffer most are the satellite economies, the producers of raw materials. Between 1929 and 1938, Latin American exports decreased by seventy per cent. In that time, hunger *did* exist in Cuba; fifty per cent of her labour force was unemployed, the national banks failed, the sugar lands were bought at bargain prices by Americans. The myth collapsed. If economies were complementary, as the classical theory states, our standard of living should be equal to yours.

In order to overcome the effects of economic liberalism, many Latin American countries entered another phase after 1930: protectionist capitalism, with the aim of encouraging the internal industrialization of Latin America and making it less dependent on the export of raw materials. But this naïve and liberal capitalism was also superimposed on the feudal structure without destroying it. It abandoned to their fate the great mass of peasants and workers, and reserved progress for an urban minority. It ended by crystallizing a dual society in Latin America: the modern capitalistic society of cities and the feudal society of the countryside. The minority society became richer at every turn, face-to-face with a majority society becoming more miserable at every turn. In the last few years, the abyss between the two has done nothing but grow. That is why capitalism has not succeeded in solving the problems of Latin America. It has been unable to destroy the legacy of feudalism. It has been unable to promote true collective development in Latin America.

This is what Latin America is: a collapsed feudal castle with a cardboard capitalistic façade.

This is the panorama of the historical failure of capitalism in Latin America:

Continuous monoproductive dependence. In Brazil, coffee constitutes seventy-four per cent of the exports; tin in Bolivia, sixty per cent; copper in Chile, sixty-three per cent; bananas in Costa Rica, sixty per cent; coffee in Colombia, eighty-two per cent; bananas in Honduras, seventy-five per cent; coffee in Haiti, sixty-three per cent; oil in Venezuela, ninety-five per cent; coffee in Nicaragua, fifty-one per cent; sugar in the Dominican Republic, sixty per cent.

A continuous system of 'latifundio'. In Chile and Brazil, two per cent of the population owns fifty per cent of the workable land. In Venezuela, three per cent of the population owns ninety per cent of the land. In general, in Latin America, with the exception of Mexico and Cuba, five per cent of the population owns half of the land. More than half of all Latin Americans are peasants who work under conditions close to slavery. However, only twenty-four per cent of the land in Latin America can be cultivated. Of this percentage, enormous expanses are out of active production, either to maintain the earnings of the owners or through pure irrationality. Most Latin American countries must import a good part of their food; only Uruguay and Argentina are relatively self-sufficient. The productivity of agriculture is extremely low in relation to the manpower employed. And international prices of the agricultural products fluctuate and are constantly declining.

Continuous underdevelopment. The present systems are unable to increase production and use natural resources in the rhythm required by our increase in population. As a result, the average annual increase in production per inhabitant in Latin America which in 1955 was 2·2 per cent, declined in 1959 to one per cent, and in 1960 to 0·0 per cent. In other words, at present, in its double feudal-capitalistic system, Latin America *does not progress.*

Continuous political stagnation. The continued existence of the feudal structure forbids the masses access to education and assures the concentration of political power in the hands of a fistful of landlords and city capitalists. Latin American armies financed and equipped by the United States, support this system, as we have just seen in Argentina, Ecuador, and Guatemala.

Continuous general injustices. At present, four per cent of the Latin American population receives fifty per cent of the combined national incomes. The higher classes have hoarded more than fourteen billion dollars in foreign banks. A great percentage of their local investments are unproductive ones: fixed-income securities, real estate, luxury goods.

Continuous dependence on foreign capital. At present, a good part of the Latin American economy is not serving its own development, but is nothing more than an extension of foreign economies, particularly that of the United States. Iron and oil in Venezuela, copper in Chile, Peruvian minerals, do not remain in those countries to promote economic development: they are a possession of the American economy and benefit only that economy. But since this is a topic very closely related to you, we will talk about it later.

The key question is this: How can the causes of underdevelopment in Latin America be chopped away? There is no room for doubt in the answer: stabilization of prices of raw materials in the short run, and economic diversification – industrialization – in the long run. But you want it to be done through peaceful evolution and the Alliance for Progress. And we think: through revolution. Let us examine both solutions.

The Alliance for Progress

The only structural reform foreseen in the Alliance for Progress is agrarian reform. Now, please consider that in Latin America the base of political power is the landlords. Do you sincerely believe that a leading class whose roots are in the ownership of land is going to let go of its reason for being? Agrarian feudalism is the basis of the wealth and political dominion of the governing classes in Central America, Chile, Peru, Argentina, Brazil, Venezuela, Colombia, Ecuador; do you believe these classes are going to commit suicide voluntarily? A Peruvian oligarch recently told me: 'If the gringos force us to divide the land, we will answer by expropriating their mining companies.' No, my American friends: an agrarian reform in Latin America, as demonstrated by Mexico and Cuba, is only made through revolution, with weapons in hand. This is what the share-croppers of Peru, the peasants of north-eastern Brazil, the pariahs of Chile, Ecuador, and Colombia are beginning to do. They are not allowing themselves to be cheated by 'false' agrarian reforms: the distribution of sterile lands, without credit, without machinery, without schools or hospitals. Those governing classes can deceive

226

you, but they are not going to swindle the peasant masses or stifle their revolutionary impetus.

The Alliance is going to be used by governments that do not truly represent their people, by governments representing the old feudal order whose only interest is to keep its privileges. Look where your dollars are going to: as in South Vietnam, as in South Korea, as in Iran and Spain – to the bank accounts of a handful of people, to the importation of luxurious automobiles, to the construction of apartment houses.

The Alliance does not even mention one of the basic factors of backwardness in Latin America: the economic deformation imposed by foreign domination of our economies. ...

Investments? Yes, you have invested ten billion dollars in Latin America. It is a curious thing: we have always received your investments, and we are still poor. You speak about your property in Latin America and call us thieves when we expropriate it. But why don't you ask your investors? Ask them how much they invest and how much they take back to the United States in profits. Do you want to know? Between 1950 and 1955, you invested two billion dollars, made three and a half billion, and took back to the States one and half billion. In a single year, 1959, you made 775 million, only reinvested 200 million and sent 575 million back to the United States. In the last seven years, Latin America lost, because of these shipments of money, $2,679,000,000. You take out too much, leave too little, and even this little is distributed unfairly: where is the real benefit for our economies? Is it just that these profits do nothing, not a single thing, to alleviate the horrible misery, ignorance and illness of the great majority of the Latin Americans who, with their slavery, made them possible? You, as Americans, tell me if that is just.

And tell me also whether you have not recovered more than your investments, whether it is not right that this squandered wealth should be recovered and directed towards improving the lot of everyone, because it was created by the work of everyone though today it benefits only a dozen corporations.

Finally, in its year of life, The Alliance for Progress has been accompanied by acts of public aggression that prostitute it

227

completely. These acts are the Cuban invasion in April, 1961, and the violation of the inter-American law in Punta del Este in January, 1962.*

*The United States attempt to use Cuban exiles to invade Cuba and overthrow its government on 15 April 1961 proved abortive (Bay of Pigs). On Washington's insistence the Eighth Meeting of Consultation of the Organization of American States was called the following January at Punta del Este in Uruguay in order to impose sanctions on Cuba. In spite of enormous pressure this move failed. And the major Latin American countries, Brazil, Mexico, Argentina, Chile, Bolivia and Ecuador refused to support an illegal U.S. resolution expelling Cuba from the O.A.S.

13. LIN PIAO

*

The Upsurge of 'People's Wars' *

Carlos Fuentes has represented the way in which some analysts in the Third World see their own economic and political situation as part of the world economy and polity. Another polemical account of the ways in which imperialism in the post-war period creates problems for Third World peoples is Lin Piao's *Long Live the Victory of People's War*, from which the next passage is taken. Lin Piao (b. 1908) joined the Chinese revolutionaries in Canton (see p. 99) while still a youth, and soon achieved great distinction by his brilliance in revolutionary warfare as well as politics. He wrote his essay on the revolutionary upsurge in the Third World to mark the twentieth anniversary of Japan's surrender. In it he sees the world of 1965, and especially the struggles like that in Vietnam, through the prism of China's national liberation war against Japanese imperialism. Next to Mao Tse-tung as the leader of the 'proletarians' in China, Lin Piao was one of the people most responsible for the initiation and success of the Cultural Revolution in China.

Defeat U.S. Imperialism and its Lackeys by People's War

Since the Second World War, U.S. imperialism has stepped into the shoes of German, Japanese and Italian fascism and has been trying to build a great American empire by dominating and enslaving the whole world. It is actively fostering Japanese and West German militarism as its chief accomplices in unleashing a world war. Like a vicious wolf, it is bullying and enslaving various peoples, plundering their wealth, encroaching upon their countries' sovereignty and interfering in their internal affairs. It is the most rabid aggressor in human history and the most ferocious common enemy of the people of the world. Every people or country in the world that wants revolu-

*From *Long Live the Victory of People's War* (Peking: Foreign Languages Press, 1965).

tion, independence and peace cannot but direct the spearhead of its struggle against U.S. imperialism.

Just as the Japanese imperialists' policy of subjugating China made it possible for the Chinese people to form the broadest possible united front against them, so the U.S. imperialists' policy of seeking world domination makes it possible for the people throughout the world to unite all the forces that can be united and form the broadest possible united front for a converging attack on U.S. imperialism.

At present, the main battlefield of the fierce struggle between the people of the world on the one side and U.S. imperialism and its lackeys on the other is the vast area of Asia, Africa and Latin America. In the world as a whole, this is the area where the people suffer worst from imperialist oppression and where imperialist rule is most vulnerable. Since the Second World War, revolutionary storms have been rising in this area, and today they have become the most important force directly pounding U.S. imperialism. The contradiction between the revolutionary peoples of Asia, Africa and Latin America and the imperialists headed by the United States is the principal contradiction in the contemporary world. The development of this contradiction is promoting the struggle of the people of the whole world against U.S. imperialism and its lackeys.

Since the Second World War, people's war has increasingly demonstrated its power in Asia, Africa and Latin America. The peoples of China, Korea, Vietnam, Laos, Cuba, Indonesia, Algeria and other countries have waged people's wars against the imperialists and their lackeys and won great victories. The classes leading these people's wars may vary, and so may the breadth and depth of mass mobilization and the extent of victory, but the victories in these people's wars have very much weakened and pinned down the forces of imperialism, upset the U.S. imperialist plan to launch a world war, and become mighty factors defending world peace.

Today, the conditions are more favourable than ever before for the waging of people's wars by the revolutionary peoples of Asia, Africa and Latin America against U.S. imperialism and its lackeys.

Since the Second World War and the succeeding years of revolutionary upsurge, there has been a great rise in the level of political consciousness and the degree of organization of the people in all countries, and the resources available to them for mutual support and aid have greatly increased. The whole capitalist–imperialist system has become drastically weaker and is in the process of increasing convulsion and disintegration. After the First World War, the imperialists lacked the power to destroy the new-born socialist Soviet state, but they were still able to suppress the people's revolutionary movements in some countries in the parts of the world under their own rule and so maintain a short period of comparative stability. Since the Second World War, however, not only have they been unable to stop a number of countries from taking the socialist road, but they are no longer capable of holding back the surging tide of the people's revolutionary movements in the areas under their own rule.

U.S. imperialism is stronger, but also more vulnerable, than any imperialism of the past. It sets itself against the people of the whole world, including the people of the United States. Its human, military, material and financial resources are far from sufficient for the realization of its ambition of dominating the whole world. U.S. imperialism has further weakened itself by occupying so many places in the world, over-reaching itself, stretching its fingers out wide and dispersing its strength, with its rear so far away and its supply lines so long. As Comrade Mao Tse-tung has said, 'Wherever it commits aggression, it puts a new noose around its neck. It is besieged ring upon ring by the people of the whole world.' *

When committing aggression in a foreign country, U.S. imperialism can only employ part of its forces, which are sent to fight an unjust war far from their native land and therefore have a low morale, and so U.S. imperialism is beset with great difficulties. The people subjected to its aggression are having a trial of strength with U.S. imperialism neither in

* The statement of Chairman Mao Tse-tung in Support of the People of the Congo (Leopoldville) Against U.S. Aggression, 28 November 1964.

Washington nor in New York, neither in Honolulu nor Florida, but are fighting for independence and freedom on their own soil. Once they are mobilized on a broad scale, they will have inexhaustible strength. Thus superiority will belong not to the United States but to the people subjected to its aggression. The latter, though apparently weak and small, are really more powerful than U.S. imperialism.

The struggles waged by the different peoples against U.S. imperialism reinforce each other and merge into a torrential world-wide tide of opposition to U.S. imperialism. The more successful the development of people's war in a given region, the larger the number of U.S. imperialist forces that can be pinned down and depleted there. When the U.S. aggressors are hard-pressed in one place, they have no alternative but to loosen their grip on others. Therefore, the conditions become more favourable for the people elsewhere to wage struggles against U.S. imperialism and its lackeys.

Everything is divisible. And so is this colossus of U.S. imperialism. It can be split up and defeated. The peoples of Asia, Africa, Latin America and other regions can destroy it piece by piece, some striking at its head and others at its feet. That is why the greatest fear of U.S. imperialism is that people's wars will be launched in different parts of the world, and particularly in Asia, Africa and Latin America, and why it regards people's war as a mortal danger.

U.S. imperialism relies solely on its nuclear weapons to intimidate people. But these weapons cannot save U.S. imperialism from its doom. Nuclear weapons cannot be used lightly. U.S. imperialism has been condemned by the people of the whole world for its towering crime of dropping two atom bombs on Japan. If it uses nuclear weapons again, it will become isolated in the extreme. Moreover, the U.S. monopoly of nuclear weapons has long been broken; U.S. imperialism has these weapons, but others have them too. If it threatens other countries with nuclear weapons, U.S. imperialism will expose its own country to the same threat. For this reason, it will meet with strong opposition not only from the people elsewhere but also inevitably from the people in its own country.

Even if U.S. imperialism brazenly uses nuclear weapons, it cannot conquer the people, who are indomitable.

However highly developed modern weapons and technical equipment may be, and however complicated the methods of modern warfare, in the final analysis the outcome of a war will be decided by the sustained fighting of the ground forces, by the fighting at close quarters on battlefields, by the political consciousness of the men, by their courage and spirit of sacrifice. Here the weak points of U.S. imperialism will be completely laid bare, while the superiority of the revolutionary people will be brought into full play. The reactionary troops of U.S. imperialism cannot possibly be endowed with the courage and the spirit of sacrifice possessed by the revolutionary people. The spiritual atom bomb which the revolutionary people possess is a far more powerful and useful weapon than the physical atom bomb.

Vietnam is the most convincing current example of a victim of aggression defeating U.S. imperialism by a people's war. The United States has made South Vietnam a testing ground for the suppression of people's war. It has carried on this experiment for many years, and everybody can now see that the U.S. aggressors are unable to find a way of coping with people's war. On the other hand, the Vietnamese people have brought the power of people's war into full play in their struggle against the U.S. aggressors. The U.S. aggressors are in danger of being swamped in the people's war in Vietnam. They are deeply worried that their defeat in Vietnam will lead to a chain reaction. They are expanding the war in an attempt to save themselves from defeat. But the more they expand the war, the greater will be the chain reaction. The more they escalate the war, the heavier will be their fall and the more disastrous their defeat. The people in other parts of the world will see still more clearly that U.S. imperialism can be defeated, and what the Vietnamese people can do, they can do too.

14. HAN SUYIN

*

The Second Decade of Independence*

Han Suyin (b. 1917) was born in China and educated in Peking, Brussels and London. A doctor by profession, she lives in Singapore, and has worked there and in Malaya. But she is also a novelist, and a writer and lecturer on contemporary world politics, especially on China. What follows is taken from her *China in the Year 2001*. The radical standpoint from which she surveys the same scene as Lin Piao is one she shares with a large number of politically-conscious non-Communists in the Third World.

IN the ten years from 1955 to 1965, the conspicuous features of the non-affluent world, the two-thirds of humanity who emerged out of colonial bondage in 1945, are the disintegration of non-alignment, the disappearance of bourgeois democratic copies of parliamentary type left in place by European colonial powers in their withdrawal, the withering of many illusions nurtured and entertained about the intentions of the affluent towards the needy, the emergence of arbitrary right-wing repressive and dictatorial military warlords' regimes. Besides these political failures of 'democracy', Western-style, there is an even more tangible and more crucial economic deterioration, and a rising quota of upheavals, rioting and discontent. The steps of this swift and irrevocable disintegration have been fully documented both by international organizations and many other economic studies – growing deficits in balances of payments, increasing poverty, increasing hostility to imperialist (mostly American) financial penetration and military manifestations, even in the Philippines and Thailand. In very many of these countries, financial neo-colonialism has preceded or accompanied deliberately provoked *coups*, bringing to power rulers 'favourable' to the United States. The backing of retrograde and military rulers has made

*From *China in the Year 2001* (London: Watts, 1967).

a mock of pretensions to democracy and duplicates the state of China in the early twentieth century, when the West backed the most feudal and reactionary warlords, in the end destroying any chance of Western type of democracy implanting itself. The situation is paradoxical; the West is its own worst enemy; for it is not because of China's emergence that the unrest, upheavals and economic deterioration occur, but because of imperialism's continued policies of domination under the forms of financial stranglehold and military suppression practised in the name of 'anti-communism'. The disappearance of all forms of democratic structure, the loss of non-alignment, the growing ascendancy of extreme right-wing military satrapism, necessarily reliant upon U.S.A. subsidies for suppressive forces to quell the risings of their own peoples, the Balkanization of many countries, and the resurgence of tribalism, dismember and tear the Third World into a chaos which shakes and confuses. This fragmentation is greeted with joy by the 'democracies', for the attendant weakness and disunity bring hopes for another 'vampire gorging', as in China in the 1890s. The subservience and servility of many Western-oriented ruling *élites* in the Third World help this new colonial domination. In fact, the 'comprador middleman' class, which Western capitalism established in China, is reproduced on a global scale.

In the decade since the Bandung Conference of 1955, hopes of an Afro-Asian solidarity of the poor against the rich have seemingly evaporated. The state of the Third World, in 1965, is much worse economically, than in 1945. Famine stalks the millions, but instead of putting the blame where it lies, on ever more oppressive exploitation, increase in population is blamed for all evils. Termed 'population explosion', it is another in a long list of hypocrisies; for neither Africa nor Latin America are over-populated. Though population increase does mitigate against a swiftly rising standard of living, population control by itself will neither arrest, nor retard, nor indeed solve any of the economic problems of exploitation. Obsession with 'the demographic factor' indicates the disquiet at the power of world-wide people's wars against imperialism. As Fritz Baade points out, the world could sustain twenty times its present population were its resources well used. In the 'wealthiest' countries, such as South Africa, a vast majority live at substandard level, because the mineral wealth of the country is in the hands of a small racialist minority.

The so-called 'failures' of Chinese foreign policies towards the Third World in the last five years have been a feature of the Western Press. In Indonesia, in Africa, the hostility of extreme right-wing ruling cliques, brought in by military *coups*, is held up as an example. Why does China no longer woo the 'non-aligned' is the question asked. At one time China's 'wooing of the non-aligned' was seen as a sinister move to be countered by the break-up of neutralism.

This break-up has been accomplished; sixty-eight military *coups,* many openly engineered by Western agencies, have contributed to it; the failure is not China's, but of the Western type of democracy, and a vindication of Mao Tse-tung's thesis that 'bourgeois-democratic rule' can no longer exist and is doomed, especially in the two-thirds of the needy world. That this destruction was accomplished by imperialism itself is not surprising. So it was in China. Therefore the way of armed struggle, with a two-stage national revolutionary process remains the only way which eventually all nations demanding true independence (both political and economic) will have to follow: the 'road of Chingkang mountain'. And it is being brought about by the very actions undertaken by the U.S.A. to 'stamp out communism'.

15. CELSO FURTADO

*

The Political Consequences of
Underdevelopment*

Celso Furtado (b. 1920), sociologist and economist, formerly an
official in the Economic Commission for Latin America, Executive
Director of the Agency for the Development of Brazil's North-east,
Brazil's Minister of Planning, and Professor at Yale and Paris
Universities, has made weighty contributions to the scholarly understanding within the Third World of its problems. This excerpt is
from his *Diagnosis of the Brazilian Crisis*, which was written before
the right-wing military *coup* of 1964.

UNDERDEVELOPMENT must be initially understood in terms
of the social structure. The fact that the better studied and better known aspects of underdevelopment are the economic ones,
is a simple confirmation of the general theory that the dominant role in the process of social development is generally
played by economic factors. The characterization of underdevelopment in purely economic terms, being a much simpler
task, is a perfectly legitimate initial formulation of the problem. It would be completely wrong, however, to expect that
economists, using the analytical methods at their disposal,
could exhaust a subject which involves important aspects that
can only be approached by sociologists or political scientists.
Consideration of underdevelopment in terms of income *per
capita* is, however, one of the obsessions of our time and
creates a serious handicap for understanding the problem on
the historical plane. It was the economists who undertook the
difficult task of pioneering in the field of social research, but it
is no longer possible to continue simply to use their work as a
basis for studying this complex subject. We still speak of economic planning as if it were a question of choice among tech-

*From *Diagnosis of the Brazilian Crisis* (Berkeley: University of
California Press, 1965).

niques elaborated by able economists, when in fact planning presupposes the formulation of policy, and specific attitudes towards the rationality aimed at in political economy. It is obvious that politics cannot be considered except in terms of the factors conditioning the exercise of power, and this involves going beyond 'analytical models' to consider 'practical human activity' within a given historical reality.

In underdeveloped social structures, by virtue of the simple fact that the inelastic supply of productive factors (particularly the land) is of relatively major importance, division of social work and private appropriation of the means of production is reflected in the marked differentiation of classes. In effect, most of the underdeveloped countries are basically agricultural; the bulk of the population is made up of peasants opposed to a minority of land-owners and merchants. However, this clear social differentiation has contributed nothing to the formation of class consciousness. As Engels had already noted: 'The agricultural populace, in view of the fact that it is spread over a wide area, and that it experiences difficulty in finding the basis for understanding, never initiates an independence movement.' The reason for the weakness of class-consciousness among the peasants is simple: in an agricultural economy, particularly where feudal or semi-feudal forms still predominate, antagonism of class interests does not play a dominant role. Since the harvest depends on weather conditions, the responsibility for 'good years' and 'bad years' is credited to nature. Where paid agricultural work is introduced, it seems progressive, since it nearly always represents a rise in real wages and affects only a fraction of the agricultural population. The urban artisan who became proletarianized felt that he was going down in the social scale, but the small rural sharecropper who manages to get paid work imagines that he has gone up.

The relative importance of the land as a productive factor and the 'social peace' that traditionally reigned in the country areas, in contrast to the atmosphere of the cities, always gave the land-owning class tremendous political ascendancy in underdeveloped countries. Under these conditions, the state tends to acquire a large number of the characteristics of an instrument for domination by one class. Nevertheless, it would be wrong to see in it the 'repressive force' to which Engels so often referred. For the state to become a repressive force (and in many cases this does happen), the class struggle must first have assumed great importance in the society. This is not the case in underdeveloped countries, particularly in the agricultural sector, which is the principal base of political power in these societies.

What we have regarded as underdevelopment is less the existence of a basically agricultural economy – in this case we would merely be dealing with a *backward* economy – than the occurrence of a strong dualism. This originates when, owing to certain historical conditions, a wedge of typically capitalist economy is introduced into a 'backward' agricultural economy, creating an imbalance at the factors level (to use the economic jargon) with repercussions throughout the social structure. The conditions created by this structural dualism cannot easily be explained in terms of a stable equilibrium model. The dynamic scheme of cumulative causation, elaborated by Myrdal, is much more effective in explaining this case. Given the existence of two forms of remuneration for work, two technologies at extremely different levels, two concepts of organization of production, a dual economy is intrinsically unstable.

If we consider the social structure of an underdeveloped system as a whole, we can distinguish two factors that could provide a dynamic impulse: the internal conflicts of the capitalist sector, and the tensions created between this sector and the pre-existing economy. There are important aspects of these interrelations that give a specific nature to the developmental process in a dual structure. Thus, development of the capitalist sector is achieved mainly by absorbing factors from the former economy or, whenever it suits the capitalists, by absorbing new techniques. This possibility of alternative solutions gives the capitalist class particular advantages over the industrial workers. In effect, the existence of a large reserve of manpower at the disposal of the capitalists is a factor that inhibits the whole process of class struggle. In this way, the capitalist sector in underdeveloped economies is, as a rule, not very dynamic. The ruling class becomes accustomed to a high rate of profit that is never effectively challenged by the class struggle. This is why, in many underdeveloped economies, the capitalist sector remains practically at a standstill, achieving the same social peace that characterized the old feudal structure, synonymous with stagnation and once described as 'the peace of the tomb'. A good example of this situation was the north-eastern textile industry in Brazil, created towards the end of the last century, which was exactly like the sugar industry in the paternalistic methods it employed.

We do not intend, at this point, to raise the problem of the growth of an underdeveloped country directly, but it must be remembered that in the early stages of this growth, a fundamental role is played by exogenous factors, through the activities of the exporting sector. The impulse given by this sector for growth is decisive for the development of the capitalist 'wedge', both with regard to activities related to export and those related to the domestic market. What needs to be stressed is the reduced internal dynamism of a dual economy, deriving from characteristics peculiar to its capitalist sector. However, the relations of this sector to the existing agricultural economy go much further than the simple transfer of manpower. The increased demand for agricultural products in the urban areas, generated by development of the capitalist sector, necessarily has strong effects on the rural sector by causing it to submit part of its activities to the direct control of capital entrepreneurs. Consequently, an unstable situation is created for the former land-owning class, which attempts to find support for the protection of its privileges in political institutions. As the stability of the old social structure is reduced, the struggle for power gains in importance, and, as a rule, it then becomes an important new factor in this very instability.

The ruling class in an underdeveloped country tends to be divided into three main groups: the original nucleus of landowners, the group controlling interests connected with external trade (always with wide foreign links) and the capitalists basically supported by the internal market. The first group is, generally, in favour of free trade and has an anti-state bias, i.e. it is opposed to any change in the *status quo*, which it thinks would have to come through state action. The second group also favours free trade, but its liberalism is already qualified, since it soon learns to use the state-machine in order to defend its external trade. The third group is protectionist, and in many ways has a pro-state bias, attempting to use the state-machine through credit, exchange, control, and other means, in order to transfer resources for its own benefit. The discrepancies between these groups are not very different from those that could have been observed in Europe at the time industrial capitalism was implanted, between the rural aristocracy, the financial 'grand bourgeoisie', and the industrial bourgeoisie. However, whereas in nineteenth-century Europe, genuine class struggle between wage-earners and capitalists grew in importance and conditioned the whole social process, in underdeveloped structures this does not occur. In the absence of a genuine challenge within the underdeveloped structure itself, the dominant groups remain unable to solve their internal contradictions, and this affects social development in an adverse way. Thus, the land-owning group that controls a large part of the political power through its rural 'basis', and acts as a depressive force on the developmental process, can maintain its dominating influence for a considerable length of time. In the same way, foreign interests linked to the exporting sector, can, for the benefit of this sector, hinder the growth of an internal market without provoking reactions of any great consequence within the economic system itself. Hence the notorious tendency to stagnate that characterizes many present-day underdeveloped economies has roots deep in their social structures.

We must call attention to one final point in the characterization of underdeveloped economies. This is the extraordinary importance that the state tends to assume in these structures. In addition to the numerous causes of the growth of the state-machine in modern times, regardless of the degree of development, the internal instability of the ruling class involves an increase in the value attributed to positions of power. Domestic capitalism, faced with the free-trade bias of the exporting

and agricultural sectors in general, requires strong state protection in order to survive. The agricultural sector, under pressure from the capitalist group, needs credit support on a large
scale in order to progress, and only the state is in a position
to offer this. The exporting sector needs an underlying structure
of basic services in order to establish itself, and this calls for
decisive participation by ·the state. This rapid expansion of the
state-machine, coupled with an increase in the provision of
general services in the urban areas (to a large extent a consequence of the concentration of income), is reflected in a
vigorous expansion of the salaried middle class, concentrated
in the urban areas, with effects of no small importance in the
political sphere.

In short, the social structure corresponding to a dual economy can be outlined as follows: at the top is the ruling class
composed of various groups of interests, in many respects antagonistic to each other, therefore unable to formulate a plan
for national developments, and holding a monopoly of power
unchallenged; lower down we have a great mass of salaried
urban workers employed in services, which forms a social
stratum rather than a proper class; beneath this is the class of
industrial workers, which hardly represents one-tenth of the
active population of the country but constitutes its most homo-
geneous sector; and finally, the peasant masses, whose characteristics have already been defined. Because of the absence of
genuine class struggle characterizing a capitalist economy, the
development of class-consciousness among the workers tends
to be an extremely slow process. It is precisely through the
growth of a class-consciousness that working-class ideology is
formed, although this process can be strongly influenced by the
historical experience of other countries and the interpretation
of intellectuals. In many underdeveloped countries – and Brazil
is a good example – a prolonged inflationary process helps to
distort the original characteristics of the class struggle. In
effect, in an inflationary situation, wage increases interest the
employers as much as the employees, since it is clear that the
consumer is the one who has to pay in the end. The point at
which the consumer will pay or not is a decision that rests in

the hands of the state, whose power is thus enormously increased. Therefore, it is much more important to control the instruments of political power than to struggle against strikers, since it is through these instruments that the decision is made as to who will finally foot the bill.

In an underdeveloped country with the characteristics we have described, the political process tends to take the form of a constant struggle for power among the groups that make up the ruling class, because of the extraordinary importance of the control of the state-machine. Since there is no endogenous process in the system capable of stimulating the growth of class-consciousness among the industrial working masses, the latter remain as liable as the salaried middle-class workers to be manipulated by ruling-class ideologies designed to serve the conflicting inner factions. These ideologies, known under the generic form of populism, use the common language of what in the nineteenth century was called 'Utopian Socialism', the essence of which is the promise of some sort of redistribution of the social product, without considering the organization of production. The danger of populism is that it succeeds in redistributing income for the benefit of certain groups and to the detriment of others, even if this is only for a limited period of time. In this way, it becomes a powerful weapon in the hands of one faction of the ruling class against the others. In an inflationary period, when credit becomes enormously important, this weapon can be used with considerable effect. In populist politics, the people – the salary- and wage-earning classes and small-income groups – are invariably manipulated to frighten the enemy and permit the take-over of key positions.

*

Western Views

One of the distinctive features of revolutionary movements in the Third World is that in one way or another they have a base in the life of the peasant or the landless proletariat of the countryside. Few living people have travelled as extensively in the rural areas from China and Vietnam to Mexico and Peru as René Dumont (b. 1904), the French agronomist and university teacher. His own research and his work for the United Nations Food and Agriculture Organization have involved close study of scores of particular situations. The following account (i) is taken from *Lands Alive,* based on a worldwide survey made in 1961. The second reading (ii) is from Barbara Ward's essay *The Decade of Development – A Study in Frustration?* Barbara Ward (Lady Jackson) (b. 1914) is an economist who has made the study of world poverty one of her main interests. Peter Bauer's contribution to a discussion with Miss Ward supplies the third reading (iii) which follows. Professor Bauer is a specialist on the Economics of Underdeveloped Countries at London University. Both Miss Ward's and his essays were published together as *Two Views on Aid to Developing Countries.*

(i) OVERDEVELOPED TOWN AND
EXPLOITED COUNTRYSIDE*

A LITTLE over three per cent of Colombia is tilled annually. A good third of it is under-utilized for grazing. Its thirteen million inhabitants live in a country double the area of France, but the south-eastern half, the *llanos,* contains less than two per cent of the population. Only twenty-five *ares*† per head are cultivated here; barely more than in China – but far less intensely exploited. Thus under-nourishment is inescapable. The 'warm' lands are below 1,000 metres altitude (3,270 feet); the

---

*From *Lands Alive* (New York: Monthly Review Press, 1965).
† An *are* equals 119·6 square yards. 1 hectare equals 2·47 acres.

'cold' are above 2,000 metres (6,540 feet), the 'temperate' lie in between. Above 3,000 metres (9,810 feet) there is no agriculture; nothing beyond a little mountain pasture, *paramos*. Soils range from 'the world's richest to the world's poorest'.

A Dispossessed Peon tills the Steep Slopes of the 'Cold' Lands

'Into one state we combine both Belgium and the Congo,' once said Colombia's Minister of Agriculture. . . . Belgium is represented by Bogotá with its luxury hotels, clubs, caviare and champagne. The 'Congo' begins on the starving outskirts of the city itself. 'Some of our high school pupils habitually faint from hunger,' added the Minister. 'It is as urgent here to feed them as to teach them.' One look around is enough; large luxury buildings are jostled by slums half hidden by posters vociferating luxury goods. Even at the beginning of the nineteenth century Humboldt was writing: 'Nowhere is there such terrifying disparity in the distribution of fortune.'

Bogotá, about 2,700 metres above sea level, lies at the edge of the Savannah that bears its name, a former lake 300 kilometres long, twenty to thirty kilometres wide, that emptied out in the quaternary era. Thirty kilometres to the north-east, on the scrub-covered schist slopes of the Andes, agriculture is sedentary and at subsistence level. This Indian peon is forty-five, his wife forty-two; they have eight living children. The three eldest (the first is twenty-three) have gone; the next three work outside but still live at home. The household works ten or so *fanegadas* totalling 6·4 hectares: the tenure of this is according to the classic system for peonage: ten hours' work a day, two days a week, for the owner – gratis. This peon feels his landlord is generous, because on these working days he is fed, and this is not the case everywhere. In the morning he gets coffee and a roll; soup, rice, potatoes and bread for lunch (but seldom meat); at about three o'clock bread and *panela* (unrefined sugar) or chocolate, or coffee with milk. This Indian's ancestors, answering to no man, used once to cultivate the rich soil of the ownerless plain. Now he works for

245

nothing to gain the right to cultivate the poor slopes of the mountain.

Of his ten *fanegadas* he ploughs about two (i.e. 1·3 hectares). In December he plants one with three loads (375 kilos) of potatoes which will yield eight to ten loads five months later: less than the national average (six tons per hectare). And he will have to use a little fertilizer because of the poverty of the soil. On a biennial rotation, the second *fanegada* is sown in March with wheat, which will give a four- or five-fold yield in September. This wheat will be sold to buy a little flour or maize, for grinding on the stone. Having no draught animals our peon must hire two oxen for a week every year, at 4·50 pesos a day (equal in purchasing power to about 4s. 6d.). Wheatsheaves cut and bound by hand are piled into three little stooks reminiscent of the big *moyettes* in Auvergne. One stack of barley, the third of these mountain crops, has been brought in sheaves to feed half a dozen chickens and a couple of turkeys.

As for the eight *fanegadas* in the pasture, they offer a cover not unlike our French meadows, moist and acid – velvet and vernal grasses, a few compositae, almost no leguminosae. They provide for the pack-donkey, which is worth fifty pesos. Our peon is hardly able to amass the 150 to 200 pesos needed for the purchase of a little horse. His 'créole' cow will give him four litres of milk after calving, but dries up quickly. He also has a little pig, and his tiny garden provides him with cabbages, onions, dahlias, iris, gladioli – and couch grass.

For the Record

A farm such as this – 150 to 200 days' work a year – can neither occupy nor sustain this family. So how do they live? They are woodcutters, and are thus bringing about the complete deforestation of these slopes: the wood is felled with an axe, and tied with rushes in small faggots of kindling each weighing about 1½ lb. One hundred and fifty-four of these bundles make a load of about 225 lb., which they sell for eight pesos in the town fifteen miles away. Transport alone uses up two days with the donkey! Our Indian takes two such loads a week and the 16*s*. thus earned forms the bulk of his financial resources.

His main expenditures are for maize alcohol and brown sugar. Roughly £3 per month for four people ... his standard of living is below the Chinese average and much less likely to improve. Without the children's wages there would be stark poverty, both economic and physiological. But the tiny house with the corrugated iron roof is clean: there is a guitar, a gun (seventeenth-century model), two axes, two hoes, a watering can, and a fine cooker.

But such lean slopes, tilled for such meagre crops. What a waste of work, and tending, moreover, to accelerate erosion. Whereas the fertile plains and valleys, where it would be so easy to work the soil, remain under-utilized as more or less derelict pastureland. This paradox extends to Bolivia, where agrarian reform can only succeed through the transfer of cultivation to the plains.

Here it was the Spanish invaders who thrust the Indian back into the poorest areas. And their descendants are not visibly anxious to improve his lot. Certainly Conservatives and Liberals are only too ready, when the occasion arises, to kill each other in the name of ideology. Dictatorships are first established, then overthrown. But except perhaps for a brief moment in 1948 the landed aristocracy have remained unshakably in power. Ought one then to ask whether the unrest in outlying regions is really attributable to 'banditry', or is it revolt? These movements sprang up, until 1957, against the depredations of the dictator Pinilla and his friends. Since his downfall they have continued, indicating that the new regime has been unable to come to terms with the poorer peasants. And there is talk that 150,000 have died in twelve years. An Italian agronomist, Rafaele Chelini, who was rash enough to point out that a rationalization of the agrarian regime was an essential preliminary to any agricultural progress, left quickly for his own country, even though he had avoided the explosive words 'agrarian reform'.

A fine study by the I.L.O. has established that the usufruct of a tiny plot granted to the peon in fact enables the big estate to count on a certain and cheap labour force. The number of days' *corvée* per week varies from one to four or even five; 'and then the farmer has to till his own plot by moonlight'. Often he works one day or more for payment in kind, which allows the big land-owner to 'condemn the native workers to total immobility, in material terms as well as in those of economic progress'.

Elsewhere, 'following a strict rota, every Indian must work a whole week in the owner's estate, tending cows, keeping up the supply of wood and water, penning the calves, without any wages at all and even with no food provided'.

Certainly the I.L.O.'s study describes an extreme case, that of the so-called aboriginal population, of whom some, far to the south, still live in communities 'where there was originally common ownership of land and tools, and collective work, but which have now taken on a great number of the forms of property, and assistance in labour'. 'Numbers of these communities are on the point of disappearing, and are struggling desperately but vainly against their white cousins who use every *legal and illegal* means to move in on their lands, gradually to usurp them, and to transform the Indians into paid agricultural workers. It must be added that the individualization of title to land proved disastrous for many communities who, 'unaware of the existence or significance of such a requirement, omitted to conform to it ... whereas encroachments and alienation of land in various guises (exchange for commercial goods, foreclosure, enforced liquidation for debt, or authority with excessive powers) led to the aboriginal groups being deprived of their traditional rights and reduced to the status of landless labourers, or tenants sharing their produce with a landlord. A great many of the surviving collectives are in remote, sterile, mountainous regions where they can barely subsist. Neighbouring properties have monopolized water and wood supplies and arrogated control of essential rights of way, with the result that the aboriginal communities are obliged to work on the estates to obtain use of these resources and rights.'

A Stockbreeding Hacienda in the Flat, Fertile Bogotá Savannah

Nearly all these remarks are in fact valid for most of the Colombian peasantry. Agrarian credit 'frequently takes the form of an account payable in kind at the store, or an advance of wages ... or the mortgaging of produce with merchants or money-lenders'. Here again we see the face of usury, so familiar in poor countries. And with it, inhumanity in working conditions. 'Recruiting methods and conditions of employment give rise to a number of abuses. Transport is generally poor, in overloaded vehicles or with long journeys on foot. Overcrowded accommodation and inadequate victuals are deplorably injurious to health. Income can be low, wages paid irregularly, and advances of cash are often necessary. One form of exploitation of the labourers involves payment in produce, and the setting up of the Company stores ... ultimately resulting in permanent indebtedness. Health and insurance arrangements are far from being regularly observed.' So it is easy to understand revolt, and 'bandits'.

Let us leave Bogotá this time by the 'Madrid' road to the north-west; then, cutting north-east, we find ourselves at *El Bosque*, thirty-seven kilometres from the capital. This hacienda is a fair comparison with Monte in Alemtejo, in Southern Portugal: a big estate standing alone. It covers 320 hectares, twenty-five under wheat, ten under maize ('no longer a paying crop'), five under potatoes and $7\frac{1}{2}$ given over to labourers' own patches. This total of $47\frac{1}{2}$ hectares is just over one-seventh of the total area which is a far higher proportion than average. The remainder is entirely grazing land. 'The absorption of Indian land is more pronounced near towns, roads, railways, and wherever irrigation possibilities exist,' says the I.L.O. study. It is the same for the outer suburban savannah as for the rich plains – Spanish possession is complete. It is a kind of intra-colonization, colonization from within. And what economic advantage does it furnish the 'invader'?

249

(ii) BLOCKS TO RAPID DEVELOPMENT*

What are the blocks to more rapid development? The first I want to pick out lies in the political fact of colonial and semi-colonial dependence. Most of the 'Southern' economies were first introduced to modernization by the Western industrial countries. But the process did not leave them strictly in command of their own economies and in the first decades of the new impact they were not in the position to take a number of decisions which could, at various points, have changed the pattern and quality of their economic life.

They had been stimulated to the beginnings of economic growth by the need of the industrial powers of the North Atlantic for raw materials, for tropical products and, up to a point, for temperate food supplies. Western investment went to the other continents to open up mines, farms and plantations and Western trade organized the international markets needed to exchange 'Southern' primary products for 'Northern' manufactures. The resulting pattern was one of a very strong development of the local import/export sector but there followed very little 'spread effect' from this sector to the rest of the economy. The transactions did not naturally generate much local credit because they remained something of a closed circuit largely under foreign control. The raw materials were sent out to pay for the original investment. Profits, capital gains and sometimes a ten-fold amortization returned to the metropolitan investors. What local purchasing power was generated was mopped up by the sale of Western manufactures imported through large Western trading companies. Since the process did not stimulate much credit locally, little capital was available for investment in the modernization of food-producing agriculture. It is typical of Asia, Africa and Latin America that the old forms of agriculture have persisted largely unchanged, outside the plantations and – in a few areas – the peasants' cash crops. Nor was capital available for local

*From *The Decade of Development – A Study in Frustration?* in *Two Views on Aid to Developing Countries* (London: Institute of Economic Affairs, 1966).

industry. There were few local entrepreneurs and, in any case, the satisfaction of the market with Western manufactures was part of the essential pattern.

In this situation only strong, direct governmental intervention would have modified the situation. On the one hand it could have transformed the agricultural scene. The peasant/ landlord relationship could have been changed in Asia, freehold introduced into the communal tribal agriculture of Africa, the *latifundia* abolished in Latin America. On the other, industry could have been stimulated by governmental decisions in the field of mobilizing savings and of building up protective tariffs behind which local enterprise could have started to grow. But these were precisely the kind of decisions which are not ordinarily taken by colonial governments. Part of the reason was their traditional philosophy of *laissez faire*. Part lay in the fact that it was not in the interest of their own trading and investing circles. Even where governments were not directly colonial – as in Latin America – the small ruling groups preferred to work with the foreign investors for limited personal gains rather than risk general reforms in the economy – one reason for Latin America's long economic stagnation. All through the colonial and semi-colonial world, the century since the 1850s has seen a fair amount of economic stimulus and development. But since the continents lacked either the governmental power or the governmental will to break the bottlenecks, the barriers to a wider modernization remained intact and growth was confined to a narrow sector.

These inhibitions can be clearly seen in the striking contrast between India and Japan. In colonial India there was, in fact, a certain amount of industrial development, particularly where entrepreneurial talent was locally strong, as it was in and around Bombay. But if we compare the relative snail's pace of Indian industrial growth between 1870 and 1920 with the forced draft industrialization of Japan over the same period, it can be seen, I think, that India chiefly lacked an apparatus of political decision for breaking the deadlocks which the process of growth does not overcome of itself. In Japan, a root and branch land reform, the compensation of landlords in govern-

251

ment bonds which could only be invested in new government-established industries, the mobilization of credit in country and town, the drive to literacy, government sponsorship of overseas training – in short, an entire battery of development strategies was carried out by a vigorous and resourceful government. In India, there was no sponsorship of industry, land reform was not touched – in spite of the increasing debt of the peasants – no particular push for general education occurred and the Indian government could not even impose a tariff until 1920. It was in fact only after 1947, with the establishment of full, independent, decision-making machinery, that India began to tackle economic problems Japan had been dealing with since the 1870s.

It does not, of course, always follow that when the local government does get the power to make its own economic decisions, it makes only the right ones. My point is that, practically speaking, up to the very end of the colonial period, local leaders were in no position to make any decisions at all. Yet in any process of development there has to be a decision-making power to deal with blocks and barriers which the sheer momentum of the economic process itself does not overcome.

(iii) FOREIGN AID AND POLITICAL ATTITUDES *

It is sometimes urged that foreign aid is necessary as an instrument of Western political strategy. This argument is particularly prominent in American discussions. More specifically it is thought that without it the underdeveloped world would go communist because of continued poverty, or because only Western aid keeps its governments out of the Eastern *bloc*.

Quite apart from the question of the weight and consequence of the recipients in global politics, these arguments are insubstantial. As we have seen, the bulk of continuous aid, as distinct from *ad hoc* relief measures, has not helped to raise living standards significantly and has probably retarded their rise. But even if aid were much more productive than it is, it could

* From *Two Views on Aid to Developing Countries* (London: Institute of Economic Affairs, 1966).

not possibly affect living standards to an extent likely to influence political attitudes. Moreover, an inclination towards
communism does not depend on living standards but on a
number of quite different factors which encourage people to
embrace a messianic faith, or encourage and enable some
people to establish a communist regime.

Indeed, by promoting centralized and closely controlled economies, foreign aid supports governments which quite understandably lean towards the Eastern *bloc* – even if that *bloc*
offers them little or no aid – for they find that system more
congenial. This tendency has been strengthened by the practice
of the Western donors to favour neutrals or even enemies compared to their friends in Africa or Asia.

There are familiar psychological factors reinforcing these
influences. Recipients of aid value little what they get for nothing. The donors of aid are not the first to find that the beneficiaries resent the benefactors. It is a commonplace that people
often bite the hand that feeds them. Furthermore, the recipients
of foreign aid frequently suspect the motives of the donors. The
transfer of tax-payers' money to foreign governments without
control over its use understandably arouses suspicions of
sinister motives, notably of political domination. It engenders
a belief that it expresses a feeling of guilt by the donors and
represents a partial restitution of past wrongs. This last idea is
popular and prevalent in underdeveloped countries where it is
widely believed, partly under the influence of Marxist–Leninist
doctrines, that their material backwardness is a result of
Western exploitation. In fact, throughout the underdeveloped
world the poorest and most backward areas are those with few
or no external contacts, and, conversely, the most materially
advanced areas, which have generally progressed most rapidly
over the last century, are those with which the developed world
has established contact. Contacts with the West, so far from
being responsible for the poverty of the underdeveloped world,
have been the main instrument in the promotion of the economic advance that has taken place.

The belief that the prosperity of particular individuals,
groups or countries accounts for the poverty or material back-

wardness of others is almost always invalid. But it is emotionally attractive and politically useful. It is therefore resistant to
refutation by logical argument or empirical evidence. In the
context of foreign aid, both aspects of this matter stand out
clearly. The material and technical progress of the developed
countries is clearly not the cause of the comparative backwardness of the underdeveloped world. But the emotional and political advantages of the belief to the contrary are so pronounced
that it does not yield to argument or evidence.

The implication of guilt, which affects much of the discussion on aid, obscures these elementary considerations. It serves
also to reinforce the various political and economic pressures
and motives for the restriction of external, private and economic contacts. In this way these ideas and suggestions lead to
policies adverse to economic advance. Here again, some of
these feelings and notions would be present without foreign aid,
but its prospect and operation tend to reinforce them.

The subservient attitude of the donors and some arguments
in the advocacy of aid enhance the plausibility and appeal of
these notions. Advocates of aid insist that the susceptibilities
of the recipients must on no account be offended, least of all
their sense of equality with the donors; that the attitudes,
qualities and policies of the recipients must not be questioned
or even mentioned; and that aid must be unconditional, except for encouraging recipients to engage in development planning. Even large-scale expenditure on mere prestige projects, or
for the financing of so-called liberation movements in far distant countries, must not be questioned, nor any of the governmental policies patently adverse to economic development.

But it remains inevitable that, whatever is said in this context about the equality between donors and recipients, the operation of foreign aid arouses or enhances feelings of inferiority
and resentment in the recipients. This result comes about because the arguments for aid and its flow emphasize differences
in material progress and technical achievement. I, for one, believe that the qualities and attitudes which promote material
success and technical achievement are not always those which
are the most valuable on many other criteria. For instance,

they do not necessarily include dignity, sensitivity, a sense of harmony or a reflective turn of mind. And material success does not guarantee happiness, understanding, sympathy or contemplation. In some of these qualities and attainments, many technically or economically backward groups excel those who are materially or economically more successful. The flow of foreign aid, its method of operation and its whole emphasis divert attention from qualities and criteria other than those which conduce to technical achievement, or which reflect its attainment. The emphasis inevitably suggests to the populations of the poor countries that they are the inferiors or the victims of the donors. It also diverts the attention, and perhaps the efforts, of the recipients into directions which fail to promote either contentment or even material progress.

PART FOUR

GOALS, OBJECTIVES AND VALUES

THE emergence of the Third World as an historical reality represents, as the readings have already indicated, a new beginning for the peoples of the tricontinental south. In this area live seven-tenths of mankind, enjoying, as a whole, only about one-fifth of the real income of the world (The First World, in contrast, with one-fifth of the population, enjoys sixty per cent of the real income.) Within each national unit, before the success of the revolutionary process, access to the meagre resources available for local distribution is enjoyed by different classes of the population in similar proportions.

Almost everywhere that has been or is the inherited situation. The social structures and attitudes, and the economic and political ideologies, which tend to continue and stabilize the situation are also part of the inherited situation. They establish what is and what is not reasonable and proper, orderly and normal, in dealings between persons and groups and nations. Specifically, for example, they would assume the doctrine of the inequality in the fundamental human sense of the European and the coloured races, the universal right of access by private enterprise, and the rightness of what is. On these and similar issues what is thought and felt within the Third World appears to differ from what is thought and felt by those (both within and outside the tricontinental south) who oppose the revolutionary challenge to the universality of Europe.

It is of importance to see to what extent the characteristic values and standards of the Third World distinguish it from the others. The ways in which the given situation, and conditions in the nation and in the world as a whole are appraised reveal the characteristic features of the revolutions in which the Third World takes its historical beginnings. The appraisal implies a standpoint in a realizable future from which one

259

reaches a systematic understanding of world history and politics as well as of action which must be taken. In the readings which qualify for inclusion in Part Four (and in some other readings) there is no suggestion that orthodox models and standards are sought in the First or Second Worlds. The model is certainly neither Russian society nor North American society, and not any satellite of either superpower. Both superpower pretensions and client roles are regarded with hostility and contempt. It is not the values of Stalinist and post-Stalinist Russia or contemporary North America which are admired, but, rather, the Paris Commune, the Bolshevik Revolution and the highest Western ideals of human freedom. In independently appraising what directions need to be taken, Third World leaders see certain products and features of these First and Second World societies, as much as those of feudal and colonial societies, as obstacles and evils: we have therefore to discover what developments these have prevented, what good they deny. What do those who speak for the Third World identify, in putting some parts of their inheritance behind them, as worthy of being preserved and renewed, what as needing to be changed and replaced?

What strikes one is the evidence in a variety of specific situations of a resolution to struggle, even fight against great odds, for something other than what was available in the pre-colonial or colonial traditions, or offered in the neo-colonial order. Clearly, there is widespread agreement in placing high value on the objectives of such revolutions. One observes in the revolutionary movements of the Third World, with their distinctive local idioms, conceptions of historical excellence beyond anything conceived in capitalist or Soviet civilization, possibilities beyond those of bourgeois or Soviet man. According to the evidence it is achievements *within* the Third World that are admired as a confirmation of the expectations of national liberation, justice, democracy, peace, and brotherhood among people.

It is, partly, in the way the social and political issues are posed, that the peoples of the Third World appear to be breaking out of the rival systems of the European world order and directing themselves to new goals and objectives. What priority is given to the welfare and rights of the poorer majority? How should the worth and the capacities of hitherto subject races and classes be conceived? In what terms should the natural resources of an area be evaluated? How relevant to the present, and how 'great', is the past? How inhuman, or unjust, or intolerable, is the continuance of the old world order? What are the limits of the authority and powers of the ruling class of the United States and the Soviet Union? What relative status should be given to the interests of 'feudal' *élites*, the middle class, officials, poor peasants, industrial workers, foreign enterprise and foreign economic interests? What should be the relationship of government and people, town and village, manual and intellectual work? Is national greatness measured in power over other peoples? Is revolutionary altruism or selfishness of higher value? What do these alternatives mean for peoples and for individuals? Which is the main incentive for development – the enrichment of men or their liberation? Should attitudes to contemporary problems be imprisoned in dogmatic ideologies or be discussed and argued out? There are, literally, hundreds of millions of people in the Third World almost continually using language which is capable of subtler discriminations than that used here.

These are universal questions. But the seriousness of the answers which the most forward-looking people give to them defines the character of the Third World. Its peoples are not 'transitional' but revolutionary, and the reasons for which they are fighting for power over their lives and destinies must be connected, we can assume, with how they think and plan together as they organize for common action and decide on the kind of leadership they will follow. The choice of leaders tells us much. The quality of their leadership in summing up what is precious in the political and moral experience of the poor and the humble, in discerning the signs of the good society, in creating trust and trustworthiness, and in guiding the people to a higher stage of human community and development, is as important as its power to organize for action.

1. LU HSUN

*

Ancient Glory and Modern Living*

At the beginning of this century the Chinese, being the beneficiaries as well as the victims of the oldest of the major civilizations, found themselves on the scene of great confusion. The questions which confronted all the peoples of the non-European world confronted them in a particularly baffling way. In the midst of all that was happening in the years following the First World War, great intelligence, imagination and faith were needed to believe in the possibility of a future. The contribution of Lu Hsun (1881–1936) – his real name was Chao Shu-jen, and he was born in Shaohsing in Chekiang province – to the modernization of the Chinese consciousness was considerable, and he is held in great honour in China today not only for his writing, but also for his courage in risking arrest, torture and assassination during the years after 1927 when revolutionary nationalists were imprisoned, tortured or killed. The three short pieces here are taken from Volume Two of his *Selected Works.*

Murderers of the Present

C U L T U R E D gentlemen say, 'The vernacular is vulgar and low, beneath the contempt of the discerning'.

All that illiterates in China can do is speak, so of course they are 'vulgar and low'. Men like myself, 'because they are unlettered, are for the vernacular in order to hide their own ignorance'. We are vulgar and low as well – that goes without saying. The sad thing is that those cultured gentlemen cannot be like that waiter in the *Flowers in the Mirror* who remained cultured all the time, using the classical language to describe the pots of wine or a plate of sweetmeats. They can show their lofty, ancient character only in their classical essays, but still talk in the vulgar, low vernacular. All the sounds uttered by

*From *Selected Works*, vol. 2 (Peking: Foreign Languages Press, 1960).

China's four hundred millions are 'beneath contempt'. This is truly lamentable.

Not content to be mortals, they want to be immortal. Living on earth, they want to go up to heaven. Modern men, breathing modern air, they want to ram moribund Confucian morality and a dead language down people's throats – what an insult to the present! These are 'murderers of the present'. And by murdering the present, they are murdering the future too.

But the future belongs to our descendants.

A Sudden Notion

I used to believe the statements that the twenty-four dynastic histories were simply 'records of mutual slaughter' or 'family histories of rulers'. Later, when I read them for myself, I realized this was a fallacy.

All these histories portray the soul of China and indicate what the country's future will be, but the truth is buried so deep in flowery phrases and nonsense it is very hard to grasp it; just as, when the moon shines through thick foliage on to moss, only chequered shadows can be seen. If we read unofficial records and anecdotes, though, we can understand more easily, for here at least the writers did not have to put on the airs of official historians.

The Chin and Han dynasties are too far from us and too different to be worth discussing. Few records were written in the Yuan dynasty. But most of the annals of the Tang, Sung and Ming dynasties have come down to us. And if we compare the events recorded during the Five Dynasties period or the Southern Sung dynasty and the end of the Ming dynasty with modern conditions, it is amazing how alike they are. It seems as if China alone is untouched by the passage of time. The Chinese Republic today is still the China of those earlier ages.

If we compare our era with the end of the Ming dynasty, our China is not so corrupt, disrupted, cruel or despotic – we have not yet reached the limit.

But neither did the corruption and disruption of the last years of the Ming dynasty reach the limit, for Li Tzu-cheng and Chang Hsien-chung rebelled. And neither did their cruelty and despotism reach the limit, for the Manchu troops entered China.

Can it be that 'national character' is so difficult to change? If so, we can more or less guess what our fate will be. As is so often said, 'It will be the same old story'.

Some people are really clever: they never argue with the ancients, or query ancient rules. Whatever the ancients have done, we modern men can do. And to defend the ancients is to defend ourselves. Besides, as the 'glorious descendants of a divine race', how dare we not follow in our forebears' footsteps?

Luckily no one can say for certain that the national character will never change. And though this uncertainty means that we face the threat of annihilation – something we have never experienced – we can also hope for a national revival, which is equally unprecedented. This may be of some comfort to reformers.

But even this slight comfort may be cancelled by the pens of those who boast of the ancient culture, drowned by the words of those who slander the modern culture, or wiped out by the deeds of those who pose as exponents of the modern culture. For 'it will be the same old story'.

Actually, all these men belong to one type: they are all clever people, who know that even if China collapses they will not suffer, for they can always adapt themselves to circumstances. If anybody doubts this, let him read the essays in praise of the Manchu's military prowess written in the Ching dynasty by Chinese, and filled with such terms as 'our great forces' and 'our army'. Who could imagine that this was the army that had conquered us? One would be led to suppose that the Chinese had marched to wipe out some corrupt barbarians.

But since such men always come out on top, presumably they will never die out. In China, they are the best fitted to survive; and, so long as they survive, China will never cease having repetitions of her former fate.

'Vast territory, abundant resources, and a great population' – with such excellent material, are we able only to go round and round in circles?

The Great Wall

Our wonderful Great Wall!

This engineering feat has left its mark on the map, and is probably known to everyone with any education the whole world over.

Actually, all it has ever done is work many conscripts to death – it never kept out the Huns. Now it is merely an ancient relic, but its final ruin will not take place for a while, and it may even be preserved.

I am always conscious of being surrounded by a Great Wall. The stonework consists of old bricks reinforced at a later date by new bricks. These have combined to make a wall that hems us in.

When shall we stop reinforcing the Great Wall with new bricks?

A curse on this wonderful Great Wall!

2. OCTAVIO PAZ

*

'We Are Responsible' *

Westwards across the Third World or eastwards across the Pacific
Ocean from Shanghai, where Lu Hsun died, is Mexico. Its history
before the twentieth century was very remote from that of China.
But things have changed since popular revolution began there in
1910. For more than half a century Mexicans have tried to find their
own way forward into a modern world in which people like them
have a respected place. The achievements of Emiliano Zapata and
Lazaro Cardenas have contributed to the making of a new world.
In *The Labyrinth of Solitude: Life and Thought in Mexico*, one of
Latin America's most distinguished poets, Octavio Paz (b. 1914),
discusses questions which are being asked all over the Third World.
Octavio Paz, who has represented his country abroad, resigned as
Mexico's Ambassador in New Delhi in September 1968, when
Mexican citizens were brutally shot down in large numbers in
Mexico City in a government move to repress dissent.

FROM the viewpoint of traditional revolutionary thinking, or
even from that of nineteenth-century liberalism, the existence
of historical anomalies like the 'underdeveloped' countries or a
totalitarian 'socialist' regime, here in the middle of the twentieth century, is absolutely scandalous. Many of the prophecies
and even dreams of the nineteenth century have been realized
(the great revolutions, progress in science and technology, the
transformation of nature etc.), but in a paradoxical or unexpected manner, defying the well-known logic of history.
From the time of the utopian socialists it was claimed that the
working class would be the principal agent of world history.
Its function was to consist in bringing about a revolution in the
most advanced countries, thus creating the bases for the liberation of mankind. True, Lenin thought it was possible to take a

*From *The Labyrinth of Solitude* (New York: Grove Press, 1961;
London: Allen Lane The Penguin Press).

266

historical leap and assign the traditional task of the bourgeoisie – industrial development – to the dictatorship of the
proletariat. He probably believed that revolutions in the backward countries would precipitate revolutionary changes in the
capitalist world. It was the matter of breaking the capitalist
chain at its weakest link. ... The efforts of an 'underdeveloped'
country to industrialize itself are in a certain sense anti-
economic, and demand great sacrifices from the people; but
there is no other way of raising the standard of living. Also,
national self-sufficiency is a costly experiment and must be
paid for by the workers, consumers and peasants. However,
the nationalism of the 'underdeveloped' countries is not a
logical response: it is the inevitable explosion of a situation
which the 'advanced' countries have made unbearable. In contrast, rational direction of world economy – that is, socialism –
would have created complementary economies instead of rival
systems. Once imperialism had disappeared and prices in the
world market had been regulated to eliminate excess profits, the
'underdeveloped' nations would have been able to obtain the
resources they needed for their economic transformation. A
socialist revolution in Europe and the United States would
have facilitated the transition of all the 'backward' countries to
the modern world, and in this case in a truly rational and
almost imperceptible way.

The history of the twentieth century causes some doubt (to
say the least) as to the validity of these revolutionary theses
and especially as to the role of the working class as the embodiment of the world's destiny. Nor is it possible to claim that the
proletariat has been the decisive agent in this century's historical changes. The great revolutions of our time, not excluding the Russian, have taken place in backward countries, and
the workers have represented only one segment – almost never
the determining one – of the great popular masses made up of
peasants, soldiers, the bourgeoisie and thousands of other persons harassed by wars and crises. These formless masses have
been organized by professional revolutionaries or specialists in
coup d'état. Even the counter-revolutions like Fascism and
Nazism fit into this scheme. The most disconcerting fact of all

is the absence of a socialist revolution in Europe, the very centre of the contemporary crisis. It hardly seems necessary to underline the aggravating circumstances: the European proletariat is the best educated and best organized of all, with the oldest revolutionary tradition, and the 'objective conditions' favourable to a seizure of power have existed in Europe on a variety of occasions. At the same time, several isolated revolutions – in Spain, for example, and more recently in Hungary – have been mercilessly suppressed, without the international solidarity of the workers having manifested itself. On the contrary, we have witnessed a barbarous regression, that of Hitler, and a general rebirth of nationalism in all of the Old World. Finally, instead of a rebellion by a democratically organized proletariat, the twentieth century has seen the birth of the 'party', that is, of a national or international grouping that combines the spirit and organization of two forces in which discipline and hierarchism are the predominant values: the Church and the Army. These 'parties' are unlike the old political parties in every way. And they have been the effective agents of almost all the changes that have taken place since the First World War.

The contrast with the periphery is very revealing. The colonial and 'backward' countries, since before the First World War, have undergone a whole series of disturbances and revolutionary changes, and the tide, far from ebbing, rises year after year. Imperialism is withdrawing from Asia and Africa, and its place is being occupied by new states. Their ideologies are confused, but they share two ideas that once seemed irreconcilable: nationalism and the revolutionary aspirations of the masses. In Latin America, which was tranquil until recently, we have seen the fall of various dictatorships and a new revolutionary spirit. Almost everywhere – Indonesia, Venezuela, Egypt, Cuba, Ghana – the ingredients are the same: nationalism, agrarian reform, better conditions for the workers and, at the top, a state determined to complete the process of industrialization and thus leap from the feudal era to the modern. It is of little importance, in a general definition of the phenomenon, whether the state allies itself with certain sectors of the native bourgeoisie or, as in Russia and China, abolishes the old classes and entrusts the imposition of economic changes to a bureaucracy. The distinctive – and decisive – characteristic is that this is not a proletarian revolution in the 'advanced' nations but an insurrection of the masses and peoples who live on the periphery of the Western world. Imperialism linked them to the destiny of the West, but now they are turning to themselves, discovering their identity and participating at last in world history.

The men and the political forms that have embodied the insurrection of the 'backward' nations are widely varied. At one extreme, Gandhi; at the other Stalin; and then there is Mao Tse-tung. There are martyrs like Madero and Zapata, buffoons like Péron, intellectuals like Nehru. It is a portrait gallery with very different types: Cárdenas, Tito, Nasser. Most of these men would have been inconceivable as political leaders during the past century or even during the first third of the present. As for their language, they combine messianic formulas with the ideology of democracy and revolution. They are 'strong men' and political realists, but they are also inspired leaders, and dreamers, and – sometimes – demagogues. The masses identify with them and follow them. The political philosophy of these movements has the same variegated character. Democracy as the West understands it is mixed with new and sometimes barbarous ideas, from the 'directed democracy' of Indonesia to the idolatrous 'personality cult' of the Soviet Union. And we should not forget the respect – the veneration, even – which Mexicans show for the figure of the President.

Along with the cult of the leader there is the official party. In some countries, including Mexico, it is an open group to which almost anyone who wants to participate in public affairs can belong, and which includes great sectors of both the left and the right. This is true of the Congress Party in India. We should mention here that one of the healthiest traits of the Mexican Revolution – due, no doubt, to the lack of an orthodox political creed as well as to the open nature of the party – is the absence of organized terrorism. Our lack of an 'ideology' has saved us from committing those tortuous persecutions which characterize the exercise of power in certain countries. True, we have suffered from violence, repression, caprices, arbitrarinesses, brutality, the 'heavy hand' (*mano dura*) of certain generals, etc., but even at the worst moments it has always been human, that is, the result of passions of circumstances, even of chance and fantasy. It is very different from the spiritual aridity of a closed system with its syllogistic, police-state morality. In the Communist countries the party is a minority, an exclusive and omnipotent sect; it is at once an army, an administration and an inquisition, combining both spiritual and secular power. Thus a wholly new type of state has arisen, in which various revolutionary traits – a directed economy, for example, or the disappearance of private property – are inseparable from such archaic traits as the sacred nature of the state or the deification of its leaders. Past, present and future; technical progress and the basest of political magic, economic development and slave labour, science and a state theology: this is the prodigious and terrifying visage of the Soviet Union. Our century is a huge cauldron in which all historical eras are boiling and mingling.

How is it possible that the contemporary intelligentsia – I am thinking especially of the heirs of Europe's revolutionary tradition – has failed to make an analysis of the present situation, not from the perspective of the last century but from that of the new reality confronting us? For example, the debate between Rosa Luxemburg and Lenin regarding the 'spontaneous revolution of the masses' and the function of the Communist party as the 'vanguard of the proletariat' would perhaps gain new meaning in light of the respective conditions in Germany and Russia. In the same way, there is no doubt that the Soviet Union hardly resembles what Marx and Engels thought a worker's state should be. Nevertheless, this state exists; it is not an aberration or 'historical error'. It is a vast reality, which manifests itself in the only way possible to living things: by the solidity and fullness of its existence. Even so eminent a philosopher as Lukács, who has devoted so much energy to denouncing the 'irrationality' of bourgeois philosophy has never

OCTAVIO PAZ

seriously attempted to analyse Soviet society from the point of view of reason. Can anyone assert that Stalinism was rational? Was the Communists' use of 'dialectic' rational, or was it merely a rationalization of certain obsessions, as happens in other neuroses? And the 'theory of collective rule', and that of 'different roads to Socialism', and the Pasternak scandal ... were these rational? Also, not one left-wing European intellectual, not one 'Marxologist', has studied the blurred and shapeless face of the agrarian and nationalistic revolution in Latin America and Asia in an attempt to understand them for what they are: a phenomenon of world-wide importance which demands a new interpretation. Of course the silence of the Latin American and Asiatic intelligentsia, who live in the centre of the whirlwind, is even more discouraging. It should be clear that I am not suggesting we abandon the old methods or reject Marxism, at least as an instrument for historical analysis. But new facts, radically contrary to the predictions of theory, demand a new set of instruments or at least a sharpening of those we already possess. A little before he died, Trotsky wrote – with greater humility and perception – that if revolution did not break out in the advanced nations after the Second World War, the Marxist view of world history would perhaps require a complete revision.

The Mexican Revolution is a part of world history. Despite certain differences in degree, in methods and in 'historical time', our situation is much like that of many other countries in Latin America, Africa and the Orient. We have freed ourselves from feudalism, military bosses and the Church, but our problems are essentially the same. They are immense problems, difficult to resolve. We are surrounded by many dangers, and also by many temptations, from 'government by the bankers' (that is, the intermediaries) to Caesarism, along with nationalistic demagoguery and other spasmodic political forms. Our material resources are few and we have still not learned how to use them effectively. Our intellectual instruments are even poorer. We have done very little thinking on our own account; most of our ideas have been borrowed from the United States or Europe. The grand words that gave birth to our peoples now have

271

equivocal values and no one knows exactly what they mean. Franco is democratic and forms a part of the 'free world'. The word 'Communism' is associated with Stalin. 'Socialism' means a group of gentlemen defending the colonial order. Everything seems to be one gigantic mistake. We console ourselves by saying that everything has happened as it should not have happened. But it is we who are mistaken, not history. We must learn to look reality in the face; if necessary, we must invent new words and new ideas for these new realities that are challenging us. Thinking is the first obligation of the intelligentsia, and in certain cases it is the only one.

Meanwhile, what can we do? There are no prescriptions any longer. But there *is* a valid point of departure: our problems are our own, and we are responsible for solving them, but at the same time they are also everyone's. Our situation in Latin America is that of the majority of the peripheral countries. For the first time in over three hundred years, we have ceased to be an inert material which the strong could use as they wished. We were objects before, but now we have begun to be the agents of historical changes, and our acts and omissions affect the great powers. The image of the present-day world as a struggle between two giants, with the rest of us as their friends, supporters, servants and followers, is very superficial. The background – and, indeed, the very substance – of contemporary history is the revolutionary wave that is whelming in the peripheral countries. For Moscow, Tito is a disagreeable reality, but he is a reality. The same can be said of Nasser or Nehru for the West. A third front, then? A new club of nations, a club made up of the poor? Perhaps it is too soon. Or perhaps it is too late: history is moving swiftly and the great powers expand more rapidly than we are able to grow. But before the flow of historical life congeals completely – and the 'draw' between the great powers is leading to this – there are still opportunities for intelligent concerted action.

We have forgotten that many others are as isolated as ourselves. We Mexicans must acquire a new awareness of Latin America. These countries are waking up now. Are we going to ignore them? We have many unknown friends in the United

272

States and Europe. The struggles in the Orient are related in one way or another to our own. Our nationalism, to be more than a mental illness or self-adulation, must search the whole world. We must recognize that our alienation is not unique, that it is shared by a majority of the world's peoples. To be ourselves would be to oppose the freezing of history with the mobile features of a living human face. It is better that we have no prescriptions or patent medicines for our ills. At least we can think and work soberly and resolutely.

The object of these reflections is no different from that which troubles other men and other peoples: How can we create a society, a culture, that will not deny our humanity but will also not change it into an empty abstraction? The contradictory violence of our reactions and the explosions of our intimate selves and our history all began as a rejection of the petrified forms oppressing us; now we are attempting to resolve them by creating a society which is not ruled by lies and betrayals, by avarice and violence and dissimulation. A society that does not make man an instrument of the state. A human society.

3. SUN YAT-SEN

*

New Values for a New Age *

After his first, abortive, attempt in 1895 to overthrow the hated Manchu regime in China, Sun Yat-sen (1866–1925) lived the insecure and unsettled life of a great patriot and revolutionary. He was convinced that China was in a desperately weak and critical condition under the effete Ching dynasty, at a time when the major foreign powers had designs on what was left of China's sovereignty. The Revolution of 1911 overthrew the Chinese Empire, and established a republic, but the disintegration and ruin of China seemed only to be hastened by the 'warlords' who took control. Sun nevertheless persisted in his belief in the power of revolutionary political action to create a new China. Allying his liberal forces with the Communist Party of China to bring in people like Li Ta-chao, Mao Tse-tung and Chou En-lai, and with conservative nationalists to bring in people like Chiang Kai-shek, in 1924 in Canton Sun created a new revolutionary government which began the task of rescuing and reconstructing China. Before his death in 1925 Sun explained his ideas in a series of lectures which were published as *San Min Chu I (The Three Principles of the People)*. The revolutionary movement started by Sun in 1924 came to a disastrous end in 1927 just at the moment when, with widespread peasant and worker support behind it, its armies swept in triumph into Shanghai. But the social ethics of the Communist-led Chinese Revolution, and of the Cultural Revolution, reveal how great the influence of Sun's nationalist and revolutionary ideas and his courage and persistence were on those who were later to fulfil his dream. Both in China today and in the rest of Asia his greatness is acknowledged.

Equality

ALTHOUGH nature produces men with varying intelligence and ability, yet the human heart has continued to hope that all men might be equal. This is the highest of moral ideals and

*From *The Three Principles of the People*, translated by Frank Price (Calcutta, 1942).

274

mankind should earnestly strive towards it. But how shall we begin? We will better understand by contrasting two philosophies of life – the selfish which benefits self and the altruistic which benefits others. Those who are out for themselves are continually injuring others with no pang of conscience. When this philosophy prevailed, intelligent and able men used all their powers to seize others' rights and privileges, gradually formed an autocratic caste, and created political inequalities – that was the world before the revolutions for democracy. Those who are concerned with benefiting others are glad to sacrifice themselves. Where this philosophy prevails, intelligent and able men are ever ready to use all their powers for the welfare of others, and religions of love and philanthropic enterprises grow up. But religious power alone is insufficient and philanthropy alone cannot remedy an evil. So we must seek a fundamental solution, effect a revolution, overthrow autocracy, lift up democracy, and level inequalities. Hereafter we should harmonize the three types which I have described and give them all equal standing. Everyone should make service, not exploitation, his aim. Those with greater intelligence and ability should serve thousands and ten thousands to the limit of their power and make thousands and ten thousands happy. Those with less intelligence and ability should serve tens and hundreds to the limit of their power and make tens and hundreds happy. The saying, 'the skilful is the slave of the stupid' is just this principle. Those who have neither intelligence nor ability should still, to the limit of their individual power, each serve one another and make one another happy. In this way, although men now may vary in natural intelligence and ability, yet as moral ideals and the spirit of service prevail, they will certainly become more and more equal. This is the essence of equality.

The Obligations of National Greatness

If we want China to rise to power, we must not only restore our national standing, but we must also assume a great responsibility towards the world. If China cannot assume that responsibility, she will be a great disadvantage, not an advantage to the world, no matter how strong she may be. What really is our duty to the world? The road which the Great Powers are travelling today means the destruction of other states. If China, when she becomes strong, wants to crush other countries, copy the Powers' imperialism, and go their road, we will just be following in their tracks. Let us first of all decide on our policy. Only if we 'rescue the weak and lift up the fallen' will we be carrying out the divine obligations of our nation. We must aid the weaker and smaller peoples and oppose the great powers of the world. If all the people of the country resolve upon this purpose, our nation will prosper; otherwise, there is no hope for us. Let us today, before China's development begins, pledge ourselves to lift up the fallen and to aid the weak; then when we become strong and look back upon our own sufferings under the political and economic domination of the Powers and see the weaker and smaller peoples undergoing similar treatment, we will rise and smite that imperialism. Then we will be truly 'governing the state and pacifying the world'.

4. JAWAHARLAL NEHRU

*

Extended Reflections of a
Nationalist in Prison*

Jawaharlal Nehru's tremendous prestige and influence, in India and abroad, in the 1930s has already been referred to (see p. 152). At the time he wrote the book published in 1936 as *An Autobiography* he had considerable experience of political leadership and of mass struggle. He had been General Secretary, and then President, of the Indian National Congress. He had been in touch with the anti-imperialist struggle in other countries. For his 'lawless' and subversive activity he had spent several terms in prison. His sensitiveness and intelligence, his wide range of interests and his eloquence, as well as the tendency to vacillate, to avoid a revolutionary commitment and to be overpowered by Gandhi's personality, are all in evidence in these excerpts from his writing in Dehra Dun Jail in 1934 and 1935.

I t is easy to criticize and blame others, and the temptation is almost irresistible to find some excuse for the failure of one's plans. Was not the failure due to the deliberate thwarting of others, rather than to an error in one's own way of thinking or acting? We cast the blame on the Government and the communalists, the latter blame the Congress. Of course, there was thwarting of us, deliberate and persistent thwarting, by the Government and their allies. Of course, British governments in the past and present have based their policy on creating divisions in our ranks. Divide and rule has always been the way of empires, and the measure of their success in this policy has been also the measure of their superiority over those whom they thus exploit. We cannot complain of this or, at any rate, we ought not to be surprised at it. To ignore it and not to provide against it is in itself a mistake in one's thought.

How are we to provide against it? Not surely by bargaining

*From *An Autobiography* (London: Allen & Unwin, 1936).

277

and haggling and generally adopting the tactics of the marketplace, for whatever offer we make, however high our bid might
be, there is always a third party which can bid higher and, what
is more, give substance to its words. If there is no common
national or social outlook, there will not be common action
against a common adversary. If we think in terms of the existing political and economic structure and merely wish to tam-
per with it here and there, to reform it, to 'Indianize' it, then
all real inducement for joint action is lacking. The object then
becomes one of sharing in the spoils, and the third and controlling party inevitably plays the dominant role and hands out
its gifts to the prize boys of its choice. Only by thinking in
terms of a different political framework – and even more so a
different social framework – can we build up a stable foundation for joint action. The whole idea underlying the demand
for independence was this: to make people realize that we were
struggling for an entirely different political structure and not
just an Indianized edition (with British control behind the
scenes) of the present order, which Dominion status signifies.
Political independence meant, of course, political freedom
only, and did not include any social change or economic freedom for the masses. But it did signify the removal of the
financial and economic chains which bind us to the City of
London, and this would have made it easier for us to change
the social structure. So I thought then. I would add now that I
do not think it is likely that real political freedom will come
to us by itself. When it comes it will bring a large measure of
social freedom also.

But almost all our leaders continued to think within the narrow steel frame of the existing political, and of course social,
structure. They faced every problem – communal or constitutional – with this background and, inevitably, they played into
the hands of the British Government, which controlled completely that structure. They could not do otherwise, for their
whole outlook was essentially reformist and not revolutionary,
in spite of occasional experiments with direct action. But the
time had gone by when any political or economic or communal problem in India could be satisfactorily solved by re-

formist methods. Revolutionary outlook and planning and revolutionary solutions were demanded by the situation. But there was no one among the leaders to offer these.

The want of clear ideals and objectives in our struggle for freedom undoubtedly helped the spread of communalism. The masses saw no clear connexion between their day-to-day sufferings and the fight for *swaraj*.* They fought well enough at times by instinct, but that was a feeble weapon which could be easily blunted or turned aside for other purposes. There was no reason behind it, and in periods of reaction it was not difficult for the communalists to play upon this feeling and exploit it in the name of religion. It is nevertheless extraordinary how the *bourgeois* classes, both among the Hindus and the Muslims, succeeded, in the sacred name of religion, in getting a measure of mass sympathy and support for programmes and demands which had absolutely nothing to do with the masses, or even the lower middle class. Every one of the communal demands put forward by any communal group is, in the final analysis, a demand for jobs, and these jobs could only go to a handful of the upper middle class. There is also, of course, the demand for special and additional seats in the legislatures, as symbolizing political power, but this, too, is looked upon chiefly as the power to exercise patronage. These narrow political demands, benefiting at the most a small number of the upper middle classes, and often creating barriers in the way of national unity and progress, were cleverly made to appear the demands of the masses of the particular religious group. Religious passion was hitched on to them in order to hide their barrenness.

In this way political reactionaries come back to the political field in the guise of communal leaders, and the real explanation of the various steps they took was not so much their communal bias as their desire to obstruct political advance. We could only expect opposition from them politically, but still it was a particularly distressing feature of an unsavoury situation to find to what lengths they would go in this respect. Muslim communal leaders said the most amazing things and seemed to care not at all for Indian nationalism or Indian freedom; Hindu com-

* Self-government.

279

munal leaders, though always speaking apparently in the name
of nationalism, had little to do with it in practice and, incapable of any real action, sought to humble themselves before the
Government, and did that too in vain. Both agreed in con-
demning socialistic and such-like 'subversive' movements; there
was a touching unanimity in regard to any proposal affecting
vested interests. . . .

As our struggle [of 1933] toned down and stabilized itself at
a low level there was little of excitement in it, except at long
intervals. My thoughts travelled to other countries, and I
watched and studied, as far as I could in jail, the world situation in the grip of the great depression. I read as many books
as I could find on the subject, and the more I read the more
fascinated I grew. India with her problems and struggles became just part of this mighty world drama, of the great struggle
of political and economic forces that was going on everywhere,
nationally and internationally. In that struggle my own sym-
pathies went increasingly towards the communist side.

I had long been drawn to socialism and communism, and
Russia had appealed to me. Much in Soviet Russia I dislike –
the ruthless suppression of contrary opinion, the wholesale
regimentation, the unnecessary violence (as I thought) in carrying out various policies. But there was no lack of violence and
suppression in the capitalist world, and I realized more and
more how the very basis and foundation of our acquisitive
society and property was violence. Without violence it would
not continue for many days. A measure of political liberty
meant little indeed when the fear of starvation was always
compelling the vast majority of people everywhere to submit to
the will of the few, to the greater glory and advantage of the
latter.

Violence was common in both places, but the violence of the
capitalist order seemed inherent in it; whilst the violence of
Russia, bad though it was, aimed at a new order based on
peace and cooperation and real freedom for the masses. With
all her blunders, Soviet Russia had triumphed over enormous
difficulties and taken great strides towards the new order. While
the rest of the world was in the grip of the depression and

going backward in some ways, in the Soviet country a great new world was being built up before our eyes. Russia, following the great Lenin, looked into the future and thought only of what was to be, while other countries lay numbed under the dead hand of the past and spent their energy in preserving the useless relics of a bygone age. In particular, I was impressed by the reports of the great progress made by the backward regions of Central Asia under the Soviet regime. In the balance, therefore, I was all in favour of Russia, and the presence and example of the Soviets was a bright and heartening phenomenon in a dark and dismal world.

But Soviet Russia's success or failure, vastly important as it was as a practical experiment in establishing a communist state, did not affect the soundness of the theory of communism. The Bolsheviks may blunder or even fail because of national or international reasons, and yet the communist theory may be correct. On the basis of that very theory it was absurd to copy blindly what had taken place in Russia, for its application depended on the particular conditions prevailing in the country in question and the stage of its historical development. Besides, India, or any other country, could profit by the triumphs as well as the inevitable mistakes of the Bolsheviks. Perhaps the Bolsheviks had tried to go too fast because, surrounded as they were by a world of enemies, they feared external aggression. A slower tempo might avoid much of the misery caused in the rural areas. But then the question arose if really radical results could be obtained by slowing down the rate of change. Reformism was an impossible solution of any vital problem at a critical moment when the basic structure had to be changed, and however slow the progress might be later on, the initial step must be a complete break with the existing order, which had fulfilled its purpose and was now only a drag on future progress.

In India, only a revolutionary plan could solve the two related questions of the land and industry as well as almost every other major problem before the country. 'There is no graver mistake,' as Mr Lloyd George says in his *War Memoirs*, 'than to leap the abyss in two jumps.'

281

Russia apart, the theory and philosophy of Marxism lightened up many a dark corner of my mind. History came to have a new meaning for me. The Marxist interpretation threw a flood of light on it, and it became an unfolding drama with some order and purpose, however unconscious, behind it. In spite of the appalling waste and misery of the past and the present, the future was bright with hope, though many dangers intervened. It was the essential freedom from dogma and the scientific outlook of Marxism that appealed to me. It was true that there was plenty of dogma in official communism in Russia and elsewhere, and frequently heresy hunts were organized. That seemed to be deplorable, though it was not difficult to understand in view of the tremendous changes taking place rapidly in the Soviet countries when effective opposition might have resulted in catastrophic failure.

The great world crisis and slump seemed to justify the Marxist analysis. While all other systems and theories were groping about in the dark, Marxism alone explained it more or less satisfactorily and offered a real solution.

As this conviction grew upon me, I was filled with a new excitement and my depression at the non-success of civil disobedience grew much less. Was not the world marching rapidly towards the desired consummation? There were grave dangers of wars and catastrophes but at any rate we were moving. There was no stagnation. Our national struggle became a stage in the longer journey, and it was as well that repression and suffering were tempering our people for future struggles and forcing them to consider the new ideas that were stirring the world. We would be the stronger and the more disciplined and hardened by the elimination of the weaker elements. Time was in our favour. ...

For long a mental tussle had been going on within me. I had not understood much that Gandhiji had done. His fasts and his concentration on other issues during the continuance of Civil Disobedience, when his comrades were in the grip of the struggle, his personal and self-created entanglements, which led him to the extraordinary position that, while out of prison, he was yet pledged to himself not to take part in the political

282

movement, his new loyalties and pledges which put in the shade the old loyalty and pledge and job, undertaken together with many colleagues, while yet that job was unfinished, had all oppressed me. During my short period out of prison I had felt these and other differences more than ever. Gandhiji had stated that there were temperamental differences between us. They were perhaps more than temperamental, and I realized that I held clear and definite views about many matters which were opposed to his. And yet in the past I had tried to subordinate them, as far as I could, to what I conceived to be the larger loyalty – the cause of national freedom for which the Congress seemed to be working. I had tried to be faithful and loyal to my leader and my colleagues, for in my spiritual make-up loyalty to a cause and to one's colleagues holds a high place. I fought many a battle within myself when I felt that I was being dragged away from the anchor of my spiritual life. Somehow I managed to compromise. Perhaps I did wrong, for it can never be right for anyone to let go of that anchor. But in the conflict of ideals I clung to my loyalty to my colleagues, and hoped that the rush of events and the development of our struggle might dissolve the difficulties that troubled me and bring my colleagues nearer to my viewpoint.

And now? Suddenly I felt very lonely in that cell in Alipore Jail. Life seemed to be a dreary affair, a very wilderness of desolation. Of the many hard lessons I had learnt, the hardest and most painful now faced me: that it is not possible in any vital matter to rely on any one. One must journey through life alone; to rely on others is to invite heartbreak.

Some of my accumulated irritation turned to religion and the religious outlook. What an enemy this was to clearness of thought and fixity of purpose, I thought; for was it not based on emotion and passion? Presuming to be spiritual, how far removed it was from real spirituality and things of the spirit. Thinking in terms of some other world, it has little conception of human values and social values and social justice. With its preconceived notions it deliberately shuts its eyes to reality for fear that this might not fit in with them. It based itself on truth, and yet so sure was it of having discovered it, and the whole of it, that it did not take the trouble to search for it; all that concerned it was to tell others of it. The will to truth was not the same as the will to believe. It talked of peace and yet supported systems and organizations that could not exist but for violence. It condemned the violence of the sword, but what of the violence that comes quietly and often in peaceful garb and starves and kills; or worse still, without doing any outward physical injury, outrages the mind and crushes the spirit and breaks the heart?

And then I thought of him again who was the cause of this commotion within me. What a wonderful man was Gandhiji after all, with his amazing and almost irresistible charm and subtle power over people. His writings and his sayings conveyed little enough impression of the man behind; his personality was far bigger than they would lead one to think. And his services to India, how vast they had been. He had instilled courage and manhood in her people, and discipline and endurance, and the power of joyful sacrifice for a cause, and, with all his humility, pride. Courage is the one sure foundation of character, he had said, without courage there is no morality, no religion, no love. 'One cannot follow truth or love so long as one is subject to fear.' With all his horror of violence, he had told us that 'cowardice is a thing even more hateful than violence'. And 'discipline is the pledge and the guarantee that a man means business. There is no deliverance and no hope without sacrifice, discipline and self-control. Mere sacrifice without discipline will be unavailing.' Words only and pious phrases perhaps, rather platitudinous, but there was power behind the words, and India knew that this little man meant business. ...

The industrial age has brought many evils that loom large before us; but we are apt to forget that, taking the world as a whole, and especially the parts that are most industrialized, it has laid down a basis of well-being which makes cultural and spiritual progress far easier for large numbers. This is not at all evident in India or other colonial countries as we have not profited by industrialism. We have only been exploited by it and in many respects made worse, even materially, and more so culturally and spiritually. The fault is not of industrialism but of foreign domination. The so-called Westernization in India has actually, for the time being, strengthened feudalism, and instead of solving any of our problems has simply intensified them.

This has been our misfortune, and we must not allow it to colour our vision of the world today. For under present conditions the rich man is no longer a necessary or desirable part of the productive system or of society as a whole. He is redundant and he is always coming in the way. And the old business of the priest to ask the rich man to be charitable and the poor to be resigned, grateful for their lot, thrifty and well-behaved, has lost its meaning. Human resources have grown tremendously and can face and solve the world's problems. Many of the rich have become definitely parasitical and the existence of a parasite class is not only a hindrance but an enormous waste of these resources. That class and the system that breeds them actually prevent work and production and encourage the workless at either end of the scale, both those who live on other people's labour and those who have no work to do and famish. Gandhiji himself wrote some time ago: 'To a people famishing and idle, the only acceptable form in which God dare appear is work and promise of food as wages. God created man to work for his food, and said that those who ate without work were thieves.'

To try to understand the complex problems of the modern world by an application of ancient methods and formulae when these problems did not exist, is to produce a confusion and to invite failure. The very idea of private property, which seems to some people one of the fundamental notions of the world, has been an ever-changing one. Slaves were property at one time, and so were women and children, the seigneur's right to the bride's first night, roads, temples, ferries, public utilities, air and land. Animals are still property, though legislation has in many countries limited the right of ownership. During wartime there is a continuous infringement of property rights. Property today is becoming more and more intangible, the possession of shares, a certain amount of credit, etc. As the conception of property changes, the State interferes more and more, public opinion demands, and the law enforces, a limitation on the anarchic rights of property-owners. All manner of heavy taxes, which are in the nature of confiscation, swallow up individual property rights for the public good. The public good becomes the basis of public policy, and a man may not act contrary to this public good even to protect his property rights. After all, the vast majority of people had no property rights in the past, they were themselves property owned by others. Even today a very small number have such rights. We hear a great deal of vested interests. Today a new vested interest has come to be recognized, that of every man and woman to live and labour and enjoy the fruits of labour. Because these changing conceptions of property and capital do not vanish, they are diffused, and the power over others, which a concentration of them gave to a few, is taken back by society as a whole.

Gandhiji wants to improve the individual internally, morally and spiritually, and thereby to change the external environment. He wants people to give up bad habits and indulgences and to become pure. He lays stress on sexual abstinence, on the giving up of drink, smoking, etc. Opinions may differ about the relative wickedness of these indulgences, but can there be any doubt that even from the individual point of view, and much more so from the social, these personal failings are less harmful than covetousness, selfishness, acquisitiveness, the fierce conflicts of individuals for personal gain, the ruthless struggles of groups and classes, the inhuman suppression and exploitation of one group by another, the terrible wars between nations? Of course he detests all this violence and degrading conflict. But are they not inherent in the acquisitive society of today with its law that the strong must prey on the weak, and its motto, that, as of old, 'they shall take who have the power and they shall keep who can'? The profit motive today inevitably leads to conflict. The whole system protects and gives every scope to man's predatory instincts; it encourages some finer instincts no doubt, but much more so the baser instincts of man. Success means the knocking down of others and mount-

286

ing on their vanquished selves. If these motives and ambitions are encouraged by society and attract the best of our people, does Gandhiji think he can achieve his ideal – the moral man – in this environment? He wants to develop the spirit of service; he will succeed in the case of some individuals, but so long as society puts forward as exemplars the victors of an acquisitive society and the chief urge is the personal profit motive, the vast majority of mankind will follow this course.

But the problem is no longer a moral or an ethical one. It is a practical and urgent problem of today, for the world is in a hopeless muddle, and some way out must be found. We cannot wait, Micawber-like, for something to turn up. Nor can we live by negation alone, criticizing the evil aspects of capitalism, socialism, communism, etc., and hoping vaguely for the golden mean, which will produce a happy compromise combining the best features of all systems, old and new. The malady has to be diagnosed and the cure suggested and worked for. It is quite certain that we cannot stand where we are, nationally and internationally; we may try to get back or we may push forward. Probably there is no choice in the matter, for going back seems inconceivable.

And yet many of Gandhiji's activities might lead one to think that he wants to go back to the narrowest autarchy, not only a self-sufficient nation, but almost a self-sufficient village. In primitive communities the village was more or less self-sufficient and fed and clothed itself and otherwise provided for its needs. Of necessity that means an extremely low standard of living. I do not think Gandhiji is permanently aiming at this, for it is an impossible objective. The huge populations of today would not be able even to subsist in some countries, they would not tolerate this reversion to scarcity and starvation. It is possible, I think, that in an agricultural country like India, so very low is our present standard, that there might be a slight improvement for the masses with the development of village industries. But we are tied up, as every country is tied up, with the rest of the world, and it seems to me quite impossible for us to cut adrift. We must think, therefore, in terms of the world, and in these terms a narrow autarchy is out of the question. Personally I consider it undesirable from every point of view.

Inevitably we are led to the only possible solution – the establishment of a socialist order, first within national boundaries, and eventually in the world as a whole, with controlled production and distribution of wealth for the public good. How this is to be brought about is another matter, but it is clear that the good of a nation or of mankind must not be held up because some people who profit by the existing order object to the change. If political or social institutions stand in the way of such a change, they have to be removed. To compromise with them at the cost of that desirable and practical ideal would be a gross betrayal. Such a change may partly be forced or expedited by world conditions, but it can hardly take place without the willing consent or acquiescence of the great majority of the people concerned. They have therefore to be converted and won over to it. Conspiratorial violence of a small group will not help. Naturally, efforts must be made to win over even those who profit by the existing system, but it is highly unlikely that any large percentage of them will be converted.

The khadi movement,* hand-spinning and hand-weaving, which is Gandhiji's special favourite, is an intensification of individualism in production, and is thus a throwback to the pre-industrial age. As a solution of any vital present-day problems it cannot be taken seriously, and it produces a mentality which may become an obstacle to growth in the right direction. Nevertheless, as a temporary measure, I am convinced that it has served a useful purpose, and it is likely to be helpful for some time to come, so long as the State itself does not undertake the rightful solution of agrarian and industrial problems on a country-wide scale. There is tremendous unrecorded unemployment in India and even greater partial unemployment in rural areas. No attempt has been made by the State to combat this unemployment, or help in any way the unemployed. Economically khadi has been of some little help to these wholly and partially unemployed, and because this improvement has

*The movement for spinning and weaving cloth in every home.

288

come from their own efforts it has raised their self-respect and given them some feeling of self-confidence. The most marked result has indeed been a psychological one. Khadi tried with some success to bridge the gap between the city and the village. It brought nearer to each other the middle-class intelligentsia and the peasantry. Clothing has a marked psychological effect on the wearer as well as the beholder, and the adoption of the simple white khadi dress by the middle classes resulted in a growth of simplicity, a lessening of vulgarity and ostentation, and a feeling of unity with the masses. The lower middle classes no longer tried to ape the richer classes in the matter of clothes or feel humiliated in their cheaper attire. Indeed they felt not only dignified but a little superior to those who still flaunted silks and satins. Even the poorest felt something of this dignity and self-respect. It was difficult in a large gathering to distinguish between the rich and the poor, and a spirit of camaraderie grew up. Khadi undoubtedly helped Congress to reach the masses. It became the uniform of national freedom. ...

In spite of all these present-day advantages of the khadi movement in India it seems to me after all a transitional affair. It may continue even later as an auxiliary movement easing the change-over to a higher economy. But the main drive in the future will have to be a complete overhauling of the agrarian system and the growth of industry. No tinkering with the land and a multitude of commissions costing lakhs of rupees and suggesting trivial changes in the superstructure, will do the slightest good. The land system which we have is collapsing before our eyes, and it is a hindrance to production, distribution and any rational and large-scale operations. Only a radical change in it, putting an end to the little holdings and introducing organized collective and cooperative enterprises, and thus increasing the yield greatly with much less effort, will meet modern conditions. The land will not and cannot absorb all our people, and large-scale operations will (as Gandhiji fears) lessen the workers required on the land. The others must turn, partly it may be, to small-scale industry, but in the main to large-scale socialized industries and social services.

289

Khadi has certainly brought some relief in many areas, but this very success it has attained has an element of danger. It means that it is propping up a decaying land system and delaying, to that extent, the change-over to a better system. The effect is not substantial enough to make a marked difference, but the tendency is there. . . .

If we consider non-violence and all it implies from the religious, dogmatic point of view there is no room for argument. It reduces itself to the narrow creed of a sect which people may or may not accept. It loses vitality and application to present-day problems. But if we are prepared to discuss it in relation to existing conditions it can help us greatly in our attempts to refashion this world. This consideration must take into account the nature and weaknesses of collective man. Any activity on a mass scale, and especially any activity aimed at radical and revolutionary changes, is affected not only by what the leaders think of it but by existing conditions and, still more, by what the human material they work with thinks about it.

Violence has played a great part in human history. It is today playing an equally important part, and probably it will continue to do so for a considerable time. Most of the changes in the past have been caused by violence and coercion. W. E. Gladstone once said: 'I am sorry to say that if no instructions had been addressed in political crises to the people of this country except to remember to hate violence, to love order, and to exercise patience, the liberties of this country would never have been attained.'

It is impossible to ignore the importance of violence in the past and present. To do so is to ignore life. Yet violence is undoubtedly bad and brings an unending trail of evil consequences with it. And worse even than violence are the motives of hatred, cruelty, revenge and punishment which very often accompany violence. Indeed violence is bad not intrinsically, but because of these motives that go with it. There can be violence without these motives; there can be violence for a good object as well as for an evil object. But it is extremely difficult to separate violence from these motives, and therefore it is desirable to avoid violence as far as possible. In avoiding it, however, one cannot accept a negative attitude of submitting to other and far greater evils. Submission to violence or the acceptance of an unjust regime based on violence, is the very negation of the spirit of non-violence. The non-violent method, in order to justify itself, must be dynamic and capable of changing such a regime or social order.

Whether it can do so or not I do not know. It can, I think, carry us a long way, but I doubt if it can take us to the final goal. In any event, some form of coercion seems to be inevitable, for people who hold power and privilege do not give them up till they are forced to do so, or till conditions are created which make it more harmful to them to keep these privileges than to give them up. The present conflicts in society, national as well as class conflicts, can never be resolved except by coercion. Conversion, of course, there must be on a large scale, for so long as large numbers are not converted there can be no real basis for a movement of social change. But coercion over some will follow. Nor is it right for us to cover up these basic conflicts and try to make out that they do not exist. This is only a suppression of the truth, but it directly leads to bolstering up the existing order by misleading people as to the true facts, and giving the ruling classes the moral basis which they are always seeking in order to justify their special privileges. In order to combat an unjust system the false premises on which it is based must be exposed and the reality laid bare. One of the virtues of non-cooperation is that it exposes these false premises and lies by our refusal to submit to them or to cooperate in their furtherance.

Our final aim can only be a classless society with equal economic justice and opportunity for all, a society organized on a planned basis for the raising of mankind to higher material and cultural levels, to a cultivation of spiritual values, of cooperation, unselfishness, the spirit of service, the desire to do right, goodwill and love – ultimately a world of order. Everything that comes in the way will have to be removed, gently if possible, forcibly if necessary. And there seems to be little doubt that coercion will often be necessary.

5. MOHANDAS GANDHI

*

Freedom for the People *

Born on 2 October 1889 (three years after Sun Yat-sen, a year before Lenin) Mohandas Gandhi, when he was assassinated in 1948, was the most distinguished citizen of the independent India he had above all others helped to bring into being. He was probably also, of all persons in the Third World, the best known at that time. Gandhi knew the Indian people very well, and he was a master of the political tactics he considered necessary in the struggle to achieve the end of British rule in India. The Indian National Congress became virtually a new organization from the time he returned to India in 1915, after his stay abroad. His readiness to resort to direct mass action, his adoption of the loin-cloth as his regular dress, his personal disregard for caste and religious differences, his personal courage, all gave a new style to Indian nationalist politics. But the task he set himself of freeing a society as vast and complex as India raises, as the last reading suggests, questions about the adequacy of his tactics. Did he examine the traditional social structure of India radically enough to discover what changes were demanded by the need for emancipating the poor for whom he cared so deeply? One form in which Gandhi and his followers protested against what they saw as Britain's economic ruining of the Indian people was the renunciation, and the burning, of clothes manufactured abroad, and the wearing of nationally manufactured products. To this campaign the poet and philosopher Rabindranath Tagore objected, on the ground that 'we must refuse to accept as our ally the illusion-haunted magic-ridden slave-mentality that is at the root of all the poverty and insult under which our country groans'. Gandhi responded with an article in the journal *Young India* (August, 1921) from which the following excerpt is taken. He explains the objectives of the national campaign for the widespread use of so primitive a tool as the *charka*, the spinning wheel, and defends the enthusiasm of his youthful followers.

*From *Young India*, August 1921.

WHEN there is war, the poet lays down the lyre, the lawyer his law reports, the schoolboy his books. The poet will sing the true note after the war is over, the lawyer will have occasion to go to his law-books when people have time to fight among themselves. When a house is on fire, all the inmates go out, and each one takes up a bucket to quench the fire. When all about me are dying for want of food, the only occupation permissible to me is to feed the hungry. It is my conviction that India is a house on fire because its manhood is being daily scorched, it is dying of hunger because it has no work to buy food with. Khulna* is starving not because the people cannot work, but because they have no work. The Ceded Districts are passing through a fourth famine. Orissa is a land suffering from chronic famines. Our cities are not India. India lives in her seven and a half lakhs of villages, and the cities live upon the villages. They do not bring their wealth from other countries. The city people are brokers and commission agents for the big houses of Europe, America and Japan. The cities have cooperated with the latter in the bleeding process that has gone on for the past two hundred years. It is my belief based on experience that India is daily growing poorer. The circulation about her feet and legs has about stopped. And if we do not take care, she will collapse altogether.

To a people famishing and idle, the only acceptable form in which God can dare appear is work and promise of food as wages. God created man to work for his food, and said that those who are without work were thieves. Eighty per cent of India are compulsorily thieves half the year. Is it any wonder if India has become one vast prison? Hunger is the argument that is driving India to the spinning wheel. The call of the spinning wheel is the noblest of all. Because it is the call of love. And love is Swaraj. The spinning wheel will 'curb the mind' when the time spent on necessary physical labour can be said to do so. We must think of millions who are today less than animals, who are almost in a dying state. The spinning wheel is the reviving draught for the millions of our dying countrymen and countrywomen. 'Why should I who have no need to

* South-east Bengal.

293

work for food, spin?' may be the question asked. Because I am eating what does not belong to me. I am living on the spoliation of my countrymen. Trace the course of every piece that finds its way into your pocket, and you will realize the truth of what I write. Swaraj has no meaning for the millions if they do not know how to employ their enforced idleness. The attainment of Swaraj is possible within a short time and it is so possible only by the revival of the spinning wheel.

I do want growth. I do want self-determination. I do want freedom, but I want all these for the soul. I doubt if the steel age is an advance upon the flint age. I am indifferent. It is the evolution of the soul to which the intellect and all our faculties have to be devoted. I have no difficulty in imagining the possibility of a man armoured after the modern style making some lasting and new discovery for mankind, but I have less difficulty in imagining the possibility of a man having nothing but a bit of flint and a nail for lighting his path or his matchlock ever singing new hymns of praise and delivering to an aching world a message of peace and goodwill upon earth. A plea for the spinning wheel is a plea for recognizing the dignity of labour.

It was our love of foreign cloth that ousted the wheel from its position of dignity. Therefore I consider it a sin to wear foreign cloth.

6. TRUONG CHINH

*

People's Power and Just Wars *

Political and ethical issues of a related nature are raised in a different way by Truong Chinh (see p. 92), when he talks about the preservation and armed defence of Vietnamese independence. The first of the two passages is from *The August Revolution*, from which we have already had an excerpt; the other is from an English translation of articles written in 1947 during the war against the French.

Independence in Every Respect

WHAT is complete independence? The whole of Vietnam from Muc Nam Quan to Ca Mau must be placed under the people's power organized by the people; there should be no foreign troops on the territory of Vietnam; Vietnamese economy must be independent, not tied to French economy or that of any country; Vietnam must develop its national culture. In a word, the Vietnamese people must be the masters of their country in every respect and the Revolution for national liberation must complete its task of shattering all imperialist bonds.

The Just War of Resistance

In history, there are two kinds of wars: just wars and unjust wars. Just wars are wars against oppressors and conquerors to safeguard the freedom and independence of the peoples. Unjust wars are wars aimed at the seizure of territories, at usurpation of the freedom and happiness of the majority of the people of such territories.

Our people are fighting the reactionary French colonialists in order to regain freedom and independence, to defend and liberate themselves; therefore, our resistance war is a revolu-

*From *The August Revolution* (Hanoi: Foreign Languages Publishing House, 1946).

295

tionary war, a people's war of self-defence, a just and progressive war. On the other hand, the French colonialists are invading our country with the aim of oppressing and exploiting our people as before; therefore, the aggressive war of the French colonialists is an unjust and reactionary war. . . .

A just war always enjoys warm support from people of goodwill, and from progressive nations all over the world. Sound public opinion and the peace-loving peoples always spurn and hold in contempt an unjust war.

We are not surprised that, so far, world opinion has not supported France, but that on the contrary, many countries (especially India, Burma, Indonesia and Malaya) uphold and encourage us. This is one of the many factors which weaken the morale of the French soldiers and strengthen the determination of our army.

On the other hand, although the August Revolution won power for the Vietnamese people, it did not completely liberate the whole country. The present resistance war will fulfil the task of national liberation.

Though the August Revolution set up the regime of the Democratic Republic of Vietnam, this regime is not yet perfect. The present resistance war will extend and consolidate the democratic republican regime of Vietnam and develop it on the basis of new democracy.

That is why Vietnam's armed resistance has not only the character of national liberation, but also that of new democracy. Is it not part of the great democratic movement now blazing forth throughout the world?

7. DUNDUZU CHISIZA

*

A World of Diversity on Indigenous Foundations*

In the transition from the state of being subject to foreign powers and cultures to that of realizing authentic independence in the modern world can particular traditional values survive? Can what indigenous traditions have done to enrich and dignify life have value in the post-colonial, technologically modern age? Dunduzu Chisiza (1930–62) who was General Secretary of the Malawi National Congress and then a senior administrator in Nyasaland (as it was at the time of his early death) explains the determination of Africans to preserve the African outlook as a force making for modern African states controlled by their own people. Chisiza's discussion of the African personality continues what was begun in the Nineteenth Century by Edward Blyden.

DIFFERENT as colonial and free Africa may appear to be in temper, in immediate objectives, and in some of the problems which they face, they have one thing in common, and that is their determination to preserve the substance of the African outlook. It is true that there is no uniform outlook. But it is possible to single out certain features which are always present in almost every African community.

Unlike easterners, who are given to meditation, or westerners, who have an inquisitive turn of mind, we of Africa, belonging neither to the East nor to the West, are fundamentally observers, penetrating observers, relying more on intuition than on the process of reasoning. We excel in neither mysticism nor in science and technology, but in the field of human relations. This is where we can set an example for the rest of the world. Since time immemorial we have never claimed to have penetrated to the heart of truth. As a result we believe that there is a lot to be learned from other

*From *The Journal of Modern African Studies*, vol. 1, no. 1.

cultures. That is why novelty has such a great pull for us, and that is why we do not impose our beliefs on other people.

There is a tendency in the West, whether the westerners themselves know it or not, for people to assume that man lives to work. We believe that man works to live. This view of life has given rise to our high preference for leisure. With us, life has always meant the pursuit of happiness rather than the pursuit of beauty or truth. We pursue happiness by rejecting isolationism, individualism, negative emotions, and tensions, on the one hand, and by laying emphasis on a communal way of life, by encouraging positive emotions and habitual relaxation, and by restraining our desires, on the other. We live our lives in the present. To us the past is neither a source of pride nor a cause of bitterness. The 'hereafter', we realize, must be given thought, but we fail to revel in its mysteries.

Our attitude to religion has more often than not been determined by our habitual desire for change. We adhere to a religious faith only so long as it is the only faith we know. If some other faith comes our way we do not insulate ourselves against its influence. The result is that often we are reconverted, to the dismay of those who converted us first. Sometimes we linger undecided between two faiths while at other times we just marvel at the claims of various religious persuasions. That we behave in this way is no proof that we are fickle; rather it is an indication of the fact that in each one of the religious faiths which we encounter there is an element of divine truth whose fascination we fail to resist. And this is as it should be, for religion is one. Iqbal has told us, 'There is only one religion but there are many versions of it'. Rumi has said, 'There are many lamps but the light is one'.*

In Africa, we believe in strong family relations. We have been urged by well-meaning foreigners to break these ties for one reason or another. No advice could be more dangerous to the fabric of our society. Charity begins at home. So does the love of our fellow-human beings. By loving our parents, our brothers, our sisters, cousins, aunts, uncles, nephews,

* Mohamad Iqbal (1876–1938), a distinguished Indian Muslim poet and philosopher. Rumi (1207–73) was one of the great Persian poets.

and nieces, and by regarding them as members of our families, we cultivate the habit of loving lavishly, of exuding human warmth, of compassion, and of giving and helping. But I believe that, once so conditioned, one behaves in this way not only to one's family, but also to the clan, the tribe, the nation, and to humanity as a whole.

If independent African states succeed in subordinating national loyalties to international loyalty they will do so because they have a solid foundation of lesser loyalties. To foster internationalism among people who are steeped in individualism is to attempt to build a pyramid upside down. It cannot stand, it has no base and will topple over. How can a person who has no real affection for his brothers or sisters have any love for a poor Congolese or Chinese peasant? When we talk about international peace, understanding and goodwill, we are actually talking about universal love. But this does not grow from nothing; its root is family love, without which it cannot grow. The unification of mankind ultimately depends on the cultivation of family love. It would seem, therefore, that in this respect we in Africa have started towards that noble goal from the right end.

Although hitherto Africans have been the least involved in the strains and stresses of international wars, the threat of nuclear war has the same perturbing effects on us as it has on the rest of mankind. In the past we have lagged behind in various walks of life. We have now rolled up our sleeves; we are bending down to do a good job of work, to develop our countries and to make up for lost time. But it is at this very moment in history that the threat of the indiscriminate annihilation of the human race looms on the horizon.

We condemn war because it interferes with man's development, because it causes untold yet avoidable human suffering, and because it is unnatural to man. We believe that in the final analysis war is a habit. Those people who engage in wars are people who, on the one hand, have conditioned themselves to answer provocation with guns and bombs and who, on the other, have become unconsciously addicted to the rhythm: war – peace – war – peace. When peace goes on for a considerable period they get bored with it; they unconsciously want a change, they want something exciting, sensational – war.

Wars are not usually waged when the politicians are busy building nations. They are indulged in when the party in power has run out of useful development ideas. They are possible because there is no effective authority above the nation-state. In Africa tribal wars were possible only in the absence of a higher authority above the tribe-state. As soon as colonial powers set up national governments 'to maintain peace, law, and order', tribal warfare bade us good-bye. It is an irony of fate that those who prescribed this antidote for the ills of Africa hesitate to treat their own ills with it. To secure the outbreak of peace on our planet we must uncondition ourselves; we must learn to answer provocation not with bombs but with tolerance, forgiveness, and love; we must change our governments just before they have finished executing their major projects; and we must form an international government charged only with the duty of maintaining world-wide peace, law, and order.

In human relations, we like to slur over 'I' and 'mine', and to lay emphasis instead on 'we' and 'our'. Put differently, this means the suppression of individuals. Ours is a society where if you found seven men, and one woman amongst them, you might never know, unless told, whose wife she was. There just isn't that forwardness in us to indicate our 'personal' ownership of anything. If I happen to have some head of cattle, a car, a house, a daughter, a fishing net, or a farm, it is 'our' net, it is my house, just as it is my brother's, my father's, my cousin's, my uncle's, or my friend's house. Individualism is foreign to us and we are horrified at its sight. We are by nature extroverts.

Love for communal activities is another feature of our outlook. Look at any African game or pastime and you notice right away that its performance calls for more than one person. Our dances are party dances demanding drummers, singers, and dancers. Game hunting is done in parties. (Even those Africans who own guns cannot abandon the habit of taking some friends along with them when going out for a hunt!) The telling of fables and stories calls for a group of boys and girls, not just one or two. Draw-net fishing is done by a group of people. Fishing with hooks is done also in canoe parties, each canoe taking at least two people. The preparation of fields, the weeding, the sowing of seeds, the harvesting, the pounding of food – all these activities are done in parties of either men or women. Even looking after cattle is not a one-man affair. A boy might start out alone from his cattle *kraal* but he is sure to take his cattle to where his fellow-herdsmen are. Beer-drinking is not only a group affair but it often means also drinking from the same pot and from the same drinking stick. Above all, to see Africans mourn the death of someone is to believe that few things are done individually here.

Such an outlook can only emanate from genuine love for each other – and unconscious love which has existed in our society since time immemorial. Here is that selfless love which all the prophets of God have preached. It isn't something that has just been inculcated into us nor anything that has been imported from without us; it is something springing from within us. Instead of foreign missionaries teaching Africans how to love each other, they would do well to sit back and observe with amazement that the very relationship they would like to bring about is already existing in the selfless love manifested in the African way of life.

We are also famous for our sense of humour and dislike for melancholy. Gloom on the face of an African is a sure sign that the wearer of that expression has been to a school of some kind where he might have got it into his head that joy and melancholy can be bed-fellows in his heart. Otherwise our conception of life precludes, as far as possible, the accommodation of dejection. An African will not hesitate to leave a job if he sees that he does not get a kick out of it. Many times I have observed people avoid the intellectual, the reticent type of African as much as they avoid rattlesnakes, if only by so doing they can escape from the melancholy of the intellectual. Even if there are real causes for sorrow, somehow our people manage to make molehills of these and mountains of the causes for happiness. The mainstay of our life is humour. So

301

characteristic of Africa is this that most foreigners know this continent as 'The Land of Laughter'. Of course, laughter relieves tension. People who laugh easily are relaxed persons, and possess one of the most prized qualities in this wearisome world.

Our society abhors malice, revenge, and hate, with the result that we are relatively free from these cankers. Were we disposed to avenge the wrongs that have been meted out to us by foreigners down through the ages, the course of human events would have taken a different turn altogether. Were we addicts of hate, the Gospel of Jesus would have been defeated on the shores of the seas that border this troubled continent. Were we to harbour malice, the African empires that flourished – like those of Monomotapa, Songhai, Mali, and Ghana – would have extended beyond the confines of Africa to the detriment of the human race. But God spared us all that. As a result we tolerate on our soil even neurotic crowds of foreigners who could not be tolerated in their own countries; we waste love on those who are inveterately selfish, individualistic, and ungrateful. Above all, we do not look forward to planning nefarious schemes against any race.

We have a reputation for taking delight in generosity, kindness, and forgiveness. It has been said with great truth by foreigners that few Africans will ever get rich because we tend to be too generous. Well, we do not want to be rich at the cost of being mean! Our society hinges on the practice of mutual aid and cooperation, whose corollary is generosity. When our chiefs and kings gave acres and acres of land to foreigners they were not prompted by bribes or stupidity, but by this self-same habit of generosity – the life-blood of our society. Even more precious, I think, is our spirit of kindness. For me to be able to walk into the home of any African between Khartoum and Durban and be certain to be accorded the utmost hospitality is to my mind a pulsating example of what quality of human relationship our society is capable of producing.

Nor is the scope of our kindness limited to our own race. Many are the days when we have preserved the life of one

302

foreigner or another. Times without number we have gone out of our way to hunt for water, eggs, milk, chicken, fish, meat, fruit, and vegetables for a choosy stranger. We have carried literally thousands of foreigners on our heads and shoulders; we have washed their clothes; we have reared their children; we have looked after their homes; we have stood by their sides in peril; we have defended them in times of war; we have given them our land, we have given them our precious minerals, nay, we have given them our all. But the gratitude we often get is ridicule, contempt, ill-treatment, and the belief on their part that God created us to be 'hewers of wood and drawers of water'. No. God knows our kindness does not stem from a feeling of inferiority. God knows we are not kind because we are fools, but because He ordained that we should be kindness-drunk rather than pride-drunk.

And yet, in spite of all this ingratitude, we are still capable of forgiving and forgetting. We are in a position to do this because in our society forgiveness is the rule rather than the exception. ...

Another outstanding characteristic of our outlook is our love for music, dance, and rhythm. This three-pronged phenomenon is indeed the spice of our life. Our throats are deep with music, our legs full of dance, while our bodies tremble with rhythm. We sing while we hoe. We sing while we paddle our canoes. Our mourning is in the form of dirges; we sing in bereavement just as on festive occasions. Our fables nearly always include a song. We sing to while away the monotonous hours of travel. The pulse of our drums evokes in us song responses. We sing under the canopy of the blue sky, we sing through moonlit nights. Gramophone music entrances us not because it is foreign or something unusual, but just because it is music.

We have war dances, victory dances, remedial dances, marriage dances, dances for women only, mixed dances, dances for the initiated, dances for the young – but all indulged in with ecstatic abandon. We nod our heads, rock our necks, tilt our heads and pause. We shake our shoulders, throw them back and forth, bounce breasts, and halt to intone thanks to him

303

who ordained that we be alive. Dance! What a world of emotions that word calls forth in us!

There is rhythm in the winnowing and pounding of grains, there is rhythm in the gait of our women folk; there is highly-developed rhythm in coition, there is rhythm in the groan of a sick person, there is complex rhythm in milking a cow or pulling a draw-net to the shore; there is rhythm that beggars description in the beats of our tom-toms. The difference between us and other peoples is that we consciously cultivate rhythm in almost everything we do.

Finally, we have a strong dislike for imposing our beliefs on other people. British people established themselves overseas with the self-assuredness of angels. They believed with puritanical fervour that the British way was the God-vouchsafed way of doing things. Their way of living was what mankind was destined to evolve up to; their ideas the gospel truth; their beliefs the paragons of man's triumph over 'superstition'. No other way – least of all the colonial people's way – could measure up to it, still less be better than it. So they believed there was nothing for them to learn from their colonial subjects, while the colonial indigenes had to be recast into the British mode of life, thought, and belief.

That was all very well for purposes of empire building. To rule a people successfully you have got to drill it into their heads that you are in every way superior to them and that, therefore, it is the right thing for them to be under you. But that way of thinking tends to arrest progress. The advancement of man uncompromisingly demands a ceaseless synthesis of ideas, a blending of ways of living, a give and take of beliefs, and above all a willingness to believe that the best is yet to come.

If persisted in, this attitude of finality, superiority, and self-deception can only promote hate and racial discord. When other peoples do not assert themselves, they may still have something to be proud of, something that they believe is unrivalled, but it is just that they have not got the same vulgarity of throwing their weight about and imposing themselves and their beliefs on other people. They are willing to live and let live. Further, they have the satisfaction of knowing that a listener with an open mind has the 'open sesame' to the fortune of knowledge and wisdom. There is a great deal that foreigners, in Africa as well as overseas, have to learn from the colonial peoples.

Such are the currents and cross-currents of emotions which help to determine the shape of things in Africa. If we do not accept the good advice of foreign experts, if we are lackadaisical towards certain of their brilliant ideas, and if we do not get on well with some of them, it may be because of the things mentioned above. The experts do not stand to lose anything if their advice is not acted upon. We should be the losers. However, since most experts want to feel, as we should expect them to, that their efforts to help fellow-human beings are bearing fruit, they might do a lot worse than take time off to gain insight into our aspirations, outlook, and problems, so that they might be better equipped to render advice which will be readily acceptable.

8. JULIUS NYERERE

*

Original Rather than Ready-Made Solutions*

What Nehru said at the Bandung Conference about the Afro-Asian determination not to be camp-followers of the two super-power *blocs* is developed in the following passage from a talk to students by Julius Nyerere (see p. 125) in 1961 entitled 'Groping Forward'. He relates this to the question of democracy in a situation where 'new forms of social construction' have to be conceived and created by the community.

W E have committed ourselves to building in this country a society very different from the present one. We struggled to get independence so that we could do something about improving the conditions under which our people live. Now that we have an opportunity to begin this work, we find ourselves in a divided world, each side anxious to involve us in the conflict so as to increase their strength.

I have said before that we do not intend to be involved in these power conflicts; we care too much about the progress of mankind to allow this to happen. The intensity of the international conflict – the heat of the Cold War – which makes powerful nations anxious to get even so new and poor a country as Tanganyika on their side, results from the arrogant assumption on both sides that they have evolved the perfect pattern of society. They believe that all that remains to be done is to get this 'perfect society' implemented in all parts of the world; conflict arises because the other people hold, equally fanatically, to their different version of the perfect society.

We reject this attitude. It implies that the human race has developed socially as far as it can; that mankind has no need to continue his struggle towards divinity. All that it has to do is

*From *Freedom and Unity – Uhuru na Umoja* (Oxford: O.U.P., 1967).

to adopt universally a form of social organization already existing in some part of the world. Quite apart from the physical dangers the world now faces, consequent to this belief, the emotional attitude brings great danger to the progress of Man. There is no standing still in life; even the most primitive biological cell experiences constant change. Society, like everything else, must either move or stagnate – and in stagnation lies death. A mind unused atrophies, and man without mind is nothing.

At present the very existence of conflict about which of two different forms of social organization is perfection, does cause the protagonists to think, and thus to develop. But it restricts their thinking to certain channels, and results in the development of warped and neurotic men and societies. Thinking about the development of new material goods, and about new forms of mass destruction continues unabated; but thinking about new forms of social construction is already becoming inhibited, not only in frankly dictatorial countries, but also in the others. The fear of losing this priceless possession – the final solution to the problems of man in society – causes increasing social pressure to be placed on the man who does not wish to conform to the ideas and attitudes of the people surrounding him. The intellectual freedom of man, without which progress cannot take place, is confined by the prison wall of dogmatism. All international and other problems of man's relations with his fellows are then considered on the basis of whether or not the people involved are on the side of the 'ultimate truth'; the issue becomes secondary.

We in Tanganyika do not believe that mankind has yet discovered ultimate truth – in any field. We do not wish to act as if we did have such a belief. We wish to contribute to Man's development if we can, but we do not claim to have any 'solution'; our only claim is that we intend to grope forward in the dark, towards a goal so distant that even the real understanding of it is beyond us – towards, in other words, the best that man can become.

This means that the people who anxiously watch to see whether we will become 'Communist' or 'Western Democrats' will both be disconcerted. We do not have to be either. We shall grope forward, and it may be that we shall create a new synthesis of individual liberty and the needs of man in society; freedom for each individual to develop the spark of divinity within himself at the same time as he contributes and benefits from his membership of a community.

9. MAO TSE-TUNG

*

Revolutionary Leadership and the
Good of the Whole People *

What Julius Nyerere was talking about has long been one of the main preoccupations in the thought and work of Mao Tse-tung. For Mao, however, the elimination of dogmatism and search for truth is less a matter of groping forward than of struggle against contradictions. He has insisted that democracy is the right to rebel against, and to overthrow, the old order, in which, according to him, 'it was right to oppress, it was right to exploit, and it was wrong to rebel'; and on his insistence on the 'truths' of Marxism he has in his long career been willing to compromise for only short periods. A political philosophy which is popularly discussed in such terms as 'serve the people', 'putting politics in command', 'from the masses, to the masses', 'antagonistic and non-antagonistic contradictions', the struggle between oppressors and oppressed, counter-revolutionary violence and revolutionary counter-violence, the world as belonging to the people, etc., has claims also to being the most substantial body of contemporary political teaching originating in the Third World. No attempt can be made here to illustrate the range of its thoughts on goals, values, strategy in the modernization of predominantly peasant masses in the given historical conditions. The first two of the three excerpts given below are from Mao's important speech in 1957 'On the Correct Handling of Contradictions among the People'. (Mao's ideas met with resistance from some influential colleagues, but this statement of revolutionary principles was reaffirmed during the Cultural Revolution.) The third is a saying which was quoted in the newspaper of the People's Liberation Army in August 1967. It was the serious determination of the Maoists to take their revolutionary principles seriously that led to the upheaval of the Cultural Revolution.

*From *On the Correct Handling of Contradictions Among the People* (Peking: Foreign Languages Press, revised translation, 1966).

Socialist Democracy and 'Truth'

'LET a hundred flowers blossom, let a hundred schools of thought contend' and 'long-term coexistence and mutual supervision' – how did these slogans come to be put forward? They were put forward in the light of China's specific conditions, on the basis of the recognition that various kinds of contradictions still exist in socialist society, and in response to the country's urgent need to speed up its economic and cultural development. Letting a hundred flowers blossom and a hundred schools of thought contend is the policy for promoting the progress of the arts and the sciences and a flourishing socialist culture in our land. Different forms and styles in art should develop freely and different schools in science should contend freely. We think that it is harmful to the growth of art and science if administrative measures are used to impose one particular style of art or school of thought and to ban another. Questions of right and wrong in the arts and sciences should be settled through free discussion in artistic and scientific circles and through practical work in these fields. They should not be settled in summary fashion. A period of trial is often needed to determine whether something is right or wrong. Throughout history, new and correct things have often failed at the outset to win recognition from the majority of people and have had to develop by twists and turns in struggle. Often correct and good things have first been regarded not as fragrant flowers but as poisonous weeds. Copernicus's theory of the solar system and Darwin's theory of evolution were once dismissed as erroneous and had to win through over bitter opposition. Chinese history offers many similar examples. In a socialist society, conditions for the growth of the new are radically different from and far superior to those in the old society. Nevertheless, it still often happens that new, rising forces are held back and rational proposals constricted. Moreover, the growth of new things may be hindered in the absence of deliberate suppression simply through lack of discernment. It is therefore necessary to be careful about questions of right and wrong in the arts and sciences, to encourage free discussion and avoid hasty conclusions. We believe that such an attitude can help to ensure a relatively smooth development of the arts and sciences.

Marxism, too, has developed through struggle. At the beginning, Marxism was subjected to all kinds of attack and regarded as a poisonous weed. It is still being attacked and is still regarded as a poisonous weed in many parts of the world. In the socialist countries, it enjoys a different position. But non-Marxist and, moreover, anti-Marxist ideologies exist even in these countries. In China, although in the main socialist transformation has been completed with respect to the system of ownership, and although the large-scale and turbulent class struggles of the masses characteristic of the previous revolutionary periods have in the main come to an end, there are still remnants of the overthrown landlord and comprador classes, there is still a bourgeoisie, and the remoulding of the petty bourgeoisie has only just started. The class struggle is by no means over. The class struggle between the proletariat and the bourgeoisie, the class struggle between the different politica! forces, and the class struggle in the ideological field between the proletariat and the bourgeoisie will continue to be long and tortuous and at times will even become very acute. The proletariat seeks to transform the world according to its own world outlook, and so does the bourgeoisie. In this respect, the question of which will win out, socialism or capitalism, is still not really settled. Marxists are still a minority among the entire population as well as among the intellectuals. Therefore, Marxism must still develop through struggle. Marxism can develop only through struggle, and not only is this true of the past and the present, it is necessarily true of the future as well. What is correct invariably develops in the course of struggle with what is wrong. The true, the good and the beautiful always exist by contrast with the false, the evil and the ugly, and grow in struggle with the latter. As soon as a wrong thing is rejected and a particular truth accepted by mankind, new truths begin their struggle with new errors. Such struggles will never end. This is the law of development of truth and, naturally, of Marxism as well.

It will take a fairly long period of time to decide the issue in the ideological struggle between socialism and capitalism in our country. The reason is that the influence of the bourgeoisie and of the intellectuals who come from the old society will remain in our country for a long time to come, and so will their class ideology. If this is not sufficiently understood, or is not understood at all, the gravest mistakes will be made and the necessity of waging the struggle in the ideological field will be ignored. Ideological struggle is not like other forms of struggle. The only method to be used in this struggle is that of painstaking reasoning and not crude coercion. Today, socialism is in an advantageous position in the ideological struggle. The main power of the state is in the hands of the working people led by the proletariat. The Communist Party is strong and its prestige stands high. Although there are defects and mistakes in our work, every fair-minded person can see that we are loyal to the people, that we are both determined and able to build up our motherland together with them, and that we have already achieved great successes and will achieve still greater ones. The vast majority of the bourgeoisie and intellectuals who come from the old society are patriotic and are willing to serve their flourishing socialist motherland; they know they will be helpless and have no bright future to look forward to if they turn away from the working people led by the Communist Party.

People may ask, since Marxism is accepted as the guiding ideology by the majority of the people in our country, can it be criticized? Certainly it can. Marxism is scientific truth and fears no criticism. If it did, and if it could be overthrown by criticism, it would be worthless. In fact, aren't the idealists criticizing Marxism every day and in every way? Aren't those who harbour bourgeois and petty-bourgeois ideas and who do not wish to change – aren't they also criticizing Marxism in every way? Marxists should not be afraid of criticism from any quarter. Quite the contrary, they need to temper and develop themselves and win new positions in the teeth of criticism and in the storm and stress of struggle. Fighting against wrong ideas is like being vaccinated – a man develops greater im-

312

munity from disease as a result of vaccination. Plants raised in hot-houses are unlikely to be sturdy. Carrying out the policy of letting a hundred flowers blossom and a hundred schools of thought contend will not weaken but strengthen the leading position of Marxism in the ideological field.

What should our policy be towards non-Marxist ideas? As far as unmistakable counter-revolutionaries and saboteurs of the socialist cause are concerned, the matter is easy: we simply deprive them of their freedom of speech. But incorrect ideas among the people are quite a different matter. Will it do to ban such ideas and deny them an opportunity for expression? Certainly not. It is not only futile but very harmful to use summary methods in dealing with ideological questions among the people, with questions concerned with man's mental world. You may ban the expression of wrong ideas, but the ideas will still be there. On the other hand, if correct ideas are pampered in hot-houses without being exposed to the elements or immunized from disease, they will not win out against erroneous ones. Therefore, it is only by employing the method of discussion, criticism and reasoning that we can really foster correct ideas and overcome wrong ones, and that we can really settle issues.

Overall Planning

By overall planning we mean planning which takes into consideration the interests of the 600 million people of our country. In drawing up plans, handling affairs or thinking over problems, we must proceed from the fact that China has a population of 600 million people, and we must never forget this fact. Why do we make a point of this? Yes, everyone knows this, but when it comes to actual practice, some people forget all about it and act as though the fewer the people, the smaller the circle, the better. Those who have this 'small circle' mentality resist the idea of bringing all positive factors into play, of uniting with everyone that can be united with, and of doing everything possible to turn negative factors into positive ones so as to serve the great cause of building a socialist society. I hope these people will take a wider view and really recognize that we have a population of 600 million, that this is an objective fact, and that it is an asset. Our large population is a good thing, but of course it also involves certain difficulties. Construction is going ahead vigorously on all fronts and very successfully too, but in the present transitional period of tremendous social change there are still many difficult problems. Progress and at the same time difficulties – this is a contradiction. However, not only should contradictions be resolved, but they definitely can be. Our guiding principle is overall planning and proper arrangement. Whatever the problem – whether it concerns food, natural calamities, employment, education, the intellectuals, the united front of all patriotic forces, the minority nationalities, or anything else – we must always proceed from the standpoint of overall planning which takes the whole people into consideration and must make proper arrangements, after consultation with all circles concerned, in the light of the specific possibilities of the particular time and place. On no account should we complain that there are too many people, that they are backward, that things are troublesome and hard to handle, and so shut the problem out. Does this mean that the government alone must take care of everyone and everything? Of course not. In many cases, they can be left to the care of the public organizations or of the masses directly – both are quite capable of devising many good ways of handling things. This also comes within the scope of the principle of overall planning and proper arrangement. We should give guidance to the public organizations and the masses of the people everywhere in this respect.

The Choice of Leaders

It is necessary to train a great many people as vanguards of the revolution. People who are politically far-sighted. People imbued with the spirit of struggle and self-sacrifice. People with largeness of mind who are loyal, active and upright. People who never pursue selfish interests, but are whole-heartedly for the liberation of the nation and society. People who fear no difficulties, but remain steadfast and advance courageously in the face of difficulties. People who are neither high and mighty

314

nor seekers after the limelight, but are conscientious and full of practical sense. If China has large numbers of such vanguards, the tasks of the Chinese revolution can be successfully accomplished.

10. JOSUE DE CASTRO

*

Both Bread and Steel*

Does what Mao Tse-tung has said about the need to take into account the multifarious human requirements of *all* the people apply to other, less populous countries? What follows is a passage from Josue de Castro's discussion of the Brazilian situation. It continues directly from the end of p. 217. De Castro, writing from an ideological position somewhat different from Mao's, develops in other parts of his discussion his demand that 'the tabu of agrarian reform – a dangerous and not quite decent subject – [must be faced] with the same courage with which we confront the tabu of hunger'. 'What [public authorities] must do,' he concludes, 'is to direct our economy towards the goal of the social wellbeing of the whole people.'

ECONOMIC development constitutes the only real solution to the problem of underdevelopment, with its fundamental characteristics of underemployment, underproductivity and general pauperism. Our people have become aware of Brazilian social reality, and this idea-force has taken hold of the masses, that only by real economic development can we free ourselves from the oppression and economic slavery that bear down the majority of our people. No one today can have any other attitude than to cooperate idealistically so that the economic development of our country can proceed at a rapid rate and without distortions. To think otherwise is to serve anti-national interests, it is to play the game of the international trusts, which are interested in holding back the surge of progress in the regions of primary economy, suppliers of raw materials for the great industrial combines that dominate the world economy.

The policy of development represents what is called a

*From Ignacy Sachs (ed.) *Agriculture, Land Reforms and Economic Development* (Warsaw: Polish Scientific Publishers, 1964).

historical necessity, an imperative from which we cannot escape.

We should therefore feel no hesitation as to the necessity and opportunity of a pro-development policy for Brazil. Our doubts and possible divergencies are to be found in the field of execution of this policy, in the elements put into play to animate and orientate our economic emancipation. The government of President Kubitschek, desiring to speed up the rhythm of our economic expansion and impregnated with the idea that only by intensive industrialization can we free ourselves economically, has carried out his programme of goals in such a way as to raise a certain apprehension in our minds, apprehension as to whether the order of priorities for application of our scant economic resources has been the best possible.

We take our place among those who consider it necessary to promote industrial development, but without undue sacrifice of investment in the farm economy sector. Concentration of the whole effort in only one sector is equivalent to stimulating an unbalanced development, and this imbalance, after a certain time, will begin to retard the rate of expansion. Economic planning should take account of a whole integrated economic system, so as to avoid distortions which eventually turn into factors of strangulation. ...

In the task of promoting the economic development of the country, the government stood somewhat perplexed before the dilemma of *bread or steel*, that is, the choice as to whether to invest the scarce available resources in producing consumer goods, or to concentrate them on intensive industrialization, thus sacrificing for a time the people's aspiration for a better life. The predominant tendency among economists is that the whole effort should be concentrated, at the beginning, on steel, on industrialization, while the people are obliged to participate, with their sacrifice, in the work of national recuperation. This is known as paying the cost of progress, which is indispensable to economic emancipation.

Nevertheless, we ought not to exaggerate this cost, or be too dogmatic about it. Social reality is not limited only to economics, but is rather the social-economic expression of a

317

whole people. The solution to the dilemma does not lie in taking care exclusively of bread or of steel, but of attacking the problems of bread and steel simultaneously, in proportions imposed by social circumstances and existing economic resources. Any attempt to require the public to pay the cost for progress beyond what is tolerable runs the risk of creating resentment and dangerous social tensions. It is my impression that the Brazilian people today, imbued with the idea of development and social progress, is prepared to pay its quota of sacrifice so that the country can develop and emancipate itself economically. But it is necessary that this public should be convinced that the sacrifice is equally distributed among all the groups and social classes that make up the nation. And I am not very sure that this is happening. In carrying out its programme of economic development the government should pay more attention to the needs of human groups that live in the agricultural sector. It should also seek to promote a more equitable regional distribution in the field of credit and investment, so that the Brazilian giant does not grow up twisted and crippled. If we aim at the development of only one part of the nation, immolating to this new Moloch the disadvantages and maladjustment of other still more underdeveloped areas, we will falsify the meaning of true economic development, which is the supreme aspiration of the whole Brazilian people.

11. CHOU EN-LAI

*

Mutual Cooperation for Development *

During 1963–4 Chou En-lai (b. 1898) who, since he became Prime Minister of China in 1949 had been concerned mainly with national reconstruction, made an extended tour of the rest of the Afro-Asian region. He had discussions with Presidents Nasser (Egypt) and Ben Bella (Algeria), King Hassan of Morocco, Presidents Bourguiba (Tunisia), Nkrumah (Ghana), Keita (Mali), Sekou Touré (Guinea), Abboud (Sudan), Emperor Haile Selassie (Ethiopia) and Prime Minister Ali Shermake (Somalia), before going on to see General Ne Win (Burma), President Ayub Khan (Pakistan) and Mrs Bandaranaike (Ceylon). One of the most important statements of the tour was his speech at Mogadishu, in Somalia, in February 1964, in the course of which he gave an authoritative explanation of China's principles in giving and receiving foreign aid for development.

IN order to consolidate their national independence, it is necessary for the new emerging Asian–African countries to develop their national economies and gradually remove the poverty and backwardness caused by colonial domination. In order to develop their national economies, it is necessary for the Asian and African countries to rely, first of all, on their own efforts, on the strength of their own peoples and on the full use of their own resources. Self-reliance does not preclude foreign aid and it is also necessary to have economic cooperation among all friendly countries. The important thing is that all foreign aid and economic cooperation should conform to the principle of equality and mutual benefit with no privileges and conditions attached. This aid and cooperation should really help to develop the independent national economy and should not be a means to control and manacle the Afro-Asian countries.

*From *Afro-Asian Solidarity Against Imperialism* (Peking: Foreign Languages Press, 1964).

In providing economic aid to other countries, the Chinese Government has always strictly abided by the following eight principles: One, the Chinese Government always bases itself on the principle of equality and mutual benefit in providing aid to other countries. It never regards such aid as a kind of unilateral alms but as something mutual and helpful to economic cooperation. Two, in providing aid to other countries, the Chinese government strictly respects the sovereignty and independence of the recipient countries, and never attaches any conditions or asks for any privileges. Three, China provides economic aid in the form of interest-free or low-interest loans and extends the time limit for the repayment when necessary so as to lighten the burden of the recipient countries as far as possible. Four, in providing aid to other countries, the purpose of the Chinese Government is not to make the recipient countries dependent on China but to help them embark step by step on the road of self-reliance and independent economic development. Five, the Chinese Government tries its best to help the recipient countries build projects which require less investment while yielding quicker results so that the recipient governments may increase their income and accumulate capital. Six, the Chinese Government provides the best quality equipment and material of its own manufacture at international market prices. If the equipment and material provided by the Chinese Government are not up to the agreed specifications and quality, the Chinese Government undertakes to replace them. Seven, in giving any particular technical assistance, the Chinese Government will see to it that the personnel of the recipient country fully master such technique. Eight, the experts and technical personnel despatched by China to help in construction will have the same standard of living as the experts and technical personnel of the recipent country. The Chinese experts and technical personnel are not allowed to make any special demands or enjoy any special amenities.

At present, the mutual aid and economic cooperation between Asian–African countries are still limited in scale. However, inasmuch as we share the same experience and are in similar positions and so best understand each other's needs, our mutual aid and economic cooperation are dependable, conformable to actual needs, equitable and of mutual benefit, and helpful to the independent development of various countries. Along with the development of national construction in Asian–African countries, there is no doubt that this mutual aid and economic cooperation will continuously expand in scope and increase in quantity.

12. FRANTZ FANON

*

Decolonization, National Liberation and Violence as Values*

In 1961 the West Indian psychiatrist, writer and revolutionary Frantz Fanon died, at the age of thirty-six. He had adopted Algeria as his home. By then there were many doubts and questions within the Third World about the process of decolonization. Fanon, because his thinking was genuinely indigenous to the Third World, has become one of the major interpreters of the revolutionary upsurge among its peoples. He committed himself to revolutionary action in the Algerian war of liberation, and his *Studies in a Dying Colonialism* was based on the insights he gained into the revolutionary process. The passages which follow are taken from his more famous *Les Damnés de la Terre (The Wretched of the Earth)*. In them the issues discussed by Nehru, Mao Tse-tung, Chou En-lai and others recur.

Violence and Decolonization

NATIONAL liberation, national renaissance, the restoration of nationhood to the people, commonwealth: whatever may be the headings used or the new formulas introduced, decolonization is always a violent phenomenon. At whatever level we study it – relationships between individuals, new names for sports clubs, the human admixture at cocktail parties, in the police, on the directing boards of national or private banks – decolonization is quite simply the replacing of a certain 'species' of men by another 'species' of men. Without any period of transition, there is a total, complete and absolute substitution. It is true that we could equally well stress the rise of a new nation, the setting up of a new State, its diplomatic relations, and its economic and political trends. But we have precisely chosen to speak of that kind of *tabula rasa* which characterizes at the outset all decolonization. Its unusual im-

*From *The Wretched of the Earth* (London: MacGibbon & Kee, 1965).

portance is that it constitutes, from the very first day, the
minimum demands of the colonized. To tell the truth, the proof
of success lies in a whole social structure being changed from
the bottom up. The extraordinary importance of this change is
that it is willed, called for, demanded. The need for this change
is equally experienced in the form of a terrifying future in the
consciousness of another 'species' of men and women: the
colonizers.

Decolonization, which sets out to change the order of the
world, is, obviously, a programme of complete disorder. But it
cannot come as a result of magical practices, nor of a natural
shock, nor of a friendly understanding. Decolonization, as we
know, is a historical process: that is to say that it cannot be
understood, it cannot become intelligible nor clear to itself
except in the exact measure that we can discern the movements
which give it historical form and content. Decolonization is
the meeting of two forces, opposed to each other by their very
nature, which in fact owe their originality to that sort of sub-
stantification which results from and is nourished by the situation in the colonies. Their first encounter was marked by
violence and their existence together – that is to say the
exploitation of the native by the settler – was carried on
by dint of a great array of bayonets and cannon. The settler
and the native are old acquaintances. In fact, the settler
is right when he speaks of knowing 'them' well. For it is the
settler who has brought the native into existence and who perpetuates his existence. The settler owes the fact of his very
existence, that is to say his property, to the colonial system.

Decolonization never takes place unnoticed, for it influences
individuals and modifies them fundamentally. It transforms
spectators crushed with their inessentiality into privileged
actors, with the grandiose glare of history's floodlights upon
them. It brings a natural rhythm into existence, introduced by
new men, and with it a new language and a new humanity.
Decolonization is the veritable creation of new men. But this
creation owes nothing of its legitimacy to any supernatural
power; the 'thing' which has been colonized becomes man
during the same process by which it frees itself.

In decolonization, there is therefore the need of a complete calling in question of the colonial situation. If we wish to describe it precisely, we might find it in the well-known words: 'The last shall be first and the first last.' Decolonization is the putting into practice of this sentence. That is why, if we try to describe it, all decolonization is successful.

The naked truth of decolonization evokes for us the searing bullets and bloodstained knives which emanate from it. For if the last shall be first, this will only come to pass after a murderous and decisive struggle between the two protagonists. That affirmed intention to place the last at the head of things, and to make them climb at a pace (too quickly, some say) the well-known steps which characterize an organized society, can only triumph if we use all means to turn the scale, including, of course, that of violence.

You do not turn any society, however primitive it may be, upside-down with such a programme if you are not decided from the very beginning, that is to say from the actual formulation of that programme, to overcome all the obstacles you will come across in so doing. The native who decides to put the programme into practice, and to become its moving force, is ready for violence at all times. From birth it is clear to him that this narrow world, strewn with prohibitions, can only be called in question by absolute violence. . . .

As soon as the native begins to pull on his moorings, and to cause anxiety to the settler, he is handed over to well-meaning souls who in cultural congresses point out to him the specificity and wealth of Western values. But every time Western values are mentioned they produce in the native a sort of stiffening or muscular lock-jaw. During the period of decolonization, the native's reason is appealed to. He is offered definite values, he is told frequently that decolonization need not mean regression, and that he must put his trust in qualities which are well-tried, solid and highly esteemed. But it so happens that when the native hears a speech about Western culture he pulls out his knife – or at least he makes sure it is within reach. The violence with which the supremacy of white values is affirmed and the aggressiveness which has permeated the victory of these values

324

over the ways of life and of thought of the native mean that, in revenge, the native laughs in mockery when Western values are mentioned in front of him. In the colonial context the settler only ends his work of breaking in the native when the latter admits loudly and intelligibly the supremacy of the white man's values. In the period of decolonization, the colonized masses mock at these very values, insult them and vomit them up.

This phenomenon is ordinarily masked because, during the period of decolonization, certain colonized intellectuals have begun a dialogue with the bourgeoisie of the colonialist country. During this phase, the indigenous population is discerned only as an indistinct mass. The few native personalities whom the colonialist bourgeois have come to know here and there have not sufficient influence on that immediate discernment to give rise to nuances. On the other hand, during the period of liberation, the colonialist bourgeoisie looks feverishly for contacts with the *élite*, and it is with these *élite* that the familiar dialogue concerning values is carried on. The colonialist bourgeoisie, when it realizes that it is impossible for it to maintain its domination over the colonial countries, decides to carry out a rear-guard action with regard to culture, values, techniques and so on. Now what we must never forget is that the immense majority of colonized peoples is oblivious of these problems. For a colonized people the most essential value, because the most concrete, is first and foremost the land: the land which will bring them bread and, above all, dignity. But this dignity has nothing to do with dignity of the human individual: for that human individual has never heard tell of it. All that the native has seen in his country is that they can freely arrest him, beat him, starve him: and no professor of ethics, no priest has ever come to be beaten in his place, nor to share their bread with him. As far as the native is concerned, morality is very concrete; it is to silence the settler's defiance, to break his flaunting violence – in a word, to put him out of the picture. ...

But it so happens sometimes that decolonization occurs in areas which have not been sufficiently shaken by the struggle for liberation, and there may be found those same know-all, smart, wily intellectuals. We find intact in them the manners and forms of thought picked up during their association with the colonialist bourgeoisie. Spoilt children of yesterday's colonialism and of today's national governments, they organize the loot of whatever national resources exist. Without pity, they use today's national distress as a means of getting on through scheming and legal robbery, by import–export combines, limited liability companies, gambling on the stock-exchange, or unfair promotion. They are insistent in their demands for the nationalization of commerce, that is to say the reservation of markets and advantageous bargains for nationals only. As far as doctrine is concerned, they proclaim the pressing necessity of nationalizing the robbery of the nation. In this arid phase of national life, the so-called period of austerity, the success of their depredations is swift to call forth the violence and anger of the people. For this same people, poverty-stricken yet independent, comes very quickly to possess a social conscience in the African and international context of today; and this the petty individualists will quickly learn.

Violence in the International Context

We have pointed out many times in the preceding pages that in underdeveloped regions the political leader is forever calling on his people to fight: to fight against colonialism, to fight against poverty and underdevelopment, and to fight against sterile traditions. The vocabulary which he uses in his appeals is that of a chief of staff: 'mass mobilization'; 'agricultural front'; 'fight against illiteracy'; 'defeats we have undergone'; 'victories won'. The young independent nation evolves during the first years in an atmosphere of the battlefield, for the political leader of an underdeveloped country looks fearfully at the huge distance his country will have to cover. He calls to the people and says to them: 'Let us gird up our loins and set to work', and the country, possessed by a kind of creative madness, throws itself into a gigantic and disproportionate effort. The programme consists not only of climbing out of the morass but also of catching up with the other nations using the

326

only means at hand. They reason that if the European nations have reached that stage of development, it is on account of their efforts: 'Let us therefore,' they seem to say, 'prove to ourselves and to the whole world that we are capable of the same achievements.' This manner of setting out the problem of the evolution of underdeveloped countries seems to us to be neither correct nor reasonable.

The European states achieved national unity at a moment when the national middle classes had concentrated most of the wealth in their hands. Shopkeepers and artisans, clerks and bankers monopolized finance, trade and science in the national framework. The middle class was the most dynamic and prosperous of all classes. Its coming to power enabled it to undertake certain very important speculations: industrialization, the development of communications and soon the search for outlets overseas.

In Europe, apart from certain slight differences (England, for example, was some way ahead), the various states were at a more or less uniform stage economically when they achieved national unity. There was no nation which by reason of the character of its development and evolution caused affront to the others.

Today, national independence and the growth of national feeling in underdeveloped regions take on totally new aspects. In these regions, with the exception of certain spectacular advances, the different countries show the same absence of infrastructure. The mass of the people struggle against the same poverty, flounder about making the same gestures and with their shrunken bellies outline what has been called the geography of hunger. It is an underdeveloped world, a world inhuman in its poverty; but it is also a world without doctors, without engineers and without administrators. Confronting this world, the European nations sprawl, ostentatiously opulent. This European opulence is literally scandalous, for it has been founded on slavery, it has been nourished with the blood of slaves and it comes directly from the soil and from the subsoil of that underdeveloped world. The well-being and the progress of Europe have been built up with the sweat and the dead bodies of Negroes, Arabs, Indians and the yellow races. We have decided not to overlook this any longer. When a colonialist country, embarrassed by the claims for independence made by a colony, proclaims to the nationalist leaders: 'If you wish for independence, take it, and go back to the Middle Ages', the newly-independent people tend to acquiesce and to accept the challenge; in fact you may see colonialism withdrawing its capital and its technicians and setting up around the young state the apparatus of economic pressure.* The apotheosis of independence is transformed into the curse of independence, and the colonial power through its immense resources of coercion condemns the young nation to regression. In plain words, the colonial power says: 'Since you want independence, take it and starve.' The nationalist leaders have no other choice but to

* In the present international context, capitalism does not merely operate an economic blockade against African or Asian colonies. The United States with its anti-Castro operations is opening a new chapter in the long story of man's toiling advance towards freedom. Latin America, made up of new independent countries which sit at the United Nations and raise the wind there ought to be an object lesson for Africa. These former colonies since their liberation have suffered the brazen-faced rule of Western capitalism in terror and destitution.

The liberation of Africa and the growth of consciousness among mankind have made it possible for the Latin American peoples to break with the old merry-go-round of dictatorships where each succeeding regime exactly resembled the preceding one. Castro took over power in Cuba, and gave it to the people. This heresy is felt to be a national scourge by the Yankees, and the United States is now organizing counter-revolutionary brigades, puts together a provisional government, burns the sugar-cane crops, and generally has decided to strangle the Cuban people mercilessly. But this will be difficult. The people of Cuba will suffer, but they will conquer. The Brazilian president, Janio Quadros, has just announced in a declaration of historic importance that his country will defend the Cuban Revolution by all means. Perhaps even the United States may draw back when faced with the declared will of the peoples. When that day comes, we'll hang out the flags, for it will be a decisive moment for the men and women of the whole world. The almighty dollar, which when all is said or done is only guaranteed by slaves scattered all over the globe, in the oil-wells of the Middle East, the mines of Peru or of the Congo, and the United Fruit or Firestone plantations, will then cease to dominate with all its force these slaves which it has created and who continue, empty-headed and empty-bellied, to feed it from their substance. (F.F.)

328

turn to their people and ask from them a gigantic effort. A regime of austerity is imposed on these starving men; a disproportionate amount of work is required from their atrophied muscles. An autarchic regime is set up and each state, with the miserable resources it has in hand, tries to find an answer to the nation's great hunger and poverty. We see the mobilization of a people which toils to exhaustion in front of a suspicious and bloated Europe.

Other countries of the Third World refuse to undergo this ordeal and agree to get over it by accepting the conditions of the former guardian power. These countries use their strategic position – a position which accords them privileged treatment in the struggle between the two *blocs* – to conclude treaties and give undertakings. The former dominated country becomes an economically dependent country. The ex-colonial power, which has kept intact and sometimes even reinforced its colonialist trade channels, agrees to provision the budget of the independent nation by small injections. Thus we see that the accession to independence of the colonial countries places an important question before the world, for the national liberation of colonized countries unveils their true economic state and makes it seem even more unendurable. The fundamental duel which seemed to be that between colonialism and anti-colonialism, and indeed between capitalism and socialism, is already losing some of its importance. What counts today, the question which is looming on the horizon, is the need for a redistribution of wealth. Humanity must reply to this question, or be shaken to pieces by it.

It might have been generally thought that the time had come for the world, and particularly for the Third World, to choose between the capitalist and socialist systems. The underdeveloped countries, which have used the fierce competition which exists between the two systems in order to assure the triumph of their struggle for national liberation, should, however, refuse to become a factor in that competition. The Third World ought not to be content to define itself in the terms of values which have preceded it. On the contrary, the underdeveloped countries ought to do their utmost to find their own particular values and methods and a style which shall be peculiar to them. The concrete problem we find ourselves up against is not that of a choice, cost what it may, between socialism and capitalism as they have been defined by men of other continents and of other ages. Of course we know that the capitalist regime, in so far as it is a way of life, cannot leave us free to perform our work at home, nor our duty in the world. Capitalist exploitation and cartels and monopolies are the enemies of underdeveloped countries. On the other hand the choice of a socialist regime, a regime which is completely oriented towards the people as a whole and based on the principle that man is the most precious of all possessions, will allow us to go forward more quickly and more harmoniously, and thus make impossible that caricature of society where all economic and political power is held in the hands of a few who regard the nation as a whole with scorn and contempt.

But in order that this regime may work to good effect so that we can in every instance respect those principles which were our inspiration, we need something more than human output. Certain underdeveloped countries expend a huge amount of energy in this way. Men and women, young and old, undertake enthusiastically what is in fact forced labour, and proclaim themselves the slaves of the nation. The gift of oneself, and the contempt for every preoccupation which is not in the common interest, bring into being a national *morale* which comforts the heart of man, gives him fresh confidence in the destiny of mankind and disarms the most reserved observers. But we cannot believe that such an effort can be kept up at the same frenzied pace for very long. These young countries have agreed to take up the challenge after the unconditional withdrawal of the ex-colonial countries. The country finds itself in the hands of new managers; but the fact is that everything needs to be reformed and everything thought out anew. In reality the colonial system was concerned with certain forms of wealth and certain resources only – precisely those which provisioned her own industries. Up to the present no serious effort has been made to estimate the riches of the soil or of mineral resources. Thus the young independent nation sees itself obliged to use the economic channels created by the colonial regime. It can, obviously, export to other countries and other currency areas, but the basis of its exports is not fundamentally modified. The colonial regime has carved out certain channels and they must be maintained or catastrophe will threaten. Perhaps it is necessary to begin everything all over again: to change the nature of the country's exports, and not simply their destination, to re-examine the soil and mineral resources, the rivers, and – why not? – the sun's productivity. Now, in order to do all this, other things are needed over and above human output – capital of all kinds, technicians, engineers, skilled mechanics, and so on. Let's be frank: we do not believe that the colossal effort which the underdeveloped peoples are called upon to make by their leaders will give the desired results. If conditions of work are not modified, centuries will be needed to humanize this world which has been forced down to animal level by imperial powers.*

The truth is that we ought not to accept these conditions. We should flatly refuse the situation to which the western countries wish to condemn us. Colonialism and imperialism have not paid their score when they withdraw their flags and their police forces from our territories. For centuries the capitalists have behaved in the underdeveloped world like nothing more than war criminals. Deportations, massacres, forced labour, and slavery have been the main methods used by capitalism to increase its wealth, its gold or diamond reserves, and to establish its power. Not long ago Nazism transformed the whole of Europe into a veritable colony. The governments of the various European nations called for reparations and demanded the restitution in kind and money of the wealth which had been stolen from them: cultural treasures, pictures, sculptures, and stained glass have been given back to their owners. There was only one slogan in the mouths of Europeans on the morrow of

*Certain countries who have benefited by a large European settlement come to independence with houses and wide streets, and these tend to forget the poverty-stricken, starving hinterland. By the irony of fate, they give the impression by a kind of complicit silence that their towns are contemporaneous with independence. (F.F.)

the 1945 VE-day: 'Germany must pay.' Herr Adenauer, it must be said, at the opening of the Eichmann trial, and in the name of the German people, asked once more for forgiveness from the Jewish people. Herr Adenauer has renewed the promise of his people to go on paying to the state of Israel the enormous sums which are supposed to be compensation for the crimes of the Nazis.*

In the same way we may say that the imperialist states would make a great mistake and commit an unspeakable injustice if they contented themselves with withdrawing from our soil the military cohorts, and the administrative and managerial services whose function it was to discover the wealth of the country, to extract it and to send it off to the mother countries. We are not blinded by the moral reparation of national independence; nor are we fed by it. The wealth of the imperial countries is our wealth too. On the universal plane this affirmation, you may be sure, should on no account be taken to signify that we feel ourselves affected by the creations of Western arts or techniques. For in a very concrete way Europe has stuffed herself inordinately with the gold and raw materials of the colonial countries: Latin America, China and Africa. From all these continents, under whose eyes Europe today raises up her tower of opulence, there has flowed out for centuries towards

*It is true that Germany has not paid all her reparations. The indemnities imposed on the vanquished nation have not been claimed in full, for the injured nations have included Germany in their anti-Communist system of defence. This same preoccupation is the permanent motivation of the colonialist countries when they try to obtain from their former colonies, if not their inclusion in the Western system, at least military bases and enclaves. On the other hand they have decided unanimously to forget their demands for the sake of NATO strategy and to preserve the free world; and we have seen Germany receiving floods of dollars and machines. A Germany once more standing on its feet, strong and powerful, was a necessity for the Western camp. It was in the understood interests of so-called free Europe to have a prosperous and reconstructed Germany which would be capable of serving as a first rampart against the eventual Red hordes. Germany has made admirable use of the European crisis. At the same time the United States and other European states feel a legitimate bitterness when confronted with this Germany, yesterday at their feet, which today metes out to them cut-throat competition in the economic field. (F.F.)

that same Europe diamonds and oil, silk and cotton, wood and exotic products. Europe is literally the creation of the Third World. The wealth which smothers her is that which was stolen from the underdeveloped peoples. The ports of Holland, the docks of Bordeaux and Liverpool were specialized in the Negro slave-trade, and owe their renown to millions of deported slaves. So when we hear the head of a European state declare with his hand on his heart that he must come to the help of the poor underdeveloped peoples, we do not tremble with gratitude. Quite the contrary; we say to ourselves: 'It's just a reparation which will be paid to us.' Nor will we acquiesce in the help for underdeveloped countries being a programme of 'sisters of charity'. This help should be the ratification of a double realization: the realization by the colonized peoples that *it is their due*, and the realization by the capitalist powers that in fact *they must pay*.* For if, through lack of intelligence (we won't speak of gratitude) the capitalist countries refuse to pay, then the relentless dialectic of their own system will smother them. It is a fact that young nations do not attract much private capital. There are many reasons which explain and render legitimate this reserve on the part of the monopolies. As soon as the capitalists know – and of course they are the first to know – that their government is getting ready to decolonize, they hasten to withdraw all their capital from the colony in question. The spectacular flight of capital is one of the most constant phenomena of decolonization.

Private companies, when asked to invest in independent countries, lay down conditions which are shown in practice to

* 'To make a radical difference between the building up of socialism in Europe and our relations with the Third World (as if our only relations with it were external ones) is, whether we know it or not, to set the pace for the distribution of the colonial inheritance over and above the liberation of the underdeveloped countries. It is to wish to build up a luxury socialism upon the fruits of imperialist robbery – as if, inside the gang, the swag is more or less shared out equally, and even a little of it is given to the poor in the form of charity, since it's been forgotten that they were the people it was stolen from.' Marcel Péju. 'To die for De Gaulle?', article appearing in *Temps Modernes*, no. 175–6, October–November 1960. (F.F.)

333

be unacceptable or unrealizable. Faithful to the principle of immediate returns which is theirs as soon as they go 'overseas', the capitalists are very chary concerning all long-term investments. They are unamenable and often openly hostile to the prospective programmes of planning laid down by the young teams who form the new government. At a pinch they willingly agree to lend money to the young states, but only on condition that this money is used to buy manufactured products and machines: in other words, that it serves to keep the factories in the mother country going.

In fact the cautiousness of the Western financial groups may be explained by their fear of taking any risk. They also demand political stability and a calm social climate which are impossible to obtain when account is taken of the appalling state of the population as a whole immediately after independence. Therefore, vainly looking for some guarantee which the former colony cannot give, they insist on garrisons being maintained or the inclusion of the young state in military or economic pacts. The private companies put pressure on their own governments to at least set up military bases in these countries for the purpose of assuring the protection of their interests. In the last resort these companies ask their government to guarantee the investments which they decide to make in such-and-such an underdeveloped region.

It happens that few countries fulfil the conditions demanded by the trusts and monopolies. Thus capital, failing to find a safe outlet, remains blocked in Europe, and is frozen. It is all the more frozen because the capitalists refuse to invest in their own countries. The returns in this case are in fact negligible and treasury control is the despair of even the boldest spirits.

In the long run the situation is catastrophic. Capital no longer circulates, or else its circulation is considerably diminished. In spite of the huge sums swallowed up by military budgets, international capitalism is in desperate straits.

But another danger threatens it as well. In so far as the Third World is in fact abandoned and condemned to regression or at least to stagnation by the selfishness and wickedness of Western nations, the underdeveloped peoples will decide to continue their evolution inside a collective autarchy. Thus the Western industries will quickly be deprived of their overseas markets. The machines will pile up their products in the ware-houses and a merciless struggle will ensue on the European market between the trusts and the financial groups. The closing of factories, the paying off of workers and unemployment will force the European working class to engage in an open struggle against the capitalist regime. Then the monopolies will realize that their true interests lie in giving aid to the underdeveloped countries – unstinted aid with not too many conditions. So we see that the young nations of the Third World are wrong in trying to make up to the capitalist countries. We are strong in our own right, and in the justice of our point of view. We ought on the contrary to emphasize and explain to the capitalist countries that the fundamental problem of our time is not the struggle between the socialist regime and them. The Cold War must be ended, for it leads nowhere. The plans for nuclearizing the world must stop, and large-scale investments and technical aid must be given to underdeveloped regions. The fate of the world depends on the answer that is given to this question.

Moreover, the capitalist regime must not try to enlist the aid of the socialist regime over 'the fate of Europe' in face of the starving multitudes of coloured peoples. The exploit of Colonel Gagarin doesn't seem to displease General de Gaulle, for is it not a triumph which brings honour to Europe? For some time past the statesmen of the capitalist countries have adopted an equivocal attitude towards the Soviet Union. After having united all their forces to abolish the socialist regime, they now realize that they'll have to reckon with it. So they look as pleasant as they can, they make all kinds of advances, and they remind the Soviet people the whole time that they 'belong to Europe'.

They will not manage to divide the progressive forces which mean to lead mankind towards happiness by brandishing the threat of a Third World which is rising like the tide to swallow all of Europe. The Third World does not mean to organize a great crusade of hunger against the whole of Europe. What it expects from those who for centuries have kept it in slavery is that they will help it to rehabilitate mankind, and make man victorious everywhere, once and for all. But it is clear that we are not so naïve as to think this will come about with the cooperation and the good will of the European governments. This huge task which consists of re-introducing mankind into the world, the whole of mankind, will be carried out with the indispensable help of the European peoples, who themselves must realize that in the past they have often joined the ranks of our common masters where colonial questions were concerned. To achieve this, the European peoples must first decide to wake up and shake themselves, use their brains, and stop playing the stupid game of the Sleeping Beauty.

13. WESTERN VIEWS

*

The first reading below (i) is taken from *Diplomacy and Economic Development*, a book based on lectures given in 1960 at Tufts University in the United States by Eugene R. Black when he was President of the International Bank for Reconstruction and Development. Mr Black's interest in the developing countries has continued since he left the World Bank. He has worked for President Johnson and been Chairman of the Board of Trustees of the Brookings Institution.

The second excerpt (ii) is from the end of *Oriental Despotism* by Karl A. Wittfogel. Wittfogel is held in very high repute in the West as a scholar in the field of the sociology of Asiatic societies and this book is a study of the relation of hydraulic societies to despotic political forms which was acclaimed with enthusiasm in academic circles when it first appeared in 1957.

The third excerpt (iii) is from a statement made by a group of people in Britain actively and professionally engaged in the work of organizations concerned with aid to developing countries. They came together in January 1968 and drew up what has come to be called the *Haslemere Declaration*.

(i) THE NEW ENLIGHTENMENT IN THE UNDERDEVELOPED WORLD*

THAT vast stretch of the planet, extending eastwards from Latin America, through Africa and the Middle East, to South and South-east Asia, which we have come to call the underdeveloped world, is an area of great diversity. Here can be found virtually every race and creed which exists on earth, every kind of geographical environment and climate, and communities in widely differing stages of development. If most

*From *Diplomacy and Economic Development* (Cambridge, Mass.: Harvard University Press, 1962).

people are poor in the material things of life, there is in much of this area a wealth of resources waiting to be tapped. If the land in some places is dangerously overcrowded, in other places it could support two or three times the present population, even without much economic advance. These parts of the world would seem to defy generalizations.

However, by characterizing the nations of the underdeveloped world as entering upon an age of enlightenment I mean to suggest that they do have something in common. In fact, they have shared a common experience and are reacting to that experience in roughly similar ways. By choosing a phrase out of the literature of Western philosophy, I mean to suggest that the common experience they have shared is to have their traditional ways of life upset by the impact of the West's own Enlightenment as it found expression in the industrial revolution of the Western world.

Ever more widely over the past two hundred years, the philosophy and technology associated with the West's own Enlightenment have spread among societies whose customs and habits had hardly changed for centuries. In some places change came with the first Western traders and investors who introduced plantation agriculture and an exchange economy where a subsistence economy had been the rule. In others it came with the mission schools where ideas of man's responsibility to better himself were taught and came into conflict with traditional obligations of the individual to his caste, tribe, or village community. It came with the mission doctor battling successfully against disease and robbing the witch doctor of his authority. It came with the first Western colonizers who interfered with the traditional structure of tribal or dynastic rule and started people on the road to thinking of themselves as nations in the Western sense.

The impact of these ideas and achievements was greatly reinforced with each scientific invention and each improvement in communications and transport. International wars played their part in exposing more and more millions to the paraphernalia of modern economic life. The cumulative result of all these invasions and intrusions has been to disturb the peace

338

of tradition in almost every nook and cranny of the globe and touch off an historic transformation which today embraces the great majority of the world's people. ...

So it is wrong to say that the distinguishing feature of this so-called revolution of rising expectations is a universal desire to abandon old habits and attitudes towards life and work in favour of new ones. That might have been the case if the impact of Western ideas and philosophies had been as pervasive as the impact of Western science and technology. The apostles of a new life, as was the case in most modern revolutions, are the minority, typically those whose close contact with Western education, Western political thought, and Western material living standards has led them to want greater opportunities to practise their knowledge, greater outlets for their ambition, and a better material lot for their countrymen. Among these are the new leaders who make it possible for me to say that the underdeveloped world is entering on an age of enlightenment.

This class in the underdeveloped world constitutes a group privileged in relation to their countrymen, but a frustrated group nonetheless. The education and economic growth from which they are already benefiting have done much more to raise their aspirations and their desire for power than they have to provide them with opportunities for a productive life and outlets for their ambition. And there is no more explosive material than the doctor who knows what modern medicine can do but does not have the facilities to put his knowledge to work; or the teacher who must teach, if at all, without textbooks; or the engineer without access to capital equipment; or the businessman without a place of business; or the politician without a following that understands what he is talking about.

This educated class is providing, quite logically, more and more of the architects and administrators of government in the underdeveloped world. In most former colonies they have already led their people to national independence. In all countries this aroused group now faces the infinitely more difficult task of carrying out a revolution within their own societies to prepare their people for modern economic life.

Few, if any, leaders in history faced a more ambitious task or one whose outcome was more uncertain. The governments in these countries are the primary agents of change in societies in which large numbers of people are resisting change. That government plays this role is not so much a matter of ideology as it is a matter of necessity. The politician and the bureaucrat in these countries are very literally leaders as well as rulers; they are taking the lead in trying to adapt to modern economic life ancient traditions which have been rendered tragically inadequate by the passage of time.

There is very little in the early development of Western countries which bears comparison with this task. In the age of inventions governments did not need to take many development initiatives; then the rate of growth was determined largely by the rate at which man could push ahead the frontiers of technology; then it made sense to allow the policies of government to be dictated to a large extent by the needs and initiatives of the private innovator. But now the knowledge about what it takes for a society to grow rich exists; the rate of growth, therefore, depends initially on how quickly society adapts itself to use this knowledge. In these circumstances it is hardly surprising that governments are performing many more innovating functions themselves and trying more deliberately to manipulate the lot of society. Such tendencies are spurred on by the fact that people are awakening more or less abruptly to the variety of achievements possible in modern economic society and are coming to want those achievements all at once. Leaders are driven to try to leap over the many contradictions in the economic development process, to try to settle once and for all the inevitable conflicts between growth and justice, growth and equality, growth and national power and prestige. No leaders in the early stage of the West's development faced anything like the range and complexity of choices which are faced by the new leaders of the underdeveloped world today.

And of course, those who man the governments of the underdeveloped countries today are in a hurry; they are eager to imitate the technology which made Western nations rich and powerful. Often they have to hurry if they are to keep the in-

340

exorable pressure of population at bay. But they are also driven by a more fundamental urge; they are driven by a renewed pride in their own racial and cultural heritage – a pride born partly of a genuine renaissance and partly of accumulated resentment over the gross inequalities in wealth among nations today and over real or imagined subjugation of their countries in the past. Nationalism is perhaps even more of a motive force among these new leaders than the drive to escape poverty. And often it is a nationalism that is only one part patriotism for every two parts an obsession that their poverty and discontent stem solely from having been held in tutelage by the strong.

It is difficult to exaggerate the importance of these new leaders. Their decisions will in large part determine not only the future course of their own countries, but increasingly the shape of international politics as well. And it is largely through these leaders that the old Western world, divided as it is into the camp of freedom and the camp of Communism, will exert whatever influence it will have on the revolution of rising expectations.

Communism has an insidious appeal to the new leaders of the underdeveloped world. On the one hand Communism blames all frustration, inequality, and poverty on Western exploitation. It plays heavily on the legacy of suspicion and animosity against the free West which the new leadership has inherited almost as an inevitable result of the transformation through which their countries are going. The world, according to the Communists, is riven by a sort of hideous class warfare between the have-not nations and the haves.

(ii) WHITHER REVOLUTIONARY ASIA*

Whither Asia? When answering this question, we must remember that capitalist colonization during the three hundred years of its dominance failed in the Orient to develop multicentred societies based on a strong middle class, organized labour, and an independent peasantry. We must remember that most constitutions of the new sovereign Asian nations, directly or in-

*From *Oriental Despotism* (New Haven: Yale University Press).

341

directly, proclaim statism as a basic feature of their government.* We must remember that in many cases – we exclude Ataturk – the will to statism was bulwarked by democratic–socialist principles and that, in most of these cases – we exclude Sun Yat-sen – the professed democratic socialists were also professed admirers of Marx.

The student of Asia naturally wants to know how seriously the Asian socialists take Marx's Asiatic ideas: his theory of the Asiatic mode of production, which stresses private property as a key necessity for overcoming state-heavy Asiatic society; his multilinear concept of development, which warns against any simple scheme of unilinear development; his definition of socialism, which includes popular control as an essential element and which makes it impossible to call Communist Russia and Communist China socialist or proto-socialist; and his 'Oriental' interpretation of Tsarist Russia, which made Plekhanov and Lenin consider the dangers of an Asiatic restoration.

Strange as it may seem, the Asian socialists are as indifferent to these ideas as are the Asian Communists. And this is true for the spokesman of socialist parties as well as for socialists like Nehru who do not belong to any such organizations. Nehru, who found 'Marx's general analysis of social development ... remarkably correct', apparently was unimpressed by Marx's analysis of the social development of India, which he can hardly have missed seeing, since Marx's writings on this subject circulated in India in several editions.

To be sure, the official representatives of the various Asian socialist parties sharply attack Russian and Chinese Communism for their totalitarianism. But disregarding Marx's views on Asiatic society and socialism, they disregard what, from the standpoint of 'scientific socialism', would be the decisive critical test. And they hide the grave implications of their own societal past by calling this past 'feudal' and by placing it into a crude scheme of unilinear development.

*The principle of statism is solemnly proclaimed in Article 2 of the Turkish Constitution. Semantically, this principle is also invoked in the constitutions of Nationalist China, India, Burma, and Indonesia. (K.A.W.)

342

Such procedures cannot be excused by asserting that the democratic Marxists of Europe also neglected Marx's Asiatic views. For while the European socialists did not draw the political conclusions Plekhanov drew, they certainly recognized Marx's concept of the Asiatic mode of production. In fact, Rosa Luxemburg, who is highly esteemed by the leading Indian socialist Mehta, expressly discussed the hydraulic and stationary character of Oriental societies.

But even if the European socialists had neglected these societies, which to them constitute a remote issue, this would not excuse the Asian socialists. Being concerned primarily with Asia, they should have paid particular attention to what Marx had to say on this subject. However, instead of doing this, they remain stubbornly aloof from Marx's and Engels's theory of Asiatic society.

This omission does not keep the Asian socialists from opposing the 'excessive growth of bureaucracy' in their own part of the world and from rejecting the Russian and Chinese Communist regimes. However, it gives tacit support to a policy which endeavours to abandon as soon as possible what Marx called 'the greatest desideratum of Asian society' – private property in land.

And far from precluding, it indirectly encourages a sympathetic appraisal of the managerial statism of the U.S.S.R. and Communist China. In the 1930s Nehru viewed the Soviet Union as 'run by representatives of the workers and peasants' and as being 'in some ways ... the most advanced country in the world'. In the 1940s he approvingly cited Tagore's opinion that the U.S.S.R. 'is free from all invidious distinction between one class and another', its regime being based not on exploitation but on cooperation. And in the 1950s he equated the despotic masters of Communist Russia and China and their peoples; and he depicted Mao and his lieutenants as advancing the freedom of those they rule.

Like his Indian counterpart, the prime minister of Burma, U Nu, is not aware of the dangers of Communist expansion. But in 1954 he noted with pride the internal and external strength of Mao's regime. And he lauded the Chinese Communists for having abolished corruption and for improving the condition of the 'down-trodden teeming millions'. He said this about a regime which openly and repeatedly had admitted being plagued by corruption. And he said it at a time when Mao's policy of enforced 'cooperativization' was breaking the backbone of the Chinese peasantry.

Excepting Japan – which never was a hydraulic civilization – and making full allowance for regional differences, we find most non-Communist nations of the Orient institutionally ambivalent and influenced by a semi- or crypto-Communist ideology which, by enhancing the authority of Marxism–Leninism, as the Leningrad discussion of 1931 explained, tends to weaken their political independence.

Does this mean that one after the other the ideologically penetrated countries will cease resisting the political erosion to which Communist strategy is exposing them? Such a turn is entirely possible. And although its consequences would entail far more than an 'Asiatic restoration', in one respect it deserves this title: it would be a spectacular manifestation of a retrogressive societal development.

Whither Western Society – Whither Mankind?

Can the West prevent this development, which would extend the system of bureaucratic state slavery to two-thirds of mankind? The history of pre-Bolshevik Russia shows that countries of the Oriental type which are independent and in close contact with the West may vigorously move towards a multi-centred and democratic society. As described above, a diversive transformation of this kind has begun in many non-communist countries of the Orient; and given time and opportunity, it may assume momentous dimensions. But will there be time? Will there be opportunity?

Time is already running out. And opportunity, if it is to be seized with any chance of success, presupposes a West whose attitude towards bureaucratic totalitarianism is both informed and bold. Today, the attitude of the West is neither.

Public opinion in the leading Western countries is ambivalent about the form and function of managerial bureaucracy;

344

and it is ambivalent also about the form and function of private property and enterprise. The Second Industrial Revolution, which we are now experiencing, is perpetuating the principle of a multi-centred society through large bureaucratized complexes that mutually – and laterally – check each other: most importantly, Big Government, Big Business, Big Agriculture and Big Labour.* But the destruction of one major nongovernmental complex may bring about the downfall of others. Under Fascism and National Socialism, the liquidation of Big Labour so strengthened Big Government that eventually Big Business and Big Agriculture were also threatened.† And in Soviet Russia the liquidation of Big Business and Big Agriculture quickly enabled Big Government to subdue labour.

These experiences should alert us to the dangers inherent in unchecked bureaucratic dominance. To what extent can we trust the members of any 'Big' group to use supreme and total power, once they gain it, to serve the people's interest and not their own? To what extent can we trust the judgement of officiating or non-officiating members of our segmented bureaucracies who view the Communist monopoly bureaucracy as a progressive form of totalitarianism? ‡

Western writers, teachers, and practising politicians who do not understand the meaning of our institutional and cultural heritage are poorly equipped to unleash its creative potential.

---

*The decrease of vertical controls from below (by voters, shareholders, and rank-and-file trade-union members) goes hand in hand with the increase of lateral controls. These last are not new (cf. the history of factory legislation in England). But while their significance has grown, the recent Communist and Fascist revolutions show that their capacity to prevent a totalitarian accumulation of power is limited. (K.A.W.)

† Before the end of the Second World War some attempts were made to analyse the institutional trends in Italian and German Fascism; but comparison with Communist totalitarianism was superficial or avoided altogether. In recent years there has been little interest in comparative studies of modern totalitarianism that include Fascism. Moscow's role in Hitler's rise to power is a similarly neglected issue. (K.A.W.)

‡When John K. Fairbank stressed 'the distinction between the fascist-conservative and *communist-progressive forms of totalitarianism*' (Fairbank, 1947: 149; italics mine), he expressed in print, and very succinctly, an opinion shared today by many intellectuals and officials. (K.A.W.)

345

And they are also poorly equipped to combat Communist totalitarianism. For however necessary military preparedness and a courageous economic policy may be, they are only two among several essentials. Equally important is the judicious implementation of institutional change. And most important, because most fundamental, is a thorough grasp of the multiform course of history and of the opportunities and responsibilities it imposes on free man.

No doubt we are in the midst of an open historical situation, and no doubt there is freedom of effective choice. But our past blunders and present deliberations show that so far we have not used our opportunities competently. We did not give full scope to the anti-totalitarian forces in the Western world. And failing to do this, we did little to strengthen the anti-totalitarian forces in the hydraulic societies in transition.

But while the realm of freedom is rapidly shrinking, the desire to defend and expand it is growing. Shocked into a vigorous reappraisal of our position, we may still learn how to wrest victory from defeat. A new insight that is fully perceived, convincingly communicated, and daringly applied may change the face of a military and ideological campaign. It may change the face of a historical crisis. Ultimately, the readiness to sacrifice and the willingness to take the calculated risk of alliance against the total enemy depend on the proper evaluation of two simple issues: slavery and freedom.

(iii) THE HASLEMERE DECLARATION

The group's main conclusions are:

Most of the 'developing world' is *not* developing. If the existing policies, complacency and lack of interest of the governments of the industrialized nations continue, it is unlikely they will ever help it to do so.

'Overseas aid' is largely a myth; at best, a wholly inadequate payment for goods received, at worst another name for the continued exploitation of the poor countries by the rich.

This exploitation takes many forms; some examples are given in this pamphlet. Principally it is the refusal of the rich

346

countries to allow the poor to own and use what material resources they possess in their own interests and in their own
way.

The international monetary and trading system was devised
by the rich to suit their needs; it ignores those of the poor.
When their interests are involved, the rich can and do break
its rules with impunity – yet complain of 'unfair competition'
when the poor try to increase their share of its benefits.

We agree with Dr Raul Prebisch, the Secretary-General of
the United Nations Conference on Trade and Development
(UNCTAD): 'In the developing world a very profound economic revolution has to take place [and] a far-reaching transformation of the social structure.... This revolution is
inevitable and we have to discuss what shape it must take,
what degree of human sacrifice, and social and political sacrifice, or moral sacrifice, this revolution of the Third World will
entail.'

That revolution has now started. There is a new Third World
that is a political force, that is starting to look inwards to its
own resources rather than outwards to us for help and an
example. We believe we must build links with it, and that these
links stem from a common goal: the changing of our world
society to make it more responsive to the needs of the individual.

We do not align ourselves with this Third World out of
charity. We do so because we are concerned with the health of
our own society, because we recognize that it, too, is damaged
by an exploitative system. A society that exploits Afro-Asia
will exploit the weaker of its own members, a system that can
no longer respond to the individual abroad will deny human
rights to those at home. At home or abroad, our technology is
used to annihilate the distance between places and widen the
gaps between men. Thus, the developed world prefers to
attempt to put a man on the moon to trying to cope with
hunger, poverty, and disease in Afro-Asia.

PART FIVE

WHAT HAS TO BE DONE

Tasks, Tactics, Programmes
and Ensuing Difficulties

THE main emphasis in the readings in Part Five is on the specific corporate decisions and actions which appear to be necessary to people in the Third World. Given their situation at any time, and the varying conditions in different spheres of activity, on the one hand, and the goals and objectives for which they are striving, on the other, what are the tasks which the responsible indigenous leaders have set themselves, the policies, the tactics and programmes which they have shown to be realistic, relevant and effective? In the course of political, economic and social action there arise continually problems which have to be solved, there come into view new obstacles which have to be overcome if progress towards the chosen goals is to be achieved. Development appears as a process of struggle, in which set-backs may follow successes. These readings indicate what in the experience of the Third World the problems and obstacles are, and how they are to be coped with. The scope of this section is so wide that some of the issues are mentioned only in passing. There is much in previous sections, and especially in Part Two, which deals with policies, programmes and tactics.

The initial task is seen as the acquisition by the people as a whole, who have suffered the authority of pre-democratic regimes – feudal, colonial and post-colonial – of supreme authority and power over the national administration and resources; and their use of these in order to transform the conditions in which they live. It is, in other words, to reorganize the nation so as to free themselves from the alien institutions, ways of thinking and values which impoverish or oppress them?

The transition away from subordination to a European-dominated world to 'authentic' freedom in a new world appears, in the thought and action of the Third World, to be a process which involves:

The nationalization of state power and sovereignty: this includes the elimination of foreign control, foreign military bases, and effective security against foreign and foreign-sponsored attempts to subvert or obstruct the autonomous exercise of democratic government.

Political reorganization: creation of new institutions and organs of political decision-making and action for the mass of the people. Realizing a modern and lasting national identity which can combine unity with local diversities. New forms of immediate contact between 'authorities' and the people. Continuing revolution to guard against bureaucracy and authoritarianism in new forms.

Reorganization of the economy: adequate food supply. Changes in land-tenure and the ownership and management of industry. Fresh thinking and action on such matters as rapid capital formation, self-reliance, development strategy, specialization, foreign trade. Rapid construction. Provision of opportunities for creative work and innovation.

Reorganization of society and culture. Ending of oppression and exploitation in family life. Expansion of educational opportunities and reorganization of the educational system. Promotion of forms of art and literature for a socialist democracy.

Reorganization of the world system. Collaboration of all peoples to create a peaceful world order, free from exploitation and terror – a world order for the maintenance of which all working people are responsible.

Problems arise in the process of this far-reaching transformation, and few countries have got to the stage of solving them. The problems arise from the very nature of what has to be done to achieve decolonization.

The readings in this and earlier sections specify such problems and obstacles as: obstruction from or subversion by superpowers or former imperial powers; romantic or unrealistic assessments of the dangers and difficulties of decolonization;

'counter-revolutionary' activity by traditional or colonial *élites* whose dominance is threatened by political movements and organization of the masses; militarism –the seizure of power by or independence from democratic control of military forces needed for national security; corruption in the political and administrative leadership; war; populism; lack of an ideology which makes sense of decolonization; shortage of capital; lack of trust in the people; the substitution of rhetoric, wishful thinking and academic speculation for hard work; incorrect theories; etc.

The 'revolutionary' programmes and prescriptions peculiar to the Third World are, in spite of the differences of viewpoint which exist, radically different from what appears to be realistic and sensible to those in Europe, North America and Japan who view the needs of the developing countries in a more orthodox way.

1. SOONG CHING-LING

*

Mass Organization for Action
against Colonial Rulers *

On p. 180 Sun Yat-sen's widow, Soong Ching Ling, described conditions in China. We now continue her article from where we left off in the earlier excerpt. Though the writer, isolated in Shanghai, and with radicals and liberals in hiding or killed, did not command any political power, she spoke and acted in the tradition of the revolutionary process which Sun Yat-sen had set in motion. In 1932, together with Lu Hsun and others, she founded the China League for Civil Rights. At the time this article was written Chiang Kai-shek was concentrating his efforts on destroying the independent soviet republics.

WHAT is our task, the task of the Chinese people? It is clear. We must take the road of national and social liberation. The Chiang Kai-shek government cannot unite China, cannot lead the national revolutionary war of the armed people against imperialism, cannot give land to the peasants. Why not? Because it is seeking always to compromise with imperialism. Because it fears the armed people more than the imperialist invaders, because it is the representative of the landlord–bourgeois *bloc* which exploits and suppresses the masses and ruins the country.

I call upon all men and women, the youth of China, and especially the workers, peasants, students and volunteers, to unite and organize this struggle for the liberation, unity and integrity of China, a struggle inseparately bound up with the efforts for the emancipation of the toiling masses from exploitation, with the fight for the rights of free speech, free press, assembly and organization, and for the liberation of political prisoners. Only through such effort will be developed the unconquerable national and social forces which will break

*From *The Struggle for New China* (Peking: Foreign Languages Press, 1952).

354

the power of imperialism and its treacherous allies. Let us remember that the Soviet Revolution demonstrated the superiority of a revolutionary people and its revolutionary armies over the forces of the whole capitalist world. The Chinese people with its already great revolutionary tradition will conquer in the same way. Not imperialist domination and the dismemberment of China, but a free, united, revolutionary China of the workers and peasants!

We must fight in every city and village for these demands:

(1) That at least eighty per cent of the armed forces of the country, with adequate equipment and all airplanes, be sent against Japanese imperialism to regain Manchuria and Jehol and to defend China;

(2) That the people be armed and that voluntary military detachments be formed;

(3) That democratic rights – free speech, free press, right of assembly and organization – be granted at once, and that the imprisonment, torture and killing of revolutionaries cease immediately;

(4) That the advance against the Soviet territories in China be stopped. Let it be emphasized that not only has the Soviet government of China declared war on Japanese imperialism, but in January of this year it offered its cooperation with any army or military detachment in the fight against Japanese imperialism, upon the condition that the advance against Soviet territory cease, that democratic rights be given to the people, and that the people be armed.

If we want to carry through these demands we must prepare to fight. We must organize in every factory, every school and university, every city and village. Our demands must be discussed in every house, shop and factory. Our demands must flood the streets. Only by arousing the masses to the seriousness of the situation and to the task of the future, will we bring action. This action will be the broad and anti-imperialist struggle culminating in the national revolutionary war of the armed people against Japanese and other imperialism. It is the duty of all national revolutionary elements to prepare for this struggle.

2. VIETNAMESE NATIONALIST LEADERS

*

Organizing the Seizure of Power *

Vietnamese nationalism, one of the oldest in the world, was never destroyed by French and Japanese rule. Not only opposition, but also active resistance to foreign rule continued throughout the colonial period. In May 1941 Ho Chi Minh and some of his colleagues took the opportunity of the war to bring the resistance forces together under the Revolutionary League for the Independence of Vietnam. Following the seizure of power from the Japanese in the August Revolution (see p. 92), the leaders of the newly independent republic issued their declaration of independence on 2 September 1945. The declaration explained what the resumption of revolutionary Vietnamese rule over the country signified politically.

'ALL men are created equal. They are endowed by their Creator with certain inalienable rights, among these are Life, Liberty, and the Pursuit of Happiness.'

This immortal statement was made in the Declaration of Independence of the United States of America in 1776. In a broader sense, this means: All the peoples on the earth are equal from birth, all the peoples have a right to live, to be happy and free.

The Declaration of the French Revolution made in 1791 on the Rights of Man and the Citizen also states: 'All men are born free and with equal rights, and must always remain free and have equal rights.'

Those are undeniable truths.

Nevertheless, for more than eighty years, the French imperialists, abusing the standard of Liberty, Equality, and Fraternity, have violated our Fatherland and oppressed our fellow-citizens. They have acted contrary to the ideals of humanity and justice.

*From Ho Chi Minh, *Selected Works* (Hanoi: Foreign Languages Publishing House, 1960).

In the field of politics, they have deprived our people of every democratic liberty.

They have enforced inhuman laws; they have set up three distinct political regimes in the North, the Centre and the South of Vietnam in order to wreck our national unity and prevent our people from being united.

They have built more prisons than schools. They have mercilessly slain our patriots; they have drowned our uprisings in rivers of blood.

They have fettered public opinion; they have practised obscurantism against our people.

To weaken our race they have forced us to use opium and alcohol.

In the field of economics, they have fleeced us to the backbone, impoverished our people, and devastated our land.

They have robbed us of our rice fields, our mines, our forests, and our raw materials. They have monopolized the issuing of bank-notes and the export trade.

They have invented numerous unjustifiable taxes and reduced our people, especially our peasantry, to a state of extreme poverty.

They have hampered the prospering of our national bourgeoisie; they have mercilessly exploited our workers.

In the autumn of 1940, when the Japanese Fascists violated Indo-China's territory to establish new bases in their fight against the Allies, the French imperialists went down on their bended knees and handed over our country to them.

Thus, from that date, our people were subjected to the double yoke of the French and the Japanese. Their sufferings and miseries increased. The result was that from the end of last year to the beginning of this year, from Quang Tri province to the North of Vietnam, more than two million of our fellow-citizens died from starvation. On 9 March, the French troops were disarmed by the Japanese. The French colonialists either fled or surrendered, showing that not only were they incapable of 'protecting' us, but that, in the span of five years, they had twice sold our country to the Japanese.

On several occasions before 9 March, the Vietminh League

urged the French to ally themselves with it against the Japanese. Instead of agreeing to this proposal, the French colonialists so intensified their terrorist activities against the Vietminh members that before fleeing they massacred a great number of our political prisoners detained at Yen Bay and Caobang.

Notwithstanding all this, our fellow-citizens have always manifested towards the French a tolerant and humane attitude. Even after the Japanese *putsch* of March 1945, the Vietminh League helped many Frenchmen to cross the frontier, rescued some of them from Japanese jails, and protected French lives and property.

From the autumn of 1940, our country had in fact ceased to be a French colony and had become a Japanese possession.

After the Japanese had surrendered to the Allies, our whole people rose to regain our national sovereignty and to found the Democratic Republic of Vietnam.

The truth is that we have wrested our independence from the Japanese and not from the French.

The French have fled, the Japanese have capitulated, Emperor Bao Dai has abdicated. Our people have broken the chains which for nearly a century have fettered them and have won independence for the Fatherland. Our people at the same time have overthrown the monarchic regime that has reigned supreme for dozens of centuries. In its place has been established the present Democratic Republic.

For these reasons, we, members of the Provisional Government, representing the whole Vietnamese people, declare that from now on we break off all relations of a colonial character with France; we repeal all the international obligation that France has so far subscribed to on behalf of Vietnam and we abolish all the special rights the French have unlawfully acquired in our Fatherland.

The whole Vietnamese people, animated by a common purpose, are determined to fight to the bitter end against any attempt by the French colonialists to reconquer their country.

We are convinced that the Allied nations which at Teheran and San Francisco have acknowledged the principles of self-determination and equality of nations, will not refuse to acknowledge the independence of Vietnam.

A people who have courageously opposed French domination for more than eighty years, a people who have fought side by side with the Allies against the Fascists during these last years, such a people must be free and independent.

For these reasons, we, members of the Provisional Government of the Democratic Republic of Vietnam, solemnly declare to the world that Vietnam has the right to be a free and independent country – and in fact it is so already. The entire Vietnamese people are determined to mobilize all their physical and mental strength, to sacrifice their lives and property in order to safeguard their independence and liberty.

3. GERMAN ARCINIEGAS

*

After Dictatorship and Despotism *

Towards the end of the following passage German Arciniegas (see p. 183) quotes former Guatemalan President Juan Jose Arevalo, the predecessor of Jacobo Arbenz, whose overthrow by the U.S. Central Intelligence Agency in 1954 made him famous. Guatemala has been the scene of one of the best organized peasant revolutionary movements in Latin America. What was it that Arevalo tried to achieve when he was elected President?

Was There Something Rotten in Guatemala?

BETWEEN 1840 and 1944 Guatemala was ruled by four dictatorships, with brief interludes of anarchy. The dictators were Rafael Carrera (1840–65), Justo Rufino Barrios (1873–85), Manuel Estrada Crabera (1898–1920), and Jorge Ubico (1931–44)....

Seventy-six years of despotism and forty spent in fruitless efforts to restore a normal way of living have maintained in poverty and ignorance the country with the proudest past in all Central America. The Mayan ruins of Petén, which John Lloyd Stephens brought to the attention of a wondering world in the nineteenth century, stand as a mute background against which their builders' Indian descendants weave bright-hued blankets. The 'ghost' city of Antigua is a testimony to the Spanish ambitions of colonial days, which had hoped to find in Guatemala a second Mexico. All this was being engulfed by nothingness until the fall of Ubico in 1944.

Of Guatemala's 3,000,000 inhabitants in 1951, sixty per cent are Indians who preserve their language and their customs. In the west are the Toltecs, to the east the Aztecs, in the south the Maya-Quichés. Illiteracy is their most tangible inheritance. Education is a difficult problem because the teachers must

*From *The State of Latin America* (New York: Knopf, 1953).

360

either know the Indian tongues or be Indians who can bridge the gulf between the native and the *ladino*. The *ladino* – the word is a corruption of *latino* – who may be a negro, a North American, or a Chinese, is one who knows about the non-Indian world and speaks a European language. Eighty-six per cent of Guatemala's Indian population speak four principal Indian languages. The rest is divided into small groups among which eleven different languages have been identified.

But the greatest stumbling block for the person who does not know Guatemala is the Spanish language. Words take on a local meaning there. The *Indian* who becomes rich is *white*. The *white* man who has no money is an *Indian*. The *dictators* are called *democrats*. *Communist* means one who opposes the *dictator*. When Juan Jose Arevala arrived from Argentina he was called a Nazi, when he was in the presidency, a Communist. Ubico began mass killings of 'Communists'. Just how far each of these expressions coincides with the universal significance is a problem in semantics the answer to which lies in the inner recesses of the Indian or *ladino* mind.

Guatemala produces coffee, bananas, chicle, sugar, cattle and Indians. Until Pearl Harbor, coffee was in the hands of the Germans and the plantation-owners of Guatemala. The property of the Germans was confiscated by the state, and today it is a national enterprise employing 200,000 workers. It is an experimental station for the improvement of coffee and an electoral reserve. The bananas have been in the hands of the United Fruit Company. The cattle and the Indians, for the most part, are the property of the land-owners....

Juan Jose Arevalo set out to accomplish a revolution in administration and in the life of the people of Guatemala. The undertaking was not without its risks. At the end of his six-year constitutional term of office he had survived twenty-seven attempts to overthrow him. He had said: 'I shall not remain in office one day beyond the limits established by the constitution, but not one day less, either.' He raised the school-teachers' salaries, he organized a school system for the Indians, he demilitarized education, he made the university autonomous, he created the faculties of Humanities and Agronomy, he built

135 schools, he published thousands of volumes in a series of books by the world's great authors at prices everyone could afford. He built an Olympic centre with a great stadium, a sports palace, and tennis courts, initiated a vast health and sanitation campaign, and erected seventeen hospitals.

The United Fruit Company, which prefers to do business with the weak republics of Central America – its dealings with the British Islands and the American possessions are negligible – suddenly found itself confronted by a man who said: 'If I am elected president, I shall see that our workers are treated with the consideration shown to foreigners.' United Fruit translated these words into: 'Arevalo is a Communist.' United States Ambassador Richard C. Patterson Jr was a man not overendowed with tact, and as between Guatemala and the United Fruit Company, he was unequivocally with the latter. 'Unofficially, Mr President,' he said to Arevalo one day, 'I want you to know that as far as I am personally concerned, your government will never get a dime or a pair of shoes from my government until you cease the persecution of American business.' In turn, Arevalo said to Samuel Guy Inman, who reported it in *A New Day in Guatemala* (1951), 'You do not have an ambassador of the United States here, but a representative of the United Fruit'.

Patterson made friends with the enemies of the government. Relations deteriorated to the point where as the different entries in the Olympic Games passed the reviewing stand to the sound of their respective national anthems, when the American flag came by the band broke into *'La Cucaracha'*. Arevalo finally informed Washington that Patterson was *persona non grata*, and he was recalled....

Guatemala's thorniest problem was its dealings with the United Fruit Company. United Fruit protested the Labour code and considered illegal a strike justified by law, invoking the special status it had been granted under Ubico's dictatorship. In 1951 the controversy had become so hot that United Fruit announced that it was withdrawing from Guatemala. The manager declared the demands of the workers were intolerable. 'The company,' he said (*The New York Times*, despatch from Guatemala dated 23 August 1951), 'has been charged repeatedly with exploiting the country and the people despite the fact that last year it paid $9,712,143 in salaries and wages, of which almost 93 per cent went to Guatemalans. ...' These figures need to be broken down. *The New York Times*, where these declarations appeared, published shortly afterwards a letter saying: 'Nine million dollars is certainly an impressive amount for one company to have poured into the economy of little Guatemala. Yet, when 93 per cent of this sum is divided among 97 per cent of the 37,000 workers, we find the average yearly income of the workers, including "salaried employees", to be $251·66....'

Which way is Guatemala heading? When Vicente Lombardo Toledano* and his associates – who in labour matters are considered the spearhead of Russia in Latin America – went to Guatemala, they were given an official reception, attended by four of Arevalo's cabinet ministers, Lieutenant-Colonel Jacobo Arbenz, and the leader of Congress. Serafino Ramualdi, the leader of the Interamerican Regional Organization, which represents the most vigorous anti-Communist labour group on the continent, remarked this fact, and at the same time has said: 'We have had occasion to deplore such stupid handling of the Communist issue on the part of the American interests in Guatemala.' Naturally the politics of Guatemala are affected by all these factors, which, though extraneous to the country, put stumbling blocks in the way of a normal working out of its destiny. When Arevalo turned over his office to the new President, Jacobo Arbenz, on 15 March 1951, he summed up his position in a speech from which the following is an excerpt.

I entered upon my office bent upon giving the people what they awaited from me ... It was necessary to begin with the first article of the new constitution which says: 'Guatemala is a free, sovereign and independent republic, organized for the primordial purpose of insuring to its inhabitants the enjoyment of liberty, culture,

* Head of the Confederation of Mexican Workers, who helped organize the Confederation of Latin American workers in 1938. Toledano was a supporter of President Cardenas's reforms.

economic well-being, and social justice. Its system of government is representative democracy.' ... At that time I was convinced – as I still am – that there can be no freedom for a nation as long as its individual inhabitants, each and every one, are not free, and that the dignity of the republic rests upon the sum total of the dignity actively and effectively operating in each individual inhabitant of its soil. To achieve this in Guatemala we came into conflict with the peculiar economic and social structure of the country, where the culture and economic control were in the hands of three hundred families who were the heirs of colonial privileges, or employees of foreign overlords, or members of an administrative caste. Creole feudalism ... reacted in an outraged manner against the way my government understood democracy and emphasized freedom. The banana barons, Roosevelt's fellow-citizens, rose against the insolence of a Central American president who dared to put his compatriots on a footing of equality with the honourable families of the exporters. Hitlerism has not died. ... After the gruelling, enlightening experience of the past six years, during which I have plumbed the depths of this tragi-comedy of man's inhumanity to man, what I can say is that contemporary democracy is losing ground at a dizzying speed to the Punic doctrines of Hitlerism.

4. AUNG SAN

*

The Right Foundations *

When he was assassinated, along with several colleagues, on the
eve of the withdrawal of British rule from Burma, Aung San (1915–
47) was Burma's national hero. Both in achievement and potential
he was a man of tremendous political and moral stature, he was
respected by all communities, and he was going to head the government of independent Burma. Six days before he was killed, he spoke
at a public meeting on the Constituent Assembly and on the new
Burma. The first of the following excerpts is taken from that speech.
A month earlier Aung San, speaking at a conference of government
leaders and experts, had concluded, 'Let me remind you of an old
way of ours, the classic way of getting things done, namely the
people's way of self help and mutual cooperation. We must resurrect
this classic way and stir and inspire the people to work together in
the building of a new Burma.' The second excerpt, 'The Foundations
of Burma's New Democratic Constitution', is from a speech in
May 1947 to the convention drafting the new Constitution.

The Right Foundations

THIS meeting was originally convened so that we might report, as members of the Constituent Assembly, to you as electors, on what we have so far accomplished in the Assembly. It
is the traditional practice in a parliamentary democracy for a
member to go back to his electors, when a session is over, and
report on progress and events.

Even though we were elected in April, we became the Constituent Assembly only on 10 June, when the session started in
due form. This is an Assembly which is unique in our history,
for we are writing the constitution of independent Burma, and
even though in strict law the Assembly does not enjoy
sovereign powers, it is going through the process of creating a
sovereign nation. Our present status in strict law is compli-

*From *Aung San of Burma* (The Hague: Nijhoff).

cated, but the important thing is that we are moving on to our goal.

I am a great one for uttering the brutal truth, or the painful truth, as Thakin Nu calls it. He has warned me occasionally that I should refrain from uttering these truths too frequently. But I have some to utter today; I am so full of them, I cannot contain them, and I only wish I had the time to tell them all.

Independence is coming, but it is not going to bring a heaven on earth. Some of you may dream fondly that once we are independent, there will not be the need to work, and the good things will spout out of the earth to take as you wish. That is not so.

Our people are inclined to believe that independence would mean a free-for-all. I remember visiting Henzada during the war, during the believe-it-or-not-independence that we had then. I saw people putting out tobacco leaves in the streets to dry, obstructing traffic. They thought they were independent and could do what they liked. That is not what independence means; liberty is not licence.

In a free country the people must be free to develop their individual personality and follow their own occupations in free and equal opportunity, but they must not infringe on the freedom and the rights of others.

You must also remember that you cannot have something for nothing in life. You have to work and earn what you want. You may dream of a new state like the Soviet Union, like America, or England, but dreams will not bring you the new state, you must work and build it.

Years of toil lie ahead of you. Maybe twenty years, at the least, will pass before you see the fruits of your toil. You must work with perseverance, with unity and discipline, always conscious of your duties as citizens of a free country. Rights carry responsibilities; you cannot enjoy the rights without discharging the responsibilities.

Britain is an inspiring example. We may not like the British, because they have been our rulers, but they do show many qualities as a nation which we must admire. How they fought, with back to the wall, during the war, and now after they have won they are still having to go through severe austerity, to re-build their economy. Britain makes a lot of things, but at this point the country needs to sell them abroad, and her own people have to produce while denying themselves of those goods. We too must plan our economy for the long future and persevere with our plans. There is no substitute for work.

We must build and preserve unity between the peoples in our country, people of the frontier areas and other peoples, and in unity we must work together to build our national strength. Without unity and strength, independence will be meaningless; the nation will be weak and vulnerable, whichever party may be in office. Behave like the lion, I therefore say. The lion, the king of the forest, exerts his full strength in hunting down his prey, however small or big the animal may be. We must all, therefore, put forth our very best in our endeavours to build the new nation. ...

There is a lot of nation-building to be done, and you must remember that you are building over the ashes of the war. Everywhere, we are behind, and to catch up with the world we must work far harder than other nations. Some say we should improve our education by introducing free compulsory educa-tion; make laws for that, they say. But what good are laws if we do not have the money, the teachers and the men? It will take another twenty years of persistent effort to turn out the teachers, to build the schools in every village, and have compul-sory education.

Then have a look at defence. Every citizen must give his ser-vice in the defence forces. Under British rule people got into the habit of thinking that the government would do the need-ful, and if anything went wrong they could blame the govern-ment. That is not the spirit in which you can build a free country. The needs for the defence of Burma are stupendous. We do not have an adequate Army, Air Force or Navy, and with the forces that we have we cannot stand against a modern enemy even for a few hours. The defence expenditure will be heavy if we want our defence to be adequate, and you have to remember that when we are tested here and there by aggres-sive powers we must be able to reply in no uncertain terms.

All these lead us back to this: you must work hard, be united and disciplined. Otherwise, the fruits of freedom will not be yours to enjoy, whether you have a Communist government or a Socialist government. You must mend your ways and build a New Burma together. These words I leave with you today.

The Foundations of Burma's New Democratic Constitution

Politics is inseparable from economics. When we rise to freedom we must rebuild our economy on broader foundations. The following must go into the foundations.

We must nationalize the basic industries and the vital utilities such as electricity, transport and communications. The benefits of the economy must accrue to the general welfare. We must prohibit monopolist organizations such as cartels, syndicates and trusts. We must encourage cooperative societies and enterprises.

You may ask me if it is not socialism that I preach. It is not. In fact, even if we may be eager to build socialism in Burma, conditions are not ready for it. We do not even have a proper capitalist system; we are a step below that. We cannot do without capitalism and private enterprise yet, but we must see that they do not exploit the people but serve their welfare instead. We must also write into our constitution clear definitions of the rights of workers and proper protection of the rights.

For the peasants we must pursue the policy of land for the tiller. Landlordism must be abolished by law. We must also see to it that the old landlordism is not replaced by a new one; the maximum holding must, therefore, be prescribed by law. Our immediate efforts must be to help the poor peasants and the middle-class peasant. The ultimate objective must be to nationalize agricultural land.

We need people with special skills to build the new nation. But they must serve the people, not the bosses; if they keep faith with the people, their lot will improve, their prospects will be brighter. Previously, because we were under foreign rule, many positions in the government service were not open to Burmans. Soon we shall be free, and Burmans will find opportunities to serve the country in all positions.

The national minorities must enjoy their rights to the full. The people must also be able to exercise their power effectively, and provisions must be made for them to recall their representatives in Parliament, and to make the government machinery more responsive to their wishes.

Defence is a national duty and responsibility. There must be no private armies, for they only lead to dictatorships as history has shown in Germany and Japan. We have to establish the People's Volunteer Organization to meet our special needs, but when we attain independence such organizations must go. We must be vigilant in preventing fascism, or dictatorship of any kind, from appearing. But first, we must have a clear idea about fascism. Firmness, where it is necessary to be firm, is not fascism. Nor is it a nickname to be freely applied to any person or any group which does not act as one wishes. Ruthless repression of the people by armed gangs in the name of false and narrow racial and ideological dogmas, that is fascism. We must give special care, when writing our Constitution, to devise adequate safeguards against such dogmas.

5. CHOU EN-LAI

*

A Programme of Construction
for Half of Asia*

In 1949 the power and control of the traditional ruling *élites* and of
foreign powers came to an end in China as a whole, and the reorganization of the war-ravaged country was begun. Men who had
ruled an area in the interior of China from Yenan in north-west
China had to explain to the nation and carry out an ambitious plan
for reconstructing and modernizing China. What, in general terms,
did they conceive as their task? In the passage which follows we
look at the plans from the other end, when substantial progress
had in fact been achieved. The Prime Minister, Chou En-lai
(b. 1898), looks back in his report of 1959 to what was done in the
first decade. Chou En-lai became a revolutionary in his student
days. In 1924 he was appointed political head of the Canton
government's military academy. From 1927 one of the closest
collaborators with Mao Tse-tung, he was the person whose organizing powers led and coordinated the complex tasks of reconstructing
the life of a vast country like China, which has a third of the
population of the Third World. His report, only part of which is
given here, is a record of work done by a whole nation according
to Mao Tse-tung's conception: 'We cannot just take the beaten
track traversed by other countries in the development of technology and trail behind them at a snail's pace. We must break away
from conventions and do our utmost to adopt advanced techniques
in order to build our country into a powerful modern socialist
state in not too long a historical period.' Chou En-lai stresses the
ideological and political basis on which development was planned.
At the time he gave his report he was yet to discover that the
statistical material he was using needed drastic revision, and China
was just entering a period of unprecedented natural calamities
which, combined with mistakes in planning, set her back economically. It was a decade later that it became clear that the Chinese
people were achieving rates of progress in industrialization, inno-

*From *A Great Decade* (Peking: Foreign Languages Press).

370

vation, standards of living and political democracy which were phenomenal.

EVERYBODY knows too that ten years ago the political situation in China was abysmally dark and reactionary. The lackeys of the imperialists – the comprador capitalists, feudal landlords, warlords, bureaucrats, local despots and evil-minded gentry – rode roughshod over the people and bled them white. The broad mass of the people were in a state of slavery and utterly without rights. People of many national minorities suffered national oppression under the Han rulers in addition to oppression by the imperialists, and the aristocrats, landlords and slave-owners of their own nationalities. The country remained split for a long time; imperialist wars of aggression, the free-for-all fighting among different groups of warlords and the counter-revolutionary civil wars launched by the reactionary rulers continued for several decades and played havoc with the people. During the Kuomintang regime, bandits, gangsters, superstitious sects and secret societies ran riot everywhere; appalling lawlessness and utter disorder prevailed.

What tremendous changes have taken place in all this in the past ten years! The corrupt, iniquitous government which trampled upon the people is gone and has been replaced by an honest, industrious and hard-working government which really serves the people, a government of the kind the people dreamed of for generation after generation. The situation in which the people had no rights has ended once and for all; the broadest mass of the people enjoy democracy in law and in fact to the widest extent in the administration of the public affairs of the country. National oppression has been eliminated; our motherland has become a big family in which all nationalities are completely equal and give fraternal aid to one another. The country has achieved a unity of unprecedented firmness. Bandits, gangsters, superstitious sects and secret societies as well as prostitutes, beggars, gambling houses and narcotic drugs have all been swept away; there is law and order everywhere. The broad mass of the people, united as one and full of vigour, are building their own happy life eagerly, courageously and with boundless energy.

What a pitiful position China occupied ten years ago in international affairs is well known. For many years, China had been a colonial and semi-colonial country. The imperialistic powers regarded our country as rich booty from which everyone snatched what he could. The European imperialists tried to carve China up; the Japanese aggressors wanted to devour it alone and did swallow nearly half of it between 1937 and 1945. The United States, after the Second World War, was bent on taking over the place of the Japanese aggressors. China, the most populous country in the world, was not only deprived of the rights which were its due in international political life, but was almost deprived of the right to manage its own affairs.

The colonial and semi-colonial old China has now gone for ever; the people's new China has emerged, independent and free. As Comrade Mao Tse-tung declared at the founding of the People's Republic of China: 'Our nation will henceforth join the big family of peace-loving and freedom-loving nations in the world. It will work bravely and industriously to create its own civilization and happiness and will, at the same time, further world peace and freedom.' The weakness of China is being transformed into its opposite – strength. At the same time, internationally, the situation in which China had no rights is changing to its opposite. Over all the territory which has been liberated, it fully exercises its sovereignty; it must also exercise its right to have its say on all major international questions which concern its interests and the interests of world peace. U.S. imperialism, while launching its aggressive war with Korea, seized our territory Taiwan and tried to spread the flames of aggression from Korea to the Chinese mainland in a futile attempt to strangle new-born China by force of arms. The Chinese people waged a mighty struggle to resist U.S. aggression, aid Korea, protect their homes and defend their motherland, and they crushed this aggressive scheme. Taiwan is still occupied by U.S. imperialism, but the Chinese people are determined to liberate Taiwan and no force whatsoever can prevent them from doing so. Up to now U.S. imperialism is still trying hard to isolate and exclude New China from international affairs. This attempt, however, is becoming more and more a failure with every passing day. Now we have established full or partial diplomatic relations with thirty-three countries, economic relations with ninety-three countries and regions, and cultural contacts and exchanges of friendly visits with 104 countries and regions. We are closely united with the great Soviet Union and the other Socialist countries. In accordance with the 'five principles' and the Bandung Declaration, we have established and developed relations of friendship and cooperation with many nationally independent countries in Asia and Africa, forming a vast area of peace. As one of the big powers of the world and as a member of the great socialist camp headed by the Soviet Union, we have been contributing, as is our duty, to the defence of world peace and the development of human progress.

How is all this swift, flying progress to be explained? How has it taken place?

The swift, flying progress of People's China is, in the final analysis, due to the fact that Chinese society has undergone a most thoroughgoing democratic revolution and socialist revolution and that China has established a socialist society based on public ownership of the means of production.

If the Chinese people had not overthrown imperialism, feudalism and bureaucratic-capitalism which weighed upon them like three great mountains, they would, as a matter of course, only find themselves for ever plunged in poverty and backwardness. And if, after toppling these mountains, they had not taken the road of socialism at once, had not carried out thoroughly the socialist revolution, or had not embarked on planned socialist construction, but, after achieving national independence, had taken the road of capitalism like some other countries, they could not possibly have made such rapid progress in the past ten years, not to mention the big leap forward that has taken place since last year....

China's development in the past ten years has been a process of uninterrupted revolution.

As early as the Second Plenary Session of the Seventh Central Committee of the Chinese Communist Party held in March 1949, the Central Committee and Comrade Mao Tse-tung pointed out that the founding of the People's Republic of China would mark the victory of the democratic revolution on a nation-wide scale and at the same time the beginning of the socialist revolutions.* The state power of people's democratic dictatorship led by the proletariat and based on the worker–peasant alliance established in 1949 as a result of the victory of the revolution, though including some representatives of the national bourgeoisie, was in essence already a state power of the dictatorship of the proletariat. At that time, the central question of the nation-wide democratic revolution, that of overthrowing the reactionary rule of imperialism, feudalism and bureaucrat-capitalism, had been solved and the basic contradiction within the country was already one between the proletariat and the bourgeoisie. The revolution should not stop at the stage of democratic revolution, it must continue to develop towards the victory of the socialist revolution.

In the first few years after 1949 the Chinese people still had to exert very great efforts to accomplish the tasks left over from the stage of democratic revolution – principally the carrying through of the anti-feudal land reform on a national scale. Following the nation-wide victory of the great people's revolution in 1949, however, because of the confiscation of bureaucrat-capital and the change from bureaucrat-capitalist ownership to socialist ownership by the whole people, this great people's revolution, economically speaking, went beyond the scope of democratic revolution. It had become a task of prime importance for the proletariat and the other working people to build a mighty socialist state economy and to firmly establish their leading position in the whole national economy. To counter the activities of bourgeois law-breakers in disrupting

*This report, which in characteristically Maoist terms, formulated the policy of China's continuing revolution under working-class leadership, and described the revolutionary victory of 1949 as 'only a brief prologue to a long drama' is included in *Selected Works*, Vol. iv, pp. 361–75. There was some opposition within the top leadership to this thoroughgoing 'proletarian' line.

the socialist economy, the Party in 1952 led the mass struggle 'against the three evils' (corruption, waste and bureaucracy) among government functionaries, and 'against the five evils' (bribery, tax evasion, theft of state property, cheating on government contracts and stealing the state's economic information) among bourgeois industrialists and businessmen. This dealt a crushing blow to the offensive launched by the bourgeoisie and, on the basis of this victory, pushed capitalist industry and commerce a great step forward towards state capitalism which submitted itself to the leadership of the socialist economy and accepted supervision by the working class. After the land reform, the Central Committee of the Party issued timely directives on developing the movement of mutual aid and cooperation, vigorously encouraged and stimulated the peasants who used to work on their own to advance in the direction of cooperation and carried on a sharp, persistent struggle against thinking tending in the rightist direction on this question. The Central Committee of the Party and Comrade Mao Tse-tung firmly refuted such bourgeois points of view of certain people both inside and outside the Party as those calling for the 'consolidation of the new democratic order', 'long-term coexistence between socialism and capitalism' and the 'guaranteeing of the four great freedoms in the rural areas – freedom of sale and purchase, letting and renting of land, freedom of employing farm hands, freedom of borrowing and lending money and freedom of trading' and in good time set forth the Party's general line for the transition period of simultaneously carrying out socialist transformation and socialist construction.* This general line immediately won the support of the people of the whole country and was written

*The political struggle among the Chinese leaders became acute over the question of alternative paths to modernization and development. In 1955 Mao threw himself into the struggle against the 'bourgeois' policies of Liu Shao-chi. His 'On the Question of Agricultural Cooperation' persuaded his colleagues to total support for peasants who wanted co-operatives and, later, communes. After 1959, when the 'Maoists' were superseded by the 'moderates' the 'freedoms' described here by Chou En-lai were restored. The struggle between the two lines of policy was resumed during the Cultural Revolution.

into the Constitution of the People's Republic of China. Thanks to the adoption by the Party of a series of measures for socialist transformation without loss of time, the revolutionary movement advanced steadily without interruption and culminated in the emergence of a nation-wide upsurge in agricultural cooperation in the autumn and winter of 1955. This upsurge in turn set off the upsurge in the nation-wide switchover of capitalist industry and commerce to joint state-private operation by whole trades and stimulated the upsurge in the organization of handicraft cooperatives by individual handicraftsmen. In this way, the socialist revolution in the field of ownership of means of production was completed in the main.

But the task of socialist revolution did not end here. Not long after, the Party set a new task: it is necessary to continue the socialist revolution on the political and ideological fronts and carry it through. It is necessary to make the various aspects of the superstructure further fit in with the socialist economic base and, at the same time, the relations between men and men in production should be further adjusted on the basis of the already established ownership of the means of production so that the socialist relations of production would be further perfected and expanded. This was the task of the anti-rightist struggle and the rectification campaign in 1957–58. As a result of the anti-rightist struggle and the rectification campaign, the bourgeois rightists, who opposed socialism, were completely isolated from the people and the socialist consciousness of the mass of the people was greatly raised. The contradictions among the people were further dealt with correctly, and the relations between functionaries in state organs and enterprises and the mass of workers and peasants, and the mutual relations among the various nationalities, were all further improved. Thanks to the victory of the anti-rightist struggle and the rectification campaign, the revolutionary enthusiasm of the people throughout the country for building socialism soared to unparalleled heights.

6. FIDEL CASTRO

*

Beyond Spontaneity*

The revolutionary transformation of China, which has gone on continuously since 1949, was the work of men and women who had had considerable administrative and organizational experience since 1924; it was led by a disciplined party, with a clear ideological basis. In contrast, power fell suddenly to the Cuban revolutionaries in December 1958, and they had to learn as a group what work had to be done, how to organize it, and what the social and historical forces and possibilities were. For the leaders and the people the revolutionary process has been one of discovery. At a rally at Sagua la Grande on 9 April 1968 the Cuban Prime Minister Fidel Castro (b. 1927) explained the development of the revolutionary process in Cuba from 1959 onwards. The regular and direct political meetings between Prime Minister and people were themselves an institution of revolutionary Cuba, and Castro's style is worth noting.

... THEY still underestimated our people in 1959. They said 'Them? We'll wipe them out. We'll blockade them. We'll starve them. We'll force them to bite the dust.'

And that was not all, that was not all! They laboured under the incredibly stupid delusion that they could sweep the revolution aside with a piddling mercenary invasion, or that they could sweep the revolution aside with bandit uprisings. They did not know the calibre of the people they were dealing with. They did not find our people to be the people of yesteryear. Our people had changed greatly.

And what happened? Against the bandit uprisings in the mountains, thousands of workers and farmers were mobilized in Las Villas Province, particularly in the Escambray Mountain zone. And when a real deluge of weapons was parachuted into the Escambray to foment counter-revolution, battalions of

*From *Cuba Information Bulletin.*

workers were mobilized and went into the Escambray to support the soldiers, workers and farmers in the region. Fifty
thousand workers, all militiamen, went to the Escambray.
And the counter-revolutionaries were reduced to scarcely a
hundred.

And the hundred that remained were wiped out to the last
man after a long struggle by the worker–farmer militiamen
of the Escambray. But the imperialists still had the resort of a
mercenary invasion. And they truly believed that they were
going to crush this country with a mercenary invasion, with
surprise bombing raids at dawn, by treacherously seizing a
piece of national territory from which they could call in the
O.A.S. and systematically bomb this country.

What the imperialists could not imagine was that when they
came the revolutionaries would be ready for them. As the
farmers say: 'When they came, the revolutionaries were one
jump ahead of them.'

And when they dropped the first bombs on that 17 April the
troops had already mobilized; when they landed their mercenary battalions, and when that day dawned – that is, they
staged their aerial attack on the 15th, and when they landed
their troops on the 17th we had very few planes, that's true,
and even fewer pilots than planes, but those few planes were in
the air, and at dawn they sank the enemy ships and downed
a good part of their aircraft. And the rest were downed by anti-
aircraft artillery.

Contrary to what the mercenaries had been told about their
finding here a people awaiting them as liberators, they found
a torrent of soldiers; a torrent of armed workers; a torrent of
artillery, machine-guns and tanks; before they could even
code messages and tell their imperialist master that they
had been defeated, there were no more mercenaries left in the
area.

They had obviously underestimated our people; they believed we would get down on our knees; they believed they
could starve us; they believed that through their criminal
blockade they would encourage counter-revolution; they believed that through the privations they imposed on our people

and the obstacles they put in the path of our economic development discontent would grow, and counter-revolution would have a base and finally, once and for all, they would do as they pleased with this tiny country that, ninety miles from their coast, had held to its own ideas, held to its desires for independence and carried on its Revolution.

The years that have passed have therefore been decisive years for the history and the life of our country. On the one hand there has been imperialism, with all its resources, all its experience and all its criminal methods, trying to destroy the Revolution. And on the other hand there has been a nation of workers, farmers and students; a nation beginning to build its own destiny; a nation deserted by the learned, the well-educated; a nation that has had to begin practically from scratch, without experience of any kind, that had to confront the incredibly difficult problem of self-development in the modern era and under the imperialist economic blockade of our country.

And we can certainly say that this battle is being won, that this battle is practically won. We must explain why we said that 1 January 1959 marked the triumph of the rebellion, for surely, in all truth, we cannot say that 1 January marked the triumph of the Revolution, equating the Revolution with the war, identifying the Revolution only with the process of armed struggle; actually it was the rebellion that triumphed on 1 January.

With the triumph of the rebellion on 1 January the past, all the heritage of the past, all the deformations of the past and all the ideas of the past still persisted; there were still countless revolutionary organizations – or rather, countless political organizations, a few of them revolutionary, many others tied to the past, bearing responsibility for the past, ready to co-operate with the imperialists to prevent the triumph of the Revolution, ready to cooperate with the imperialists to turn the Revolution from its path.

What did the imperialists want? They wanted the revolutionaries to cease being revolutionaries. They want the revolutionaries to listen docilely to their points of view, their proposals. But things turned out very differently, and all their efforts clashed against the iron will of the revolutionaries – that is, of the true revolutionaries and the people.

But the revolution inherited that past, the mentality of the past. There was not even a political organization that represented the will and effort of all the people. It was necessary to spend years creating the instruments of the Revolution.

In those early days could we say, in truth, that we knew what a revolution was? In those days the prevalent sentiment was the sentiment of struggle, the sentiment of rebellion, but the concept of what a revolution was did not exist among the masses, nor could it then.

What happened? The workers, oppressed for many years, exploited by the monopolies, exploited by employers, believed the triumph of the Revolution was the beginning of a reign of abundance and wealth. They could not understand that in reality we were a poor country, an underdeveloped country, sucked dry by those monopolies and capitalists, they could not understand that in reality this was a poor country getting ready to develop its wealth.

Naturally property did not change hands, nor could it change hands the first day. On the first day of the triumph of the Revolution there were still monopolies, there were still bosses and private businessmen; and the workers, oppressed for many years, naturally went in search of new gains: reduction in the workday, wage increases, and so on and so forth. That can be easily explained; it was logical. But the Revolution, of course, could not be made the first day. Revolution is a process: private property had to pass to the hands of the nation, to the hands of the people; it had to cease being private property and become collective property.

But how many were there who could not understand that a revolution did not mean that the people would simply enter an era of wealth, but that it meant that they would begin to create that wealth, begin to lay the groundwork for that era of wealth? This was a nation whose population had doubled, whose economy had not grown, which was faced with needs of all kinds and, at the same time, had to begin to develop its economy, to invest in its development, to invest in industry, to acquire factories, to develop agriculture. And what happened? There were very few who understood that reality.

There was great inequity in workers' incomes. Those who worked, for example, in banks were well-organized and won demand after demand from their bosses – who obtained great profits and could raise their wages; we found that bank employees, for example, earned four, five or six times what a cane-cutter earned and, moreover, had vacations, enjoyed a series of benefits – the workers organized in some industries, including some monopolies, could win a number of benefits relatively easily by virtue of the strength of their organization; but hundreds of thousands of workers scattered throughout the countryside, without strength, without the conditions to win those economic battles, earned a fourth, a fifth, or a sixth of what was earned by those other workers.

How could the Revolution make this situation equitable? How could the Revolution raise the sugar-cane workers' standard to that of a bank employee? It couldn't be done. What could the Revolution, faced with an underdeveloped economy, provide for the millions of hungry or undernourished people?

But these things -- the great truth that the triumph of the Revolution did not mean access to wealth but rather meant the opportunity to create that wealth – were not sufficiently understood. Many workers were accustomed to working under a boss's whip, accustomed to being able to work for only a few months, plagued by unemployment, surrounded by hundreds of thousands of unemployed who were waiting for a job to become available so they could take it over. When the Revolution triumphed those workers acquired permanent work, job security, and were no longer beset by the myriad problems that had weighed on them – the likelihood of a child dying if he became sick, the need to pay for everything, the constant threat of unemployment. All those circumstances disappeared, and many who could not understand what the Revolution was all about began to work less than they had before, began to work seven, six, five, four hours a day. The tendency in the

381

early days of the Revolution was for efforts not to increase but to fall off.

And there is something that anyone can understand, today more clearly than ever. For today our nation is increasingly a nation of workers; today there are more and more people who know what it costs to produce bread, to produce crops, to struggle against plant disease, to struggle against underbrush, to struggle against hard-to-work land, to struggle against the weather, against hurricanes. Today the workers, who know what it is to cut sugar-cane by hand or to weed cane or other crops with a hoe, can understand perfectly that only job productivity and the use of technology, water conservation and flood control works to counter drought and flood, the control of plant disease, the mechanization of work and, as a consequence, job productivity, will permit a nation to have and enjoy an abundance of all it needs.

But how can an underdeveloped country, whose job productivity is ten or fifteen times less than that of a highly developed country, expect to enjoy the material goods that a developed country can enjoy? When our country's economy is developed, distribution will not be as it is in capitalist societies, where some have a great deal, where some have ten or twenty times or even a thousand or ten thousand times more than others. No. Distribution of wealth will be equitable. And, when the preliminary phases are concluded, men will receive not according to privilege, according to fortune, but according to need. Distribution will be just; but in order to distribute something, no matter how just that method of distribution may be, you must first have something to distribute. Justice doesn't create wealth: wealth is created through work. The most that justice can accomplish is to distribute that wealth in a humane way, a just way. Justice can be the yardstick for distributing what work creates. But justice cannot replace work in the creation of wealth.

And these are the questions that our people now understand. They are matters that our people now understand with remarkable clarity. If not, how could we explain the present situation in our country? How could we explain this extraordinary mass

382

movement? How could we explain this tremendous effort in the revolutionary offensive? How could we explain the fantastic mobilization of workers from one end of the country to the other? And how could we explain how it is that the same holds true in Pinar del Rio, in Matanzas, in Havana, in Oriente, in Camaguey, in Las Villas? And now – no longer speaking of pre-revolutionary days – who would be willing to work for Señor so-and-so, or for such-and-such a monopoly?

For the people – and this is crystal clear – are only capable of doing this when they are working for their economy; when they are working for their industry, for their agriculture; when they are working to create their wealth.

And this is the contradiction that can never be overcome by the underdeveloped countries that seek to develop their economies by capitalist methods. Bourgeois governments and bourgeois politicians call on the workers to make sacrifices, to work more and to consume less in order to develop the economy; but the workers say: 'Sacrifice, for whom? Save, for whom? Lower consumption, for whom? So that a group of you can become richer? So that you can have more millions? So that you can own more factories? No! I don't care if there's only a little bit, but out of that little bit you have to give me a little more.' And that's logical, that's natural. ...

7. FIDEL CASTRO

*

Problems of the Revolution
of Rising Expectations *

A growing revolutionary consciousness among the mass of the
people also arouses and sharpens the awareness of deprivations and
of human possibilities. There is a 'revolution of rising expectations',
as transformations take place, and new problems, belonging to a
new era, are added to those of the old which have not been solved.
Young, relatively inexperienced revolutionaries had achieved rapid
success in ambitious health, education, construction and housing
programmes, but how was all this to be part of an even more
ambitious political revolution? Castro in 1966 shared some of his
problems as an administrator with the Congress of Cuban Trade
Unions. What follows is an excerpt.

WE think that the pledge of placing prime importance upon
the effort in agriculture has been a great one. In recent years
we have been concentrating the greatest part of our efforts on
agriculture. By any chance does this mean that we should abandon industry? No! Industry needs a great deal of skilled
personnel, industry needs many technicians, which, by the way,
are being formed – industry needs big investments, projects.
Any factory requires months, sometimes years, for projects,
and more years in their construction, plus scores of skilled
workers and technicians.

Our country is making a serious effort in the principal
branches of industry such as electricity, construction; you all
know that we are constructing two cement factories which
together will produce almost one million tons of cement: plans
are being made to construct more cement factories so that we
may reach a production capacity of two and a half million
tons by 1970. We are all, all of us, extraordinarily interested in
the development of the construction industry, and above all,

* From *Cuba Information Bulletin.*

384

in the production of cement. Why? Because this is germane to all of our economic plans. Coffee-growers need cement for their drying platforms; the cattle industry needs cement for the installation of dairies; hydraulic works need cement for the construction of sewers and aqueducts; in a word, all agricultural activities, and all industrial activities, need cement. It's been some time now that this country has had a cement shortage.

Now. What is the most urgent problem of all? What is the most constant demand of this population? Housing! We are aware of the fact that the problems most frequently posed to us in the street, or anywhere in the country, are problems related to housing! Something very interesting has come up concerning the housing situation. It would never have occurred to anyone before that an administrator (or a politician) could solve someone's housing problem; this never occurred to anyone. As a result of the Urban Reform, due to which a great number of people no longer pay rent, due to which the housing problem has been solved for a great number of families, the hunger for housing has made itself felt in all those who live in shacks, in all those who live in one room, in all those who live in places which are practically uninhabitable. A hunger and a need for housing is evident. Whenever we stop to talk with the public, there is always a number of people who ask us for houses. This is one of the most disagreeable problems we have to face. There are many problems that are within our capacity to solve. Scholarships? Practically everyone who has asked for a scholarship – despite the enormous rate at which the number of these requests is growing – has been able to receive one. Many problems can be attended to in this manner, but the housing problem causes us great concern because we are unable to grant the requests we are made. We are asked something we are unable to give, something which we could give only if we could use a 'Mandrake the Magician' formula; pulling the houses out of a hat. There are some people who have said to us: 'I have been waiting for a chance to see you. What a lucky break!' Here is a case where 'opportunism' comes to the surface. Why? The person says: 'Can you solve this problem?' Yes, I can solve it by harming someone else. How? Let us say we find someone who really needs a house, because the whole family – four or five – live in one room. There is a reserve of houses, comprising either the ones that have been built or those that are vacant. If any of us solves that problem by giving this family one of the houses in reserve, it may very well be a house that was already marked for someone else and for all we know, the latter's family may consist of seven people – not five – living in one room. There are still among our people – unfortunately we must say this – a series of habits left over from the past. Many people see the public figure, the administration official, the government official, as a sort of servant, to be used when the opportunity arises. We like to visit places, projects under construction, factories, farms, etc., and study all the problems of these work centres. Very often there are problems to be solved: supplies, lack of cold drinking water, which may require the use of a mobile tank. These are collective problems that we can solve. The tragic part comes once the collective problems have been taken care of. Ten people show up and say: 'This is my problem. I was waiting for a chance to talk to you, so you could get me a house.' The house, always the house. And they drop their problems into our lap.

It is our duty to visit places and concentrate upon pressing matters, to find the solution to collective problems, but often we are subjected to the torture of being asked to solve problems we cannot solve. We suffer when we realize how many people behave this way, begging for favours just as in the past. In the past, if someone needed to be admitted to a hospital, it had to be requested as a favour; for someone to receive an education, another favour; favours, favours, all the time. Our people became conditioned to thinking of the individual. Don't they realize that we are human beings? That we must think and concentrate in order to devote ourselves to fundamental questions of interest to a great many people?

Often they stop us and tell us their problem. It isn't so bad if it is something that can be remedied, but we suffer when they ask for something we cannot do anything about. Besides, look-

386

ing for a solution to their problems by using this method is not the correct thing to do. This is doing a favour by depriving someone else of his rights. This is solving problems by cheap political methods. And we cannot become 'cheap politicians'. We cannot solve anyone's problems at someone else's expense.

Is there a dire need of houses? Of course there is. Can we understand the anxiety of many families, anxious to have a house of their own? Yes, it is understandable; it is logical. And, of course, many people tormented by their plight, do not reason. We have met people who were actually in a traumatic condition: 'I live under a staircase,' they say, 'under a staircase!' and they make it sound almost as if it were our fault. What is our duty as revolutionaries? To say 'yes' to everyone and do nothing? No. To go around playing politics, and solving problems with that type of method? No. The correct solution, the revolutionary solution is for us to move ahead with the construction of houses, and above all, the production of cement, one factory, then two, then three, the problem of steel rods, installations, piping, all that is needed to build at least 100,000 houses per year. If we manage to increase housing construction to 100,000 houses per year, we can solve that problem in fifteen years. The housing shortage in this country consists of approximately one million houses. A million houses, including people who have no houses, others who live at someone else's house, and those who live in one room; those living under staircases, and in palm-thatched huts. According to research made, we need one million houses. For that we must use at least one million tons of cement. Furthermore, we must mechanize construction so that twenty or twenty-five thousand workers can build 100,000 houses, because all the man-power in construction cannot be allotted to housing only.

This is, however, a problem that will take time; a problem that depends on the previous development of the construction industry, the mechanization of construction, cement production, and all the other items needed for housing.

Because, of course, it is not only the problem of building a house. Streets must be constructed, running water has to be provided. When a water supply is installed, drains have to be laid down at the same time. If not, what happened in the town of Nueva Gerona on the Isle of Pines, occurs. The aqueduct was built there, but no drainage system was constructed suitable for a real aqueduct but rather adequate only for bucketsful of water – today, frequently the water floods into the streets of Nueva Gerona, overflowing the wells. Today, the problem must be rapidly solved. How can such a problem be solved so as to avoid epidemics? By finding water pumps to do the work that a sewer and drainage system could easily solve.

And almost every town in Cuba lacks a sewer system as well as an aqueduct. All these small towns – with reason – want a sewer system to be built and they want an aqueduct system – with reason; and these towns want schools to be built; every town wants a medical dispensary or a hospital to be constructed; they all need roads, sports fields, stadiums. Moreover, in every region there is the need for economic development. All that is quite logical. In addition, everyone wants a new house; but they also want milk delivery every morning at breakfast time, and to build the dairy, we have to have cement.

What have we acquired to date? Awareness of our needs. But in addition to awareness of our needs, we have gained the hope of solving them. But what has occurred? The pressures are tremendous and our resources are still limited.

A party comrade in Baracoa presents the problem of a movie house there. The existing movie will not hold all the people who wish to attend; a new one is needed because of the long lines to get in. Another comrade asks for something else. Everyone is requesting something because everyone can see where the needs are. Everyone wants his problem to be solved. And out resources are limited.

And the problem of the correct distribution of funds is becoming a very serious one.

I am certain that if we put the same spirit and effort into giving as we put into taking, we should be able to solve this country's problems much more rapidly.

If there is no bread because the bakery is old, this of course presents a problem of bread supply, and probably cement is required for that bakery. And so, it is first one and then another, and cement is needed for industrial plants as well. If there is no medical doctor, that is a real tragedy. The limited resources at our disposal must be invested very wisely and their distribution settled by a system of priority for each problem as it arises. However, we should understand once and for all that our citizens need to recognize the fact that our public officials are men who are carrying out a duty; that they must serve collective social interests, and that they must devote their time and energy to this task.

We are all working in the struggle, and it is not a question of delivering a sermon to someone just because we cannot solve the problem he presents. And from experience I know that there is nothing more inopportune than a sermon, when a pressing need is presented. This I understand from experience. It is ridiculous. And it is ridiculous to put ourselves in the position of delivering a sermon to some person with an urgent need because he is living in a room with eight other persons, for example. Because, what will this person think at that moment? He can only see the room, the over-crowding, and the house which is about to collapse. What philosophic explanation can this person grasp, and what non-philosophic arguments are worthwhile in such a case? He believes that this is his opportunity, that his lucky number has come up; because this is the day he will solve the problem.

Ah, no! We must educate ourselves collectively. We must develop that awareness collectively. . . .

And it's true that sometimes they have been distributing badly. But what is to be done? Men are not perfect and – unfortunately – there are people who do things badly. But the essence of the problem is not that; the essence is that a million homes are needed. Because of a series of cave-ins, it was necessary to give priority to many families who lived in homes that were on the verge of collapse. In order to do this, normal distribution through the trade unions was halted, obliging people who were at the top of the waiting list for homes to wait for months. Thus, some received apartments without being on the waiting list, because they lived in buildings in imminent danger of collapse.

Thousands of families in the capital of the Republic, literally thousands, have been moved for safety reasons, and they had to be given those homes. Very well, the need for homes is tremendous; the people of Havana need them and ask for them, the population grows. And yet, in the interior of the country, the situation is worse. The conditions in which the workers of Moa lived were appalling. It was necessary if we wanted those workers to have minimal living conditions, in order to develop that industry – to allot a given quantity of cement to the building of homes in Moa. Even more shocking was the situation in Nicaro, where it was necessary to build the village of Levisa to solve the problem.

The housing needs are worse in the interior of the country, they are worse. And, of course, all of the needs are very great, and we have to be aware of this problem.

It is healthy for the citizenry, collectively, to be conscious of their problems; it is necessary and it is very healthy. Because in the measure that we are conscious of our problems, we will all work for the solution of these problems.

In our Revolution, under socialism, between the people and the governing power there is not, nor can there be, contradictions, there is not nor can there be antithesis, our duty is to do the maximum, it is to do what we are able to and more than we are able to. Our duty is to think, to find solutions to problems, to go to the root of difficulties and resolve them. And when we cannot and if we are not capable, we must change jobs. We need only to realize that we are not being useful since the men in a revolution who have certain responsibilities – the kind of official, I mean – must be men without any vested interest in the post itself, and conscious that public work is the most demanding; the most wearing; it is work which demands that one live under tension, work, and concern oneself with the solution to problems.

And men of the Revolution are not politicians. And we must teach the people that only those who can give the maximum, to do the maximum honestly and without demagogy, without

390

deceit, and without politicking will have the right to be at the helm of their destiny.

The people and revolutionary leaders must educate themselves in these concepts, and such men have a task, a job within society, perhaps the hardest, perhaps, on many occasions, the bitterest, perhaps in many instances the tensest. And under socialism these contradictions and the solution to problems is not only the affair of those who govern, it is the affair of those who govern and of the people, of the government along with the people, and of the people along with the government.

In socialism, every citizen must be responsible, every citizen must know that a great responsibility rests upon him, and we must strive to teach this to the people. Not a cult, a fanatic cult, not blind obedience nor magic formulas conjured up by me to solve problems. We believe that individual men have a very limited role, we think that the less necessary specific individuals may be, the better it will always be.

Formerly, officials, ministers were looked upon as legendary personages. There were people who were overjoyed if an alderman shook their hand; if the mayor greeted them one day, they felt happy. How could one even dream of talking with a minister? He was a person from another world. With the Revolution these differences had to disappear. With the Revolution, these differences have disappeared. I do not know of one official of the Revolution who is like those of former times! I do not know one citizen who does not feel perfectly at ease speaking with any leader of the Revolution, without becoming nervous, or thinking that this is out of the ordinary. And people must cooperate so that men who have responsibilities maintain contact with them. They must not drive away men who occupy responsible positions by driving them mad.

There have been times when a well-known comrade has to go to the beach. Ah, but he cannot go to the beach. Why? Because he has to go where everyone goes. And then twenty people descend on that poor individual, looking for solutions to their problems. They scare him away from contact with the people. They deprive him of the possibility of going to the source from which he can learn the most, from which most can be gathered, the people.

In my revolutionary experience, I have never been better informed than when I speak with the people, than when I get together with workers, with students, with farmers. I have attended two universities in my life: one where I learned nothing and another where I learned all, and the second was my contact with people, with their interests, their worries, with their problems, with those things that concern them. There should not be one man who considers himself a political cadre who does not possess the sensitivity to feel deeply about people and their problems.

Any defect, except insensibility, can be forgiven. Therefore, the political cadre cannot be formed in a university, the political cadre cannot be formed in a school. In a school, the culture of one who has the innate capacities of a political cadre, of one who has a political vocation, can be developed. Politics is a vocation, even though it is a transitory phenomenon. The less the masses participated, the more important were the politicians. And the day must even come when there will be no politicians, when each citizen will be the political cadre. The day must arrive when this odious office of cadre disappears.

In socialism, or rather in communism, it is said that the State will disappear. The State is understood to be a coercive force. Engels said that the activity of governing people would be substituted by the administration of things. That is the society we want to see. That is the society we aspire to, the society in which the masses will have maximum participation, total participation. But exercise much caution with slogans, much caution with distorted interpretations!

8. OGINGA ODINGA

*

Organizing for Mass Democracy*

How the revolutionary political activity of the masses can be organized after independence to give political and economic substance to democracy is one of the questions which arises in the process of decolonization. From Cuba we move to Kenya. One of the political leaders who worked for and achieved the end of British Colonial Office rule in Kenya was Oginga Odinga (b. 1911). He had always been a radically anti-imperialist and outspoken politician, but, not being of the majority Kikuyu people, had not been detained during the 'Mau-Mau' emergency. Odinga was appointed Vice-President of independent Kenya, but his notions of how democracy should be strengthened and the national interest safeguarded were not shared by some of his colleagues, and he was forced out of office, and out of the Kenya African National Union, of which he was a founder. He has continued, under difficult conditions, to be active in Kenyan politics. The excerpts which follow are taken from his autobiography *Not Yet Uhuru*.

DURING the Emergency years the struggle was intensely bitter, but it was open conflict. Without the forest fighters in the so-called 'Mau-Mau' period, Kenya's independence would still be a dream in the minds of a few visionary politicians, for the rising in Kenya brought independence nearer not only for Kenya but, in precipitating an adaptation in British colonial policy, for the whole of East Africa.

But freedom for Kenya came not at victory point, as in Algeria, at the climax of the military rising, but only five years later, in staggered stages after the administrators of the colonial system had made preparations for the timing and the manner of the independence takeover. I have tried to describe in detail how every type of local separatism and tribalism was encouraged to prevent a strong national movement; how, when settler groups could no longer protect their

*From *Not Yet Uhuru* (London: Heinemann, 1967).

393

interests in the names of White parties, from the benches of the legislature, they switched to lobby, caucus and backroom activity, and then used African political movements, especially KADU and *majimbo*, to protect settler policies. By the time it became clear that KANU could not be stopped from heading the first independence government, the ground had been laid by settler activity and by careful Colonial Office planning, for the slowing down of the full achievement of our independence aims.

Some of us were, perhaps, slow to realize that the time when accession to independence was progress in itself had passed. Only the political and economic content of that independence can reveal whether it will have real meaning for the mass of the people. President Nasser has been foremost among those who have warned against the leaders of popular movements who give themselves up to deceptive constitutional façades while imagining that they have attained complete freedom.

The stage following on independence is the most dangerous. This is the point after which many national revolutions in Africa have suffered a setback, for there has been a slide back into complacency after the first victory over external control and pressure, and national governments have left too much in their countries unchanged, have not built for effective independence by transferring power and control to the authentic forces and support of the national revolution, and have forgotten that internal elements of exploitation are closely related to reactionary external pressures.

Neo-colonialism, after all, is not centred in a vacuum. It is built on the previous colonial history of the country in which it operates, from foundations that the colonial regime lays before its ostensible departure. The object of neo-colonialism is to ensure that power is handed to men who are moderate and easily controlled, political stooges. Everything is done to ensure that the accredited heirs of colonial interests capture power. This explains the pre-independence preoccupation of the colonial power with the creation of an African middle class and the frenzy to corrupt leaders at all levels with the temptations of office and property and preferably both. Throughout

394

Kenya's colonial period the colonial governments, aided by the settlers, concentrated on infiltrating the nationalist movement and creating and encouraging divisions and splits within it. The constitutions that were devised incorporated provisions that gave institutional form to the forces of distrust and dis-unity which had been fostered. Independence was on the way in East Africa, and Britain had reconciled herself, in the first instance, to the attainment of independence by Tanganyika and Uganda. But though Britain was reconciled to the fact of surrendering direct control over former colonies, she was by no means prepared to withdraw her influence completely. The strategy was to place in power in Kenya those elements that would be favourably inclined to Britain, and would safeguard her economic and military interests. This explains the never-ceasing efforts to foster moderate elements and to try to weaken the genuine progressive nationalists who recognized the forces of neo-colonialism and would not cooperate with them.

Silencing the militants and encouraging the moderate politi-cal spokesmen was one aspect of neo-colonialism; another aspect was the economic burden with which Kenya was saddled from the start of *uhuru* and the economic directions which were laid down irreversibly for us. As independence approached we we're saddled with ever-increasing financial obligations arising out of Britain's subsidization of the exodus of settlers and civil servants, and the land compensation policies estab-lished for us. Britain seemed more concerned with arranging compensation for those who were leaving Kenya than the state of things they would leave behind for the people of Kenya.

KANU, the party, it seemed to me, was the key to our advance. If the party could be associated with policy-making at all levels, including the Cabinet level, the whole national effort could be galvanized for advance. No popular policy would be possible without a strong and vigorous party. Where there was no united and powerful national movement neo-colonialism moved in and thrived.

The one-party state has become a feature of very many parts

of independent Africa. The party political system of the West-minster type grew out of a highly stratified society of conflict-ing power interests. We regarded the *uhuru* period as the culmination of the struggle for independence, when national mobilization was needed for a set of political and economic *uhuru* aims – expressed as 'African Socialism' – to which all forces and economic groups in the country would subjugate their efforts. But a one-party government could be democratic only if the mass of the people were associated with policy-making at all levels, if the people were drawn into the running of the party, if national issues were discussed in the branches, at public meetings, at conferences, in our newspapers, among our women and the youth; if careful thought was given to the role of the party in relation to the administration so that civil servants trained in pre-colonial attitudes could not, in the day-to-day running of the country, undo the best plans made by the political leadership. The existence of one party, an umbrella party, meant that all policy decisions and differences had to be hammered out within the party. There could be fierce controversy, but once majority decisions were taken through democratic process they had to be accepted. Differ-ences of opinion there would inevitably be, but they would have to be resolved within the ranks of the party, by full and open discussion, not by intrigue and manoeuvre, or the running of local or tribal support. Discipline was essential to unity. The man who appeared on a party platform one day to take part in open discussion but met the next week in a caucus of his personal or tribal followers to plan counter-decisions sabo-taged our national cause.

The party, as I saw it, was the guardian of our *uhuru* aims. A vigorous party organization that made public representatives subject to discipline and whose organizers were trained in the spirit of sacrifice for *uhuru* was the only guarantee against politicians jockeying for position to further their own ambi-tions. Since the formation of K A N U in 1960, during the general elections of 1961 and 1963, we had been pursued by the devils of personality rivalry, tribal allegiance, and the undermining of party discipline.

Two things were essential for a strong party: an independent party press and a training school for party officials. Pio Pinto was a moving spirit in the establishment of Pan-Africa Press which published a weekly in Dhluo, *Nyanza Times*, a weekly in Swahili, *Sauti ya Mwafrika*, and a bi-monthly in English, *Pan-Africa*; and in the formation of the Lumumba Institute. Kenyatta performed the opening ceremony of the Lumumba Institute at the end of 1964 during the *Jamhuri* Celebrations of the declaration of Kenya as a Republic. . . .

A year after *uhuru* several tendencies, then, were taking place simultaneously. A group in the Cabinet, growing alarmed at the strength of back-bench and popular pressure, was resorting to caucus forms of procedure and was excluding some of us in the Cabinet from decision-making procedures. The party, as the expression of the will of the ordinary people, was not being allowed to function, and despite repeated requests by branches for the holding of a conference and new elections, head office stalled on this demand. K A D U'S joining the party gave the party officials a prolonged pretext for delaying national elections and a national conference, because all the K A N U branches had to hold elections to absorb K A D U members at their local levels.

It seemed to me that our leaders in government and party were retreating from the people, that every excuse was being made to avoid consulting them, and that government by a small circle of leaders could too easily be influenced by forces against the national interest. This is not something I have ever had to learn from books; it is the experience of my accumulated years in political life. I have frequently had the experience of being manipulated by political forces, but where I have judged that national unity is the prime need, I have put up with the slander and the intrigue, the rumours and manoeuvres, because it is my conviction that in the long run the people will decide, and as they have not prestige and office to protect, but their right to land, jobs and social services, they are the best judge of policies and leaders.

I believe in making the democratic process work in the party, in government, among the people. We fought for *uhuru*

397

so that the people may rule themselves. Direct action, not underhand diplomacy and silent intrigue by professional politicians, won *uhuru,* and only popular support and popular mobilization can make it meaningful. This is one of my convictions repeated with, to some, monotonous regularity over the years. My second conviction is that at this time in history if Africa is to be really free, if we are to attain true economic independence – and let us remember that this stage is crucial for if we fail to attain true economic independence we will rob our political freedom of its lasting guarantee – we must follow a policy of non-alignment, of relations with both 'east' and 'west', with both capitalist and socialist countries. If our aid and investment come from one source only we can banish the prospect of pursuing an independent policy, for we will be brought under control by the withholding of aid, or by some other economic pressure. As an African nationalist I cannot tolerate an African regime dominated by either the 'west' or the 'east'. If non-alignment is used to justify relations with one of these worlds alone, it is not non-alignment. Kenya is still today largely part of the Western sphere of interest and investment. To reach the non-aligned position we must break this predominantly Western influence, and develop relations with the East. It was with the deliberate intent of making Kenya less dependent on the colonial powers that I have worked for relations with the socialist countries, and this, not the development of relations with the West alone, is the true policy of non-alignment for Kenya. The fiercer the attacks on the socialist countries – and on me for visiting them – the more convinced I became that we in the colonial countries struggling for full freedom can find much in common with socialist policies and economic planning, and that if the colonial powers that have tried for so long to keep us inferior are so alarmed at our efforts to seek relations with the socialist world, this must be the true path of non-alignment. Non-alignment, let us remember, means that we shall tie ourselves to no power *bloc*; and that while we shall not necessarily opt for neutrality on every issue, ours will be the freedom to decide.

The danger in Kenya has never been communism but im-

perialism and its remnant. I told the Pafmesca* conference at
Addis Ababa that the snake in the bush is less dangerous than
the snake in our house, which is imperialism. Why seek a non-
existent enemy when we already have a fight on our hands
against the remnants of imperialism? If communism were to
prove a problem in the future we would deal with it, I told the
conference. Nothing had happened in Kenya between the 1963
Addis Ababa Pafmesca Conference and the end of 1964 and
Jamhuri to make me change my mind that no communist
forces were actively plotting against Kenya. I am convinced
that the external vested interests at play in Kenya are not communist forces, but the result of the involvement of an increasing
number of politicians in British, American and West German
commerce and big business.

Political intrigue, caucus decisions and ambitions for office
cannot thrive side by side with a vigorous, popularly-based
party machine, or democratic decision-making of any kind.
KANU itself was being left to wither but the KANU Parliamentary Group was hard at work; though far from being
welcomed by the Government as a ginger group to keep contact with the people, it was resented and frowned upon.

The life and soul of the KANU Parliamentary Group, of
the pressure for federation, of the attempts to build a KANU
press and the Lumumba Institute to train grass-roots organizers, was my close friend and associate, Pio Pinto.† On the
morning of 24 February 1965 as Pio drove his car down the
drive of his home, with his year-old daughter on the back seat,
an assassin hidden behind the fence called out 'Jambo, Bwana'
and shot Pio in the stomach. Moments later he was dead.

* Pan-African Freedom Movement of East and Central Africa, formed
in 1958.
† Born 1927. Detained in 1954 at the outbreak of Mau Mau 'emergency', and released in 1959.

9. SOONG CHING-LING

*

Counter-Revolution in China: 1927*

In 1927, at the moment of victory, Sun Yat-sen's Kuomintang-
Communist-led alliance of all revolutionary forces was destroyed
from within by the seizure of power by the military under Chiang
Kai-shek in the name of anti-Communism. What was the way
forward in those circumstances? Tactically, would a change of
course be necessary? Soong Ching-ling (see p. 180) herself a member
of the Kuomintang Central Committee, issued a statement, from
which the next piece is taken.

TODAY we face a crisis and we must probe searchingly into
fundamental questions for fundamental answers. We must
answer the questions of the nature of revolution in general, of
the Chinese revolution in particular, whether it is to be a
political or social revolution, and what changes are involved.

In the last analysis, all revolution must be social revolution,
based upon fundamental changes in societies; otherwise it is
not a revolution, but merely a change of government.

To guide us in the Chinese revolution, Sun Yat-sen has
given us his Three Principles and his Three Policies. It is the
Third Principle, that of the livelihood of the people, that is at
stake at the present time, the Principle that answers the questions of fundamental social changes in China.

This Third Principle was felt by Sun to be basic in our revolution. In this Principle we find his analysis of social values and
the place of the labouring and peasant classes defined. These
classes become the basis of our strength in our struggle to overthrow imperialism and cancel the unequal treaties that enslave
us, and effectively unify the country. These are the new pillars
for the building up of a new, free China. Without their support,
the Kuomintang, as a revolutionary party, becomes weak,

*From *The Struggle for New China* (Peking: Foreign Languages Press,
1952).

chaotic and illogical in its social platform; without their support, political issues are vague. If we adopt any policy that weakens these supports, we shake the very foundation of our Party, betray the masses and are falsely loyal to Sun Yat-sen.

Today there is much talk of policy. Sun defined Three Policies, which he decided were the only means by which his Three Principles could be carried out. But today it is being said that policies must be changed to fit the needs of the time. There is some truth in this statement, but change of policy should never be carried to the point where it becomes a reversal, so that a revolutionary party ceases to be revolutionary and becomes merely an organ, operating under the banner of revolution, but actually working in support of the very social structure which the party was founded to alter.

At the moment, we face critical issues. Theoretical and practical differences have arisen between various elements of the party. Drastic solutions are suggested. It is because I feel that the carrying out of these suggested solutions would destroy the strength of the party and delay the success of the revolution, that I must speak. These solutions seem to me a part of a policy which would alienate and suppress the classes upon which our strength largely depends and for which the revolution must be fought. Such a policy, I feel, is doomed to failure.

This new policy is proposed as a corrective to mistakes that have been made. But the corrective seems to me more serious than the mistakes.

It is time now for honesty and courage. There have been mistakes, but the fact that some of us are unwilling to face is that we are at least as responsible for many of these mistakes as those whom we would now hold completely at fault. If we look back honestly at the past months in Wuhan, examine our words and decisions unflinchingly, we cannot evade this responsibility. Speeches and statements are recorded in the history of the Party. But now we would shirk the responsibility and shift it to other shoulders.

Yes, there have been mistakes, but we must face the fact that they are not only others' mistakes; they are our own as well.

We have helped to make them; we must correct them. Moreover, for revolutionary mistakes, revolutionary solutions must be found. We must not betray the people. We have built up in them a great faith. To that faith we owe our final allegiance.*

Sun Yat-sen came from the people. He told me a great deal about his early days. He came from the peasantry. His father was a farmer and the people in his district were farmers.

Sun was poor. Not until he was fifteen years old did he have shoes for his feet, and he lived in a hilly region where it is not easy to be a barefoot boy. His family, until he and his brother were grown, lived almost from hand to mouth, in a hut. As a child he ate the cheapest food – not rice, for rice was too dear. His main nourishment was sweet potatoes.

Many times Sun has told me that it was in those early days, as a poor son of a poor peasant family, that he became a revolutionary. He was determined that the lot of the Chinese peasant should not continue to be so wretched, that little boys in China should have shoes to wear and rice to eat. For this ideal he gave forty years of his life.

Yet today the lot of the Chinese peasant is even more wretched than in those days when Sun Yat-sen was driven by his great sense of human wrongs into a life of revolution. And today men, who profess to follow his banner, talk of classes and think in terms of a 'revolution' that would virtually disregard the sufferings of those millions of poverty-stricken peasants of China.

Today also we hear condemnation of the peasant and labour movement as a recent, alien product. This is false. Twenty, thirty years ago, Sun was thinking and speaking in terms of a

*The detailed history of the past years was very complicated. Madame Sun issued this statement on 14 July, 1927, when the Revolutionary Government, which had moved its capital to Wuhan, had decided to expel its Communist members and outlaw their supporters. Their fear of their own military had greater influence than their hopes of revolutionary success. The 'others' whose mistakes are referred to were Stalin and his agents, who were concerned for Russian national interests as Stalin saw them. The Kuomintang government won the approval and support of the Chinese gentry, the landlords and businessmen, and foreign interests in China, and civil war began in 1927.

revolution that would change the status of the Chinese peasant. In his early twenties he wrote to Li Hung-chang, petitioning for social and economic reforms. In 1911, he wrote an article on the agrarian question in China, printed in Geneva in *The Socialist,* in which he said that the basis of social and economic transformations in China is an agrarian revolution. All his life this was one of the big goals he had in mind. Everything he planned he saw as a means to the betterment of the life of the Chinese masses.

In 1915, when we were in Japan, he urged Liao Chung-kai to study more deeply into the peasant and labour problems.

It is only in the past few years, after four decades of struggle, that these plans for a revolution of the people have begun to bear fruit. I remember clearly the first All-Kwangtung Peasants' Conference, in Canton, in July 1924. Then for the first time, we saw the people of China, who must be her new strength, coming to participate in the revolution. From all the districts of Kwangtung the peasants came, many of them walking miles and miles, barefooted, to Canton. They were ragged, tattered. Some carried baskets and poles. I was deeply moved.

Sun Yat-sen was also. When we reached home, he said to me: 'This is the beginning of the success of the revolution', and he told me again the part the oppressed people of China must play in their own salvation.

All these years, his purpose was clear. But today we talk of recent foreign influence. Was Sun Yat-sen, the leader who was voicing the agrarian revolution for China when Russia was still under the heel of the Tsar, was he the tool of foreign scheming?

Sun Yat-sen's policies are clear. If leaders of the Party do not carry them out consistently, then they are no longer Sun's true followers, and the Party is no longer a revolutionary party, but merely a tool in the hands of this or that militarist. It will have ceased to be a living force working for the future welfare of the Chinese people, but will have become a machine, the agent of oppression, a parasite battening on the present enslaving system.

We face a serious crisis. But it is more a crisis for us as

individuals than for China as a country. Whether the present Kuomintang at this moment rises to the height of its ideals and courageously finds a revolutionary corrective for its mistakes, or whether it slumps into the shamefulness of reaction and compromise, the Three Principles of Sun Yat-sen will conquer in the end. Revolution in China is inevitable.

At this moment, I feel that we are turning aside from Sun Yat-sen's policy of leading and strengthening the people. Therefore I must withdraw until wiser policies prevail.

There is no despair in my heart for the revolution. My disheartenment is only for the path into which some of those who had been leading the revolution have strayed.

But although there are members of the Party who are straying from the path Sun charted for the revolution for China, millions of people in China who have already come under the banner of the Party will continue on this path to the final goal. This means that I shall not keep faith alone. I am certain that all true members of the Kuomintang will take this revolutionary path.

10. MEHDI BEN BARKA

*

Resolving the Ambiguities of
National Sovereignty

More than thirty years after those fighting for the peasants and factory-workers in China were confronted with the problems which Soong Ching-ling discusses, the Moroccan Mehdi Ben Barka (1920–64), contemplated what seemed like a similar trend internationally. Ben Barka, born in poverty, had from his student days been active in Morocco's fight for independence from France. He successfully mobilized mass support in the struggle against French imperial rule, and was President of independent Morocco's Consultative Assembly from 1956 to 1958 when moves by less radical elements in Morocco pushed him out. As Secretary-General of the National Union of Popular Forces he went into exile, and before his murder in France in 1964 he had begun work as organizing secretary of the first tri-continental conference. What follows was written in 1962, and addressed to revolutionaries in the tricontinental south.

OUR revolutionary optimism and our total confidence in the final outcome of the anti-imperialist stuggle must not prevent us from observing and analysing with lucidity a dangerous ebbing of the revolutionary movement on certain fronts, which risks, if no remedy is found, delaying the liquidation of the colonial system, strengthening neo-colonialism in all its forms and hindering the continuation of the struggle for the real liberation and the economic and social development of our peoples.

There is no use lamenting the tragic death of Lumumba or the disintegration of his party. Likewise, it is not enough to denounce the degeneration of some political or trades-union leader or some king or minister who, after participating in the national struggle, betrays the ideals that he held for a moment, in order to serve imperialist manoeuvres and sacrifice the vital interests of his people in the name of ephemeral advantages, real or hypothetical.

It is essential to explain and halt this phenomenon of ebbing, which is marked by failures and momentary disappointments.

In the light of experience, we can perhaps find the cause of this ebbing in the gap that exists between the revolutionary aspirations and potentialities of our popular masses on one hand and, on the other, the subjective conditions of action offered them by present-day organizations with their slogans and their programmes which are often incapable of bringing the masses to the height of their historic tasks.

The role of the revolutionaries of Africa and Asia is, first of all, to constitute a mobilizing factor, a factor of awareness and acceleration of the movement of national liberation, then to open the most effective paths of action in order to reduce the risks of setbacks or abortion of the Revolution.

A Strategy and a Tactic

We must go beyond the stage of spontaneity and improvization that has characterized the majority of the national liberation movements.

The problems that are raised now and those that will be raised in the future are more complex and can only be faced after a serious and profound study. They are to be found on different levels, depending on whether it is a question of: continuing the national liberation struggle against the traditional colonial system; a reconversion of methods vis-à-vis neo-colonialism; or the organization within the new independent states of the struggle for economic development and the social revolution.

For each of these levels, we have to define an authentically revolutionary strategy and tactic, avoiding past errors, foiling the manoeuvres of imperialism and its domestic allies, and which, finally, will permit us to overcome the difficulties and surmount the contradictions born of independence.

This work can only be carried out on the basis of precise and complete information and scientific analysis which must not lead either to the over- or underestimation of the forces of the enemy.

406

At present, this enemy is changing his tactics. He is becoming more and more difficult to detect and isolate, especially since, under local or international guise, he is re-establishing himself or strengthening his hold on the countries of Africa and Asia that have acquired political independence, sometimes profiting from the difficulties necessarily arising from the reconversion of colonial and semi-feudal economic, administrative and social structures.

The definition of this strategy and this tactic constitutes one of our basic tasks.

Thus, our militants and our cadres will be better armed ideologically to meet the enemies and his allies. They will be able to establish a sharp and clear demarcation line between the partisans of national independence and sovereignty and the promotion of the masses, on the one hand, and those of domination on the other. They will know how to end the mystifications, launch slogans for an effective action of liberation and construction, and to deflate the false ideologies of neo-liberalism, pseudo-socialism and other artificially created 'isms', which abound in the present state of confusion.

False Independences

The independence acquired by some countries is only nominal. We must understand from that the fundamental characteristic of neo-colonialism, its meaning and inner mechanism, in order to foil its manoeuvres.

The comprehension of the reality of neo-colonialism, the precise study of the means it employs, the isolation of the elements that give it support in our countries, demands a constant work of investigation and clarification.

Because of the present conjuncture created by the European Common Market and the role that certain new independent African states are called to play in it, it is important to reveal the economic bases of the neo-colonialist phenomenon that generates false independences.

Certainly, independences 'granted' by the colonizers do not constitute a novelty in colonial history (Egypt in 1922, Iraq in

407

1932, for example). But that which was only occasional between the two World Wars has become a policy conceived with
clarity and applied with perseverance.

This orientation of the traditional colonial system is only
the expression of a profound change in the structures of
Western capitalism. It is not through chance that, in the policy
of European countries with regard to their colonies, a growing 'liberalism' has appeared at the same time as a modernization, an Americanization of European capital.

In reality, from the moment when after the Second World
War, through the aid of the Marshall Plan and a greater
interpenetration with the American economy, Western Europe
left behind the structures of the nineteenth century in order to
adapt itself to American capitalism, it was inevitable that it
would also adopt the relations of the U.S.A. with its prolonga-
tion in the New World, or in other terms, that it, too, would
have its Latin America.

That is the profound meaning, in particular, of the French
policy in regards to France's former African possessions,
grouped today within the African and Malagasy Union
(U.A.M.).

In brief, it consists of 'generously' granting political independence, if need be by creating artificial states proposing a cooperation whose aim is an alleged prosperity, but whose objective bases are outside Africa.

But what is new is that, in the relations of Africa with the
colonial powers of Europe, there is a new tendency to domination not marked by direct exploitation and the colonization
of the population.

This is why we must judge in a new fashion the proposals of
the European powers and the position of the political chiefs
of the new states.

*The time when accession to independence was progressive in
itself has passed. Only the political and economic content of
that independence can reveal whether it has a progressive
meaning to it.*

Thus is raised the problem of the nature of power in these
new States. Hence, it is a question of knowing whether the

holders of power are the expression of a national will or the administrators of colonial interests.

The Problem of Power

It is quite obvious that the desire of the colonizer is that the transfer of the political power that he holds be made to the benefit of an heir (a person or a group of interests) capable of assuring him the remote control of the affairs of the new states, and, above all, of the continuity of the economic power to the profit of the metropolitan country.

But the equation is not always reduced to the colonizer's desire, especially when the popular will in the country involved is expressed through a national liberation movement. This leads to multiple solutions shown us by present-day experience.

We know the extreme case of People's China, Vietnam and Cuba, for example, where the struggle, begun at the level of national liberation, became oriented towards economic and social revolution, thanks to the conquest of power by the People's Army after a total victory over the colonial or reactionary forces.

On the contrary are the purely neo-colonialist solutions.

Between these extremes, the problem of power finds intermediary solutions as a result of negotiations which end in compromises depending upon the position of strength of the two partners. But experience shows that the same road leading to independence can result in different solutions to the problem of power.

In Guinea, the power was recovered for the profit of the people because of the action and the vigilance of the Democratic Party of Guinea (P.D.G.).

In the case of Morocco, the power held by the French, Spanish and international protectorates was transferred – under the pressure of the liberation movement – not to the king alone, although theoretically the sovereign, but to a coalition including the popular forces. It took more than six years for the accredited heirs of the colonial interests to capture the power and consolidate it.

The pseudo-constitutional method was used also at the same

time by neo-colonialism to consolidate the fascist regime in South Korea.

At the same time, we find obstinate attempts in Kenya to impose a prefabricated coalition in order to prepare for the exclusive transfer of power later to the heir-presumptive of the British authority.

All the Rest Are Illusions

What must we conclude after this general survey?

That the fundamental question in our national liberation movement is that of the political power, in order to make sure that independence is immediately followed by the effective transfer of power to the authentic representatives of the national revolution in the countries concerned, even if that should bring about the resumption of the armed struggle.

The condition that is indispensable so that independence does not lead to the creation of a neo-colonialist State is, naturally, the existence of a popular organization, whose leadership is thoroughly convinced that besides political and economic power, all the rest are illusions.

11. JUAN BOSCH

*

Dominican Revolution and
Counter-Revolution : 1965 *

In 1961, after a reign of terror over the Dominican people lasting
thirty-two years, the dictator Rafael Trujillo was assassinated.
Estimates of those tortured to death in the most obscene ways, or
otherwise murdered, go as high as 500,000. At the beginning of
1963 the liberal leader Juan Bosch (b. 1909), who had returned from
exile and been elected, became President. A democratic constitution
was promulgated in April, 1963. Bosch attempted some reforms,
but a *coup* in September 1963 by those who were threatened by
these reforms ended the period of constitutional rule. In April
1965 a popular uprising in the Dominican Republic was on the
point of succeeding in bringing back the exiled President, and restoring constitutional rule, when United States forces intervened.
Two contradictory views of what must be done in the Third World
were in conflict. Juan Bosch, writing in the American journal *New
Republic* in June 1965 explains why the attempt to restore democracy to his country was not equal to the solution of the domestic
and international problems involved.

I N most Latin American capitals newsmen writing about the
Dominican crisis are still asking: 'Why didn't Juan Bosch
return to his country?' Some say that in the first moments of
the Dominican revolution a rebel plane landed in San Juan in
Puerto Rico to take me home and I refused to use it. This is a
lie.

The constitutionalist revolution began at noon on 24 April,
in the city of Santo Domingo; the so-called government of
Reid Cabral immediately closed the international airport at
Punta Caucedo. Because San Isidro, General Wessin y Wes-
sin's base, lies between Punta Caucedo and the city of Santo
Domingo, Wessin y Wessin's control over the airport was

*From *New Republic*, 24 July 1965.

complete from the very beginning. By four in the afternoon Wessin's tanks were blockading entrances to the city via Punta Caucedo, which is the same as the route from San Isidro; and it was only after four in the afternoon that I received my first news of the revolution. I received it through a radio station in San Juan. Thus, from one in the afternoon of 24 April, to this day, Wessin y Wessin's forces, which control the Dominican air force, have completely controlled the airways and the roads to the airport.

Two Dominican air force planes came to Puerto Rico – the first a Mustang P-51 fighter which landed on Monday, 26 April, I believe, in Mayaguez, and a Douglas transport which landed next day in San Juan. Both were grounded by U.S. military authorities and have remained grounded.

I did try to reach my country. I made such efforts with Abe Fortas, the well-known American lawyer, who in the first days was unofficial liaison between the U.S. government, and Rector Jaime Benites of the University of Puerto Rico. On Saturday, 1 May, Mr Fortas informed me that a battle was imminent between U.S. Marines and Dominican constitutionalist forces. I explained to Mr Fortas that all I could do in these circumstances was to go to my country and I asked him for a plane to take me there immediately. Mr Fortas did not reply. Early on 2 May, in the presence of Rector Benites, I made the same request to Ambassador John Bartlow Martin and he refused even to consider the matter, saying that if I went to Santo Domingo I would be killed. According to him, that should not be allowed to happen as it would leave my country without leaders.

During its initial phase, for two months, the Dominican revolution was confined to the capital of the republic; as it entered its third month, the movement began to spread to the interior of the country. This was inevitable, since a revolution is not a unified military operation which can be contained within set boundary lines by military forces. Washington has remained inexplicably unaware of what is really happening.

In bottling up the revolution and keeping it confined to a portion of the city of Santo Domingo, the United States government was appraising the situation in terms of force: The revolutionary element represents a given number of men with a given number of weapons; therefore, we can subdue them and knock them out with a given number of soldiers and a given amount of arms.

It is easy to think in terms of force in this day and age, especially in the United States, where a battery of electronic computers comes up with plausible answers to problems of this type in a few minutes, perhaps even in a few seconds.

A revolution, however, is an historical development which is ill-adapted to this type of automated reasoning. Its force is derived from the hearts and minds of people. Neither of these can be measured by electronic computers.

The Santo Domingo uprising was – and is – a typical people's democratic revolution in the historic Latin American manner, generated by social, economic and political factors at once Dominican and Latin American. It is like the Mexican revolution of 1910. The United States reacted to the Dominican revolution of 1965 almost exactly as it did to the Mexican revolution of 1910. Why? Because, traditionally, the official world of North America has been opposed to democratic revolutions in Latin America. With the exception of the Kennedy years, the policy has been to reach a meeting of minds with local power groups, to use force to back them up. During the Franklin Roosevelt era the use of armed intervention was abandoned, but the policy of supporting local power groups was continued, and in the case of the Cuban revolution of 1933 North American warships made their appearance in Cuban waters as an ominous reminder. It was John Fitzgerald Kennedy who transformed outmoded concepts by putting new policies into practice; but after his demise the old idea once more took hold that power can only be exerted by means of force.

Yet this idea has been disproved by history. A revolution is not a war. Traditionally, the defeated ones in revolutions have been those who were stronger in weaponry. The thirteen American colonies were weaker than England, yet they won the War of Independence; the French masses were weaker than

Louis XVI's monarchy, yet the people won in the French Revolution; Bolívar was weaker than Ferdinand VII, yet he won the South American revolution; Madero was weaker than Porfirio Diaz, yet he triumphed in the Mexican revolution of 1910; Lenin was weaker than the Russian government, yet he won the revolution of 1917 in Russia. Without a single exception, all the revolutions which have been victorious throughout the course of history have been weaker than the governments against which they were rebelling. It is clear, therefore, that revolutions cannot be measured in terms of military power; other values must serve as their yardstick.

To distinguish between a true revolution and a mere disorder or struggle for power among rival contenders, one must study the underlying causes of the uprising, and the stand taken by the various sectors of society as it developed. It must also be viewed in its historical context. The U.S. officials failed to consider any of these aspects of the Dominican revolution. In Washington, word was received that at noon on Saturday, 24 April, there had been some restlessness in certain quarters of Santo Domingo and among the people of the city; a little later it was learned that the commander-in-chief of the Army had been taken prisoner by his subalterns. Immediately, plans to land U.S. armed forces in the little Caribbean country were contemplated. President Johnson himself so stated when, at a press conference on 17 June, he affirmed that '... as a matter of fact, we landed our people in less than one hour from the time the decision was made. It was a decision we considered from Saturday until Wednesday evening.'

Since Saturday, therefore, the United States government had considered it necessary to land troops in Santo Domingo; and we may be sure that at the time the United States government did not know what kind of revolution was developing or was going to develop in the Dominican Republic. It was obvious that the policy of the North American government was to defend the *status quo* in Santo Domingo, without any regard for the will of the Dominican people. The reaction in Washington was, therefore, the usual one: the controlling group in the Dominican Republic was threatened, and had to be defended.

414

This controlling group was pro-United States, without a doubt; but it was also anti-Dominican Republic, and this to an extreme degree. During its nineteen months of government, this preferred regime of Washington had ruined the Dominican economy, established a system of corruption and daily ridiculed the hopes of the people for a dramatic solution to the country's problems.

The Dominican revolution of April 1965 was not an improvization. It was an historical event, the origin of which was clear to see. It had been developing since the end of 1959, through the death of Trujillo in May 1961, the elections of December 1962; and finally the strike of May 1964. The *coup d'état* of September 1963 was unable to stamp out this revolution. It was a delusion of sociological and political ignoramuses that when the government over which I was presiding had been overthrown, the revolution would be vanquished. It was a delusion to believe, as did those responsible for formulating Dominican policy in Washington, that a man of 'good' social and business background was the kind of person to handle the Dominican situation.

From the time of the 1963 *coup d'état*, the country was returned to the same lack of freedom and contempt towards the mass of the people which prevailed in the days of Trujillo. Corruption of the Trujillo type became more widespread and more shameless than under the tyrant himself. The Cabral regime sought a return to Trujilloism without Trujillo, an historical absurdity which could not be continued. The middle classes and the masses came together as allies, united in a common cause, to restore the country to a regime of lawfulness.

In April 1965, a second Cuba could not have been in the making in Santo Domingo. What erupted was – and is – a democratic and nationalistic revolution. No Latin American nation today can accept a democracy which also does not offer social equality and economic justice. It was a costly political blunder to look on it as a revolution which was in danger of drifting towards Communism.

The United States will pay a price for this blunder and, in

my opinion, it will be paid within our lifetime. A measure of the grossness of the mistake is the size of the forces originally deployed to bottle up the revolution. In April, the United States had 23,000 men in Vietnam; it landed 42,000 in Santo Domingo. Washington officials look upon events in the Dominican Republic as so fraught with danger that their preparations seemed like those of a nation waging a life-and-death war. A tiny, impoverished nation, making the most heroic effort of its history to achieve democracy, was overwhelmed by huge quantities of cannons, planes, warships, and by a propaganda campaign which presented completely distorted facts to the world. The revolution did not shoot a single person; it decapitated no one, burned down not a single church, nor raped one woman. Nevertheless, allegations of these horrors were proclaimed to the world at large.

The Dominican revolution had nothing to do with Cuba, or Russia, or China. It would have ended in April had the United States not intervened. Instead, it was bottled up and consequently began to generate a force of its own, alien to its nature, and including hatred of the United States. It will be a long time before this anti-U.S. feeling disappears. When democratic nationalism is thwarted or strangled, it becomes a breeding ground to Communism. I am certain that the use of force by the United States in the Dominican Republic will produce more Communists in Santo Domingo and in Latin America than all the propaganda of Russia, China and Cuba combined.

It will be difficult to convince the Dominicans that democracy is the best system of government. They were paying for their democracy with their lives and with their blood, yet North American democracy represented their tremendous and heroic struggle to the world as a work of bandits and Communists. Force was used to prevent the Dominicans from achieving their democracy. Many Americans may not believe this is true, but I am expressing here what the people of the Dominican Republic feel and will continue to feel for many years to come, rather than trying to describe what the intentions of the United States were.

The United States was obliged to have recourse in Santo

Domingo to an expedient which would permit it to use force without exposing itself to world opprobrium. This explains the military junta headed by Antonio Imbert.* This junta was the brainchild of Ambassador John Bartlow Martin – of the United States, in other words. Rarely in modern history has so costly an error been committed in terms of U.S. prestige as placing in the hands of Imbert the power of armed Dominican troops, then advancing as an excuse for his crimes the argument of fighting Communism in Santo Domingo. The brutal killings of Dominicans and foreigners – including a Cuban priest and a Canadian priest – which were committed by Imbert's troops on the pretext of wiping out Communism will, in Dominican history, be forever laid to the acccount of the United States, and particularly to Ambassador Martin. These killings occurred while North American forces were in Santo Domingo; moreover, Ambassador Martin knew what kind of man Imbert was before inviting him to lead the junta. Imbert's tyranny was established beyond a doubt, and following as he did on the heels of Trujillo, there was no pretext strong enough to justify setting up the tyranny of Imbert.

Under the revolution, no one was shot or decapitated; but Imbert's forces shot and decapitated hundreds of persons. These crimes were not given the publicity they should have had in the United States, but they are cited in the documentation of the Commission on Human Rights of the Organization of American States and of the United Nations, with all their ghastly details of skulls crushed by gun-butts, of hands lashed behind backs with wire, of headless corpses floating in rivers, of women executed by machine-guns, of fingers smashed with hammers to prevent identification of the dead. Most of the victims were members of the Dominican Revolutionary Party (a party recognized as democratic), since the function of Imbert's 'democracy' is to wipe out all democrats in the Dominican Republic. It is a bloody irony of history that the crimes imputed to the Dominican revolution were actually

*General Imbert was one of those who led the *coup d'état* of September 1963. On 7 May 1965, after the pro-Bosch Colonel Camaano was sworn in as provisional President, the military junta was set up.

committed by Imbert. The blame will also fall on the United States and, unfortunately, upon democracy in general as a system of government. If I know my people, when the day of reckoning comes, it will be hard for the Dominicans of today and of tomorrow to be indulgent towards the United States and harsh only in their judgement of Imbert and his soldiers.

The Dominican people will not soon forget that the United States brought into Santo Domingo the Nicaraguan battalion named for Anastasio Somoza, that Central American emulator of Trujillo; that it brought in Stroessner's Paraguayan soldiers, of all elements those least qualified to represent democracy in a land where thousands of men and women had just died fighting to establish democracy; that it brought in the soldiery of Lopez Arellano, who, so far as the Dominicans are concerned, is a sort of Honduran Wessin y Wessin. A highlight in all future history texts of the Dominican Republic will be the bombardment of the city of Santo Domingo for twenty-four hours on 15 and 16 June.

All these flow from the use of force as an instrument of power in the handling of political problems. An intelligent evaluation of the events in Santo Domingo would have prevented them. President Johnson said that his Marines went into Santo Domingo to save lives; what they really did was to destroy the democratic image of the United States throughout the South American continent.

12. ALONSO AGUILAR

*

Towards Realistic Solutions *

The Mexican Revolution began in 1910, but what is regarded as the classical period of revolutionary transformation and modernization is that (1934–40) during which Lazaro Cardenas was President. In 1961, when it was obvious that a period of reaction had set in, the Mexican National Liberation Movement was created in order to continue the traditions and values of the Mexican Revolution. One of its leading members, Alonso Aguilar, also a professor of economics in Mexico City, discussed the Alliance for Progress and the needs of Latin America in a lecture he gave in March 1963. What follows is an excerpt.

THE true nature of the Alliance, its antecedents, its projection, and its scope explain why it is failing. As we have seen, the Alliance does not try to tackle the basic problems of Latin America. It projects itself into secondary fields and evades decisive issues, such as the problems of imperialism; its discussions take place within the framework of profound contradictions, and it is based on utopian principles. Its failure is due not to its disorganization or its bureaucracy, but to its inner contradictions, to the obstacles which block the realization of its programme, to the greedy illusions which cause Latin America's privileged minorities to substitute 'firmness, austerity, dedication, and sacrifice' for the betterment of the majority's living conditions.

What may we then expect from the Alliance? Has the ambitious scheme drawn up at Punta del Este† had no repercussions throughout the continent? In our view, there have

*From *Latin America and the Alliance for Progress* (New York: Monthly Review Press, 1963).

† The Alliance was proposed by President Kennedy and adopted at a special meeting of Latin American ministers in August 1961 at Punta del Este in Uruguay. Only Ernesto Guevara, for Cuba, opposed the proposal.

419

been certain conflicting influences which are, however, not mutually exclusive. The Alliance for Progress cannot help but have a certain impact on Latin American development; in fact, its impact is already being felt. In some countries, it has helped to improve the financial situation, even if on a short-term basis, raising the rate of investment or accelerating the rhythm of development; in others, it has to a certain extent stimulated the construction of housing, schools and health centres. The Alliance is very likely encouraging a number of institutional reforms; and many Latin Americans who live on the margin of privilege defending their own class interests, have begun to believe in all good faith that such reforms are of substantial significance in terms of Latin America's evolution.

In conclusion, ALPRO can point to a certain amount of success and may, for another few years, stem the tide of social and economic change for which the people of Latin America have begun to clamour. What seems equally evident, however, is that the Alliance will not be able to solve any basic problems, if only because of its dependence on forces abroad, a dependence which has been one of the decisive causes of our backwardness. Within the framework of the Alliance, this dependence cannot be broken but can only be reinforced.

The pessimists who believe that Latin American progress can be spelled only in English, in terms of American loans and investments, frequently give vent to the fear that should the Alliance fail, all will be lost. The revolution of 'great expectations' has turned into despondency, impotence, and disillusionment. The people, however, take a different view in which there is no room for frustration.

Without pretending in a few lines to set out Latin American requirements for progress and improving living conditions, I would like to mention only some of the factors which are imperative if we want to register any advance.

We must first of all destroy the old agrarian structure and remove the obstacles which have hitherto prevented the land from being owned by those who work it. From Chile and Argentina to Colombia, Peru, and Mexico, everywhere we are faced with large estates, both old and new, which must be

420

liquidated if we aspire to modern forms of agriculture, an extensive domestic market, industrialization worthy of the name, a better distribution of wealth and income, and a truly democratic form of development. It should be understood that agrarian reform, the nature of which will of course vary from country to country, will not be promoted by the land-owners but by the peasants, just as commercial reforms will not be initiated by middlemen, or the system of credit be reconstructed by bankers and speculators.

We must accelerate and reorient the process of capital accumulation; increase the rate of investment and channel available funds into those fields of activity which promise to be most productive from an economic and social point of view. In order to carry out these projects, we need to achieve a fairer distribution of national income, to reduce the lavish consumption of the rich, to raise the productivity of public expenditure, and to prevent the Latin American economy from being bled to death by means of either foreign trade or foreign capital.

We must recover the wealth which today is in the hands of foreign trusts and monopolies and incorporate it into the national patrimony. As long as silver, lead and zinc, coal and oil, magnesium and sulphur, much of our best land, the production of and trade in coffee, cotton, bananas, the richest fishing grounds, and the principal chemical and mechanical industries remain under foreign control, the Latin American economy will continue to be tributary to others and will never be able to dispose freely of its fruits or its labour and its resources.

We must revise the very premises on which Latin American industrialization is to be based, project our economic development into new paths, and direct it towards more ambitious goals, so as to provide ourselves with genuine industries which will make use of all productive potentialities.

We must understand that to raise the standard of living of the majority constitutes not only an essential social aim but is a prerequisite to economic development; we must also understand that improvement in the conditions of the working class will be achieved only in so far as workers will be able to count on independent unions loyally defending their interests.

We must tighten our commercial, political, and cultural relations with other Latin American countries and prevent foreign interests from becoming the long-run beneficiaries of this growing interchange.

Independently of any development towards a Latin American Common Market, we must adopt a policy which will result in the diversification of our foreign trade. Going to Washington to beg – and at times to implore – that our raw materials be granted better prices, and undertaking bigger and better studies as to how to stabilize the prices of our products, have not helped to solve Latin America's foreign exchange problems. To trade with all countries, and certainly with the socialist countries, which undoubtedly show a more rapid rate of economic growth and thus offer the best prospects, is today not only an economic necessity, imposed by public sentiment, but also the road to independence which none of us can ignore.

We must adopt effective measures to protect Latin America against capital flight and other levies which tend to exhaust our financial resources. We can no longer permit our national resources and our productive energy to be drained off, large sums of money to be annually transferred abroad, foreign investments to deprive us of far more wealth than they contribute.

We must aim at genuine and disinterested international cooperation, responding to the aspirations of our people for progress and well-being, respecting our sovereignty, unaccompanied by restrictive conditions – in short at cooperation which will help to transform the social order rather than defend privileges and vested interests.

We must see to it that governments plan their activities and rationalize their expenditure, and that economic and social policies correspond to the needs of the broad mass of the population.

We must guard against just claims being turned into mere phrases; we must insist that the public sector become more democratic and that the common people participate in it rather than leave it in the hands of members or representatives of the oligarchies which govern Latin America today. As long as the democratic forces are excluded from government, as long as they remain mere objects of hostility and repression in the name of anti-Communism and the defence of the Hemisphere, so long will it prove impossible to reorient economic and social policy in the sense that it will benefit the majority.

Last but not least, we must understand that no fundamental or lasting progress can be achieved on the basis of side-stepping the most serious problems and refusing to come to grips with the forces of imperialism.

Imperialism remains the principal cause of Latin America's backwardness. At the same time, it constitutes the gravest threat which hovers over our people. The constantly repeated statement that 'Castro-Communism' is the greatest danger confronting the Americas is both absurd and grotesque. Who can really believe that the Cuban Revolution has hampered our development, when Cuba today finds herself in the front line in the defence of liberty, dignity, and the principles of self-determination and non-intervention on which all Latin American sovereignty must needs be based?

The showy and pseudo-revolutionary robe which has of late cloaked American policy does not signify that imperialism has ceased to be imperialism, but merely that the old garments are worn out.

We live in an age propitious to progress. Imperialism has been weakened through the pressure of all those nations who today watch the dawn of their independence and are anxious to protect their autonomy. The struggle for full emancipation is not a blindly chauvinistic struggle, nor is it doomed to fail. It is the only struggle which will lead us forward. It is the road to national dignity, progress, independence, peace, and genuine international cooperation. Today the triumph of Cuba's Revolution – as that of Mexico's yesterday – proves the fallacy of the assumption that our people are helpless in the face of the enemy. Conscious of the dangers and obstacles, which it would be wrong to underestimate, we believe that this is the hour when we must not give way to defeatism. We must have confidence in our cause and in our own resources. We must claim our heritage with determination and without fear. We must

423

remember that national liberation is triumphant everywhere. We must unite in the beliefs of Bolívar, Morelos, and San Martín. If we base our joint efforts on these principles, conscious of the fact that the cause of each is the cause of all, Latin America will sooner or later succeed in the struggle in which she is today engaged and which is waged to secure her second independence.

13. INDIAN PLANNING COMMISSION

*

Planning in a Non-Socialist Economy *

India is not only, on account of its large population and great traditions, a major force in the Third World. It is distinguished also because popular forces in it have more than in many other cases to maintain some continuity with the ways and the ideas of the pre-Independence period. It offers the most important of the less radical answers to the question: What must be done? Though not a centrally-planned, socialist country, it set up in February 1950 a Planning Commission, to advise a government which had constitutionally committed itself to ensuring:

'(a) that the citizens, men and women equally, have the right to an adequate means of livelihood;

'(b) that the ownership and control of the material resources of the community are so distributed as best to subserve the common good; and

'(c) that the operation of the economic system does not result in the concentration of wealth and means of production to the common detriment.'

The Cabinet resolution setting up the Commission, which subsequently drafted the First Five Year Plan, assigned it certain duties, which are quoted in the first of the following excerpts (i). The second excerpt (ii) is taken from the Draft First Five Year Plan, issued in July 1951.

(i) 1. Make an assessment of the material, capital and human resources of the country, including technical personnel, and investigate the possibilities of augmenting such of these resources as are found to be deficient in relation to the nation's requirements;

2. Formulate a Plan for the most effective and balanced utilization of the country's resources;

3. On a determination of priorities, define the stages in which

*From *Draft First Five Year Plan.*

425

the Plan should be carried out and propose the allocation of resources for the due completion of each stage;

4. Indicate the factors which are tending to retard economic development, and determine the conditions which, in view of the current social and political situation, should be established for the successful execution of the Plan;

5. Determine the nature of the machinery which will be necessary for securing the successful implementation of each stage of the Plan in all its aspects;

6. Appraise from time to time the progress achieved in the execution of each stage of the Plan and recommend the adjustments of policy and measures that such appraisal may show to be necessary;

7. Make such interim or ancillary recommendations as appear to it to be appropriate either for facilitating the discharge of the duties assigned to it or on a consideration of the prevailing economic conditions, current policies, measures and development programmes; or on an examination of such specific problems as may be referred to it for advice by the Central or State Governments.

(ii) Democratic planning presupposes an overall unity of policy combined with proper diffusion of power and responsibility. In such planning, not only the governments of states but also local self-governing bodies, such as municipalities, district and *taluka* boards and *panchayats*, and various functional organizations have to play a vital part. Measures to promote a healthy growth of such institutions are, therefore, an integral part of democratic planning. We visualize that in due course it will be possible for the *panchayats* and other local, regional and functional bodies to participate actively in the preparation of plans. The role of the central planning authority will be to prepare a general framework for the Plan, to invite the appropriate local and functional bodies to send in the plans affecting their respective fields, and, when these are received, to amend and adapt them, in the light of overall needs and resources, and finally to work out, in consultation with the bodies concerned, a comprehensive National Plan. In the implementation of the Plan, again, the principle of diffusion of power and responsibility must be followed. The function of the Central Government is thus to evolve a coordinated policy and to act as an ultimate source of reference in case of conflict between local or sectional interests.

14. JAGDISH BHAGWATI

*

Dilemmas in Planning*

What decisions must be made and what action taken in order to achieve economic development while retaining forms of private enterprise? Some of the problems which arise and their solutions are discussed by Jagdish Bhagwati, an Indian economist who is professor of Economics at the Massachusetts Institute of Technology. The excerpts are taken from his *The Economics of Underdeveloped Countries.*

Developmental Targets and Methods

ECONOMIC expansion on a firm, continuing, sustained and permanent basis is naturally the overriding objective of most underdeveloped countries today. However, the task of formulating programmes to achieve it immediately raises fundamental questions. Are there not *other objectives*, different from the desire to increase the rate of growth of G.N.P. *per capita*, which these governments share? If so, might there not be a conflict between these diverse aims? How could such conflicts be resolved? Again, in attaining these objectives might there not be certain social and political *constraints* on the actions of these governments? Might not certain *methods* (such as collectivization of agriculture either of the Soviet variety or as in the Chinese Communes) be ruled out in some underdeveloped countries though not in others? These questions cannot be brushed aside; they affect and condition the advice and prescriptions that social analysts can offer to the developing countries.

Governments in fact have a wide range of objectives. A high rate of growth of income, an egalitarian distribution of income, fuller employment, the development of backward regions, the creation of strategic industries and the reduction

*From *The Economics of Underdeveloped Countries* (London: Weidenfeld & Nicolson, 1966).

of reliance on foreign trade are among the principal economic and 'non-economic' aims that animate most governments.

This is indeed a large assortment of objectives and few of them can be simultaneously achieved. A tax policy, for example, which is geared to the redistribution of income in favour of the poor may reduce the growth of G.N.P.; the poor may save less while the rich save more, so that the net effect of the redistributory policy may be a reduction in the national savings and hence in investment. Again, a policy of developing backward regions may involve the use of scarce resources in areas where the returns are low. Hence the result may be a low level of current G.N.P. The development of backward regions would thus be in conflict with an increase in the national income.

The conflict may even be between the *same* objective at *different* points in time. Thus a policy of promoting full employment in the immediate future may be an obstacle to full employment later. Suppose everyone was employed right away in a typical, overpopulated country such as Turkey or Indonesia. This would mean that jobs would have to be created although complementary factors such as spades, shovels, buses, looms and factories were not available. The bulk of the people would thus have to be 'employed' in unproductive ways. Two conductors might be put on a bus where only one is necessary; and so on. The result would be an inflation of the wage-bill at the expense of profits. This would cut into the nation's capacity to save and severely impair its capacity to accumulate capital. In consequence there would be a correspondingly slower rate of expansion of those very cooperating factors (such as machinery and equipment) that would otherwise have led to genuine employment of greater numbers in the future. More jobs today would then conflict with more jobs tomorrow. This is indeed a dilemma which recurs everywhere. More consumption today means less consumption tomorrow; and so on.

If then these conflicts between objectives can occur both at one point of time *and* between different time periods, what is to be done? The objectives will naturally have to be weighed one against the other.

The Political Economy of Development

One of the most difficult questions raised by development concerns its effect on the distribution of wealth. Rapid growth, in a mixed economy, with private ownership of property and the means of production, produces conditions under which concentration of wealth and economic power are likely to thrive. There are several reasons for this phenomenon. The primary factor, however, is the scarcity of private entrepreneurs with both organizing ability *and* financial resources. Often, even when the number of entrepreneurs is more numerous, the licensing authorities find the bigger and established firms more efficient and therefore regard them as better candidates. Typically, therefore, a few business 'houses' develop extensive industrial, financial and trading interests. In India, for example, the topmost business complexes have amassed capital investments which are not merely immense in relation to national wealth but also extensive in their range. This situation leads, in the first place, to monopolistic practices which may be economically inefficient – a result which must be weighed against the advantages of more efficient organization and management which these business houses may offer. More important, these large complexes develop considerable political influence. After a certain stage it becomes impossible to reverse the political situation by evolutionary, reformist methods; the government becomes dependent for party finance on economic giants and impervious to any *genuine* control of the concentration of wealth and economic power.

The close link which develops between vested interests and governments is worrying not merely in itself but because it threatens eventually to stand in the way of economic progress. Growing concentration of wealth and influence, for example, shields the wealthier classes from heavy taxation. This in turn prevents governments from taxing other, not-so-affluent groups. The whole tax effort thus gets compromised. And so on.

In fact, the existence of vested interests and pressure groups holds up economic progress over a vast range of issues. Land reform is a typical example. Frequently, stiff legislation is put

430

on the statute books to silence radical criticism. In practice, the legislation is implemented with cynicism and widely avoided.

This raises a more general point. Practically no measure aimed at economic progress will be universally beneficial. Some individuals and classes will gain and others will lose. It is rarely practicable to compensate the losers. Thus, no policy of economic development can be carried out unless the government has the capacity to adhere to it, no matter how organized and systematic the opposition to it by the losers – who may well be powerful pressure groups. Quite often, however, democratic governments lose equanimity and determination in the face of opposition. In the Indian case, for example, measures aimed at reducing wasteful expenditure on gold and increasing savings through a compulsory deposit scheme were substantially withdrawn in the light of public agitation, despite a state of emergency in the country.

This is the dilemma of most democratic governments. While the majority of the electorate certainly want rapid economic progress, few of them are willing to concede that the government's measures to achieve it are either necessary or desirable. It is common practice, for example, for people to criticize taxation while becoming indignant about the poverty which that taxation is aimed at eliminating. It is not surprising that most democratic governments, even when enlightened and willing to initiate and encourage economic progress, feel it necessary to go about their business with caution and often to retreat from sound policies.

It is here that socialist countries, such as the Soviet Union and mainland China, have an immense advantage: their totalitarian structure shields the government from the rigorous and reactionary judgements of the electorate. The Soviet government's firm control on expansion in consumption over the last few decades could hardly ever be attempted by a democratic government. Another advantage of the socialist countries is their passionate conviction and dedication to the objective of economic growth – which contrasts visibly with the halting and hesitant beliefs and actions of most democracies. The firm and purposive sense of direction which the Chinese maintained

431

through the early 1960s, in the face of floods, drought and other economic disasters, is in pointed contrast to the extensive revisions and changes in policies and methods which are prompted by minor setbacks in most democratic governments and which produce a sense of drift and helplessness.

The political economy of development poses, in this respect, a cruel choice between rapid (self-sustained) expansion and democratic processes.

15. V. K. R. V. RAO

*

Self-Reliance in Agricultural Production*

Given the situation that was described earlier by Dr Rangnekar,
what had to be done to develop the agricultural sector of the Indian
economy? One of India's leading economists and a member of its
Planning Commission, V. K. R. V. Rao, published this article in
October 1965. Dr Rao has since then been appointed India's
Minister of Education.

I⊤ is not befitting either the dignity or the self-respect of a
nation with a total cropped area of nearly 390 million acres
and a net irrigated area of seventy million acres to be an im-
porter of food-grains. The position becomes worse when it is
remembered that even with imports, the availability of food
in nutritional terms is much less per head in India than in many
other countries with a much smaller area under cultivation.
That after fifteen years of planning India should still find herself in a state of dependence on foreign supplies to keep her
food economy going is not a matter of pride to the planner.
Above all, it is a matter for profound regret that the bulk of
the food-grains we import from abroad is not even paid for by
us from our free foreign exchange resources but comes as a
gift and a loan under various PL 480 provisions from the
United States. Recent events have brought in a new dimen-
sion to the problem and faced the country with the possibility
of a break-down in its food supplies at a time when she is
fighting for the very survival of her sovereignty and the maintenance of the secular, democratic and socialist ideals of her
polity. In the circumstances, it is not surprising that both the
national leadership and the Planning Commission have declared that food production should command the highest
priority in our plans for economic development and that India

*From *Yojana*, October 1965.

433

must reach self-sufficiency in food at the earliest possible moment. Can we do it?

I have no doubt in my mind that India can attain self-sufficiency in food if only she really makes up her mind to do so and is willing and able to put through the necessary policies and programmes for increasing her agricultural production. While it is true that Indian agriculture still continues to be a gamble in rain it is also a fact that she has perhaps the largest irrigated area in the world, and this becomes still larger if minor irrigation works are also taken into account. The average yields per acre in India are among the lowest in the world. But this is not due to the infertility of the soil or any technical impossibility of increasing production. It is due to the fact that we are not making the best use of the secure supplies of water that our irrigation system has provided us with. It is due to the fact that the efficiency of our minor irrigation works is at a low level because of the comparative absence of rural electrification for drawing water from our wells, tanks, rivers and rivulets. It is also due to the fact that our soil does not get replenished through the use of chemical fertilizers nor our crops protected by pesticides. It is also the result of our using seeds of low germinating quality, our failure to use hybrid seeds with high yield potentialities, and our sticking to seeds that are not capable of standing high fertilizer doses and therefore incapable of recording significant increases in yield. Our agricultural implements are still, generally speaking, of the primitive variety used by our ancestors during the days of the Ramayana and the Mahabharata. Our agricultural practices are still largely of pre-scientific age and our system of crop-rotation prior even to the European agricultural revolution of the eighteenth century. The destruction of even a part of the food we grow by rats, rodents, birds, and bad storage adds to the dismal tones of the picture that I am drawing of Indian agriculture.

The dark shades of the picture grow more bleak when we look at the state of our animal husbandry and our failure to use the large potential of fisheries that our long coastline and our abundant supply of inland water areas gives us. Surely, there has been something wrong with India if she has allowed these facts to continue in spite of the pressing national necessity both for more food and for freedom from dependence on imports.

Potentialities of Doubling Output

I feel overwhelmed by the magnitude of the indictment I have made of ourselves as a nation. I feel even more appalled at the implication this has on the success of our planning and the efficiency both of our planners and the implementation of the plans. But there is no need to despair. On the contrary the very facts that I have given show the vast potentialities that exist for doubling and even trebling our agricultural production. And when it is remembered that our food deficit at current levels of consumption is less than ten per cent it should be a matter of comparative ease to make up this deficit.

Not only are our potentialities much above our immediate or even longer-term requirements, but we also know what is wrong and therefore what should be done to right the position. And we have been trying also to apply the right remedies, even though our efforts in this direction have not been adequate or sufficiently efficient to meet the needs of the situation. Thus during the fifteen years of our planning we have increased our production of cereals by thirty million tonnes. The index of agricultural production as a whole has been showing an average annual rise of more than three per cent. But population has been growing at the rate of 2·2 to 2·4 per cent a year, the base levels from which we started have been sub-standard from the point of view of nutritional requirements, and our distribution system has been unable to cope with the growing requirements of food in a developing economy. Hence it is that in spite of a considerable measure of success in absolute terms in the agricultural field, we continue to depend on imports and live from hand to mouth in regard to this most basic necessity of human existence.

What the food situation in India reveals is not that we have done nothing to cope with it but that we should do far more

435

than we have done so far, and do that with more vigour, more systematic planning, and a better sense of basic priorities.

Beginnings of a National Movement

This is precisely what we are now trying to do. The Fourth Plan centres on the fulcrum of self-reliance and our highest priority is the maximization of food production. Recent events have been a blessing in disguise, for they have made the country much more conscious of the need to solve our food problem even for national survival. The national will to become self-sufficient in food not only in terms of current consumption but also in terms of better nutritional standards has now begun to emerge in unmistakable fashion. Government, planners, and the public are all beginning to combine in one great national movement for self-reliance and self-sufficiency in food. The climate is now right for attempting a great leap forward in our agricultural production.

But mere will is not enough. What is needed is better planning and more efficient implementation. This is precisely what the Planning Commission is now trying to do. I outline below in summary form the main elements of the new agricultural planning with which we hope the country will move towards self-reliance and self-sufficiency in food:

(1) It is not enough to go in for more irrigation or increased supplies of water for agricultural purposes. It is also important to see that our water supplies are put to the most efficient use. Water management has to be accompanied by suitable systems of crop patterns and crop rotation, use of high-yielding seed, application of adequate and appropriate quantities of chemical fertilizers and pesticides, and adoption of improved and scientific agricultural practices. This is now being attempted in the I.D.P. and the I.A.D. districts; and attempts will be made to step up both the coverage and the efficiency of these programmes during the Fourth Plan period. In addition, special area development programmes will be undertaken in the newly irrigable command areas with a view to getting the best economic returns from the supplies of water newly made available.

436

(2) Special 'crash programmes' will be undertaken to utilize the irrigation potential created by the major and medium irrigation works by planned reduction of the time-lag between potential and utilization. Simultaneously, attempts will be made for reducing the time span between the start and completion of major and medium irrigation works.

(3) More systematic attention will be paid to the stepping up of the efficiency of minor irrigation works by the installation and energization of pump sets, accompanied by an appropriate demonstration and supply programme of agricultural facilities and techniques aimed at maximizing production. Simultaneously, attempts will be made not only to increase the number of minor irrigation works but also to see that the existing ones are kept in a proper state of maintenance and those needing repair like silted tanks, wells with lower water tables, etc., brought into a state of efficiency. All this will enable the country to get quicker and larger dividends from the investment in minor irrigation.

(4) Soil conservation is another programme to which more attention will be paid. This will aim not only at quantitative expansion but at a more scientific base, taking into account water sheds, forest areas, nature and contour of the soil, and built-in provision for both maintenance and effective utilization of the area taken up by the bunds.

(5) Seed is another, and in some ways a more important, component in the agricultural planning that we are undertaking. Hybrid jowar, hybrid bajra and hybrid maize are all capable of bringing about substantial increases in yield; they are also the crops whose greater efficiency will improve the economic conditions of our smaller and poorer farmers. Recent experiments have shown that certain foreign varieties of wheat and rice like the Mexican Senora 64, Lerna Rojo and V.18 in the case of wheat and Taichung Native 1 in the case of rice are capable of bringing about large increases in yield, given water and fertilizers. Indo-Japanese varieties of paddy also promise substantial results. Attention will therefore be concentrated during the Fourth Plan period on comprehensive seed programmes, including its multiplication, certification and utiliza-

tion, especially in areas where the availability of water and the supply of fertilizers make it possible for them to reach their maximum potential yields. The possibilities of this programme are seen from the expectation of an additional production of twenty-five million tonnes by its application to an area of only 32·5 million acres during the Fourth Plan period.

(6) Fertilizers of course constitute the most important input for a massive increase in agricultural production. The Fourth Plan therefore contemplates a substantial stepping up in the use of chemical fertilizers to the tune of more than three to three-and-a-half times the level reached at the end of the Third Plan period, and along with it the application of appropriate quantities and varieties of pesticides. All this will involve a terrific organizational effort in terms of education, research, demonstration, supplies and distribution.

(7) Increasing the efficiency of agricultural implements is another important way of increasing agricultural production. During the Fourth Plan emphasis will be laid on modern implements like tractors, power tillers, harvesters and the like, and also on improving the efficiency of implements that can be worked by animal power. Provision on an extensive scale for repair and maintenance facilities will be made, for without such facilities it would be impossible to bring about any substantial increase in their use.

(8) Account is also being taken of the need to link up credit and marketing facilities with programmes for increased agricultural production. While every attempt will be made to improve the efficiency of the cooperative system in this regard, alternative institutions will also be set up where necessary to see that lack of credit and marketing facilities does not hold up or hamper individual or area programmes for production.

(9) Modernizing agriculture does not just mean provision of material inputs. Research and extension are an essential precondition of agricultural progress. Accordingly, the Fourth Plan envisages a comprehensive programme for coordinating and expanding agricultural resesearch on a nation-wide scale, linking it up with the complexity and variety of the problems

on the field natural to a vast country like India, giving a practical bias to the training given in our agricultural colleges and diploma institutions, and tying them up with concrete development programmes in the agricultural areas in their vicinity. The Fourth Plan also includes a comprehensive programme for rural adult education, the training of practising farmers, setting up of junior agricultural schools, and the promotion of an agricultural and scientific bias in our system of elementary and secondary education.

(10) Agriculture is essentially a local industry; and unless it is tackled in a planned, integrated and comprehensive manner at the local levels, no amount of national planning or national supplies will lead to the desired increase in agricultural production. That is why so much stress is being laid in the Fourth Plan on district and block plans for agricultural development, with an agricultural planning cell at the state headquarters for bringing about the necessary dovetailing and coordination between local and state plans for increasing agricultural production.

(11) In our system of administration – for that matter, in any system of administration – it is not possible to bring under one administrative department all the facilities and activities that go to make up a comprehensive programme for increasing agricultural production. Irrigation, Power, Credit, Roads, Fertilizers, Seeds, Implements, Research, Education, Extension – all these are vital to agriculture and yet they are and cannot but be under separate ministries and departments. Hence the need for coordination at both the ministerial and official levels, both at the Centre and in the states. This has been recognized and action taken to secure the necessary machinery for the purpose, though I cannot say that this machinery is working with the requisite efficiency or firmness, clarity or purpose or dynamism so essential for a massive programme in agriculture. Thus we have an Agricultural Production Board at the centre, Cabinet sub-committees for agricultural production programmes in the states, Agricultural Production Commissioners in the states and their counterparts in the districts, and other appropriate bodies of officials at various levels. What is needed is more efficient

working of these boards and officials and also better inter-communication and coordination with non-official individuals and organizations in the field. The Fourth Plan will concentrate special attention on this factor.

(12) Finally, and in some ways this is the most important advance that has been made in our agricultural planning, the Fourth Plan is based on a recognition of the need for having an integrated agricultural plan within the framework of the overall Plan. Thus, we will have during the Fourth Plan period an agricultural plan that will bring together not only the various programmes and targets relevant thereto but also identify and give priority to all activities in other sectors which have a bearing on the implementation of the agricultural plan. All these have to be planned in such a manner as to give them not only the appropriate intersectoral balances including both availabilities and outlets, but the required time-phasing and programming as well. The integrated agricultural plan will cover all the appropriate and inter-connected sectors; it will also include commodity-wise, programme-wise, and area-wise sections, all of which in turn will have the necessary intersectoral tie-up. It is this integrated and comprehensive agricultural plan that needs to be given the highest priority if we mean what we say by the statement that agriculture will command the highest priority in the Fourth Plan. Thus, fertilizers, pesticides, and agricultural implements should command higher priority than other sectors in industry; and agricultural education and research in education, rural transport in transport, rural electrification in electrification, and agricultural needs in allotment of cement, bricks, iron and steel, and foreign exchange. In order to see that this is done and to emphasize the comprehensive and inter-sectoral character of maximizing agricultural production, it is proposed to bring out separate volumes for the agricultural plan of the country as a whole as well as for the different states which make the Indian Union.

The Fourth Plan also contains significant programmes for animal husbandry, fisheries, poultry, piggery, subsidiary foods like potatoes, sweet potatoes and tapioca, horticulture, storage and warehousing and improved processing. Space does not permit me to elaborate on any of these items, but it is necessary to mention them to complete the record.

I hope what I have said above gives some justification for the optimistic undertones of this article in spite of the pessimistic overtures with which it has been started. I do believe it is possible for India to reach self-reliance in her food supplies at current levels of consumption before the end of the Fourth Plan period. I also believe that my faith is based on scientific and realistic reasoning and not on just wishful thinking. Self-sufficiency at current levels of consumption is of course not enough. What we need is also a rise in the levels and quality of our food consumption so that we may reach nutritional standards comparable to those of the developed countries. All this should be true not only for our classes, but also for our masses. I am sure we will do this too, though it may take us two more plan periods before we reach this goal. But, as Gandhiji used to say, one step at a time is enough. Our immediate task is to rid the country of the stultifying and nationally dangerous dependence on imports for our food supplies. This, I think, can be done by implementing the agricultural programmes and the comprehensive multi-sector integrated agricultural plan that the Planning Commission intends to put before the country for the Fourth Plan period.*

*The Indian Fourth Five-Year Plan was to have began in 1966, but was put off for three years.

16. PEOPLE'S REPUBLIC OF CHINA MARRIAGE LAW (1950)

*

The Modernization of the Family*

The strongly authoritarian, male-dominated traditional family system was one of the main cultural and institutional foundations of pre-revolutionary China. It had existed for two thousand years. On 1 May 1950, the Government of the People's Republic of China passed a new Marriage Law, which, by giving a new status to women and children, revolutionized relationships within a hundred million families throughout the country. The reform was taken very seriously, and the shock of personal radical 'liberation' so immediate and close to the day-to-day life of the people was at first severe. Part of the Marriage Law is given below.

Chapter I General Principles
Article 1.   The feudal marriage system which is based on arbitrary and compulsory arrangements and the superiority of man over woman and ignores the children's interests shall be abolished.

The New-Democratic marriage system, which is based on the free choice of partners, on monogamy, on equal rights for both sexes, and on the protection of the lawful interests of women and children, shall be put into effect.

Article 2.   Bigamy, concubinage, child betrothal, interference with the re-marriage of widows, and the exaction of money or gifts in connexion with marriages, shall be prohibited.

Chapter II The Marriage Contract
Article 3.   Marriage shall be based upon the complete willingness of the two parties. Neither party shall use compulsion and no third party shall be allowed to interfere.

*Peking: Foreign Languages Press.

Article 4. A marriage can be contracted only after the man has reached twenty years of age and the woman eighteen years of age. . . .

Article 6. In order to contract a marriage, both the man and the woman shall register in person with the people's government of the district or *hsiang* in which they reside. If the marriage is found to be in conformity with the provisions of this Law, the local people's government shall, without delay, issue marriage certificates.

If the marriage is not found to be in conformity with the provisions of this Law, registration shall not be granted.

Chapter III Right and Duties of Husband and Wife

Article 7. Husband and wife are companions living together and shall enjoy equal status in the home.

Article 8. Husband and wife are duty bound to love, respect, assist and look after each other, to live in harmony, to engage in productive work, to care for the children and to strive jointly for the welfare of the family and for the building up of the new society.

Article 9. Both husband and wife shall have the right to free choice of occupation and free participation in work or in social activities.

Article 10. Both husband and wife shall have equal rights in the possession and management of family property.

Article 11. Both husband and wife shall have the right to use his or her own family name.

Article 12. Both husband and wife shall have the right to inherit each other's property.

Chapter IV Relations between Parents and Children

Article 13. Parents have the duty to rear and to educate their children; the children have the duty to support and to assist their parents. Neither the parents nor the children shall maltreat or desert one another.

The foregoing provision also applies to foster-parents and foster-children. Infanticide by drowning and similar criminal acts are strictly prohibited.

Article 14. Parents and children shall have the right to inherit one another's property.

Article 15. Children born out of wedlock shall enjoy the same rights as children born in lawful wedlock. No person shall be allowed to harm them or discriminate against them.

Where the paternity of a child born out of wedlock is legally established by the mother of the child or by other witnesses or by other material evidence, the identified father must bear the whole or part of the cost of maintenance and education of the child until the age of eighteen.

With the consent of the mother, the natural father may have custody of the child.

With regard to the maintenance of a child born out of wedlock, in case its mother marries, the provisions of Article 22 shall apply.

Article 16. Husband or wife shall not maltreat or discriminate against children born of a previous marriage.

Chapter V Divorce

Article 17. Divorces shall be granted when husband and wife both desire it. In the event of either the husband or the wife alone insisting upon divorce, it may be granted only when mediation by the district people's government and the judicial organ has failed to bring about a reconciliation.

In cases where divorce is desired by both husband and wife, both parties shall register with the district people's government in order to obtain divorce certificates. The district people's government, after establishing that divorce is desired by both parties and that appropriate measures have been taken for the care of children and property, shall issue the divorce certificates without delay.

When only one party insists on divorce, the district people's government may try to effect a reconciliation. If such mediation fails it shall, without delay, refer the case to the county or municipal people's court for decision. The district people's government shall not attempt to prevent or to obstruct either party from appealing to the county or municipal or people's court. In dealing with a divorce case, the county or municipal people's court must, in the first instance, try to bring about a reconciliation between the parties. In case such mediation fails, the court shall render a verdict without delay.

In the case where, after divorce, both husband and wife desire the resumption of marital relations, they shall apply to the district people's government for a registration of re-marriage. The district people's government shall accept such a registration and issue certificates of remarriage.

Article 18. The husband shall not apply for a divorce when his wife is with child. He may apply for divorce only one year after the birth of the child. In the case of a woman applying for divorce, the restriction does not apply. . . .

Chapter VI
Maintenance and Education of Children after Divorce . . .

Article 22. In the case where a divorced woman re-marries and her husband is willing to pay the whole or part of the cost of maintaining and educating the child or children by her former husband, the father of the child or children is entitled to have such cost of maintenance and education reduced or to be exempted from bearing such cost in accordance with the circumstances. . . .

Chapter VIII By-laws

Article 26. Persons violating this Law shall be punished in accordance with law. In cases where interference with the freedom of marriage has caused death or injury, the person guilty of such interference shall bear responsibility for the crime before the law.

Article 27. This Law shall come into force from the date of its promulgation. In regions inhabited by national minorities, the people's government (or the Military and Administrative

Committee) of the Greater Administrative Area or the provincial people's government may enact certain modifications or supplementary articles in conformity with the actual conditions prevailing among national minorities in regard to marriage. But such measures must be submitted to the Government Administration Council for ratification before enforcement.

17. HAN SUYIN

*

Mobilizing the Creative Powers
of the People *

A variety of specific changes proceeded simultaneously in almost every area of Chinese society, economy and politics. In 1967, Han Suyin (see p. 234), after eleven visits in one decade to China, describes aspects of the development process from the point of view of a non-Marxist radical in South-east Asia.

Population – a National Resource

T H E population of India increased by over eighty million from 1920 to 1947; in China, the greatest increase has come about after 1949. In 1953 the first communist census of population in China gave over 583 million; until then figures had hovered between 450 and 500 million. Infants up to four years old constituted 15·6 per cent of the 583 million; which gives a round figure of ninety million infants under four years old in 1953. This astronomic increase in four years was due to the nation-wide and compulsory public health measures taken immediately when the communist government came to power, the immediate uplift in conditions in the countryside.

In the census of 1953, the total juvenile population up to age seventeen was 41·1 per cent of the total population. This gives us a figure of near 240 million juveniles in 1953.

No census of population figures have been published since; but the trend has continued towards a net increase as in India; the rate quoted by Chou En-lai being 2–2·2 per cent a year.†
An inspired guess that forty-five per cent of the population is under eighteen years old and fifty per cent under twenty-one does not appear extreme. In 1966, the population was quoted

* From *China in the Year 2001* (London: Watts, 1967).
† Interview with author, September, 1965; also with Edgar Snow, March, 1965. (H.S.)

447

as '700 million' by leaders of the government. If we take this figure of 700 million, we have a possible 315 million juveniles under eighteen in China, or 350 million under twenty-one years old.

The implications of these figures, by themselves, are sobering. A large young population, whose reproductive rate in the next decade will be very high, represents 'consumption' rather than 'production'. This is adding to the already weighty problems of China. How are these 300 odd million young to be fed, clothed, educated and given a better life than their parents? If 'normal' Western standards are used, the task is obviously impossible.

Is this enormous young population a relative or an absolute factor in retarding China's progress? Can it be handled, as Mao Tse-tung says: 'so that a bad thing becomes a good thing'?

The first notion we must clarify is that of over-population. There is no 'over-population' in China.* A population of 700 million in China gives us a proportion of around 190 people per square mile, the average of Europe today. In India, one third the size of China, the population of 520 million today gives us an average of 350 per square mile, less than half the number of inhabitants per square mile in Belgium, Holland and Japan. We must, I think, agree that population is also a cultural appraisal, and its evaluation depends on the development of resources, and their distribution and working. It is, in fact, a function of the economic system and of industrial development.

The *distribution* of population in China is uneven, the eastern seaboard, the deltas, the more fertile agricultural areas, low-lying rice-producing basins with double or treble cropping have a crowded countryside with 1,000 people per square mile; two thirds of the Chinese population live on one sixth of the area of China. The rest is sparsely populated; some areas have fewer than one person per square mile.

* As Baade points out in his book, *The Race to the Year 2000*, the world could support ten times its present population, if all its resources were well used. (H.S.)

This uneven distribution corresponds to the Key Economic Areas of feudal China,* labour-intensive fields with almost certain harvests and established systems of irrigation. Historical attitudes, as well as the low level of tools, and the feudal system itself, prevented the clearing and pioneering of new settlements. Superimposed upon the primitive means of production was a superstructure of inhibiting social habits and traditions such as filial duty, clan relations and superstitions.

The non-monetarized rural economy, laws restricting travel and commerce, inland transport taxes, landlordism and debt contributed to stagnation and lack of incentive to pioneer.

The tradition of the clan tended to keep all its members together, so as to have enough labour hands for the harvests. Tools and means of production were owned by the clan and could not be removed.

Today, the picture is different. Decentralization moves the young from the cities to new areas; wholesale commune-centred family planning, new methods of part-work part-study education are spreading out the population, limiting births, and cutting down the cost of education and consumption.

Education is an investment in human capital, enhancing and multiplying its effectiveness. The scientific peasant, the worker–inventor, creates wealth. The forms, modalities, directions, emphases of education are therefore of particular importance. Making the whole system of education in China a part-work part-study system is restoring the juvenile half of the population in varying degrees to the production sector. On this all-important subject of turning consumers into producers, and turning education into a self-reliant, self-sufficient, self-feeding, self-paying sector of the economy, a new policy is being worked out; it is only possible to be sure of one thing, that all schools will be part-work part-study schools, and the same for colleges and universities.

At the same time birth control at commune level throughout the land is also intelligently directed towards the most reproductive group, the under-thirties.

Late marriage and contraceptive techniques are being advo-

*Chi Chao-ting, *Key Economic Areas in Chinese History.*

cated with the same methods of appeal to revolutionary priority, this priority being not the self, but 'production for the revolution'. If within the next decade the population control techniques succeed, a stabilization of the population growth at around 1·5 per cent increase per year is possible. The emphasis on the absence of fear, and on the voluntary cooperation of married couples in wise family planning is, psychologically, the best approach and the most relevant to human worth and dignity.

If this succeeds, then by the year 2000 it can be safe to assume that the population could be stable round about 1·2 thousand million people or less, assuming that at the moment, with half the population under twenty-one and the family planning drive in the communes only beginning it takes another decade before reaching the desired rate. If the yield per acre has doubled and in some areas trebled, the food production will be sufficient. But it is a race, at the moment, between increased yield and increasing numbers of healthy babies.

Science – Development and Research

This subject, like so many facets of the Chinese policies of development, tends to be confused by contradictory reports. Studied emphasis is placed, as Dr Ping Chia-kuo pointed out, on 'certain aspects ... which are important only as symptoms, while deeper, historical trends often forgotten amidst the crises and passions of the day, and yet of lasting significance' are either omitted or ignored. *The interpretation of what happens in China is a function of the attitudes towards China,* and what happens in China cannot be studied apart from what the Chinese themselves take as a guide to their actions, namely, the ideological factors (known as the Thought of Mao Tse-tung); these, so far, have not received in the West the attention that is due to them.

Scientific research in China has received close attention since 1956. All of it has been overshadowed by the constant threat of encirclement, containment, and since 1962, of almost certain attack, within the foreseeable future, by the U.S.A.

Geological surveys were hampered at first by lack of personnel, but this is no longer the case. Well over 10,000 qualified geologists today, instead of the 1,200 of 1950, have discovered in China, among other things, deposits of thorium and uranium, at present used in the nuclear research programme.

Speaking of the 'new revolution in science, technique and industry produced by automation', Chou En-lai said that this was a 'revolution far exceeding in its significance the industrial revolution associated with steam and electricity'. China would have to 'leap' into the highest international standards within twelve years (1956–67). A Twelve-year Plan for long-term research projects was drawn up that year and is now coming to a close; an evaluation can therefore be made while the next long-term scientific research plan is being prepared.

In the decade since 1956, China has not only conducted the steps necessary for the first industrial revolution, but has also undertaken the second revolution necessary because of advances in automation and in the use of atomic energy; this overlapping has meant that the funds necessary for research and experimentation have been more than generous; that the creation of technological personnel has been a priority at all times, despite the political and ideological emphases on political purity which, however much it is deprecated in the West as 'stifling initiative' does not seem to have that effect.

Scientific know-how and achievement, in my opinion, coincide with the requirements of Marxism–Leninism; scientists are *also*, sometimes unconsciously, imbued with ideals of the Good Society. In the present Cultural Revolution, the movement includes *scientific experiment*, which is the spirit of innovation and research. This is significant, as is the extolling of scientific heroes and heroines and other worker-inventors.

Chou En-lai's emphasis on 'bringing our country's most vital scientific departments near to the most advanced world levels by the end of the Third Five-year Plan' (1966–70) can also no longer be looked upon as a vain boast.

It was in this speech, notably, that Chou En-lai emphasized self-reliance and independence of the U.S.S.R. 'To fulfil this task, we must discard all *servile thinking*, which is lack of national self-confidence. ...' Although Soviet assistance was needed to do away with backwardness, one should 'distinguish between what is essential and not essential ... to seek a solution from the Soviet Union to every question, great and small' was 'incorrect' and to 'send mostly middle school graduates rather than scientists' to the Soviet Union was wrong. 'The result would be *forever a state of dependence and imitation, impeding the systematic rapid development of our science....*'

The best scientific forces and the best university graduates must be concentrated 'for the earnest, and not merely nominal launching, of the march of science ... *we must grasp the time element*'. All the necessary material such as books, publications, archives, technical data, and other facilities including translation of foreign works, etc., are and have been available at all times, contrary to reports in the Western press.*

There are two aspects to this research programme; one, the high level concentration of the best brains and talent on certain projects, the second, the most widespread diffusion, communication and facilities for creating a pool of technological personnel *of all types* at worker–peasant level. And though this seemed 'impossible', it has been done, surprisingly well.

In agriculture the most important emphasis has been on the wide spread of scientific knowledge to the peasants themselves, and cooperation and coordination between scientist and peasant. Today the idea of research and the words 'study and experiment' have become part of peasant vocabulary. 'Cooperation, now a routine functional factor in China, has been a major element in the scientific and industrial success stories. ...'†

In industry each factory has its one or more lines of research, all technical problems and improvements are discussed by cooperation between scientists, workers and lower technical staff, and the administrative cadres; the practice of sending students from technical colleges to the factories also results in their discovering problems in design and manufacture, and these become their chosen subjects of work; they get full co-

*C. H. G. Oldham, 'Science and Education in China', *Contemporary China* (New York: Pantheon, 1966). (H.S.)
† *Far East Trade and Development*, October 1966. (H.S.)

operation in solving these research problems from workers and scientists as well as the approval of party cadres.

News such as, for example, that Anshan steel works has turned out one new product every day for the last two years, that technical innovations in this period are developed at an average of fifteen a day, that the steel complex has caught up or surpassed current world standards in twenty technical economic norms is a tribute to the technical innovation movement. Twenty-two special technical teams, including engineers, research workers, experienced workers and cadres, were employed on these technical questions; in the process, several young inventors (post-1962) made innovations; 40,000 technicians are employed in this one complex alone; they have produced alloy steel in open-hearth furnaces, a kind which could only be made previously in electrical furnaces; these technicians are now organizing conferences and demonstrations and sharing their experiences with other steel complexes, big and small, all over China; and the number of technicians capable of making these alloy and special steels has doubled in two years.

The pure oxygen top blown converter process introduced recently in China will not only make steel at far greater speed and lower capital investment, but also allow the recovery of waste materials (gas and soot) for the production of fertilizers and other chemicals. It takes less than one year to design and build such a converter in China.

Scientific breakthrough has occurred in all sectors, and not only in nuclear development; synthetic insulin has been produced and also synthetic benzene, a basic raw material for the manufacture of plastics and other synthetics. Fermentation dewaxing is another recent breakthrough made by young Shanghai workers and scientists. (This process removes paraffin from crude oil by bacteriological action.) A fireproof chemical which resists 1,000° C is produced by a small chemical workshop in Manchuria. In medicine, a recent * delegation of Belgian doctors reports impressive surgery techniques, even in country hospitals; research in medical and surgical fields con-

* 1966.

tinues; all medical instruments, of the most complex type, are produced and made in China; heart, lung, and liver techniques are of international standard.

The Institute of Automation of the Chinese Academy of Sciences is producing automatic control motors; already several factories, entirely automated, are functioning (as models for the future). The expansion of technological personnel is no longer a function of academic diplomas; it is at the very base, among the ordinary workers, that science begins; there must be no hierarchy among scientists confined to 'top level' men or experts or technocrats; the present Cultural Revolution reaffirms this principle and will strengthen this policy.

Like all aspects of the Chinese Revolution, the theme of research and development is accompanied by a 'two lines' contradiction; there is the contradiction between the technical and scientific personnel, who at least until 1960 were mostly of bourgeois origin, and the demands for political meetings and discussions; during the First Leap Forward there was widespread grumbling over the interruption at research level; in today's Leap Forward, however, special care has been taken to reiterate that scientific personnel must be protected, just as special care has been taken that all must proceed 'by reason and not force', and also that 'the minority is not always wrong, truth is sometimes with the minority'. Local party interference and high-handedness with intellectual personnel still occurs, and it has been more obvious in the realm of pure research than in that of practical application. However, at the 1966 Physicists Congress in Peking a galaxy of young investigators read papers on original research of international calibre. Special consideration to the scientific branches is increasing, as after 1962 more and more scientific personnel were of worker and peasant origin; the acceptance of 'intellectuals' as part of the proletarian society and their fitting into the social system is becoming easier.

18. SURENDRA J. PATEL

*

The Efficient Use of Investments *

Given the need to accelerate economic growth, what is the measure of the task which has to be accomplished? Surendra J. Patel (b. 1923) has had a special interest in comparing the process of economic growth at various periods and in various countries. Having worked as an economist for the U.N.'s Economic Commission for Europe, the Economic Commission for Africa and the Economic Commission for Asia and the Far East, this Indian economist writes out of wide experience when he states his belief that rapid growth is attainable. The essay 'Planning in India and China: Its Relevance to the Theory of Economic Growth', from which the excerpt is taken, was first published in 1959.

... Even though the data are rough and subject to a number of qualifications – particularly owing to the differences in conceptual framework, methods of computation and to some extent price comparability – they are reliable enough to permit a few observations concerning the direction of change during this period.

(1) In the initial year, that is 1950, total gross national product and gross investment in China were about one tenth higher than in India. Since the population in China was larger by about half, the level of *per capita* gross national product was about one third lower than in India. China was even poorer than India.

(2) In 1950, gross investment as a share of gross national product was between 9–10 per cent in both and the current rate of saving was about the same.

(3) Eight years later, by 1958, the gross national product rose by thirty per cent in India and by over 100 per cent in China. The annual rate of increase in India was a little over three per

*From *Essays on Economic Transition* (Bombay: Asia Publishing House, 1965).

cent; in China it was over ten per cent (or at least three times as high). The rates of growth were strikingly dissimilar in the two countries although in the initial period they had about the same volume of gross national product and of gross investment (or about the same current rate of saving).

(4) At the purely quantitative level of economic analysis, these differences seem to stem in part from the different rates of growth of investment in the two countries and in part from a more efficient use of capital in China – that is, obtaining a lower capital/output ratio. In 1950, the volume of investment in China was only slightly higher than in India, but the rate accelerated much more in China. As a result, by 1958, the absolute volume of annual capital formation in China was some three times higher than in India. During these eight years, total investments in China were about two and a half times higher than in India.

(5) Both countries began with about the same level and rate of investment, but China raised investments much faster than India. Consequently, it had a faster rate of growth of the gross national product and greater increase in the ability to invest.

China Used Capital More Efficiently

It is interesting to note that there was only a small difference between the two in the marginal savings/income ratio, or the proportion of additional income ploughed back as investment. This ratio was 0·27 for India and 0·33 for China – that is, approximately thirty per cent of the additional income was used for investment. Thus, even with similar marginal savings/income ratios, the growth in China was much more rapid. This was also due to the fact that a more efficient use of investments was made in China. The marginal capital/output ratio, or the amount of additional investment required for a unit of additional output, was 3–3·5 in India; while in China this ratio was about 2. This difference was in part due to concentration of investments in the transport and communications sector in India – a sector relatively more developed in India than in China, and yet, for reasons which will no doubt have to be sought in the non-economic fields, India poured in nearly one

456

third of the public investments in it. It was also due to obtaining larger increments in agricultural output with relatively low investments in agriculture.

The low capital/output ratio need not be interpreted as solely arising from the utilization of a very low level of technology: for instance, from the attempt – now almost abandoned – to obtain additional output of modern steel through small blast furnaces in China. The ability to attain a low capital/output ratio and thereby a much more efficient use of the scarce factor of investment is connected with the whole field of social planning; more specifically, with the ability of the planning agencies to utilize to the maximum the potential productive resources which are essential for an economy to grow. These efforts also include the use of unemployed and under-employed labour organized on a vast scale to create socially necessary capital works (local irrigation works, control of soil erosion, afforestation, roads, schools, etc.); more intensive exploitation of existing modern facilities (which are seriously under-utilized in India, despite the talk about shortage of capital – factories that work only one shift and that too inefficiently, idle capacity in the transport system, under-utilization of railway tracks and rolling stock; acres and acres of land which produces barely a little more than the seed thrown into it; the absence of the practical application of the simple but highly productive modern agricultural techniques; inefficient use of the employed labour due to the lack of the purposive application of simple organizational and technical innovations; and these are but a few examples). Yet these changes make limited demand on what is understood as capital investment, but if introduced on a large scale, can yield very significant increases in total output.

Not at Cost of Consumption

(6) The rapid increase of investment in China was not associated with any decline in aggregate consumption. In fact, the larger expansion in gross national product made possible by a larger volume of investment and more efficient allocation of it resulted in bringing about a much greater rise in consumption.

During 1950–58, the rise in consumption amounted to about one fourth in India, while it was over eighty per cent in China. In 1950 *per capita* consumption in China was approximately a third lower than in India. By 1958, it rose somewhat above that in India.

Even when all the formidable difficulties of interpretation of statistical data are taken into consideration, the examination of the developments of two countries does throw grave doubts on the current concept of the 'vicious circle' of poverty – which emphasizes the inability of the pre-industrial countries to raise investments and start a self-generating, self-propelling growth.

There is thus need for a basic re-examination of the current concepts on the theoretical relationship between investment (saving) and growth in income and consumption in both a static and a dynamic situation. In a static sense, it is correct to say that investment is an arithmetical deduction from income. Therefore if more investment is undertaken, less of the income is left for consumption: this idea is usually expressed in the oft-repeated phrase, 'you cannot have your cake and eat it'. In sciences – natural and social – the laws of statics do not always have much relevance to dynamics, where a different functional relationship among the various variables is expected to prevail. This is now accepted in all the natural sciences where experimentation in dynamics and its results have left little choice. But in the social sciences, its acceptance has remained slow.

Not Limited by Low Saving

In fact the relationship is not so simple as the current concepts assume. When one considers the question of economic growth in a dynamic situation, investment is not merely an arithmetical deduction from income but also simultaneously the generator of income; the marginal increments in income are directly related to as well as dependent upon the increments in investment. In a static case, investment has no impact on the level of income and it only tends to alter the level of consumption; but in a dynamic situation, investment has a definite and direct influence on the level of income. It is the major variable which can raise income. Higher investment would necessarily mean lower income in a static sense. But due to the dynamic functional relation between investment and income, one could derive almost a 'perverse' (from a static point of view) result in a growing economy – the larger the investment effort, the larger the rise in future consumption. The correlations, therefore, between investment and consumption are entirely different in the two situations; an inverse correlation in a static and a direct correlation in a dynamic situation.

Economic growth need not be conditioned in an absolute sense by the low current rate of saving, but can be financed, subject to an appropriate policy framework, as a draft on the future. The central aim of economic theory and policy would then be not to continue the sterile lamentations on the 'vicious circle' of poverty and the low level of savings but to elucidate and implement the steps that make possible a drawing on the future growth.

Drawing on the Future, Not Deficit Financing

The argument therefore may be stated thus: that a country that undertakes a larger investment effort can attain a larger increment both in total output and consumption. There is nothing obscure and incomprehensible in the idea of drawing on the future growth. Modern methods of finance, evolved during the last two centuries, indicate that a large part of the grant of a line of credit – for a month, three months, a year or longer – to an individual or an enterprise is essentially a draft on the future growth of income which is expected to be realized through the efforts of an individual or an enterprise. If the individual or the enterprise succeeds, the line of credit is repaid in the stipulated period and the financing is considered a successful venture; otherwise not. It is ultimately the confidence in the future that makes such an extension of credit possible. As with individuals, so also with economies. Future growth, therefore, need not be conditioned by the level of current savings but could be financed as a draft on the future.

A distinction must be made between drawing on the

future and deficit financing. When the latter is resorted to without a plan to plough back the future growth in output, it usually leads to more of it, and to serious inflationary pressures. It is here that the nature and the quality of social planning – the organization of social drives and motivations, the control of the flows of output and income, the ability to cut down sharply conspicuous consumption, the most efficient and economic use of the resources – has a far greater importance than the capacity of the economic planning agency to produce attractive statistical formulae.

Investment-Consumption Correlated

The line of reasoning in this paper would suggest two conclusions which have great relevance for planning in the pre-industrial countries:

(1) That over a period of time, raising investment in order to attain higher rates of growth does not require a decline in aggregate consumption; in fact, the rise in investment and consumption is directly correlated. Only those economies which raise the volume of investments faster can expect an increase in consumption.

This possibility can have important social consequences. In a large measure, the haunting fear of the need for a decline in consumption has so far been an important element in discouraging a bolder investment programme. It has been said that only authoritarian measures can succeed in restraining consumption. Once it is admitted that there is a direct correlation between the growth of consumption and investment, part of the hesitation in planning may be easier to overcome.

(2) That over a period of time there is no absolute connexion between the current rate of saving and the potential rate of growth. Subject to adequate policies, economic growth could be financed as a draft on future expansion of resources. In this respect, economic growth may approximate the movement of a self-propelling body. The initial motion would begin not so much due to the push given by the present rate of savings but due to the ability to discount the future. Once begun, it can be self-perpetuating.

460

Growth is Attainable

This analysis does not indicate that planning for economic growth is simple, that there is little to be done except to take an overdose of optimism. But merely to emphasize the economic difficulties and the scarcity of resources is to look into an empty medical chest. Most of what has been said above is simple and obvious, except perhaps to those who have the 'dogmatism of the untravelled'. In the quest for the complex, the simple and obvious has too often been overlooked.

If the limiting role wrongly assigned to it is wrested from the current rate of saving and the paralysing fear of the need to reduce consumption is overcome, it would then seem that most countries have the possibility of attaining and maintaining high rates of growth – amounting to some 8–10 per cent per year. A rate of growth of this order would raise the present level of output by fifty to 120 times in half a century. When this is realized, it is a matter of simple arithmetic (and the knowledge of the great force with which high rates cumulate when compounded over a period of time) to indicate that closing the gap – even at its widest – between the richest and the poorest country is not an impossible task. It does not require hopeless and endless centuries but less than half a century – no more than the adult life of a person. The central task of the theory of planning would then be to demonstrate how best to achieve the attainable – the abolition by the end of this century of the economic problem which has engaged throughout the ages more than ninety per cent of the people for most of their active lives.

19. JOSE MA SISON

*

Peace, Order and Security
for the People*

When Senator Claro M. Recto died in 1957, the Philippines lost one of its most distinguished nationalists. Recto was a liberal who struggled for what he regarded as the true independence and dignity of the Filipino people. In the next excerpt a much younger man, Jose Ma Sison (b. 1939), speaks in the same tradition, and in the same forthright manner, when he addresses a group at the Philippines Military Academy at Fort del Pilar in October 1966 on 'The Correct Concept of National Security'. Sison invokes memories of the great revolutionary nationalists of the 1890s. He discusses both the correct role of the military in a genuine democracy and the problem of guarding against foreign subversion of national independence and sovereignty. There has been a good deal of evidence that Filipino popular opinion supports these views and arguments.

I UNDERSTAND that an increasing number of officers and rank and filers of the Armed Forces of the Philippines are re-considering their traditions and the basic postulates by which commands have been sent down from the top with the most rigid discipline characteristic of the military establishment.

In the Philippine Military Academy, I would presume that the fresher minds of young men are striving to clarify that the true military tradition which every Filipino must be proud of and whose spirit he must imbue should hark back to the Katipunan and the Philippine Revolution.

At least on the surface, every soldier of the government carries with him the initial of the Katipunan on his uniform. The Philippine Military Academy carries the name of the great anti-imperialist general, Gregorio del Pilar, who fought both

*From *Struggle for National Democracy* (Quezon City: Progressive Publication, 1967).

against Spanish colonialism and American imperialism. He died fighting American imperialism, faithful to the sovereignty of the Filipino people but betrayed by a fellow-Filipino who showed the imperialist soldiers how, in familiar Yankee slang, to rub him out at Tirad Pass.

We are once again at a point in our national history where the body politic is pervaded by the collective desire to assert our people's sovereignty and to give substance to those forms of seeming independence that a foreign power has acceded to us as a measure of compromise and chicanery in its favour. There is now an evident political flow involving all patriotic classes, groups and individuals. Our people as a whole, including those who have been conservative, are beginning to re-examine the status of our national life and the strategic relations that have bound us from the beginning of this century.

An intensive inquiry is now being made as to how our economy has remained agrarian and colonial in character; as to how our political life has not actually permitted the masses of our people to enjoy the bounty of genuine democracy; as to how an imperialist culture wedded to a colonial culture has persisted; as to how we have persisted in considering ourselves under the protection of a foreign power which extracts superprofits from us and which constantly involves us in its selfish enmities throughout Asia and throughout the world in the guise of a religious crusade called anti-communism.

We fear aggression and supposedly we prepare for it. But many of us forget the aggression that has succeeded in perpetuating itself within our shores. Many of us lose sight of the fact that actually a foreign aggression persists within our territory, causing petty confusion among our people and constantly trying to reduce our officialdom into a mere board of directors for its selfish imperialist interests.

Perhaps, it takes a conservative man like Speaker Cornelio Villareal to state for us, as he has done so in a series of articles in the *Manila Times*, that the Joint United States Military Advisory Group (JUSMAG) has developed a built-in control of our armed forces through its firm control of logistics, intelligence, planning and personnel training on a strategic level.

Guided no less by his experience, Rep. Carmelo Barbero, an ex-army officer, has also made statements in support of the contention that an undue amount of foreign control exists within the very machinery upon which people are supposed to depend for their national security.

It should be pertinent to ask ourselves whether we should allow the Armed Forces of the Philippines to continue in the mercenary tradition of the Civil Guards of the Spanish times, the Macabebes, the Philippine Scouts and the USAFFE under direct American command and the Ganaps and puppet constabulary of the Japanese imperialists. Is the military willing to reject this mercenary tradition and replace it with the revolutionary spirit of Katipunan? ...

We have gained experience and confidence in the people's war of resistance against the Japanese, nevertheless. Although we have again fallen into the hands of American imperialists, we gained experience as a people in the anti-Japanese war of resistance. We have shown our mastery of the techniques of guerrilla war and our ability to merge with the masses in time of crisis: but we need now to realize that we have to be guided by a thorough understanding of the tasks of a genuine national and social liberation and the motive forces that need to be impelled with the proper demands so as to move correctly against the current enemy and then the subsequent one, both of whom we should clearly identify.

We fought successfully against Japanese imperialism; we were successful in fighting and in arming ourselves. But we were inadequate in so far as it concerned arming ourselves ideologically and politically. We were too gullible about America's promise of independence; we thought genuine independence could be had; instead the independence that we got has now been thoroughly exposed as empty of substance, particularly for the masses of our people. By arming ourselves with the correct thoughts, we could have acted more independently and used our resistance forces to assert our independence from both Japan and the United States. For instance, we could have allowed the peasant masses all over the archipelago to enjoy land reform immediately on the lands abandoned by the

464

landlords who sought safety in Manila under the care of the Japanese imperialists and in Washington under the care of the American imperialists. Instead, we let a few Americans lead the USAFFE and the leadership of the guerrilla movement was submitted to them on a silver platter. The mercenary backpay mentality tainted the patriotic movement. Until now, we suffer the humiliation of mercenaries; of constantly begging for veterans' payments from a foreign government to which perhaps many of our people owe more loyalty than to the Philippine government that remains a mere poor appendage of that exploiting power. However, subservience to that foreign government is concealed by the representation of its interests as automatically those of our government and of our own people.

If an occasion like the anti-Japanese struggle should again arise, we must make use of all our lessons as a people and strike out on our own as an independent force, independent of the strategic demands of a foreign power like the United States. It is not only that we on our own have learned our lessons or that we have developed as a more forceful nation, but it is also that we find ourselves now on a certain level of world development that is far higher than that on which we found ourselves during the Japanese occupation. National liberation movements are now all over the world; the socialist states have become more powerful. These two forces combined have now the capability of scattering and weakening the imperialist power of the United States; U.S. imperialism is increasingly weakened by the very over-extension of its power and the consistent opposition of peoples all over the world.

The diabolic stories of 'communist aggression' circulated by American propaganda have become too over-used in the Philippines. More and more students are reading about the experience of the socialist countries and how on the other hand the Soviet Union and the People's Republic of China have been the ones who have suffered from imperialist intervention. The true facts about the Korean War and Sino-Indian border dispute are now coming to light before the Filipino intelligentsia; and the American aggression against South and North Vietnam, the hundreds of U.S. intrusions into Chinese territory and the American support for Chiang Kai-shek in Taiwan are certainly more evident than the claim that China is the No. 1 aggressor and the United States is the No. 1 peacemaker.

'Communist aggression' is one of the myths we are beginning to perceive with greater clarity. As a matter of fact, our reactionary leaders have started to use contradictions of terms such as 'internal aggression' and 'aggression by proxy'. Whenever there are labour or peasant unrests and strikes, or anti-imperialist demonstrations of students and the youth, the pathological anti-communists see in these dynamic expressions of popular demands 'the scheming hands of foreign communists using local agents'. If we truly want democracy to develop in this country for the masses, we should never begrudge the use of constitutional rights for the peaceful redress of their grievances. These rights were formally recognized to countervail the obvious legal superiority of the landlords and capitalists who themselves made the laws through their political agents.

The soldiers of the government should ask themselves why in strikes they find themselves categorically on the side of the capitalist establishment or in peasant conflicts on the side of the landlords. In anti-imperialist demonstrations, they also find themselves together with the police lined up against unarmed ordinary citizens. Oftentimes, they find themselves being briefed that these strikers and demonstrators are subversive agitators.

I know for a fact that most of the enlisted men of the Armed Forces of the Philippines come from the peasantry. But why is it that in disputes between the landlords and the peasants, the soldier who is actually a peasant in government uniform, finds himself being used as a tool of the landlord? Why point your guns to the masses and not to the foreign comprador and feudal interests who exploit the people?

The officers and rank and filers of the Armed Forces of the Philippines should have the honour and conviction to fight for the interests of the people. If they should find themselves being ordered from the top to take the side of the American imperialists, the compradors and the landlords and fight the

466

peasant masses, the workers, progressive intelligentsia, they should have the honour and conviction of changing their sides and throw in their lot with the oppressed who have long suffered from their exploiters.

Peace and order or rule of law has become the convenient slogan for motivating the soldier against the masses who resort to their right of free assembly and expression. In the first place, it should be asked: Peace and order for whom? Rule of whose law? The exploited masses who daily suffer from deprivation and exploitation must be allowed to organize and express themselves freely. Why should they be quieted down by the force of arms, under the pretext of maintaining peace and order and rule of law? Why should they be prevented from making clear their demands? In taking your side against the oppressed masses, you become no different from the civilian guards of the landlord and the private security guards of the capitalists and of the American Embassy and military bases.

In tracing the chain of armed power in the country, we can see that the process of arms is attached to property as indicated by the licence laws. So, the private entities who have most private arms are landlords, capitalists and their political agents in the executive and legislative departments of the government and yet they have the most access to the use of the government police and armed forces. When a certain local situation cannot be taken care of by the civilian guards, the municipal police comes in and in a series, the Philippine Constabulary, the Philippine Army and in the very end, American military intervention. It has been said that the chain of armed power leads to American imperialism; so it is also said that the most strategic armed protection for the exploiters of this society comes from American imperialism. With this understanding, the masses begin to have a strategic hatred for American imperialism. The exploiters and their armed satellites are recognized as being within the same hierarchy of power, with American imperialism as the presiding power.

American imperialist propaganda keeps on harping that there would be no more serious threat to national security and internal peace and order without the communists here and

467

abroad. We are made to hate communists or those whom we think are communists in the same way that the Spaniards and the friars tried to play up hatred against Filipinos who were called Masons and *filibusteros*. The Philippine military is indoctrinated to feel a violent unreasoning hatred for communists in the same way that the Civil Guards were indoctrinated to hate *filibusteros* by the Spaniards in order to maintain their colonial loyalty.

We must realize that the masses will always be restless so long as they are exploited. At certain stages, they may actually be quieted down by the violent force of the state. But when they rise up again, their previous rising, though defeated, serves as a mere dress rehearsal for a more powerful and sweeping revolution. In 1872, our colonial masters thought they had finished once and for all the secularization movement. Only fourteen years after, they reaped a whirlwind – not only a stronger wave of the secularization movement but a widespread separatist movement which wanted national independence, no less.

During the 1950s, the American imperialists might have thought that they had suppressed the national-democratic movement for good. But if they continue to deprive the Filipino people of true independence, they shall certainly reap a whirlwind – the whirlwind of true national independence. If the compradors and landlords have repressed the peasant masses for so long, they await a time when the people shall in a revolutionary tempest sweep them away from the land.

American imperialism and landlordism are not the creation of communist agitators. They are the objective results of extended historical processes. . . .

At present, a movement within the Armed Forces of the Philippines should be started to reclaim alienated territory of the Philippine government from the U.S. government. We must uphold Filipino sovereignty over the American military bases in the Philippines. We must place these military bases under Filipino command. We should demand the immediate termination of the Military Bases Agreement as an instrument nullifying our sovereignty.

The true sons of Bonifacio, Emilio Jacinto, Gregorio del Pilar and Antonio Luna within the armed forces should reject American military dictation. They should reject the Military Assistance Pact and the JUSMAG as instruments of foreign control and influence over the Philippine military. They should reject all psychological warfare measures, such as 'civic action' and others, that have been proposed by American counter-insurgency experts to deceive the people who must be patriotically assisted in their struggle to liberate themselves from imperialism and feudalism.

Let us develop our munitions industry locally. Let us diversify our sources of military supplies. Let us not depend on one power which abuses our sovereignty and takes advantage of our people. Let us stop American indoctrination in the armed forces and the police force so that an anti-imperialist and democratic orientation can be propagated among them. Let us allow the armed forces to plan and conduct their actions in accordance with the interests of our people. Or else they remain the mercenaries of the imperialists, compradors and landlords.

We should rely on the patriotism, courage and capability of the people in defending themselves. We demonstrated in the anti-Japanese struggle that we could actually convert the enemy into a supplier of arms for the masses by capturing them. Let us dismiss the imperialist presumption that we can only be under the protection of a foreign power.

In this era of world-wide people's war against colonialism, imperialism and neo-colonialism, we are in a position not only to learn from our anti-Japanese experience but also from the struggles of so many other peoples. Let us not repeat the mistakes of Aguinaldo in the Filipino–American War. Let us not again make the mistake of being fooled by American imperialism. In this era of mounting world-wide anti-imperialist movements, the main enemy has become unmistakably clear and objectively the national struggle shall be assisted by external developments to a higher extent than at any other point in Philippine history. ...

Let us withdraw from the Mutual Defense Treaty because it

is a licence for the United States to intervene militarily in our internal affairs.

Let us withdraw from the South-East Asia Treaty Organization because it is essentially an anti-South-East Asian compact controlled by non-South-East Asian imperialist powers who would help the United States intervene in the internal affairs of the Philippines. Let us redeem ourselves in the eyes of our fellow-Asians from the ignominy of our having long remained as the servile tools of American imperialism.

We have long been curtained off by the United States from a huge part of the world. We have long believed in the servile line that the enemies of the United States are also the enemies of the Philippines.

We would better serve our national security if we broaden our diplomatic relations and we increase our friends. Let us be more aware of the present world reality. Let us be aware and let us take advantage of the contradictions among capitalist powers and the contradiction between socialism and capitalism. Let us be aware of the alliances against American imperialism. Let us turn the present world situation to our national-democratic advantage.

*

Andrew Shonfield, from whose book *The Attack on World Poverty* the following excerpt is taken, was director of Studies at the Royal Institute of International Affairs ('Chatham House') in London.

Trade Within the Underdeveloped World

ONE way in which the undeveloped countries could surely help to relieve the pressure on their balance of payments is by trading more among themselves. It is not just a matter of taking in each other's washing. Surplus production of a commodity runs to waste in one country, while in another people go short of it, because the mechanism of exchange fails to function efficiently. A lot more food could and would be grown in the great surplus agricultural area of Asia which runs from Burma across the South-East Asian peninsula, if there were an assured market for it. But it only needs one good rice harvest for Burma to be faced with the nightmare of surplus stocks. That is what has happened recently. There are no adequate storage facilities, the rice rots, the price falls – and next time the peasant does not bother to grow so much or to bring it to market.

The reason given for the Burmese failure to sell the rice to the Indians is simply that the Indians cannot afford it. That is true in the sense that the Indian government is not prepared to allocate anything out of its very inadequate reserves of foreign exchange to pay for additional imports of rice. It is clear, in fact, that if there is to be any substantial increase in this or in any other trade among the undeveloped countries – who are almost certain to be short of foreign exchange as soon as they try seriously to speed up their economic development – it will be necessary to by-pass the normal machinery for

*From *The Attack on World Poverty* (London: Chatto & Windus).

making payments. If Burma demands to be paid, like everyone else, in sterling or some other convertible currency, it will be left holding its surplus rice, and everybody will be that much poorer.

Indeed, one should have thought it elementary that these nations should be encouraged to engage in barter trade, wherever this helps them to put their actual or potential surpluses of production to some useful purpose. It came as a shock, therefore, when I was in India at the end of 1959, to run into a mission from the International Monetary Fund engaged in a vigorous effort to break up an Indo-Burmese barter agreement. The I.M.F. started by hurling anathemas. What the Indians were doing was a sin against the principle of untrammelled multilateral trade, with equal freedom for all exporters to enter a market. Only by holding to this principle could a nation be assured that it was buying its goods in the cheapest market and so keeping its own costs competitive. Moreover, the I.M.F. was able to back up its doctrine by brandishing a big deterrent. The Indians happened to owe it a lot, and the debt was going to fall due for repayment in 1961–2; they also knew that they were likely to need to borrow some more.

The particular object of the Fund's wrath was a clause in the Indo-Burmese trade agreement which committed the Indians to take an extra 150,000 tons of Burmese rice, paying for this out of the proceeds of any margin of *additional* Indian exports to Burma above the average level of the previous five years. In other words, the Burmese were promised a market for their rice if they agreed to import more Indian goods than they had up till then. A barefaced picture of bilateralism, certainly: the I.M.F. no doubt congratulated itself on having stamped on it in time. But people who are not devout worshippers of an economic doctrine, which was after all designed primarily to provide a set of decent rules to govern the commercial contests between developed capitalist countries, may wonder why such violent objection should be taken to a sensible scheme for raising the level of consumption and output in some undeveloped ones.

The I.M.F. under the leadership of Mr Per Jacobsson, the

conservative Swedish economist who became its managing
director in the middle 1950s, has been most active in smelling
out heresies in trade policies in the underdeveloped world. His
men move in with determination to snuff out the trouble before it has time to spread. It is a strange experience to see them
at work, because they bring to it some of the spirit of a cru-
sading order defending the true faith. They have a kind of
moral self-confidence, which seems to belong to another century – certain that however painful the decisions which they
force on poor nations, they are truly defending them, for their
own sakes, against their evil natures. Usually, the issues on
which the I.M.F. asserts the primacy of its doctrines are so
obscure to the ordinary person that he has not the intellectual
patience to understand, and resent, its interventions in national
policy. But every now and then there is an eruption, as for instance when the students in Rio de Janeiro came out on to the
streets to demonstrate against the Monetary Fund. It so happened that in this case the issue had by then become involved
in local politics, and justice was by no means all on the
Brazilian government's side.

Bibliography

Aguilar, Alonso, *Latin America and the Alliance for Progress* (New York: Monthly Review Press, 1963).

Ahmad, Egbal, 'Radical But Wrong', (*Monthly Review*, July–August 1968).

Ahmed, J. M., *The Intellectual Origins of Egyptian Nationalism* (Oxford, New York: O.U.P., 1960).

Alavi, Hamza, 'The Army and the Bureaucracy in Pakistan', *International Socialist Journal*, No. 14, March–April 1966.

Alstyne, Richard van, *The Rising American Empire* (New York: O.U.P., 1960).

Angell, Alan, 'Party Systems in Latin America' (*Political Quarterly*. Vol. 37. No. 3. July–September 1966).

Arciniegas, German, *The State of Latin America* (New York: Knopf, 1953; London: Cassell).

Arevalo, Juan Jose, *The Shark and the Sardines* (New York, Lyle Stuart, 1961).

Aung, Maung Htin, *The Stricken Peacock. Anglo–Burmese Relations 1752–1948* (The Hague: Nijhoff, 1965).

Awolowo, Obafemi, *Path to Nigerian Freedom* (London: Faber and Faber, 1947).

Bailey, F. G. *et al., Political Systems and the Distribution of Power*, A.S.A. Monographs No. 2. (London: Tavistock, 1965).

Bailey, F. G., *Tribe, Caste and Nation* (Manchester: Manchester University Press, 1960).

Baran, Paul, *The Political Economy of Growth* (London: Calder, 1957).

Barnett, Donald L. and Njama, Karari, *Mau Mau from Within: Autobiography of Kenya's Peasant Revolt* (New York: Monthly Review Press, 1966).

Barraclough, Geoffrey, *An Introduction to Contemporary History* (London: Watts, 1964).

Ben Barka, Mehdi, *Conditions de la Réforme Agraire au Maroc* in Ignacy Sachs (ed.). *Agriculture, Land Reform and Economic Development* (Warsaw: Polish Scientific Publishers, 1964).

Bettelheim, Charles, *India Independent* (London: MacGibbon & Kee, 1968).

474

Blackburn, Robin, 'Prologue to the Cuban Revolution' in *New Left Review* No. 21, October 1963.

Blyden, Edward W., *African Life and Customs* (1908).

Bodde, Derk, *Peking Diary 1948–9. A Year of Revolution* (Greenwich: Fawcett Publications, 1967).

Bohannan, Paul, 'Africa's Land', in George Dalton (ed.) *Tribal and Peasant Economies. Readings in Economic Anthropology* (New York: Natural History Press, 1967).

Bonilla, Frank, 'Brazil', in James S. Coleman (ed.) *Education and Political Development* (Princeton: Princeton University Press, 1965).

Borg, Dorothy, *American Policy and the Chinese Revolution. 1925–1928* (New York: Macmillan, 1947).

Bosch, Juan, *The Unfinished Experiment: Democracy in the Dominican Republic* (New York: Praeger, 1965).

Brandenburg, Frank R., *The Making of Modern Mexico* (Englewood Cliffs, N.J.: Prentice Hall, 1964).

Brecher, Michael, *Nehru. A Political Biography* (Oxford: O.U.P., 1959).

Brogan, D. W., *Worlds in Conflict* (London: Hamish Hamilton, 1967).

Buchanan, Keith, *The Southeast Asian World. An Introductory Essay* (London: Bell, 1967).

Buck, John Lossing, *Land Utilization in China* (Chicago, 1937).

Burchett, Wilfred G., *Vietnam: Inside Story of a Guerilla War* (New York: International Publishers, 1965).

Burchett, Wilfred G., *Vietnam North. A First-Hand Report* (London: Lawrence and Wishart, 1966).

Casanova, Pablo Gonzalez, 'Mexico: A Semicapitalist Revolution', in Ignacy Sachs (ed.) *Planning and Economic Development* (Warsaw: Polish Scientific Publishers, 1964).

Castro, Fidel, *History Will Absolve Me* (Havana: Guairas, 1967).

Chandrasekhar, S., *Infant Mortality in India. 1901–1955* (London: Allen & Unwin, 1959).

Chatterji, B. R., *Southeast Asia in Transition* (Meerut: Meenakshi Prakashan, 1965).

Chen Po-ta, *A Study of Land Rent in Pre-Liberation China*, 2nd edn (Peking: Foreign Languages Press, 1966).

Chen Yi, *Vice-Premier Chen Yi Answers Questions Put by Correspondents* (Peking: Foreign Languages Press, 1966).

Chou En-lai, 'Speech at the Mass Rally of Welcome in Mogadishu',

3 February 1964, in *Afro-Asian Solidarity Against Imperialism* (Peking: Foreign Languages Press, 1964).

Coedes, G., *The Making of Southeast Asia* (Berkeley: University of California Press, 1966).

Collingwood, *The Idea of History* (Oxford: O.U.P., 1946).

Coomaraswamy, Ananda, *The Religious Basis of the Forms of Indian Society* (New York: Orientalia, 1946).

Coser, Lewis A., *The Functions of Social Conflict* (Glencoe, Illinois: The Free Press, 1956).

Costa Pinto, L. A., 'Portrait of Developing Man: The Processes of Social Changes in Latin America', in Irving Louis Horowitz (ed.) *The New Sociology* (Oxford and New York: O.U.P., 1964).

Curtis, Robert, 'Malaysia and Indonesia', in *New Left Review* No. 28, November–December 1964.

Datta, Amlan, *Socialism, Democracy and Industrialization* (London: Allen and Unwin, 1962).

Davidson, Basil, *Black Mother* (London: Gollancz, 1961).

Davidson, Basil, *The Liberation of Guiné* (Harmondsworth: Penguin, 1969).

de Bary, Theodore (ed.) *Approaches to the Oriental Classics* (New York: Columbia University Press, 1959).

de Jesus, Carolina Maria, *Beyond All Pity* (London: Souvenir Press, 1962).

de Jouvenel, Bertrand, *Efficiency and Amenity*, Fortieth Earl Grey Memorial Lecture (Newcastle-upon-Tyne, 1960).

Dellinger, Dave, *What is Cuba Really Like?* (New York: Liberation Reprint, 1964).

Dobb, Maurice, *Studies in the Development of Capitalism* (London: Routledge & Kegan Paul, 1946).

Dorticos Torrado, Osvaldo *et al.*, *The Declarations of Havana* (Peking: Foreign Languages Press, 1962).

Dozer, Donald Marquand (ed.) *The Monroe Doctrine. Its Modern Significance* (New York: Knopf, 1965).

Dube, S. C., 'Bureaucracy and Nation Building in Transitional Societies', in *International Social Science Bulletin* Vol. XVI, No. 2, 1964.

Dube, S. C., *India's Changing Villages. Human Factors in Community Development* (Ithaca: Cornell University Press, 1958).

Dumont, René, *False Start in Africa* (New York: Praeger, 1966).

Dumont, René, *Lands Alive* (New York: Monthly Review Press, 1965).

Economic Commission for Latin America, 'Fifteen Years of Economic Policy in Brazil', in *United Nations: Economic Commission for Latin America*, Vol. IX, No. 2., November 1964.

Edwardes, Michael, *The Last Years of British India* (London: Cassell, 1963).

Elsbree, W. H., *Japan's Role in Southeast Asian Nationalism* (London, 1953).

Fals Borda, Orlando, 'Violence and the Break-up of Tradition in Colombia', in Claudio Veliz (ed.) *Obstacles to Change in Latin America* (Oxford: O.U.P., 1965).

Fanon, Frantz, *Studies in a Dying Colonialism* (New York: Monthly Review Press, 1959).

Fanon, Frantz, *The Wretched of the Earth* (London: MacGibbon and Kee, 1965).

Fei Hsiao-tung, *Peasant Life in China: A Field Study of Country in the Yangtse Valley* (London: Routledge & Kegan Paul, 1939).

Fischer, Joseph, 'Indonesia', in James S. Coleman (ed.) *Education and Political Development* (Princeton: Princeton University Press, 1965).

Fisher, C. A., *Southeast Asia* (London: Methuen, 1964).

Fleming, D. F., *The Cold War and Its Origins*, Vol. 2 (New York: Doubleday, 1961).

Forman, Harrison, *Report from Red China* (London: Hale, 1947).

Frank, Andre Gunder, 'On the Mechanisms of Imperialism – the Case of Brazil', in *Monthly Review*, Vol. 16, No. 5. September 1964.

Frank, Andre Gunder, 'The Sociology of Development and Underdevelopment of Sociology', in *Catalyst*, Summer, 1967.

Freyre, Gilberto, *New World in the Tropics* (New York: Knopf, 1959).

Fuentes, Carlos, *et al.*, *Whither Latin America?* (New York: Monthly Review Press, 1963).

Furnivall, J. S., *Colonial Policy and Practice. A Comparative Study of Burma and Netherlands India* (Cambridge: C.U.P., 1948).

Furtado, Celso, *Diagnosis of the Brazilian Crisis* (Berkeley and Los Angeles: University of California Press, 1965).

Gadgil, D. R., *Planning and Economic Policy in India* (Bombay: Asia Publishing House. 1961).

Garcia, J. A. and C. R. Calle (eds), *Camilo Torres: Priest and Revolutionary* (London: Steed & Ward, 1968).

477

Gerassi, John, *North Vietnam. A Documentary* (London: Allen & Unwin, 1968).

Gettleman, Marvin E. (ed.), *Vietnam – History, Documents and Opinions on a Major World Crisis* (New York: Fawcett, 1965).

Giap, Vo Nguyen, *People's War, People's Army* (Hanoi: Foreign Languages Publishing House, 1961).

Gil, Frederico G. and Parrish, Charles J., *The Chilean Presidential Election of September 4, 1964,* Parts 1 & 2. (Washington Institute for the Comparative Study of Political Systems).

Gilly, Adolfo, 'The Guerilla Movement in Guatemala', in *Monthly Review*, Vol. 17, Nos. 1 & 2, May and June 1965.

Gourou, Pierre, *The Tropical World. Its Social and Economic Conditions and Its Future Status*, 4th edn (London: Longmans, 1966).

Graaff, J. de V., *Theoretical Welfare Economics* (Cambridge: C.U.P., 1957).

Greene, Felix, *A Curtain of Ignorance* (New York: Doubleday, 1964).

Han Suyin, *China in the Year 2001* (London: Watts, 1967).

Han Suyin, *The Crippled Tree* (London: Jonathan Cape, 1965).

Han Suyin, *The Mortal Flower* (London: Jonathan Cape, 1966).

Hay, Stephen and Qureshi, I. H. (compilers), *Sources of Indian Tradition*, Vol. ii (New York: Columbia University Press, 1958).

Heimsath, Charles H., *Indian Nationalism and Hindu Social Reform* (Princeton: Princeton University Press, 1964).

Hensman, C. R., *China: Yellow Peril? Red Hope?* (London: S.C.M. Press, 1968).

Hensman, C. R. (ed.), *The Public Services and the People* (Colombo: Community Institute, 1963).

Hensman, C. R. (ed.), *Organizing for Development, Progress and Reaction in Ceylon. 1947–1963* (Colombo: Community Institute, 1964).

Hinton, William, *Fanshen – A Documentary of Revolution in a Chinese Village* (New York: Monthly Review Press, 1966).

Hirschman, Albert O., *Journeys Towards Progress. Studies of Economic Policy-Making in Latin America* (New York: Doubleday, 1963).

Hodgkin, Thomas, *African Political Parties* (Harmondsworth: Penguin Books, 1961).

Horowitz, Irving Louis, *The Three Worlds of Development* (New York and Oxford: O.U.P., 1966).

478

Huang Sung-kang, *Lu Hsun and the New Culture Movement of Modern China* (Amsterdam: Djambatan, 1957).

Huberman, Leo and Sweezy, Paul, *Cuba. Anatomy of a Revolution* (London: Routledge & Kegan Paul, 1961).

Humphreys, R. A. and Lynch, John, *The Origins of the Latin American Revolutions* (New York: Knopf, 1966).

Imam, Zafar, 'The Effects of the Russian Revolution on India 1917–1920', in S. N. Mukherjee (ed.), *St Anthony's Papers* No. 18 (Oxford: O.U.P., 1966).

Indian Council of World Affairs, *Asian Relations – Proceedings and Documentation of the First Asian Relations Conference* (New Delhi, 1948).

Isaacs, Harold R., *No Peace for Asia* (New York: Macmillan, 1947).

Iyer, Raghavan (ed.), *The Glass Curtain Between Asia and Europe* (New York: O.U.P., 1965).

Jaffe, Philip, *New Frontiers in Asia. A Challenge to the West* (New York: Knopf, 1945).

Jagan, Cheddi, *The West on Trial. My Fight for Guyana's Freedom* (London: Michael Joseph, 1966).

Jaguaribe, Helio, 'The Dynamics of Brazilian Nationalism', in Claudio Veliz (ed.) *Obstacles to Change in Latin America* Oxford: O.U.P., 1965).

Jalee, Pierre, 'Third World? Which Third World?' in *Revolution* (Vol. I, No. 7, November 1963).

Jansen, G. H., *Afro-Asia and Non-Alignment* (London: Faber and Faber, 1966).

Juliao, Francisco, 'Brazil, a Christian Country', in Carlos Fuentes *et al.*, *Whither Latin America?* (New York: Monthly Review Press, 1963).

Kahin, George McT., 'Indonesia' in Kahin (ed.), *Major Governments of Asia* (Ithaca: Cornell University Press, 1963).

Kahin, George McT. and Lewis, John W., *The United States in Vietnam* (New York: Delta, 1967).

Kidron, Michael, *Foreign Investments in India* (New York: O.U.P., 1965).

Kiernan, Victor, 'The New Nation States', in *New Left Review*, No. 30, March–April 1965.

Lach, Donald F., *China in the Eyes of Europe. The Sixteenth Century* (Chicago: University of Chicago Press, 1968).

Lach, Donald F. and Flaumenhaft, Carol, *Asia on the Eve of Europe's Expansion* (Englewood Cliffs, N.J.: Prentice-Hall, 1965).

479

Lacouture, Jean, *Ho Chi Minh* (London: Allen Lane The Penguin Press, 1968).

La Feber, Walter, *The New Empire – An Interpretation of American Expansion 1860–1898* (Ithaca: Cornell University Press, 1963).

Lattimore, Owen, Oldham, C. H. G. and Robinson, Joan, 'China Today', in *The Journal of the Royal Society*, Vol. CXVI, No. 5144, July 1968.

Lattimore, Owen, *Solution in Asia* (Boston: Little Brown, 1949).

Lattimore, Owen, *The Situation in Asia* (Boston: Little Brown, 1949).

Legum, Colin and Margaret, *South Africa: Crisis for the West* (London: Pall Mall, 1964).

Lens, Sidney, *The Futile Crusade – Anti-Communism as American Credo* (Chicago: Quadrangle Books, 1964).

Lewis, Gordon K., *The Growth of the Modern West Indies* (London: MacGibbon & Kee, 1968).

Lewis, W. Arthur, *Politics in West Africa* (New York: O.U.P., 1965).

Lin Piao, *Long Live the Victory of People's War* (Peking: Foreign Languages Press, 1965).

Lomax, Louis E., *Thailand: The War That Is, The War That Will Be* (New York: Knopf, 1967).

Lu Hsun, *Selected Works* (Peking: Foreign Languages Press, 1964).

Macpherson, C. B., *The Real World of Democracy* (Oxford: Clarendon Press, 1966).

Magdoff, Harry, 'The Age of Imperialism' in *Monthly Review* (June, October, November 1968).

Mandela, Nelson, *No Easy Walk To Freedom*, Articles, Speeches, and Trial Addresses. (New York: Basic Books, 1965; London: Heinemann).

Mao Tse-tung, *Selected Readings* (Peking: Foreign Languages Press, 1968).

Marshall, T. H., *International Comprehension In and Through Social Science*, Hobhouse Memorial Lecture (London: Athlone Press, 1959).

Mazrui, Ali A., *Towards a Pax Africana. A Study of Ideology and Ambition* (London: Weidenfeld and Nicolson, 1967).

Memmi, Albert, *The Colonizer and the Colonized* (New York: Orion Press).

Merton, Robert K., 'Social Problems and Sociological Theory', in Robert K. Merton and Robert A. Nisbet (ed.), *Contemporary Social Problems* (London: Hart-Davis, 1964).

Mondlane, Edourdo, *The Struggle for Mozambique* (Harmondsworth: Penguin, 1969).

Moore, Barrington, *The Social Origins of Dictatorship and Democracy. Lord and Peasant in the Making of the Modern World* (Boston: Beacon Press, 1967; London: Allen Lane The Penguin Press).

Morgan, D. J., *British Private Investment in East Africa* (London: Overseas Development Institute, 1965).

Mukerji, D. P., 'Mahatma Gandhi's Views on Machines and Technology', in *International Social Science Bulletin*, Vol. VI, No. 3, 1954.

Myrdal, Gunnar, *An International Economy – Problems and Prospects* (New York: Harper, 1956).

Myrdal, Jan, *Report from a Chinese Village* (New York: Pantheon Books, 1965; London: Heinemann).

Naipaul, V. S., *An Area of Darkness* (London: André Deutsch, 1964).

Needham, Joseph, *Science and Civilisation in China*, Vols. 1 and 2 (Cambridge: C.U.P., 1954 and 1956).

Needham, Joseph, 'The Dialogue of Europe and Asia', in *United Asia*, Vol. 8, No. 5, 1956.

Nehru, Jawaharlal, *An Autobiography With Musings on Recent Events in India* (London: John Lane The Bodley Head, 1936).

Nisbet, Robert A., *The Quest for Community* (Oxford: O.U.P., 1953).

Nisbet, Robert A., 'The Study of Social Problems', in Robert K. Merton and Robert A. Nisbet, *Contemporary Social Problems* (London: Hart-Davis, 1963).

Nkrumah, Kwame, *Neocolonialism: The Last Stage of Capitalism* (London: Nelson).

Nove, Alexander, *Communism at the Crossroads* (Leeds: Leeds University Press, 1964).

Nyerere, Julius, *Freedom and Unity – Uhuru na Umoja* (Oxford: O.U.P., 1967).

O'Brien, Patrick, *The Revolution in Egypt's Economic System, From Private Enterprise to Socialism 1952–1965* (Oxford: O.U.P., 1966).

Odinga, Oginga, *Not Yet Uhuru* (London: Heinemann, 1967).

Onslow, Cranley (ed.), *Asian Economic Development* (London: Weidenfeld and Nicolson, 1965).

Panikkar, K. M., *Asia and Western Dominance* (London: Allen & Unwin, 1953).

481

Panikkar, K. M., *The Foundations of New India* (London: Allen & Unwin, 1963).

Parsons, Talcott, *Social Structure and Personality* (Glencoe, Illinois: The Free Press, 1964).

Patel, Surendra J., *Essays on Economic Transition* (Bombay: Asia Publishing House, 1965).

Paz, Octavio, *The Labyrinth of Solitude. Life and Thought in Mexico* (New York: Grove Press, 1961; London: Allen Lane The Penguin Press).

Pike, Frederick B., 'Social Conditions in Mid-Twentieth Century Chile: Old Problems Acquire New Urgency'. Chapter 10 of *Chile and the United States 1880–1962* (Notre Dame: University of Notre Dame Press, 1963).

Polanyi, K., Arensberg, C. M. and Pearson, H. W., *Trade and Market in the Early Empire* (Glencoe: Free Press, 1957).

Pomeroy, William, 'Pacification in the Philippines 1898–1913', in *France Asie*, Summer, 1967.

Prebisch, Raul, *Towards a New Trade Policy for Development* (New York: United Nations, 1964).

Ramos, Samuel, *The Profile of Man and Culture in Mexico* (New York: McGraw Hill, 1962).

Roig de Leuchsenring, Emilio, *Marti Anti-Imperialist* (Havana: Book Institute, 1967).

Rockerfeller, David, 'What Private Investment Means to Latin America', *Foreign Affairs*, Vol. 44. No. 3, 1966.

Romein, Jan, *The Asian Century* (London: Allen & Unwin, 1962).

Sachs, Ignacy (ed.), *Agriculture, Land Reforms and Economic Development* (Warsaw: Polish Scientific Publishers, 1964).

Sarkar, N. K., *The Demography of Ceylon* (Colombo: Government Press, 1957).

Sayeed, Khalid Bin, *Pakistan: The Formative Phase* (Karachi: Pakistan Publishing House, 1960).

Schram, Stuart, *Mao Tse-tung* (Harmondsworth: Penguin Books, 1966).

Schurmann, Franz, *Ideology and Organization in Communist China* (Berkeley: University of California Press, 1966).

Seers, Dudley (ed.), *Cuba – the Economic and Social Revolution* (Chapel Hill: University of North Carolina Press, 1964).

Segal, Ronald (ed.), *Political Africa* (London: Stevens, 1961).

Segal, Ronald, *The Race War* (London: Jonathan Cape, 1966).

Senghor, Leopold-Sedar, *On African Socialism* (New York: Praeger, 1964).

Shamuyarira, Nathan M., *Crisis in Rhodesia* (New York: Transatlantic Arts, 1966).

Sison, Jose Ma, *Struggle for National Democracy* (Quezon City: Progressive Publications, 1967).

Sithole, Ndabaningi, *African Nationalism*, 2nd edn (Oxford: O.U.P., 1968).

Sjahrir, Soetan, *Out of Exile* (New York: Day, 1949).

Smelser, Neil J., 'Toward a Theory of Modernization', in George Dalton (ed.), *Tribal and Peasant Economies. Readings in Economic Anthropology* (New York: Garden City Press, 1967).

Snow, Edgar, *Red Star Over China* (London: Gollancz, 1937).

Snow, Edgar, *Journey to the Beginning* (London: Gollancz, 1959).

Soong Ching Ling, *The Struggle for New China* (Peking: Foreign Languages Press, 1952).

Srinivas, M. N., *Caste in Modern India and Other Essays* (Bombay: Asia Publishing House, 1962).

Srinivas, M. N., *Social Change in Modern India* (Berkeley: University of California Press, 1966).

Sun Yat-sen, *San Min Chu I* (Calcutta, 1942).

Tabata, I. B., 'From October to the Cultural Revolution', in Leo Huberman and Paul M. Sweezy, *50 Years of Soviet Power* (New York: Monthly Review Press, 1967).

Tagore, Rabindranath, *Towards Universal Man* (Bombay: Asia Publishing House, 1961).

Tawney, R. H., *Land and Labour in China* (London: Allen & Unwin, 1932).

Teng Ssu-yu and John K. Fairbank, *China's Response to the West: A Documentary Survey 1839–1923* (Cambridge, Mass.: Harvard University Press, 1954).

Thiam, Doudou, *The Foreign Policy of African States* (New York: Praeger, 1965).

Thornton, A. P., *The Habit of Authority – Paternalism in British History* (London: Allen & Unwin, 1966).

Toynbee, Arnold J., *America and the World Revolution* (New York and Oxford: O.U.P., 1962).

Toynbee, Arnold J., *The Study of History Volume VIII* (Oxford: O.U.P., 1954).

Tsuru, Shigeto, 'Merits and Demerits of the Mixed Economy in Economic Development. Lessons from India's Experience', in Ignacy

Sachs, *Planning and Economic Development* (Warsaw: Polish Scientific Publishers, 1968).

United Nations, *The Economic Development of Latin America in the Post-War Period* (New York: U.N., 1964).

United Nations, *Economic Survey of Latin America 1963* (New York: United Nations, 1965).

Veliz, Claudio (ed.), *Obstacles to Change in Latin America* (Oxford O.U.P., 1965).

Viet Report, Vol. 3. Nos. 4 & 5, January 1968.

Walker, Kenneth R., *Planning in Chinese Agriculture: Socialisation and the Private Sector. 1956–1962* (Chicago: Aldine, 1965).

Weber, Max, *The Theory of Social and Economic Organization* (Glencoe, Illinois: Free Press, 1947).

Weinberg, Albert K., *Manifest Destiny. A Study of Nationalist Expansionism in American History* (Baltimore: Johns Hopkins Press, 1935).

White, Theodore H. and Jacoby, Annalee, *Thunder Out of China* (New York: Sloane, 1946).

Williams, Eric, *Capitalism and Slavery* (Chapel Hill: University of North Carolina Press, 1944).

Williams, William Appleman, *The United States, Cuba and Castro* (New York: Monthly Review Press, 1962).

Williams, William Appleman (ed.), *The Shaping of American Diplomacy Vol. I. 1750–1900. Readings and Documents in American Foreign Relations* (Chicago: Rand McNally, 1956).

Wolf, Eric R., 'Types of Latin American Peasantry. A Preliminary Discussion' in Dalton (ed.), *Tribal and Peasant Economies. Readings in Economic Anthropology* (New York, 1967).

Woodruff, William, *Impact of Western Man. A Study of Europe's Role in the World Economy 1750–1960* (London and New York: Macmillan, 1966).

Worsley, Peter, *The Third World* (London: Weidenfeld and Nicolson, 1964).

Yang, C. K., *Chinese Communist Society: The Family and the Village* (Cambridge, Mass.: M.I.T. Press, 1965).

Yglesias, Jose, *In the Fist of the Revolution* (New York: Pantheon, 1968; London: Allen Lane The Penguin Press).

Zimmer, Heinrich, *The Art of Indian Asia. Its Mythology and Transformations.* 2 vols. (New York: Pantheon, 1955).

Index

D
843
.H43
1969

D
843
.H43

1969